TRANSITIONS IN
CARIBBEAN LAW

TRANSITIONS IN CARIBBEAN LAW

Law-Making, Constitutionalism and the Convergence of National and International Law

Edited by
DAVID S. BERRY AND TRACY ROBINSON

The Caribbean Law
PUBLISHING COMPANY
Kingston

First published in Jamaica, 2013 by
The Caribbean Law Publishing Company
an imprint of Ian Randle Publishers
11 Cunningham Avenue
Box 686
Kingston 6
www.ianrandlepublishers.com

NATIONAL LIBRARY OF JAMAICA
CATALOGUING-IN-PUBLICATION DATA

Transitions in Caribbean law : law-making, constitutionalism and the
    convergence of national and international law / edited by David S.
Berry and Tracy Robinson

    p. ; cm.
Bibliography : p. - Includes index.
ISBN 978-976-8167-64-4 (pbk)

1. Jurisprudence – Caribbean, English-speaking
2. Constitutional law – Caribbean, English-speaking
3. International law – Caribbean, English-speaking
I. Berry, David S.   II. Robinson, Tracy

349.729   - dc 22

Cover and book design by The Caribbean Law Publishing Company
Printed in the United States of America

Table of Contents

some distinguished Caribbean judges to the development of 'fi wi law,' notably Chief Justice Wooding and Justice Telford Georges.[4] From the perspective of international law (Berry), administrative law (Ventose) and constitutional law (Robinson), three chapters closely look at the CCJ's most significant early decision, a death penalty appeal decided in 2006, a year and half after the inauguration of the Court in April 2005, *AG v Joseph*.[5]

This case epitomizes the transitions in law in the Caribbean over the last decade. The litigants, Lennox Boyce and Jeffrey Joseph, are well known to Caribbean public law. Their appeal was one of the last major decisions heard by the Privy Council from Barbados, which became one of the first Caribbean countries to accept the appellate jurisdiction of the CCJ. They had lost their appeal before the Privy Council in 2004 in the legendary case, *Boyce v R*,[6] by a slim 5: 4 majority on the interpretation of the general savings law clause and its protection of the mandatory death penalty.[7] Two years later, the same litigants succeeded before the CCJ on different grounds, which carefully reviewed a series of earlier Privy Council decisions. The CCJ focused on the men's legitimate expectation that they would have access to international human rights tribunals before the death penalty was carried out and their right to procedural fairness before the local body considered the exercise of the prerogative of mercy. To come full circle – an illustration of the force of international legal commitments – a year after the CCJ decision, in November 2007, the Inter-American Court of Human Rights held Barbados responsible for violations committed against these men by, among other things, the mandatory nature of the death penalty in Barbados.[8] Barbados agreed to repeal the mandatory death penalty and to constitutional reform to remove the infamous protection of existing laws secured by the general savings law clause in the Barbados Constitution.[9]

The chapters in this book contend with the themes directly addressed in this early decision of the CCJ and others that circle the establishment of this transnational court.

---

4. See Jackson, Chapter 1.
5. See (n 2).
6. [2004] UKPC 32, (2004) 64 WIR 37 (Bdos)
7. Barbados Constitution 1966 s 26.
8. *Boyce v Barbados* (Preliminary Objections, Merits, Reparations and Costs), Inter-American Court of Human Rights, Judgment of 20 Nov 2007, Series C, No 169 <http://www.corteidh.or.cr/casos. cfm> accessed 19 April 2011.
9. For example, Death Penalty Project, 'News Release, May 2009 – Barbados' Compliance with Inter-American Court Ruling' <http://www.deathpenaltyproject.org/content_pages/7> accessed 19 Apr 2011, *Case of DaCosta Cadogan v Barbados* (Preliminary Objections, Merits, Reparations and Costs), Inter-American Court of Human Rights, Judgment of 24 September 2009, Series C, No 204 <http://www.corteidh.or.cr/casos.cfm> accessed 19 Apr 2011, 103–4.

Transitions in Caribbean Law: An Introduction

David S. Berry and Tracy Robinson

This book explores both concrete and conceptual developments in the legal systems of the Commonwealth Caribbean.[1] Although at first glance the individual chapters may appear unrelated, a closer look reveals that they explore and offer insights into a number of cross-cutting themes that are at the front of Caribbean regional jurisprudence – from the challenges involved in applying abstract (sometimes regional, often extra-regional) rules to concrete and differing societies, to those posed by the elucidation and clarification of the different sources of Caribbean law, to the institutional challenges involved in making and interpreting the law. Several of these themes need to be unpacked, as well as others tentatively explored, in order for the contribution of the pieces in this book to be appreciated. What, for example, can we learn about a 'Caribbean jurisprudence'? Is there such a thing? Is there a kind of transnational Caribbean law – especially a 'confluence' of national and international law[2] – and what is its effect on the legal institutions of the region? How do small jurisdictions make law – or is law made for them – in a global economy? Is there a trend towards 'transjudicialism' and how is this reflected in new institutions like the Caribbean Court of Justice (CCJ)?

The chapters in this book are the first to ask these questions in the context of contemporary developments in Caribbean law and legal systems and particularly the establishment and early jurisprudence of the CCJ. The only posthumous publication to date by the late Professor Margaret Demerieux, who died in November 2005, sets the stage by evaluating the early legacy of the Judicial Committee of the Privy Council in constitutional human rights cases from the Caribbean.[3] Leighton Jackson looks squarely at the intellectual contribution of

---

1. Almost all of the papers in the present volume were first presented as part of the UWI Faculty of Law 'Faculty Workshop Series.' Some of them were part of a special tribute to Public Law Professor Emeritus Albert Fiadjoe on the eve of his retirement.
2. *AG v Joseph* [2006] CCJ 3 (AJ), (2006) 69 WIR 104 (Bdos) 151 [106] (de la Bastide P and Saunders J).
3. See Demerieux, Chapter 8. Professor Demerieux's article is published with the permission of her executor and estate.

1. The Concept of a Caribbean Jurisprudence

There have been two central tenets – truisms perhaps – in the development of Caribbean regional legal institutions and legal education: firstly, that there is already a West Indian law or a *common* Caribbean law, which is judged as flawed and inadequate, and, secondly, that we need the development of something described as a 'Caribbean jurisprudence' upon which to found more relevant and responsive Caribbean lawmaking. In conferences held in England in the early 1960s on 'English Law in the West Indies,' Sir Hugh Wooding, the former Chief Justice of Trinidad and Tobago, who was both a pioneer of Caribbean legal education and the region's premier nationalist judge, described the existing system of law in the West Indies as 'hopelessly inadequate to fulfil the requirements of our society and in many respects so unrelated to the verities of our life, economy and customs as to need urgent revision and thorough reform.'[10] In a later speech on regional integration in 1967, Sir Hugh Wooding spoke of an urgency to 'cultivate a Caribbean legal philosophy' that accorded with Caribbean legal realities, while maintaining the ethos of the common law.[11]

This preoccupation of jurists in the 1960s, on the eve of the establishment of regional legal education in 1970, with the need for *a* Caribbean legal philosophy has been sustained into the twenty-first century. Underlying the call are familiar nationalist and regionalist anxieties – can the Caribbean develop the self-confidence to make law consistent with its 'identity' and will lawmakers and the legal profession accept the Caribbean on its own terms?[12] While other aspects of Caribbean life are said to represent idiosyncratic Caribbean culture, law is seen as an anomaly that has not come 'home.'[13]

These chapters engage with, and re-present, this problematic of a Caribbean jurisprudence. They illustrate the durability of the concomitant anxieties, hopes and feelings of community shared by lawyers in the Caribbean that are embedded within it. In the same breath, by pointing to legal interchange across and beyond the region, and the diversity amongst small Caribbean states in their history, political and business

---

10. H. Wooding, 'Foreword' in K. Patchett (ed), *The Law in the West Indies: Some Recent Trends* (Commonwealth Series No 6, British Institute of International and Comparative Law, London 1966) vii.
11. H. Wooding, 'Address at the Institute of International Relations, UWI, St Augustine Trinidad, 28th June 1967: Legal Problems of Political Integration' in H. Fraser (ed), *A Collection of Addresses by the Rt Hon Sir Hugh Wooding* (Government Printing Office, Trinidad and Tobago 1968) 114–23, 122 (emphasis added).
12. See R-M Antoine, Chapter 3.
13. B. Chevannes, 'If the Shoe Doesn't Fit: Law and the African-Caribbean Family' (2002) 27(2) J of Eastern Carib Studies 80, 94, L. Jackson, Chapter 1.

culture, and social and economic development, the contributions to this book also unmoor 'a Caribbean jurisprudence' as the foundational issue for Caribbean legal thinkers. By asking what the sources of law in the Caribbean are, how law is made and what law means in a transnational Caribbean, they point us towards a concrete examination of law in the Caribbean that does not over-privilege an autonomous, sovereign and homogeneous Caribbean arena in which we can readily discern 'the emotion[s] of the people.'[14]

In his contribution to this book, Leighton Jackson suggests that law in the Caribbean be 'creolised,' thus making a positive association between creolization and creativity and resilience.'[15] Though the term is not easily defined, the understanding of creolization that Jackson appeals to, arguably, is that of a framework for the 'development of new traditions, aesthetics, and group identities out of combinations of formerly separate peoples and cultures,' a creative interplay that generates something new and worthwhile out of the loss wrought by colonialism.[16] By choosing this concept of creolization, which is so heavily identified with the Caribbean, Jackson also posits the idea of an indigenous Caribbean legal tradition.

But perhaps Jackson's creole jurisprudence may be more helpful as cultural concept already at play in the making and understanding of Caribbean law and the Caribbean than as a present goal of Caribbean legal thought. Anthropologist Aisha Khan warns against 'construing creolization...as about needing to find something to celebrate and recover some optimism from a typically bleak portrayal.'[17] Crucially, she observes that calls for creolization – and we would add calls for a Caribbean or creole jurisprudence – tend to stay in the realm of the theoretical or abstract.[18] That abstract 'Caribbean' philosophy provides little direction when faced with concrete problems – such as should Caribbean lawmakers adopt the Business Judgment Rule that limits director liability when a director reasonably believed her or his decision was in the best interests of the company,[19] or how should the doctrine of *uberrimae fidei*, or utmost good faith, in insurance contracts be applied in the Caribbean,[20] or how should Caribbean public law respond

---

14. D. Simmons, 'Judicial Legislation for the Commonwealth Caribbean: The Death Penalty, Delay and the Judicial Committee of the Privy Council' (1998) 3 Carib L B 1, 10.

15. L. Jackson, Chapter 1.

16. N.R. Spitzer, 'Monde Créole: The Cultural World of French Louisiana Creoles and the Creolization of World Cultures' (2003) 116 Journal of American Folklore, 58–59.

17. A. Khan, 'Journey to the Center of the Earth: The Caribbean as Master Symbol' (2001) 16 Cultural Anthropology 271, 282.

18. Ibid.

19. S. Goldson, Chapter 2.

20. L. Walcott, Chapter 4.

to 'new blends of public and private power,'[21] or when can a legitimate expectation arise in relation to an unincorporated treaty,[22] or what are the proper limits of implied constitutional norms.[23]

Moreover, if we regard a creole jurisprudence critically, then we will recognize that it is not 'neutral' and that 'certain elements of representation...are always chosen, [and] certain others get left out' of what is deemed Caribbean.[24] Creolization invokes an essentialized Caribbean, with a distinct, limited and readily identifiable logic.[25] Certain images figure more prominently than others as emblematically Caribbean – like children born out of wedlock and common law marriage in working-class black families. This concept can conceal the extent to which the Caribbean is imagined, including through the law, to be a space to which some belong and not others, distinctions and hierarchies which may be determined by race, gender, sexuality, class and origin.[26] For example, only towards the end of the twentieth century do we see what Godfrey Smith describes as a 'constitutional space' starting to emerge for indigenous people in the Caribbean.[27] Indigenous people have been, until recently, largely invisible as citizens of the Caribbean.

Further, when notions of unique Caribbeanness are wedded with the abstract nature of legal discourse, injustice and inequality are further masked and disempowerment entrenched.[28] Sir Hugh Wooding, for example, in 1967 identified the need for Caribbean law to recognize the ubiquity of heterosexual couples living together without the benefit of marriage but in 'the true spirit of a husband-and-wife relationship.'[29] A Caribbean legal philosophy would insist, he said, that the common law husband be treated like a *de jure* husband, entitled to some exculpation if he 'caught his woman in an act of quasi-adultery,' the paradigmatic act of provocation at common law.[30] But the call for a Caribbean jurisprudence here, Tracy Robinson argues, merely obscures the gendered assumptions that underlie the common law rule of provocation – that men have proprietary rights in women's bodies and sexuality – and it betrays the way in which privilege, in the name of the developing Caribbean nation, is appropriated for certain subjects and not others.[31]

---

21. A. Aman, 'Globalizations, Democracy, and the Need for a New Administrative Law' (2003) 10 Indiana J Glob Legal Studies 125, 129. See Antoine, Chapter 3.
22. D. Berry, Chapter 5, E. Ventose, Chapter 6.
23. T. Robinson, Chapter 11.
24. Khan (n 17) 292.
25. T. Robinson, 'A Caribbean Common Law' (2007) 49 Race and Class 118, 123.
26. Ibid 121.
27. G. Smith, Chapter 10.
28. E. Mertz, *The Language of Law School: Learning to 'Think Like a Lawyer'* (OUP, Oxford 2007) 213.
29. H. Wooding (n 11).
30. Ibid.
31. Robinson (n 25).

For such reasons, the project of defining and identifying *a Caribbean jurisprudence,* as a search for an emancipatory truth and a distinct and separate way of seeing the world, may not be as worthwhile an undertaking as has been assumed for decades. Still, we should not abandon it entirely, but instead view it as a form of cultural discourse or legal consciousness. When structured distinctions and hierarchies are taken into account, law in the Caribbean emerges as having different meanings for different people, not only in the past, but as a feature of the present.[32] Jackson's interest in a legal realist analysis of Caribbean law is helpful here, and even more so what Sally Merry terms a 'new legal realism.'[33] The latter continues the focus on the operation of law in everyday life but with a new interest in tracking 'the flows of people, ideas, laws, and institutions across national boundaries,' recognising the importance of 'local cultural understandings of law' and foregrounding 'interactions in situations of unequal power.'[34]

Rose-Marie Antoine's detailed inquiry into how judges balance the public/private divide in employment, and how they should do so is very much in this vein. Courts and lawmakers today have to contend with institutional arrangements designed for very different political, social and economic times. Caribbean constitutions set up mechanisms for tempering the plenitude of governmental power, including an elaborate scheme, through service commissions, for regulating the government's status as the single most important and the most powerful employer. But there now is a global trend towards reducing the size of government by privatizing some of the functions carried out by the state. Public sector reform designed to improve efficiency and accountability is a corollary to privatization in the Caribbean. Many of the privatization initiatives do not transfer resources and responsibilities entirely to the private domain, but preserve an important role for the state, creating what some now call the 'third sector.'[35] This is characterized by centralization of policymaking and strategy and a decentralization of operational management,[36] or a hybrid of 'public direction and private enterprise.'[37] Antoine points out a challenge faced by Caribbean courts in balancing public and private in this new terrain, namely, whether to extend public

---

32. R. Cotterrell, 'Transnational Communities and the Concept of Law' (2008) 21 Ratio Juris 1, 5.
33. S. Merry, 'New Legal Realism: New Legal Realism and the Ethnography of Transnational Law' (2006) 31 Law & Soc Inquiry 975.
34. Ibid 976, 978.
35. P. Vincent-Jones, 'The New Public Contracting: Public Versus Private Ordering?' (2007) Indiana Journal of Global Legal Studies 259, 259–60.
36. N. Deakin and K. Walsh, 'The Enabling State: The Role of Markets and Contracts' [1996] Public Administration 33, 36–37.
37. Vincent-Jones (n 35) 275.

law protection and judicial review to contracts of employment or instead to focus on private law remedies. She prefers interventionist approaches by Caribbean courts to protect persons who are in effect employees of the state and vulnerable to the exercise of the tremendous state power.

2. Making Law in Small Jurisdictions: Legal Transplantation and the Problem of 'Fit'

Legal change and reform are important tools of development in the Caribbean. For at least four decades, Caribbean jurists have questioned the blind transplantation of foreign statues in the region and the heavy reliance on foreign, particularly English, precedents in the Caribbean. The principal concerns have been the lack of fit between the Caribbean and legal rules developed elsewhere and the need for more autochthonous legal solutions.

Many chapters in this book indicate how extensively the courts of the Commonwealth Caribbean rely upon the decisions of the House of Lords and English Court of Appeal for the development of the common law.[38] Lesley Walcott, for example, offers an overview of the issues facing contemporary Caribbean insurance law, particularly focusing on the doctrine of *uberrimae fidei*, or utmost good faith, and she raises questions about the impact of English law. She notes the heavy reliance upon English cases like the House of Lords' decision in *Pan Atlantic Insurance*,[39] and argues that the Commonwealth Caribbean jurisprudence itself has yet to provide clear answers to the nature and scope of *uberrimae fidei*. Jackson, in contrast, offers a trenchant critique of lawmaking in the Caribbean, by legislatures as well as judges, and their unquestioning adoption of English statutes and precedents. He concedes that the transplanted laws meant for other societies become 'West Indian,' but argues that they rest on the Caribbean like 'the illfitting garment of a loved one.'[40]

Similarly, Suzanne Ffolkes-Goldson illustrates the 'lack of fit' with Caribbean corporate governance regimes. These have been transplanted from developed countries to the Caribbean and she argues that they are not well suited for the corporate culture of the region. The dilemma is magnified by the heavy reliance on precedents from the donor jurisdiction in which the original donor law has often undergone significant amendment. Both judges and academics struggle with whether to have regard to precedents from the donor jurisdiction when there are notable differences that now exist between the donor and transplanted laws. For

---

38. See, e.g., L. Walcott, Chapter 4, L. Jackson, Chapter 1, E. Ventose, Chapter 6.
39. [1995] 1 AC 501 (HL).
40. L. Jackson, Chapter 1.

example, many Caribbean countries have adopted versions of Canadian company legislation. But recent amendments to the Canadian legislation in 2004 have been interpreted as importing the American-styled 'Business Judgment Rule' which creates a presumption that directors are not liable for a breach of care, diligence and skill for a decision, if there was no conflict of the director's duty and interest, the director was informed and reasonably believed the decision was appropriate at the time it was made, and that the director had a rational belief that it was in the best interest of the company. Goldson notes the difficulties in determining whether this Rule should also apply to Caribbean countries which have enacted earlier versions of the Canadian law.

Using Jonathan Miller's typology of legal transplants, the Canadian company legislation might be described as a 'legitimacy-generating transplant' that is adopted in part because of the prestige of the foreign model.[41] Miller explains that since the legitimacy here lies in the prestige of the foreign model, local actors often cede future control over the interpretation of their version.[42] Future interpretations from the donor country are adopted even though they rest on amendments or changes in the donor statute.[43] Furthermore, if the transplanted model loses prestige in the donor country and is radically amended, this affects its continued prestige and attractiveness in the transplanting country.[44]

Further, Kamille Adair's analysis of the recent introduction of human trafficking legislation in Guyana, Jamaica and Belize points to the dangers of the 'externally-dictated transplant.'[45] She shows how those statutes were adopted as a result of external pressures, primarily from the United States, and without the necessary domestic needs assessment or any critical evaluation of the existing domestic norms or international norms which were 'carbon copied' into the legislation. Thus, the Caribbean statutes fail to effectively differentiate between the recruitment and transportation aspects of trafficking, on the one hand, and the forced labour or slavery-like practices that result, on the other. As such, the anti-trafficking statutes of Belize, Guyana and Jamaica do not provide for the offence of exploitation in and of itself, independently from the chain process of recruitment, transportation and receipt. This provokes Adair to argue for the incorporation of three different perspectives into anti-trafficking legislation: the law enforcement, human rights, and

41. J. Miller, 'A Typology of Legal Transplants: Using Sociology, Legal History and Argentine Examples to Explain the Transplant Process' (2003) 51 Am J Comp L 839, 854.
42. Ibid 859.
43. Ibid.
44. Ibid 869.
45. See K. Adair, Chapter 7, Miller (n 41) 847.

labour rights approaches. She argues that by focusing too intently on the punitive law enforcement side of trafficking, Caribbean states run the risk of violating the labour and human rights of trafficking victims.

Ultimately, it is perhaps Ffolkes-Goldson who most clearly identifies the lack of fit of transplanted laws as well as shows how fraught the very question of 'fit' or suitability of transplanted laws for the Caribbean can be. The corporate culture in the Caribbean is one of closely-held companies with interlocking directorships.[46] Corporate governance regimes from developed countries would negatively impact these interlocking directorships. Yet it is hardly an answer to say these corporate governance rules are unsuitable because they would circumscribe an entrenched aspect of Caribbean corporate culture. Disruption of these interlocking directorships might be viewed as a worthwhile undertaking. The question of what is Caribbean or 'fits' Caribbean culture and society does not take us far enough. The more pointed and useful interrogation is what do reformers want to accomplish and how do they wish to balance competing interests at stake in a changing global economy.

Some scholars like Ann and Robert Seidman say quite categorically that legal transplants do not work and that the transfer of law from the developed to developing world will not aid the latter's development.[47] They argue that transplanted law will not produce the same behaviour in both places because the operation of 'pre-existing, country specific non-legal factors' will generate different responses.[48] Kevin Davis's point of departure, that making laws has different cost/benefit implications for large and small jurisdictions, provides another way of thinking about legal transplants in the Caribbean.[49] He assumes that when lawmakers assess whether to create indigenous laws or transplant foreign ones, there is no *a priori* answer. Lawmakers must weigh a range of considerations, including cost. Using insolvency rules, he identifies many reasons why Jamaica might not want to transplant foreign laws, reasons very comparable to Ffolkes-Goldson's. These include differences in the Jamaica economy and that of developed countries and the absence of specialized commercial courts that will determine complex cases.[50] He does not end there, and weighs this against the relative lack of experience of local lawmakers in the area and the relatively low volume of economic activity likely to benefit from their hard work, and the high costs of

---

46. See H. Beckles, *Corporate Power in Barbados, The Mutual Affair: Economic Injustice in a Political Democracy* (Lighthouse Communications, Bridgetown 1989).
47. A. Seidman and R. Seidman, *State and Law in the Development Process: Problem-Solving and Institutional Change in the Third World* (MacMillan Press, Basingstoke 1994) 46.
48. Ibid 46.
49. K. Davis, 'Law-Making in Small Jurisdictions' (2006) 56 U Toronto L J 151.
50. Ibid 176.

communicating the indigenous rules in a small jurisdiction.[51] Ironically, he concludes that the best solution might be to adopt the pre-2005 Canadian legislation that contains a large number of broad standards, recognizing that it 'is not perfectly tailored to fit local circumstances and may generate legal uncertainty.'[52] Even with these shortcomings, he says this may be a better approach because 'the costs of achieving a better fit between legal norms and the society to which they apply, and of resolving legal uncertainty, are more likely to be prohibitive in small jurisdictions than in large ones.'[53] Davis presents no clear winner, but indicates hard pragmatic assessments small jurisdictions must make in the development of their law.

On this approach legal transplantation is not inherently good or bad. Jackson is right to be suspicious of a formal mode of analysis that says being successors to the 'heritage of English law'[54] is 'reason enough' to adopt English law in the Caribbean without scrutinizing the substance of the laws imported to determine their value.[55] He is most concerned about how the rigid rules of precedent inhibit Caribbean judges from following a course of their own. At the same time we should see the transmigration of legal concepts and institutions as a normal and essential element of the development of law.[56] Professor Esin Orucu notes that 'innovation in law is small and borrowing and imitation is of central importance in understanding the course of legal change.'[57] The small jurisdictions of the Caribbean must now give closer attention to why, when, how, what and from where we borrow laws, rather than an outright rejection, or uncritical adoption, of transplantation.[58] The starting point must be the needs and context of the Caribbean and the costs of lawmaking. Models from other jurisdictions, and these increasingly today include other Caribbean countries, should be considered only if they are functional, can reasonably meet these identified needs and be 'tuned' to address issues of compatibility.[59] The sobering reality is that the most satisfactory and optimal outcomes are not likely to be perfect ones in small Caribbean jurisdictions.

---

51. Ibid.
52. Ibid.
53. Ibid.
54. K. Patchett, 'English Law in the West Indies: A Conference Report' (1963) 12 ICLQ 922, 922.
55. See Sujit Choudhry's analysis of the genealogical argument for comparative constitutional law in 'Globalization in Search of Justification: Toward a Theory of Comparative Constitutional Interpretation' (1999) 74(3) *Ind LJ* 819, 910.
56. E. Orucu, 'Law as Transposition' (2002) 51 ICLQ 205, 205.
57. Ibid 206.
58. Ibid.
59. Ibid 207–8.

3. Law in the Caribbean: Transnational Dimensions

Another major theme in this book is the transnational nature of law in the Caribbean. Roger Cotterrell's analysis that 'the firmly defined jurisdiction of the nation state and the politically organized national society [are not] the terrain from which all legal phenomena can be observed and evaluated' is very apt for the Caribbean.[60] One dimension of this transnational law is regional, and it has distinctly imperial roots that have received postcolonial succour. Saunders J of the Caribbean Court of Justice (CCJ) concedes that the Privy Council as a final court of appeal contributed to the identity of a transnational Caribbean law because 'so far as the judicial power is concerned, we have been practically united.'[61] This he described as a 'solid edifice' on which shared law and judicial decision-making has been built.[62] When the founders of Commonwealth Caribbean legal education created a *common* law programme to serve several Caribbean states that did more than elucidate 'West Indian law.' It served as an interpretive community that made it more real. Notwithstanding the obvious localized dimensions of law in the region – each country had its own Parliament and courts – the Faculty of Law asserted the existence of a *common* regional law and aimed at producing lawyers who could practise *anywhere*. It is little wonder that Mindie Lazarus-Black's review of the early history of Caribbean legal education concludes that the products of the Faculty of Law 'were global before that concept held currency.'[63]

Transnational here has a second meaning, describing what the CCJ calls that 'confluence' between national and international law.[64] Forged in a colonial context, and often described as the first site of modernity and the 'proving ground' for international capitalism,[65] the Caribbean would almost inevitably today have laws with strong transnational dimensions, that is 'a kind of hybrid between domestic and international law that can be downloaded, uploaded, or transplanted from one national system to another.'[66] Modern constitutions, for the most part, were shaped in the image of each other and Westminster. The justiciable bills of rights introduced in the constitutions were modelled on African

---

60. R. Cotterrell, 'Transnational Communities and the Concept of Law' (2008) 21 Ratio Juris 1, 5.
61. A. Saunders, 'The Caribbean Court of Justice and the Legal Profession: Promoting our Caribbriprudence,' address delivered to the OECS Bar Association, Grenada (21 September 2007) 2.
62. Ibid.
63. M. Lazarus-Black, 'After Empire: Training Lawyers as a Postcolonial Enterprise' (2008) 25 Small Axe 38, 39.
64. *AG v Joseph* [2006] CCJ 3 (AJ), (2006) 69 WIR 104, 151 [106].
65. B. Maurer, 'Book Review of Sheller, Consuming the Caribbean: From Arawaks to Zombies' (2004) 78 New West Indian Guide/ Nieuwe West-Indische Gids 305, 305.
66. H. Koh, 'Why Transnational Law Matters' (2006) 24 Penn St Int'l L Rev 745, 753.

predecessors' which in turn used the European Convention on Human Rights as a template.[67] Recent legislative initiatives in the US against human trafficking took their cues from the Palermo Protocol to prevent, suppress and punish trafficking in persons. As Adair shows, it was then translated into US foreign policy directives and legislation in the Caribbean and elsewhere.[68] International financial calamities from the North have blown new corporate governance regimes southwards.[69] While rule of law initiatives in transitional democracies and developing countries have become a global phenomenon, in a parallel move, the CCJ seems to be institutionalizing the rule of law as an implied constitutional fundamental, not just at the level of national constitutions but in the Caribbean Community.[70]

References to decisions of foreign Commonwealth or common law courts and international human rights norms are now commonplace in the interpretation of the bills of rights of Caribbean constitutions.[71] Margaret Demerieux's chapter on the Privy Council, which is published posthumously, reveals that cosmopolitanism did not characterize the early period of Privy Council adjudication in the Caribbean.

More recently, in a series of Privy Council decisions and the inaugural CCJ decision of *AG v Joseph* discussed throughout this book, the relationship between national and international law in the Caribbean has been brought into sharp relief. These death penalty cases have raised issues about whether domestic tribunals can refer to international law, for what purpose, and whether international law – including the practices of treaty bodies and tribunals – can have tangible effects in national legal systems.

In exploring the complexities of these cases, David Berry, argues that the common law rules regarding use of international law within the domestic courts invoked before the Privy Council and CCJ are not vague or contradictory. Rather, these rules are precise, comprehensive and comprehensible. He argues that their application by the Privy Council in death penalty cases has been problematic, especially in light of the apparent incompatibility of the jurisprudence of the members the Privy Council with their own reasoning while sitting as the House of Lords. He observes that the Privy Council treats the Caribbean as more susceptible to international law than the United Kingdom, without explaining why.

---

67. See *Minister of Home Affairs v Fisher* (1979) 44 WIR 107 (PC Ber) 112.
68. K. Adair, Chapter 7.
69. S. Goldson, Chapter 2.
70. See *AG v Joseph* [2006] CCJ 3 (AJ), (2006) 69 WIR 104 (Bdos), *TCL v Caribbean Community* [2009] CCJ 4 (OJ), (2009) 74 WIR 319 [46], *TCL v Guyana* [2009] CCJ 5 (OJ), (2009) 74 WIR 302 [27].
71. See C. McCrudden, 'A Common Law of Human Rights? Transnational Judicial Conversations on Constitutional Rights' (2000) 20 OJLS 499.

For this reason, Berry is critical of Privy Council decisions like *Thomas v Baptiste,* which in effect, allowed international legal processes to have domestic effect without incorporation into the domestic law, and *Reyes,* in which the Privy Council treated the ECHR as having been directly applicable to Belize before independence. Even the CCJ's doctrine of legitimate expectation does not resolve the tension. Berry argues that under a strict dualist understanding of the relationship of international law and municipal law, it is difficult to see how one could have a *legitimate* expectation about a process which is not *legal* under domestic law, let alone even part of that domestic legal system.

Berry argues that if we want to modify the dualist approach, we must do so in a principled way. Wit J's approach in the case of *AG v Joseph* offers one model, but others more in keeping with the common law also can be developed and utilized. He suggests a wide range of legitimate ways in which international law can be used by national tribunals, from referring to international law as a non-binding, comparative and potentially persuasive authority, to more profound roles in which international law can play significant roles through incorporation, legislative transformation or interpretation. Customary international law, for example, becomes part of the law of the land – the common law – so long as it is not contradicted by statutory or judicial authority. Treaties can be transformed into domestic law through legislation and ambiguous domestic law, including both common and statutory law, can be interpreted in the light of international law, including unincorporated treaties. Finally, he suggests that Commonwealth Caribbean judges have a role to play in establishing the types of statutes capable of being viewed as transformation statutes – in other words, those implementing treaty obligations in domestic law. In this vein, Berry suggests that state actions before treaty bodies may demonstrate an understanding by the executive that particular, previously-enacted statutes are to be understood as implementing (subsequent) treaty obligations. Such actions may allow a judge, when arriving at an informed interpretation of the meaning of that statute, to look to the treaty which it is *now* meant to transform. Berry argues that by using such techniques Caribbean judges do not fall foul of the problems inherent in bringing international law in through the back door. Rather, they will simply be exercising the normal judicial function of arriving at an informed interpretation of domestic statutory and common law.

From the perspective of administrative law, Eddy Ventose takes a more sanguine view of the CCJ's treatment of the doctrine of legitimate expectations. Like Berry, he is critical of the Privy Council's contribution. On the question of legitimate expectations and unincorporated treaties, he describes the law generated by the Judicial Committee in death penalty cases as in a state of disarray, with differently constituted boards of the Privy Council coming to different conclusions and the 'dissents of yesterday became the majority decisions' of today, producing uncertainty.

Ventose agrees with the CCJ's conclusion that legitimate expectations arise in this narrow case of condemned prisoners and says that this will not amount to a wholesale enforcement of unincorporated treaties because the following must be established: (a) ratification (which clearly was not of itself sufficient to found a legitimate expectation – properly understood); (b) positive statements by the state to abide by the Convention; (c) an established practice by the state of allowing condemned persons to allow their petitions to be processed before execution; and (d) Parliament in making that amendment impliedly recognized that it was the practice and indeed the obligation of the state to await the Commission's process, at least for some period of time. He anchors the appropriateness of the application of legitimate expectations in the doctrine of the rule of law, that to allow the state to renege on its promise or change its policy amounts to an abuse of power. The rule of law dictates that the court should not be impotent to provide a remedy where there has been abuse of power by the executive. Where the executive promises to preserve existing policy for a specific group who would be substantially affected by the change in policy, it must keep its promise.

Transnational law has a third little explored element in the Caribbean. Most of the Caribbean law discussed in this book falls within orthodox definitions of law – case law, legislation, international conventions. Still, these chapters describe a much more expansive sphere of transnational rules and regulation that sit on the edge of and challenge conventional definitions of law. The Private Sector Organization of Jamaica (PSOJ)'s draft Corporate Governance Code, and the recommended Caribbean Code of Corporate Governance in Securities Markets and Caribbean Corporate Governance Principles discussed by Goldson are all attempts at private regulation that lack the imprimatur of the state, but significantly impact corporate culture and governance in the Caribbean. On the other hand, Goldson shows how state actors who are not lawmakers greatly impact the meaning and interpretation of the law. Jurisprudence, she shows, develops from the offices of registrars of companies as legal practitioners seek the advice of registrars on statutory interpretation. These evolving standards are shared across jurisdictions and thus contribute to the wider transnational nature of Caribbean law.

4. 'The Habits of Constitutionalism' [72]

Constitutionalism, according to Richard Kay, 'entails an attempt "to keep a government in order."'[73] In other words, it 'implements the rule of law.'[74] Over the last half century, the Caribbean has been coming to terms with a system of limited government subject to written constitutions with entrenched bills of rights. It took time for the Judicial Committee of the Privy Council as the primary interpreter of these new constitutions, to appreciate fully the implications of judicial review under a written constitution with an entrenched bill of rights.[75] In the early post-independence period, constitutional adjudication was unfamiliar, and, as Lord Bingham acknowledged, some courts resisted giving the written constitutions and their protection of fundamental rights full effect as the supreme law.[76] The familiar approach of early Caribbean courts and the Privy Council was to subordinate the constitutions to the common law, one dimension of the Caribbean's common law constitutionalism.[77]

By tracing the trajectory of the jurisprudence of the Judicial Committee of the Privy Council from its early cases, Margaret DeMerieux reveals how the Board over time weaned itself from its absolute reliance upon the common law. Foundational cases such as *Nasralla*[78] reveal the Privy Council deciding issues on the basis of the existing law and the common law, even in the face of stated constitutional rights. The old approach was to treat constitutional bills of rights as codifying or leaving the common law unchanged. Demerieux notes a shift, by the end of the 1970s and early '80s, to recognizing that the constitutional provisions provided for rights differing in scope from those available at common law, including new rights, and could found an independent cause of action. The Board's decisions in *Maharaj No*[79] and *Thornhill*[80] opened new ground by not permitting the assertion of common law to defeat the fundamental rights expressed in the bills of rights. DeMerieux offers a vision of a broader compatibility between the common law and the bills of rights. Both the common law and the interpretation of the bills of rights are matters

---

72. L. Ackermann, 'The Obligations on Government and Society in our Constitutional State to Respect and Support Independent Constitutional Structures' (2000) 3 Potchefstroom Electronic Law Journal/Potchefstroomse Elektroniese Regsblad 1, 4.
73. R. Kay, 'American Constitutionalism' in L Alexander (ed), *Constitutionalism* (CUP, Cambridge 1998) 16.
74. L. Alexander, 'Introduction' in L. Alexander (ed), *Constitutionalism* (CUP, Cambridge 1998) 1, 4.
75. *Bowe v R* [2006] UKPC 10, (2006) 68 WIR 10 (PC Bah) [42].
76. Tom Bingham, *Widening Horizons: The Influence of Comparative Law and International Law on Domestic Law* (The Hamlyn Lectures) (CUP, Cambridge 2010) 69.
77. See M. Demerieux, Chapter 8, T. Robinson, 'Gender, Nation and the Common Law Constitution' (2008) 28(4) OJLS 735.
78. (1967) 10 WIR 299 (PC Ja).
79. (1978) 30 WIR 310 (PC T&T).
80. (1976) WIR 498 (PC T&T).

for judges, and *common law adjudication* can itself develop human rights, or recognize and create new rights. This accords with Fraser JA's understanding of the common law as a 'pragmatic system of rules and principles fashioned by the courts to meet the needs of society as those needs changed from time to time.'[81]

With few exceptions, the post-1960 constitutions marking self-government or independence from Britain all contained bills of rights, a dramatic turnaround in British decolonization policy.[82] The thinking at the time the bill of rights in the 1960 Nigerian Constitution was drafted, which became the model for the Commonwealth including the Caribbean, was that an entrenched bill of rights would better protect minority groups. Ironically, Caribbean independence constitutions have been the least durable in the most plural and ethnically diverse Caribbean countries: Belize, Guyana and Trinidad and Tobago. The last two – Guyana and Trinidad and Tobago, now republics, are the only countries in the region that enacted new constitutions after independence. Belize's independence constitution of 1981 still governs, but it has undertaken far more radical reforms than its Caribbean neighbours with much older independence constitutions.

Stark gaps can be found between the constitution on paper and its workings in Caribbean countries, evidence that the habits of constitutionalism are not always well entrenched. Arif Bulkan shows how 'bare' constitutional protections for judicial independence in Guyana have been evaded or manipulated by governments outright.[83] For example, judicial appointment processes have been subverted by the creation of new judicial offices, by a failure to adhere meaningfully to consultation requirements and by a refusal to consent to the appointment of a replacement judicial officer when a position became vacant, thereby requiring temporary appointments. Judicial independence has also infringed by post-retirement extensions of judicial tenure, which by their nature are precarious and subject to political influence. While judicial independence can be threatened by the erosion of the jurisdiction of the Court, as forewarned in the early decision in *Hinds*,[84] Bulkan argues that the same occurred by removing, without replacement, a layer of appellate protection when the jurisdiction of the Judicial Committee of the Privy Council was abolished in Guyana.

Guyana became the third English-speaking Caribbean country to gain independence in 1966; Belize in 1981 was one of the last. Godfrey

---

81. *Lassalle v AG* (1971) 18 WIR 379 (CA T&T) 404. See T. Robinson, Chapter 11.
82. C. Parkinson, *Bills of Rights and Decolonization: The Emergence of Domestic Human Rights Instruments in Britain's Overseas Territories* (OUP, Oxford 2007).
83. A. Bulkan, Chapter 9.
84. (1975) 24 WIR 324 (PC Ja).

Smith points out one distinct advantage of later independence. In the case of Belize, it had the benefit of 20 years of vicarious constitutional experience from its neighbours in the Caribbean and Commonwealth to guide it in the constitution making process. To begin with, it did not include many of the stultifying aspects of the earlier constitutions. Its general savings law clause had limited application, it gave explicit right to redress for breaches of the opening section to the bill of rights and it included the right to work. Smith argues that these changes gave judges a head start in expanding the frontiers of constitutional interpretation.

It is plain that the advancement of constitutionalism is not the 'exclusive province of the judiciary.'[85] Constitutional reforms introduced to ensure greater respect for the rule of law can be sidestepped by the executive. On the other hand, there is some indication that Caribbean legislatures can play a meaningful role in developing the habits of constitutionalism. Smith describes in Belize a 'symbiotic, mutually re-enforcing dynamic between the judicial and the legislature' in which the Belize legislature has been 'proactive, even aggressive' in developing the constitution since independence. Most amendments, almost counterintuitively, expanded citizen rights, strengthened judicial independence and gave the Senate unprecedented power. And he observes that most reforms have come from recommendations of broad-based political reform processes or election manifesto promises. It is that 'dynamic complementarity' between judiciary and legislature that he explains finally created a 'constitutional space' for indigenous people in Belize.[86]

Despite the hope that legislatures will deepen constitutionalism through ethical constitutional reform, undertaken alongside broad-based consultations, Bulkan and Robinson think that in the immediate future, more will turn on what judges do. Since 1991, virtually every single Commonwealth Caribbean country has been engaged in some constitutional reform process. These have been stalled by oppositions with sufficient parliamentary force to veto reforms on partisan political grounds or by new governments unwilling to pursue reforms already underway. The question is whether the development of unwritten or implied constitutional norms by the judiciary could buttress constitutionalism in the Caribbean. Bulkan stresses that the need for such norms is most evident where the constitutional texts, in particular the bills of rights, are lacking. Resort to the constitution's underlying values, such as the separation of powers, the rule of law, democracy, and judicial independence, can clarify contradictory constitutional provisions

---

85. G. Smith, Chapter 10. See A. Bulkan, Chapter 9.
86. G. Smith, Chapter 10.

and resolve difficult cases. Robinson argues that articulating and giving effect to 'our inherent constitution' – implied constitutional norms – could make the constitutions more *our own*. Her argument is that given the vagaries of the political scene, people will turn to the courts to maintain core fundamental constitutional values. Though implied constitutional norms will generate a measure of uncertainty, she argues that they can help chart progress in the face of 'imperfect' constitutions. Ralph Carnegie dared Caribbean constitutional lawyers to, on occasion, read the texts of their 'imperfect' constitutions lightly and focus more of them on a form of poetry, laden with symbolism and open to different meanings over time.[87] In his view, rather than the text revealing all, it would be 'experience and reasonableness and restraint in its administration [that would determine] its effective working.'[88]

5. Transjudicialism and Institutional Redesign

In terms of institutional challenges, perhaps the key change alluded to peripherally in several of the chapters in this book is the creation of the CCJ.[89] The CCJ plays two roles in the region, and thus can simultaneously influence different levels of Caribbean jurisprudence: (1) it sits as a final appellate court, and thus can interpret national laws and the common law, and (2) it sits as a treaty-interpreting tribunal, empowered to interpret and apply norms governing CARICOM's Single Market and Economy and, at least potentially, regional customary international law.[90]

The formation of the CCJ, a unique 'hybrid institution' and a regional court designed to advance economic integration and a Caribbean jurisprudence, is understood commonly in nationalist terms, as 'completing the independence' of Caribbean states. Still, the concept of the independent nation-state that propelled the decolonization process in the mid-to-late twentieth century has been altered dramatically by the forces of globalization and the internationalization of law. As

---

87. A.R. Carnegie, "The Importance of Constitutional Law in Jamaica's Development' October (1985) WILJ 43, 50
88. Ibid 45.
89. Created by the Agreement Establishing the Caribbean Court of Justice (adopted 14 Feb 2001, entered into force 23 Jul 2002) <http://www.caribbeancourtofjustice.org/court_ instruments.html> accessed 17 Aug 2010 ['CCJ Agreement']. The status of this treaty was obtained from: CARICOM Secretariat, 'Matrix of Agreements' (updated to July 2010, but specified to be 'a work in progress') (on file with authors) ['Matrix']. The 2006 version of the Matrix of Agreements is available online at <http://www.caricom.org/jsp/secretariat/legal_ instruments_index.jsp?menu=secretariat> accessed 17 Aug 2010.
90. The following 12 states are contracting parties to the CCJ Agreement and are thereby subject to the Court's original jurisdiction: Antigua and Barbuda, Barbados, Belize, Dominica, Grenada, Guyana, Jamaica, St Kitts and Nevis, St Lucia, St Vincent and the Grenadines, Suriname, and Trinidad and Tobago. Matrix (n 89).

demonstrated by Janet McClean, globalization is connected to the experiences of empire; she argues that the colonial experience of looking outside national borders at different sources of law and seeking to be a part of a broader legal community created 'habits of mind that help ease the transition to new supranational tribunals and supranational law.'[91] Likewise today the Caribbean Court of Justice has noted the 'distinct, irreversible tendency towards confluence of domestic and international jurisprudence.'[92] Arguably, the establishment of the court exemplifies the trend towards 'judicial globalization,' which is described a 'process of judicial interaction across, above and below borders, exchanging ideas and cooperating in cases involving national as much as international law.'[93] The establishment of a transnational regional/international court, that is the final arbiter of domestic legal matters in sovereign countries is, if nothing else, a concession to cosmopolitanism and interdependence.[94]

With respect to the CCJ's appellate jurisdiction, although for a time, only Barbados and Guyana allowed such cases to go to the court. They recently have been joined by Belize, and the number of countries allowing such appeals is likely to increase in the future.[95] Although similar to the jurisdiction of the Privy Council, the CCJ's appellate jurisdiction may possess a greater potential to change the nature of Commonwealth Caribbean law. This is because as a post-independence, regionally-created appellate court, the CCJ automatically will be vested with a legitimacy that must be envied by the Privy Council. Judges are selected by an independent Regional Judicial and Legal Services Commission,[96] are safeguarded in terms of autonomy and independence by regional treaties,[97] and bring with them considerable personal experience of

---

91. J. McLean, 'From Empire to Globalization: The New Zealand Experience' (2004) 11 Indiana J Glob Legal Studies 161, 180.
92. *Boyce v AG* [2006] CCJ 3 (AJ), (2006) 69 WIR 104 [106].
93. A-M Slaughter, 'Judicial Globalization' (2000) 40 Virginia J Int'l Law 1103, 1104.
94. T. Robinson (n 25) 123.
95. Belize recently replaced the Privy Council with the Caribbean Court of Justice: A. Ramos, 'Sayonara, Privy Council! Hello, CCJ!' *Amandala Online* (Belize City 14 May 2010) <http://www.amandala.com.bz/index.php?id=9837> accessed 19 Aug 2010.
96. For example, the CCJ Agreement, art V.
97. For example, the CCJ Agreement, arts IV and V (appointment and removal), VII and XXX (privileges and immunities), IX (tenure of office), XXVIII (finances). See also the Revised Agreement Establishing the Caribbean Court of Justice Trust Fund (adopted 12 January 2004, entered into force 27 January 2004); Protocol on the Privileges and Immunities of the Caribbean Court of Justice and the Regional Judicial and Legal Services Commission (adopted and entered into force 4 July 2003); Protocol to the Agreement Establishing the Caribbean Court of Justice Relating to Security of Tenure of Members of the Regional Judicial and Legal Services Commission (adopted and entered into force 6 July 2006); Protocol to the Agreement Establishing the Caribbean Court of Justice Relating to the Tenure of Office of Judges of the Court (adopted 26 May 2007, provisionally applied from 7 June 2007, not yet in force). The latter four treaties are all available through the website of the Caribbean Court of Justice at <http://www.caribbeancourtofjustice.org/court_instruments.html> accessed 17 August 2010. Status information is from Matrix (n 89).

the cultural, social and legal norms of Commonwealth Caribbean jurisdictions.

In its second role the CCJ is the original, exclusive, compulsory, and final interpreter of CARICOM's constituent treaty, the Revised Treaty of Chaguaramas (Revised Treaty),[98] and other relevant rules of international law.[99] This original jurisdiction is not subject to significant commentary in the chapters of this book, but is worth highlighting because it may prove to be another source of unification for the Caribbean. Sitting in its original jurisdiction, the CCJ can overtly influence Caribbean integration by interpreting, implementing and enforcing the rules, values and overarching legal architecture of the Revised Treaty. But it can also do so in a subtler manner, in a way similar to the Privy Council. The decisions of the Privy Council – by drawing parallels between constitutional and legal provisions from several Commonwealth Caribbean states – push states to rethink their laws whenever similar provisions elsewhere are found wanting, and also inculcate a regional 'comparative law' habit. So too can the CCJ push states to compare, and at times borrow from, regional legislative developments which are meant to implement CARICOM rules. Further, the CCJ may force Caribbean countries to think more deeply about our regional enterprise, since the task of interpreting and enforcing the Revised Treaty will require the Court to deal with the real economic practicalities of regional trade and economic interaction. For example, several of the first original jurisdiction decisions deal concretely with the requirements for upholding, or seeking waiver of, the common external tariff (CET) on a fundamental natural resource necessary for regional development – cement.[100] In these cases, the CCJ initiated a bold new regional jurisprudence on issues concerning the requirements for *locus standi* of persons before the Court, the rules of treaty interpretation, the

---

98. Revised Treaty of Chaguaramas Establishing the Caribbean Community Including the CARICOM Single Market and Economy (adopted 5 July 2001, entered into force 1 January 2006) <http://www.caricomlaw.org/agreements.php> accessed 17 August 2010. The Revised Treaty entered into force in accordance with Article I of the Agreement to Enable the Entry Into Force of the Revised Treaty of Chaguaramas Establishing the Caribbean Community Including the CARICOM Single Market and Economy (adopted 21 December 2005, entered into force 9 February 2006) <http://www.caricomlaw.org/agreements.php> accessed 17 August 2010. Article I of the Agreement was intended to have retroactive effect: Statement by Safiya Ali, General Counsel, CARICOM Secretariat (Personal email correspondence 24 August 2010).

99. CCJ Agreement, art XVII.

100. The eight original jurisdiction decisions of the CCJ as of May 2011 are: *TCL v Guyana* (Interim Order) [2008] CCJ 1 (OJ); *TCL v Guyana* (Jurisdiction) [2009] CCJ 1 (OJ), (2009) 74 WIR 302; *TCL v Caribbean Community* (Jurisdiction) [2009] CCJ 2 (OJ), (2009) 74 WIR 329; *Doreen Johnson v CARICAD* (Jurisdiction) [2009] CCJ 3 (OJ); *TCL v Caribbean Community No 2* (Judgment) [2009] CCJ 4 (OJ), (2009) 75 WIR 194; *TCL v Guyana No 2* (Judgment) [2009] CCJ 5 (OJ), (2009) 75 WIR 327; *TCL v Guyana* (Decision on extension) [2009] CCJ 6 (OJ); *TCL v Guyana No 3* (Judgment on contempt) [2010] CCJ 1 (OJ), (2010) 76 WIR 312. All of the Court's judgments are available through <http://www.caribbeancourtofjustice.org/judgments.html> accessed 17 August 2010.

nature of CARICOM, the purpose of the Single Market and Economy, and the availability of forms of relief in the original jurisdiction. More profoundly, these original jurisdiction decisions already reveal that by ratifying the Revised Treaty Member States of the Caribbean Community have changed the legal nature of the region. They have conferred upon private economic entities 'rights capable of being enforced directly on the international plane,'[101] and created 'a regional system under the rule of law,'[102] one which implies a power of judicial review[103] and the potential for state liability in damages for breach of the Revised Treaty.[104] In these decisions, the CCJ also has signalled its willingness to interpret and apply general rules of customary international law, general principles of international law, and general principles of Community law.[105] The latter could serve as the basis for a number of far-reaching legal developments, as seen in other jurisdictions. In the jurisprudence of the European Court of Justice, for example, general principles of Community law were used as the judicial foundation for the principle of fundamental rights, long before human rights were recognized in the EU treaty regime.[106] In the Inter-American system of human rights, the rules of treaty interpretation have been construed to enable the use of regional declaratory instruments to read human rights into the broader treaty regime,[107] and a similar development could take place in the jurisprudence of the CCJ through interpretation of the Revised Treaty in light of the human rights principles of CARICOM's Charter of Civil Society.[108] Such developments, and potential developments, augur well for increased regional integration which, although in this instance focused on the CARICOM Single Market and Economy, may have broader long term implications for the development of both regional and national legal systems, including human rights systems. By acting on both the national and regional planes the CCJ is at the forefront of developing national, and perhaps even regional, constitutional law.

---

101. *TCL v Guyana* [2009] CCJ 1 (OJ) [18].
102. *TCL v Caribbean Community* [2009] CCJ 2 (OJ) [32].
103. *TCL v Caribbean Community No 2* [2009] CCJ 4 (OJ) [38].
104. *TCL v Guyana No 2* [2009] CCJ 5 (OJ) [27].
105. *TCL v CARICOM* [2009] CCJ 2 (OJ) [41] (referring to 'general principles of law common to Member States').
106. For example, *Stauder v Ulm* (Case 29/69) [1969] ECR 419 (ECJ), *Nold v Commission* (Case 4/73) [1974] ECR 491 (ECJ), *Roquette Frères SA v Directeur Général de la Concurrence de la Consommation et de la Répression des Fraudes* (Case C-94/00) [2002] ECR I-9011(ECJ).
107. *Interpretation of the American Declaration of the Rights and Duties of Man within the Framework of Article 64 of the American Convention on Human Rights*, Advisory Opinion OC-10/89 of 14 July 1989, Inter-American Court of Human Rights, Series A, No 10 <http://www.corteidh.or.cr/opiniones.cfm> accessed 19 April 2011.
108. Charter of Civil Society for the Caribbean Community, adopted at the Eighth Inter-Sessional Meeting of the Conference of Heads of Government of the Caribbean Community on 19 February 1997 <http://www.caricom.org/jsp/secretariat/legal_instruments/chartercivilsociety.jsp> accessed 19 April 2011.

I.

LAWMAKING
IN THE CARIBBEAN

Fi We Law: The Emergence of Caribbean Jurisprudence and the Doctrine of Precedent

Leighton M. Jackson

1. Introduction

When speaking of 'Commonwealth Caribbean jurisprudence,' one is faced with the difficulty that the term may be without meaningful content on a conceptual level. The laws in our states – constitutional, statutory and judge-made – are for the most part, the rules originally devised for and meant to govern societies other than our own. This does not deny the comfortable but deceptive feeling of ownership – like wearing the ill-fitting garment of a loved one; you have a feeling of belonging in it, its ill-fit and your refusal to make alterations is proof of your commitment or sacrificial reverence. Even in light of the modern day trumpeting of 'globalisation' the texture of Caribbean life – cultural, social, economic and political – remains significantly different from the place from which these laws come and continue to come.

The question is why this lag between law and society has remained so long after the institution of independent and sovereign legislatures, native judges and lawyers, local legal education and world-acclaimed local university scholarship in the social sciences. Keith Patchett, then an Assistant Lecturer at the University of Sheffield, and who, a decade later, became the first Professor and Dean of the newly created Faculty of Law, University of the West Indies (UWI), promised in 1963 that we would be well on our way to creating a Caribbean jurisprudence when certain prerequisite institutions were in place: secondary sources, such as textbooks and journals, current and full indices and digests of legislation, law reporting with proper indexing and digests, a systematic approach to law reform, especially in the matters of 'lawyers law,' critical commentary on judicial decisions as a salutary check upon judicial scholarship, a West Indian law school which teaches the law in use in the West Indies, and not just in England, and the special problems facing the West Indian lawyer, and, as an important unifying factor, a court of appeal with an all-embracing jurisdiction.[1] Much of these have been attained, perhaps not

---

1. K. Patchett, 'English Law in the West Indies: A Conference Report' (1963) 12 ICLQ 922, 962–66.

perfectly but certainly, substantially, yet there has not been a satisfying movement in the direction of a Caribbean jurisprudence.

The question therefore remains, what has stultified the movement for the emergence of laws, judicial decision-making and an institutional framework of law, which reflects and responds readily and meaningfully to the realities of Caribbean societies? The answer is the lack of commitment of our rulers – legislators, judges, lawyers and legal educators – to the kinds of discourse, the kinds of argumentation, to justify the meanings of our legal rules based on our existential reality.[2] In short, there has not been a creolization of the inherited laws and institutions, as has happened in much else of Caribbean life and institutions. The role of the types of legal argumentation or discourse in the creolization of law in the Caribbean is what this work is about. I advocate an approach that restricts the formalist application of case law precedent; one that promotes a greater engagement of the other modes of legal argumentation from a realist perspective. This will facilitate a more speedy evolution of a legal system to one that is not a mere subsidiary of a foreign nation's jurisprudence, but a self-conscious, self-evolving, self-evaluating dialogue for the emergence of *fi we law*.[3]

2. English Law in the Caribbean or Caribbean Law in English?

Dorcas Elizabeth White, one of the intellectual giants of 'Commonwealth Caribbean Jurisprudence,' not long after her graduation from the new Faculty of Law of the University of the West Indies in 1974 and joining the Faculty as a lecturer, wrote two seminal unpublished papers in which she sought to contain her seethe at Patchett's notion that there wasn't any such thing as 'West Indian law.'[4] She presented a two-pronged attack. First, at the continuing efficacy of the Privy Council

---

2. In speaking of the advancements in the arts, Rex Nettleford observed that 'To the one dimensional mind this spells schizophrenia, but to the Caribbean person living in his/her existential crossroads of existence, it is a source for creative action.' R. Nettleford *Inward Stretch, Outward Reach: A Voice from the Caribbean* (Macmillan Caribbean, London 1993) 9. However, we have not expressed our existential reality in our jurisprudence because, according to Simeon McIntosh, of the commitment of our 'discourse' to the British political idiom. S. McIntosh, 'West Indian Constitutional Discourse: A Poetics of Reconstruction' (1993) 1 Carib L R 12, 17.

3. The meaning of 'fi' is 'for.' When used with 'we' it means 'our.' E. Adams, *Understanding Jamaican Patois: An Introduction to Afro-Jamaican Grammar* (Kingston Publishers, Kingston 1991) 18.

4. D. White, 'Jettison the Judicial Committee? You T'ink It Easy?' (on file with the UWI Faculty of Law Library, nd); D. White, 'Patterns of Law Making in the West Indies' (on file with the UWI Faculty of Law Library, nd), The term 'Commonwealth Caribbean' seems now preferred to the term 'West Indian' especially in relation to law, as West Indies speaks of Columbus's geographical mistake as well as the fact that Commonwealth Caribbean indicates not only geography but is limited to those states that received English law and legal system.

4

dictum in *Robins v National Trust Co*[5] which proclaimed the indivisibility of 'English law,' its binding nature on 'colonial' courts and the supremacy of the House of Lords as the authority to settle what this 'English law' is. Second, and even more intensely, she seethed at the way the local Commonwealth Caribbean courts literally followed this commandment, necessarily viewing themselves as 'colonial courts.' While the objective of White's essays was to set the legal record straight,[6] she made as her central point the fact that acceptance of this heretical doctrine, together with the existence of the Privy Council as the highest court of appeal for our jurisdictions, meant that 'the courts of the Commonwealth Caribbean have been hedged in' and that this 'foreclose[d] any "opportunity to... contribute to" the development of any "common pool of case law"' in the way in which other ex-colonial common law jurisdictions such as Australia, Canada and the United States did.[7]

As a first step, White rejected the indivisibility of English law and asserted that the concept of Jamaican law or Barbadian or Trinidad and Tobagan or Guyanese law is not a myth. She said that 'When law once derived from the traditional English source has been received into a territory that law without losing its textual similarity to English law in force in England assumes a new identity and becomes the law of the "receiving" territory.'[8] White was clear that there is no confusion between the textual similarity with the source of the rules and the identity of those rules; 'its identity is inextricably bound up with the "receiving" territory.'[9] She acknowledged that the law in force in the Caribbean was derived 'almost *in toto* from a foreign source' and might not be very relevant to the region's needs, but she said,

> The fact is: West Indian law may be bad law, it may be irrelevant law, unsuitable to the peculiar circumstances of the region; It may be imposed law – that is, the law directed to the colonies by the British Parliament; it may be all that or even worse but it is still West Indian law.[10]

'This,' White says, 'is *the* only starting point.'[11] But *only* the starting point.

---

5. [1927] AC 515 (PC Can) 519.
6. She was seeking to counter the views proclaimed by Prof. Patchett in 'English Law in the West Indies' (n 1).
7. White, 'Jettison' (n 4) 19.
8. Ibid 15.
9. Ibid 16.
10. White, 'Patterns of Law Making' (n 4) 1–2.
11. Ibid 2 (emphasis added). It must be remembered that White, among the first graduates of the new Faculty of Law, to learn the law from the Caribbean perspective in the Caribbean rather than studying English law at British Universities and dining in the Inns of Court, would naturally rebel against the hegemony of all things English and specifically the notion that we have no law of our own.

Creolization of English Law

The question then is where have we gone from this starting point; or more pertinently, where do we go? Put another way: How do we make this law that is ours relevant and suitable? Patchett in his ironically titled article, 'English Law in the West Indies: A Conference Report,'[12] concluded that, 'At the present time it is premature to speak of "West Indian" law.'[13] Though Patchett was a lifelong exponent of the need to make the law fit the peculiar needs of the society in which it is meant to govern, his approach was more pedantic than robust, calling for the establishment of a host of institutions and 'mechanics' before this can take place, rather than resorting to resistance and rebellion and the use of our own creative ingenuity as lawyers and judges.[14] While the institutions mentioned by Patchett are important, one can believe that even then we will only have a Caribbean jurisprudence when we have the cultural self-confidence to own up to the fact that we will have as much ownership of law as we make our own. The fact is that most of the institutions that Patchett advocated are now in place but the journey must now be charted. From 'the starting point,' moving on has to be based on our methods of argumentation, which White caustically refers to as 'the dreaded opportunity to think.'[15] Caribbean realism must inform the interpretation and application of the rules – the creolization of English law.

The push by the first cohort of graduates against the immorality of a jurisprudence looking outwards for its values is in line with the views of the early social scientists produced by the UWI. Edward Brathwaite and others like him clearly saw the indigenous creations of these societies. This he describes as creolization, the summary of the 'cultural action—material, psychological and spiritual—based upon the stimulus/response of individuals within the society to their environment and—as white/black, culturally discrete groups—to each other' as the integral factor for the creation of an autonomous society.'[16]

Law is one of the last remaining institutions in the Caribbean that has resisted local residence – the process of creolization. The resistance is accomplished mainly by the obsequious adoption of English legislation and the overemphasis on English precedent and tradition as the preferred methodology of argumentation utilized by Caribbean lawyers and judges.

---

12. See Patchett (n 1).
13. Ibid 962.
14. Ibid 962–66.
15. White, 'Jettison' (n 4) 20.
16. E. Brathwaite, *The Development of Creole Society in Jamaica 1770–1820* (OUP, NY 1971; reissued Ian Randle Publishers, Kingston 2005) 296.

This insulates the legal system from the local reality while embracing traditions and precedents created elsewhere. We have not begun to start; the start is to recognize that we have what we can call our own and thereby mobilize the outgrowth through the use of the creative intellect.

White, writing in 1976 refused to discuss judicial law making in the Caribbean 'for the simple reason that there has been none because the West Indian judiciary seemed singularly lacking in creative initiative mainly because they have taken the judicial Committee's dictum [that House of Lords' precedents dictate the law in the Caribbean] too literally.'[17] More than 30 years later, we have not moved much further because the methods by which Caribbean lawyers and judges resolve legal issues place too much emphasis on the doctrine of precedent in its formal sense, at the expense of discourse that is 'real.' It succumbs too credulously to what Professor Edward H. Levi refers to as 'the pretense' that assumes the law is a system of *known* rules applied by a judge.[18] Thus we go searching relentlessly for that case or that dictum that is on all fours with the facts presented for resolution and limit the usefulness of even the doctrine of precedent by looking to facts rather than the principles for differences or similarities.

The failure is not to be laid solely at the door of the judges and the legislators, but also in the halls of the legal academy, the academics and the lawyers it has spawned, for the lack of searching theoretical and philosophical discourse and critique. This has its roots in our legal education and its pedagogy that emphasize the principle of precedent, even in statute-based subjects, through the memorization, or at best, familiarization with as many cases as possible per topic, with the hope that every conceivable nuance of fact may be uncovered not through abstraction but by crude analogy. Also, by failing to stress the skill of handling primary sources of law, authoritative texts and journal articles that critically guide the approach to legal analysis over pre-digestion of these materials that produce second-hand knowledge of the law, the student is unaware of and incapacitated to other structures of legal argumentation. Their instinct, like the argument of counsel and the judge, becomes a predictable recitation of case after case, without any incisive and critical analysis of principle or evaluation of outcome.

The evolution of law in other common law states show that the doctrine of precedent by itself is a slow and unproductive source for the

---

17. White, 'Patterns of Law Making' (n 4) 4. For similar views see F. Alexis, 'The Case Against West Indian Appeals to the UK Privy Council' (1975) 4 Bull of E Caribb Aff 1; A. Burgess, 'Judicial Precedent in the West Indies' (1978) May WILJ 27.

18. E. Levi, *An Introduction to Legal Reasoning* (University of Chicago Press, London 1949) 1.

transformation of law. Law was not all about precedents, but in truth about 'the felt necessities of the time, the prevalent moral and political theories, intuitions of public policy, avowed or unconscious, even the prejudices which judges share with their fellow-men' and even more that 'the law embodies the story of a nation's development through many centuries and cannot be dealt with as if it contained only axioms and corollaries of a book of mathematics.'[19] Like all societies, the Caribbean has a story to tell through its laws; a story yet to be told.

However, notwithstanding that the establishment of legal education in the Caribbean was to be based on the ideals of legal realism and sociological jurisprudence, the praxis of law in the region maintains its foundations in the formalist traditions.[20] Our preoccupation with a formal version of the doctrine of precedent is not only the product of a postcolonial psychosis, which, despite independence, has not seen the kind of self-confidence in the legal culture that is exhibited in indigenous areas of Caribbean life, such as in the art, dance, literature and music, but it is re-enforced by our system of legal education. A broader use of the different methods of argument that is part of the accepted common law legal culture is the only way to manumit our legal system from its colonial moorings and into the sea of dialogue about ourselves. Patchett reminds us that Caribbean courts 'have been empowered to take into account the circumstances which obtain in the West Indies and in their decisions they could well contribute to the development of a differently conceived democratic society.'[21] However, he quite rightly observes that this is a potential development that depends on the guts of the persons occupying judicial office 'as well as their understanding of the role in which they have been cast.'[22]

This is an argument for *a consciousness-of-self approach* to legal reasoning and it finds useful analogy with the experience of the United States over the self-same terrain, which has the great advantage of speaking out aloud and critically about what their judges do in legal reasoning. Finally, it is urged that we must make a transformation in the curriculum of the Faculty of Law that will be more conducive to producing the kind of graduate fit for the task.

---

19. Holmes, *The Common Law* (Dover Publications, NY 1991) 1.
20. See UWI, 'Report of Committee on Legal Education' under the Chairmanship of Sir Hugh Wooding (UWI Mona, Jamaica 1965) (hereafter the 'Wooding Report').
21. Patchett (n 1) 928.
22. Ibid. See also Burgess (n 17) 27.

3. The Legal Culture of Decision-Making

What is commonly accepted as the skills of practical reason in the acknowledged methods of thought and the distinctive grammar of the common law legal system are all part of the *legal culture of decision-making* in which lawyers, legislatures and courts operate.[23] Wilson Huhn identifies five types of legal argument accepted by the legal culture: Text, Intent, Precedent, Tradition, and Policy.[24] He says that these arguments operate like 'rules of recognition.' These types of legal arguments function like 'rules of recognition' as they 'tell us what is and what is not a valid legal argument. The five types of legal argument are the kinds of argument that lawyers and judges accept as legitimate.'[25] The types of argument and reasoning that may legitimately be made to influence or rationalize decision-making in law do not consist of tight compartments of logic but interrelate as well as conflict.

The importance of the method of legal argument is that the method employed and the manner in which it is employed determines to a large measure the decision reached. The frequency of the reliance on one source rather than another also demarcates one legal speaker from another, one legal culture from another and, ultimately, the historical evolution of a legal system. In other words, it is functionally related, as is the suggestion of this chapter, to whether one can speak of one's legal system as one's own. It is from this point of view that we can talk about Caribbean/West Indian jurisprudence, not in the purely existential sense used by Dorcas White – 'West Indian law may be bad law...*but it is still West Indian law*,'[26] – but in the sense spoken about by, for example, Professor Rose-Marie Antoine, as an 'indigenous jurisprudence' one that is 'unique,' in which courts/judges do not 'surrender their judicial sovereignty to English courts' and which is more reflective of 'West Indian reality.'[27]

A. Meaning of Legal Reasoning

Huhn begins by positing that the five types of legal argument are rules of evidence for determining what the law is. He compares legal arguments to determine what the disputed law is to witnesses and exhibits that are produced to prove a disputed question of fact at a trial.

---

23. R. Sullivan, *Statutory Interpretation* (Irwin Law, Ottawa 1997) 168.
24. W. Huhn, *The Five Types of Legal Argument* (2nd Carolina Academic Press, Durham & North Carolina 2008) 13.
25. Ibid.
26. White generally (n 4).
27. R. Antoine, *Commonwealth Caribbean Law and Legal Systems* (Cavendish, London 1999) 115–18.

The facts which may be presented and their manner are controlled by rules of evidence, while the accepted mode of argumentation is regulated by the legal culture.[28] A *textual argument* considers only the constitution, statute or other legal document that is being interpreted. *Intent* focuses on the intent of the people who wrote the text.[29] Huhn says that 'Evidence of intent may be drawn from the text of the law itself, from previous versions of the text, from its drafting history, from official comments, or from contemporary commentary.'[30] *Precedent* is the statement of judges in formal legal opinions.[31] *Tradition* involves evidence of the people's historical beliefs and behaviour.[32] *Policy* is somewhat more amorphous than the others and involves judicial notice of any fact the court finds relevant to determine the question of law. A policy argument is therefore a value argument. Sullivan explains in relation to statutory interpretation:

> In determining the meaning of a provision in relation to particular facts, courts inevitably engage in policy analysis. That is, they take into account extratextual values or preferences that tend to favour one outcome over another. Although this aspect of interpretation is often played down by the courts, it is an essential and appropriate part of the interpretative process.
>
> There are many ways in which extratexual values and preferences are introduced into interpretation. They form part of the basis for inferring meaning and purpose of legislation in textual and purposive analysis and for distinguishing good from bad consequences in consequential analysis. In these types of analysis the appeal to policy is usually implicit and intuitive rather than formal and self-conscious. However, policy enters interpretation in more formal and direct ways as well: through the doctrine of strict and liberal construction, through non-application rules, and through presumptions of legislative intent....
>
> Although policy analysis involves an appeal to values and preferences that are external to the text, it is nonetheless a legitimate part of statutory interpretation because these values and preferences make up the legal culture in which legislatures and courts both operate.[33]

---

28. Huhn (n 24) 15.
29. Ibid 31.
30. Ibid 34.
31. Ibid 15.
32. Ibid.
33. Sullivan (n 23) 167–68.

B. American Legal Realism

In the common law world, the United States stands out as the most reflective and self-conscious regarding the theories of legal reasoning. This is rooted in its revolutionary constitution based on Enlightenment philosophy and liberalism. The development of university-based law schools with full-time faculties in the late nineteenth century turned philosophical exploration of what law means into discourses on theories of judicial decision-making. Writers agree that the beginning of this discourse was with Christopher Columbus Langdell who became Dean of Harvard Law School in 1870. Langdell is attributed the role of father of 'legal formalism' which, fashioning itself from features of liberalism and utilitarianism of the earlier era, envisioned a limited role for law in governance. Langdell proposed that law is a science, like any other science and that the data of that science are judicial decisions and the law library, the laboratory. He introduced what came to be known as the 'case-based method' of studying law based on the premise that the lawyer could discover the laws of society by studying cases.[34] The basic notion was that the judge was a mere mechanical applicator of rules without discretion, which could be found in legislation and previous cases. Thus text and precedent were the pre-eminent theories of decision-making. The critical feature of formalism was the dispassionate nature of decision-making that legitimated the existing inequalities of distribution of wealth and power.

Formalism was challenged by legal realism which disputed that decision-making was essentially based on either science or logic. This was part of a growing body of philosophy that viewed life and society as more susceptible to human weakness than formalism allowed and that it was out of step with reality. Kenneth Vandevelde says that 'The problem with the formalist vision of society was that it denied the relevance of social hierarchy.'[35] Harvard Law School professor and subsequently Associate Justice of the Supreme Court, Oliver Wendell Holmes Jr, led the legal realism school of thought. His basic idea was that law finds its reality in historical values and circumstances. He famously said that

> The life of the law has not been logic: it has been experience. The felt necessities of the time, the prevalent moral and political theories, intuitions of public policy, avowed or unconscious, even the prejudices which judges share with their fellow-men, have had

---

34. K. Vandevelde, *Thinking Like a Lawyer: An Introduction to Legal Reasoning* (Westview Press, Boulder CO 1996) 115.
35. Ibid 120.

a good deal more to do than the syllogism in determining the rules by which men should be governed. The law embodies the story of a nation's development through many centuries, and it cannot be dealt with as if it contained only the axioms and corollaries of a book of mathematics.[36]

Roscoe Pound, Dean of Harvard Law School, also added the voice against formalism with his sociological jurisprudence and his principle of judges being social engineers whose decision is arrived at through weighing of policy interests. 'Realists were more likely to evaluate judicial decisions according to their actual effect on society, rather than according to their consistency with prior cases or abstract rules.'[37] Towards the end of the twentieth century, others joined the debate: there was the Chicago School with its somewhat utilitarian conception of law and economics; critical legal studies which emphasized that a court deciding a case must choose from opposing values but avoiding extremes, and the rights theory of John Rawls and Ronald Dworkin arguing from a set of fundamental rights divined through intuition and deduction as a basis for decision-making that proclaims the dignity and worth of the person.

The outcome of these discourses in the halls of legal education, searching for a philosophical structure and approach to law, is the American law student well-rooted in a critical sense of legal self. The product was practitioners, judges and lawmakers whose response to their social, economic and political environment in relation to law was always critical and evaluative which could hardly confine itself, despite its inherited colonial common law origins, to any one theory of adjudication. Legal Methods, in addition to Jurisprudence, became a critical subject of study for law students, in addition to requiring pursuit of a first degree. American judges are pushed to discuss the real reason for their decisions and take into consideration how law affects society.[38]

4. 'We are not free, however, to follow a course of our own'[39]: Legal Reasoning in the Caribbean

Overwhelmingly, legal reasoning in the Commonwealth Caribbean adopts a formalist approach. Legal formalism has always been the traditional approach in England by sheer expediency of bringing certainty to the common law, which for centuries trumped legislation as the primary source of law. The doctrine of precedent always took

---

36. Holmes (n 19) 1.
37. Vandevelde (n 34) 124.
38. Huhn (n 24) 62.
39. *Johnson v R* (1966) 10 WIR 402 (CA T&T) 410 (Wooding CJ).

front stage and its coercive element of binding precedent was rigidly applied. Indeed, it was only in 1966 that the House of Lords in England admitted itself the freedom to reverse its own previous decision.[40] In the Caribbean, academic criticism was related to the imperiousness of the Privy Council imposing the authority of the House of Lords and even of the intermediate Court of Appeal and lower courts of England on the courts of the Caribbean even though they do not fall within the hierarchy of the doctrine of binding precedent and patterns of legislation which employed copying and what was referred to as the 'scissors and paste technique.'[41]

Even more stinging rebuke was reserved for the local courts and legislature for feeling itself bound by English cases and patterns of legislation and not employing any methodology of reasoning to avoid principles that were clearly unsuited to the Caribbean. The English version of the common law through this legal culture was considered supreme and neither legal practitioners nor judges generally saw beyond its foreboding shadows, regardless of the injustice that the application of the common law caused. In other words, the doctrine of precedent, both as it relates to the common law and to interpretation of legislation, mostly adopted from England, had a virtual monopoly on legal reasoning in the Commonwealth Caribbean.[42] This was seen as the cause of the difficulty in developing a Caribbean jurisprudence.

> The case law illustrates that Commonwealth courts tend to treat all English cases, even decisions from inferior or lower English courts, in this way, that is, as declaring the common law principles. This is a mechanical approach and greatly undermines the potential for creating a unique jurisprudence in the region.[43]

The difficulty was not entirely a matter of how the doctrine of precedent was being applied to the common law. It was related to the failure to resort to other sources of legal reasoning. Further, the reality is that statute and, importantly, the written constitutions with supreme law clauses and enforceable rights provisions, called on the legal profession and the judiciary to expand their vision beyond precedent to other

---

40. Practice Statement (Judicial Precedent) [1966] 1 WLR 1234.
41. See generally (n 17).
42. See White, 'Jettison,' 'Patterns of Lawmaking' (n 4), Burgess (n 17) and R. Nelson, 'New Final Appellate Courts in the Commonwealth and the Doctrine of Precedent' (Paper delivered to the Commonwealth Meeting of Justices and Registrars of First/Regional Appellate Courts in New Zealand & Australia 20–24 February, 27 February–2 March 2006) <http://www.caribbeancourtofjustice.org/papersandarticles/NEW%20FINAL%20APPELLATE%20COURTS%20-%202006.pdf> accessed 6 December 2009.
43. Antoine (n 27) 113.

theories of decision-making. There was a concentration by the critics on what was wrong with the way in which Caribbean courts were reasoning but no suggestion made as to the corrective response. There were in fact decisions, which ran against the grain of criticism that Caribbean judges failed to exhibit critical analysis, but there was no attempt to analyse those judgments to discover a methodology of reasoning that could consistently be employed in forging this new era of Caribbean jurisprudence.

Moreover, when the Privy Council made a decision that broke away from its usual formalism, as it has been doing increasingly of late, the criticism became the failure of the Privy Council to abide by the strictures of the doctrine of precedent.[44] This became even more impassioned when the Privy Council shifted legal gear in its reasoning and theories of decision-making after the judges of that court became familiar with the rights approach to legal reasoning through the enactment of a charter of rights for the United Kingdom and became immersed in the jurisprudence of the European Court of Justice. The death penalty cases especially became literal legal and political battle grounds that paradoxically found the courts of the Commonwealth Caribbean seeking to cling to its the colonial heritage of the death penalty and the British court wanting to wrest it from their bosom and bring them into the era of modern regard for human rights.

A. Sir Hugh Wooding CJ and the Supremacy of English Precedents

Sir Hugh Wooding, Chief Justice of Trinidad and Tobago at the time of the coming into force of the Independence Constitution of that state in 1962, was the pre-eminent legal mind in the Caribbean at that time. His call for transformation of the Caribbean jurisprudence was radical in 1966, addressing the County and District Court Judges Association in Toronto, Canada, he declared that 'We need change, radical, almost revolutionary change, if we are to have a juridical system to meet the needs of our social order.'[45]

As Chair of the Committee on Legal Education, he presided over the establishment of a legal education system for the Commonwealth Caribbean that initially was built upon an acceptance of legal realism

---

44. See A. Fiadjoe, *Commonwealth Caribbean Public Law* (3rd edn, Routledge-Cavendish, London & NY 2008) 204–10.
45. H. Wooding, 'Address to the Country and District Court Judges Association at the Royal York Hotel, Toronto, "Law Reform Necessary in Trinidad and Tobago" 28 April 1966,' in H. Fraser (ed), *A Collection of Addresses by the Rt Hon Sir Hugh Wooding* (Trinidad and Tobago Government Printing Office, Port of Spain 1968) 74, 77.

and sociological jurisprudence.[46] That system called for in its first year, the study of Caribbean History, Sociology, Economics, Political Science, Law and Legal Systems in the West Indies and Legal Methods and Techniques. In the second and third years, students were compelled to read courses in Law in Society I and Law in Society II respectively, requiring not lectures or examination, but tutorials only and an extended critical analysis of the effect of some laws on society. Contract and Torts were subsumed under one course – the Law of Civil Obligations. 'The Development of Constitutions and Constitutional Law in the West Indies' became a course of study for the first time.[47] The Wooding Committee recommended that the curriculum not be limited to 'strictly legal subjects'; it was 'of the utmost importance to rise above any narrow professionalism because a legal practitioner should be trained to become not only a caretaker of his client's interests but also a significant member of the society in which he lives.'[48] It said that 'law is not only a learned but also a liberal profession, to the end that its practitioners should be graduates with legal minds and a keen awareness of social issues.'[49]

However, the legal training of Wooding CJ never allowed these enlightened epistemic modalities to be brought into his judicial decision-making. He was staunchly formal in outlook. To this formalism in decision-making he so lent his colossal credentials and stature that it can be safely surmised to have had a lasting negative impact on the evolution of Caribbean judicial reasoning and governance and ultimately, the revolutionary juridical changes for which he spoke publicly.

Collymore v AG

The most famous of his decisions is *Collymore v AG*[50] delivered after his revolutionary change in jurisprudence speech. The issue in *Collymore* was not only the role of the court in relation to the new independence constitutions, but also the influence of precedent and the colonial tradition in the understanding of the new Caribbean polity. The question before the court was whether the Independence Constitution of Trinidad and Tobago 1962 in expressly guaranteeing a right to join a trade union under the provision dealing with freedom of association includes the right to withhold labour as part of union activities. Wooding stuck to his legal training. He validated the provisions of the Trinidad and Tobago

---

46. See Wooding Report (n 20).
47. UWI, 'Faculty of Law Regulations and Syllabuses for Academic Year 1971–72' (UWI Cave Hill, Barbados 1971).
48. Wooding Report (n 20) 6–7.
49. Ibid 11.
50. (1967) 12 WIR 5 (CA T&T), affd (1969) 15 WIR 229 (PC T&T).

Constitution, not by reference to the history of that movement in the social and historical development of the country which would have been in the forefront of the minds of the architects of Independence, many of who were trade unionists, but on the historical precedents of England.

> I have made this [historical] review [of precedents] not only to show why I prefer to regard the so called right or freedom to strike as what in essence it is, a statutory immunity, but more so because I think it exposes the fallacy of integrating the statutory immunity with the freedom of association. The immunity was a consequence of the free association which enabled the associates to win for themselves legislative relief from the imbalances to which the common law had made them subject. So just as the freedom of a builder to build should not be confused with the building he planned nor yet with the tools which he used for its erecting, so too freedom to associate should not be confused with the immunities with the associates secured nor yet with the means which were employed for their securing. Association, its objects and means it employs are, as always, separate and distinct in their identities.
>
> In my judgment, then, freedom of association means no more than freedom to enter into consensual arrangements to promote the common interest objects of the associating group. The objects may be any of many. They may be religious or social, political or philosophical, economic or professional, educational or cultural, sporting or charitable. But the freedom to associate confers neither right nor license for a course of conduct or for the commission of acts which in the view of Parliament are inimical to the peace, order and good government of the country. In like manner, their constitutionally guaranteed existence notwithstanding, freedom of movement is no licence for trespass, freedom of conscience no licence for sedition, freedom of expression no licence for obscenity, freedom of assembly no licence for riot and freedom of the press no licence for libel.[51]

As Antoine points out, the Chief Justice felt himself bound to adopt the English common law position that there was no right to strike, ignoring the possibilities under the new independence constitution and its explicit protection of freedom of association.[52] She criticized this judgment for betraying 'a rigid adherence to the belief that correct principles of law are only those which could be located under expositions from English courts.'

---

51. Ibid 15. In *R v ex parte Island Construction Co Ltd* (12 March 2003) BS 2003 SC 44 (Bah) 30, Moore J quoted an advisory opinion given by Georges CJ (then retired) on aspects of *Collymore* that 'Despite the traditional respect accorded the opinions of Wooding CJ it is unlikely that that approach would be adopted today.'
52. Antoine (n 27) 113.

Even though the case is renowned for Wooding CJ's famous statement that the courts are constituted the guardians of the Constitution, even this was grudging because he felt compel to note in effect that this guardianship had a judicial escape route; 'what is or is not inimical to the peace, order and good government of the country is not for the court to decide.'[53] As Margaret Demerieux commented, this 'virtually denies the claimed role of guardianship of the Constitution'[54] But the true criticism of Wooding CJ's judgment is the limited source of reasoning which was confined to precedent and a textual analysis that was entirely controlled by precedent.[55] To the extent that the historical tradition was garnered, it was not the historical tradition of the society for which Wooding was writing. There was no discussion of the consequential effect of depriving trade unions in Trinidad and Tobago of the right to strike and no evaluation of the reasonableness of the consequence. Policy, in the view of the Chief Justice, was a matter entirely for the legislature. The meaning of the provision could be garnered from an examination of precedent and deductive logic. This is formalism in its most classic sense.

Johnson v R

Wooding CJ regarded English precedents as supreme and relegated the Caribbean courts to be mere purveyors of precedent, even though, in his absolute intellectual brilliance, he was able to exhaust in the clearest way the alternative solutions and even to abstract that which was best. The precedent, if it existed, was, however, the only justification for the choice between alternatives. Even where House of Lords decisions were widely viewed as wrong, he felt constrained to follow them. The much criticized and subsequently overruled House of Lords decision *DPP v Smith*[56] was inconsistent with the rules consistently applied by the courts in Trinidad and Tobago. In giving the decision of the Court of Appeal in *Johnson v R*,[57] he made a study of the emerging law in other jurisdictions, principally the Australian High Court which had refused to follow *Smith*. Wooding CJ concluded, 'If we were free to adopt a course of our own, we would follow the approach of Taylor J [in an Australian case]—not because it is really fundamentally different from that of any of his brethren, but because it is so elemental.' But such was not to be.

---

53. (1967) 12 WIR 5, 15.
54. M. Demerieux, *Fundamental Rights in Commonwealth Caribbean Constitutions* (UWI Faculty of Law Library, Barbados 1992) 488.
55. We were never told why the Supreme Court is the guardian of the Constitution and what it meant or why the courts are forbidden to evaluate what is inimical to good governance.
56. [1961] AC 290 (HL).
57. (1966) 10 WIR 402 (CA T&T).

Holding himself bound by the House of Lords in *Smith*, he made the poignant remark, 'We are not free, however, to follow a course of our own.'[58]

White v Springle

This approach was also taken in the case of *White v Springle*[59] in which the mother and father of a child born out of wedlock tussled over custody. The reality of the situation in the Commonwealth Caribbean, including Trinidad and Tobago, is that the overwhelming majority of children of Afro-Caribbean families are born out of wedlock. English common law historically denied status to these children. The question before Wooding CJ was whether the father, against whom there was an affiliation order adjudging him the putative father of the child and assessing child support, had standing to apply for custody. Wooding acknowledged that, unlike the English legislation, the Trinidad and Tobago Affiliation Proceedings Act 1957 gave the putative father an independent right to apply for the custody of his child and gave the magistrate the power to commit custody to him.[60] Without the least hesitation, and following the English precedents, Wooding CJ held that the English common law trumped the terms of the legislation. He referred to the Infants Ordinance which dealt with proceedings before the Supreme Court, while this was a proceeding under the Affiliation Proceedings Act in the Magistrate Court. He held that 'the titles "mother" and "father" belong *prima facie* to only to those who have become so in the manner known to and approved by the law and the consequent meanings of those terms when used in a statute are not to be departed from unless a compelling reason for so doing can be found in the statute itself.'[61]

Neither the reality of the social circumstances in Trinidad and Tobago, the clear close relationship between the father and the child, the legal system's acknowledgement of paternity, including the imposition of child support payments on the father, nor the specific wording of the Affiliation Proceedings Act were 'compelling' reasons in the judge's view. Therefore, the court read down the text of the Act by inserting the words that 'it must be shown clearly that it will be detrimental to [the child's] welfare that the child should remain in her custody.'[62]

---

58. Ibid 410.
59. (1966) 10 WIR 152 (CA T&T).
60. Trinidad and Tobago Affiliation Proceedings Act 1957 s 8(5).
61. *White* (n 59) 155.
62. Ibid 157.

B. The Realism of Telford Georges

Thornhill v AG[63] was born into a judicial climate that underplayed the effect of the independence constitutions of the Caribbean and sought to affirm, like Wooding CJ did in *Collymore*, that not much had changed. Very little light emitted from the constitutions by way of judicial interpretation. Georges J, as he then was, brought a floodlight to judicial decision-making on constitutional values that made even the Privy Council take notice. Section 2(c)(ii) of the Trinidad and Tobago Constitution 1962 provided that 'no law shall abrogate, abridge or infringe or authorize the abrogation, abridgment or infringement of any of the rights and freedoms hereinbefore recognized and declared and in particular no Act of Parliament shall (c) deprive a person who has been arrested or detailed (ii) of the right to retain and instruct without delay a legal adviser of his own choice and to hold communications with him.' The question was whether an accused has a right to counsel as soon as he is detained and before legal proceedings commenced. Based on the Wooding common law/historical/precedential authority approach which was confirmed by the Privy Council in the landmark case of *DPP v Nasralla*,[64] that no new right was created by the constitutions, the answer was no. Georges J in addressing the argument clearly indicated that the Wooding formalist approach was not available that day. His recourse was not to English common law case history but to the value judgment of the ordinary citizen of Trinidad and Tobago in reading this provision which constituted his contract with the state. He laid out his realistic mode of reading the Constitution in clear and unimpeachable language.

> The first issue for determination is whether or not the applicant has the constitutional right which he asserts he has...To the layman reading the Constitution of Trinidad and Tobago which is set out as the Second Schedule to the Trinidad and Tobago (Constitution) Order in Council 1962...the answer would clearly be that he does.[65]

The profound nature of this simple declaration cannot be gainsaid. In one sentence, Georges J captured the value of the legal principle – what it means to the ordinary citizen whose life it affects, what it means for constitutional democratic governance and what the role of decision-making involves. It did not, like the formalism of Wooding CJ, require in the first instance and the last, a consistency with prior cases or abstract

---

63. (1974) 27 WIR 281 (HC T&T), affd (1976) 31 WIR 498 (PC T&T).
64. (1966) 10 WIR 299 (PC Ja).
65. *Thornhill* (n 63) 284.

concepts, but 'the layman reading the Constitution' whose life it is meant to govern. Thus, the moral relationship between the rule of the Constitution and the citizen is firmly established as the major premise. The framers of the Constitution cannot be conceived of capable of '[s]uch calculated cynicism' so as to mislead the citizen as to what is meant.[66]

Georges J then had to disarm the general savings law clause in section 3 of the Trinidad and Tobago Constitution 1962 which stated that the fundamental rights protection in sections 1 and 2 did not apply to any law that was in force at the commencement of the Constitution. This has served to preserve a common law precedential theory of adjudication as to the meaning of the fundamental rights provisions. Using the plain meaning textual approach he announced that '[t]he phrasing is quite clear,':

> There may well have been areas in which there was no law in force at the date of the Constitution. The proclamation that rights and freedoms existed in that area would then create such rights and freedoms and it would devolve upon the courts to interpret what these rights and freedoms were and to decide whether subsequent legislation abrogated abridged or infringed them. Assuming therefore that there was no such right at common law as is set out in s 2(c)(ii) I hold that the right now exists because the Constitution has proclaimed that it has always existed here and that it should continue to exist. The burden is on the State to show that there was some law existing at the date of the Constitution which qualified that right and to which therefore it remains subject by virtue that there was some law existing at the date of the Constitution which qualified that right and to which therefore it remains subject by virtue of s 3.[67]

Finally, Georges J hinted at what will highlight his signature approach to common law decision-making – that its principles are not immutable but manipulable. He dismissed the attempt to shackle the Caribbean law to English common law history during the reign of Charles II and James II to which he was referred:

> While this is doubtless an accurate description of the common law at that time, I would hesitate to think that it would be the state of affairs at the date of the Constitution. The strength of the common law as I understand it is its capacity for growth. Its concepts may seem to develop only too slowly but when the challenge of changing social conditions has to be met and an appropriate factual situation is present to the court a sensible answer can often be produced

---

66. Ibid.
67. Ibid 285.

which can be shown to have been foreshadowed in the dicta of the judges of the past.[68]

Minister of Home Affairs v Fisher

Perhaps the most important and cited case in Caribbean constitutional interpretation is *Minister of Home Affairs v Fisher*.[69] Every law student and practitioner can recite the famous statement of Lord Wilberforce in relation to the approach to constitutional interpretation as purposive and generous avoiding the austerity of tabulated legalism. It appears in most judgments in the United Kingdom and the Commonwealth dealing with constitutional interpretation. What is not generally remembered or known is that the groundwork for this decision was laid by Georges JA sitting in the Court of Appeal of Bermuda.[70] The judgment was an example of his broad and effective use of a wide range of legal arguments.

The issue in that case concerned the definition of the word 'child' in section 11(5)(d) of the Bermuda Constitution 1967. Section 11 provides protection for the freedom of movement of belongers and subsection (5)(d) defines belonger to include the child or stepchild of a Bermudan. The common law was clear. 'Child' connoted legitimate child and excluded the child born out of wedlock, deemed *filius nullius*. Further, both legislation and Caribbean constitutions recognized and enforced the dichotomy. It was therefore easy for the judge at first instance in *Fisher* to reject the claim of the plaintiff Eunice Fisher, a Jamaican married to a Bermudian, that her four illegitimate children, who were born in Jamaica to Jamaican fathers, belonged to Bermuda so as to prevent the Minister of Home Affairs from deporting them.

The issue brings into stark relief the difference between formalism as a theory underlying judicial decision-making and realism. The prevailing approach of Caribbean judges was that regardless of the reality in the Caribbean where most children are born out of wedlock, the historical common law distinction governed. In *Re Lewis*[71] Douglas CJ in the Barbados High Court declared that 'Under the common law of England, and at common law in Barbados, the father of an illegitimate child, so long as the child remains illegitimate, is not generally recognised for civil purposes. Whether this accords with the facts of life in the context of Barbados is not for me to decide.'[72]

---

68. Ibid 286.
69. (1979) 44 WIR 107 (PC Ber).
70. *Fisher v Minister of Labour and Immigration* (unrep) 15 July 1977, Civ App No 2, 3, 5 of 1977 (CA Ber), affd (1979) 44 WIR 107 (PC Ber).
71. (1970) 15 WIR 520 (HC Bdos) 521.
72. Ibid 522.

In approaching the appeal by Eunice Fisher against the deportation order of her children back to Jamaica, Georges JA referred to the fact that the doctrine of illegitimacy was not particularly suited to countries like the Caribbean where illegitimacy cannot be said to be a rare exception to the rule. He then stated the purposive approach to constitutional interpretation that was later to be adopted by Lord Wilberforce in the Privy Council. He said that in interpreting the provisions of the chapter protecting fundamental rights and freedoms, 'technical rules of law should not be invoked to exclude persons from their protection.'[73] He accepted that the concept underlying the protection of stepchildren is 'that parent should not be separated from child during the child's minority even though status cannot be transmitted.'[74] He used the intention of the framers, taken from the text, just as he did in *Thornhill*. He assumed that the drafters of the Constitutions had in mind statutory provisions dealing with children. To him, the drafter 'was dealing specifically with the subject of status. Yet he omitted to qualify the word "child" with the word "legitimate" as it is qualified in that Act. I consider the omission significant.'[75] He then resorted to a predictive and evaluative assessment of his interpretation to seal the consequentialist analysis.

> Acknowledgedly this interpretation does widen somewhat the categories of persons who 'belong to Bermuda' when compared with the categories of persons who are immune from deportation. An illegitimate male child of a male with Bermudian status would be now included. Having regard to the necessary restrictions in the way of acquiring Bermudian status, this does not seem alarming and standing by itself could not appear to be sufficient reason for applying the technical rule and excluding the illegitimate child of a woman who has Bermudian status.[76]

Watson v Morgan-Grant

On this issue of the meaning of child and parent within the social context of the Caribbean, Georges JA had a final opportunity to weigh in. It constitutes the most straightforward statement of his realist approach to judicial decision-making in this area where policy interests take precedence over abstract rules and prior cases. But his efforts to strike a chord more harmonious with the prevailing cultural milieu were rebuffed.

---

73. *Fisher* (n 70) 6.
74. Ibid 7.
75. Ibid.
76. Ibid 8.

In *Watson v Morgan-Grant*,[77] Georges JA sitting in the Court of Appeal, this time of the Cayman Islands, found himself alone in seeking to give legal recognition to the father of the child born out of wedlock and judicially declare the distinction between children at an end once and for all as a matter of policy. He returned to his methodology of treating with precedent as realists do by finding similarities in principle rather than in facts and being unswayed by outdated cases. He rejected the idea that the Caribbean courts are shackled to the previous decisions of English courts and held outright: 'I can see nothing which requires a distinction to be made between legitimate children and children born out of wedlock.'[78] This is on the basis the English decisions were merely persuasive and not binding on a Caribbean court of appeal.

He then reviewed the celebrated Jamaican case of *Clarke v Carey*[79] in which the Jamaica Court of Appeal construed the words of a similar statute to give 'mother' an unlimited meaning but restricted the meaning of 'father' to legitimate children only. Georges JA agreed with the dissenting judge in that case that such an illogical dichotomy does violence to language. His solution was simple:

> The difficulties are resolved by holding that in the context of the Law policy does not require the recognition of the distinction between legitimate and illegitimate children. Once that distinction disappears there is no need to differentiate between parents of such children. An illegitimate child is no longer *'fillius nullius'*- the child of no one.[80]

Completing his judgment, as was his method, with a consequentialist analysis, he rejected the argument that there may be problems in identifying the father of the child since it does not frequently, if at all, happen in the Caribbean that there are claims by men to paternity of children which are disputed by the mothers of the children. But more positively,

> Where paternity has been established the capacity of the father to file an application under the Law is of benefit to the child since it provides an additional channel by which the court can be apprised of the need to inquire into the desirability of intervention in the interest of the welfare of the child. The interpretation should be viewed as conferring benefits on the child rather than as conferring rights on the father.[81]

---

77. (1990–91) CILR 81 (CA Cay Is).
78. Ibid 102.
79. (1971) 12 JLR 637 (CA Ja).
80. *Watson* (n 77) 103.
81. Ibid 104.

However, Zacca JA, delivering the opinion of the majority was content to review the previous cases and conclude that they 'held that "child" does not include an "illegitimate child" [and] were correctly decided.'[82] Therefore, the relevant law 'was not intended to embrace illegitimate children.'[83] Compelled by Georges JA's stinging dissent, Zacca JA had to explain *Fisher* and to show why the injustice of the case was acceptable. In so doing, he resorted to a formalistic analogy that distinguished the facts of the cases: *Fisher* involved the interpretation of a constitutional instrument and in this case a statute. Amazingly, the judge could not see the principle that the legal recognition of family relationships, especially as close as father and child, was as fundamental a human right as any to which anyone can claim entitlement. Further, there was no reference to the goal or purpose of the law or the effect that it would have on such a large number of children and their parents in a society where the vast majority of children would be deprived of the relationship of father.[84]

A Postscript

Starting in 1976, almost all the states of the Commonwealth Caribbean passed legislation to reverse the common law of illegitimacy and to grant equality to all children regardless of the circumstances of their parents' relationship at birth. This was done with popular political fanfare as would befit the emancipation of most of the members of a society from illegitimacy to legitimacy. In Trinidad and Tobago where the Status of Children Act was passed in 1981, in *Marie v Powell*,[85] the court had to consider whether the legitimate brother and sister of the deceased intestate was entitled to letters of administration in his estate in preference to the only child of the intestate who was born out of wedlock. There is no doubt that the Act attempted sweeping reform using words that are ample for the purpose and determined in its objective. The Act provided that 'Notwithstanding any other written law or rule of law to the contrary, for all purposes of the law of Trinidad and Tobago (a) the status and the rights, privileges and obligations of a child born out of wedlock are identical in all respects to those of a child born in wedlock.'[86]

The Court of Appeal held that the case turned on the interpretation of section 4(1); specifically, the meaning of 'vested.' That section provides that the 'Act does not affect rights which became vested before its

---

82. Ibid 96.
83. Ibid 97.
84. Ibid 96.
85. (27 November 1985) TT 1985 CA 65 (T&T).
86. Trinidad and Tobago Status of Children Act 1981 Cap 46:07 s 3(1)(a).

commencement.' Subsection 2 states that 'Save as provided in subsection (1) this Act applies to persons born and instruments executed before as well as after its commencement.' If the word assumed its widest meaning, 'vested in interest,' it would limit the retrospective effect of the Act and deprive the child of the deceased of right of administration and perhaps also of inheritance. The more limited meaning, 'vested in possession' would allow her to obtain the full measure of the Act's ameliorating objective and she would be entitled both to succeed to her father's estate and to letters of administration over her uncle and aunt.

There clearly was an ambiguity between an interpretation that would advance the objectives of the Act and one that would retard that objective. Attuned to precedent and not policy, formalism and not realism, the Court of Appeal, referring to ancient fourteenth century English cases, chose the latter interpretation. Admitting that '[t]he ordinary and primary legal meaning of the word "vest" when used in conjunction with the word "right" is vest in interest as well as in possession,' the court held that since the deceased died before the passage of the Act, his daughter, being illegitimate had no right to letters of administration in her father's estate, notwithstanding the statute's provision that it applied to persons born before and instruments created before or after the Act and that all laws are to be read in conformity with the Act. '[T]he 1981 Act,' said the Court of Appeal, 'must be construed prospectively so as to preserve existing rights, and not retrospectively with the consequence of taking away any such rights.'[87]

In *McKenzie v Sampson*,[88] the plaintiff McKenzie applied for a declaration that he was the son of the deceased intestate, and entitled to succeed to his estate. The nephew of the deceased opposed his application. Under the Status of Children Act 1980 of St Vincent and the Grenadines, where a child born out of wedlock is asserting paternity in order to succeed to property, the 'paternity must have been admitted by or established during the lifetime of the father, (whether by one or more of the types of evidence specified by section 6 or otherwise).'[89] The court at first instance held that McKenzie did not satisfy the provision. Saunders JA, giving the decision of the Court of Appeal, explained that this ruling meant he could proceed with a declaration that Sampson was his father but even if he succeeded, he could not share in Sampson's estate.[90] The court viewed

---

87. *Marie v Powell* (n 85) 4. See *Johnson v Salim* GD 1993 HC 8, 11 June 1993 (Gren) where the court held that a similar provision in the Grenada Status of Children Act meant vested in possession and not just in interest and so extend the reach of the Act.
88. (28 March 2004) VC 2004 CA 7 (St V-G).
89. St Vincent and the Grenadines Status of Children Act 1980 Cap 180 s 7(1)(b).
90. *McKenzie* (n 88) 8.

it as paradoxical that there could exist two standards given the fact that the professed aim of the Act is to remove the legal disabilities suffered by children whose parents were not married to each other.[91] The judge went on to consider whether the Act was discriminatory within the terms of the St Vincent and the Grenadines Constitution. He felt forced to concede that the Constitution gave no relief against such discrimination, 'no matter how reprehensible.'[92]

In *K and Minister of Foreign Affairs,*[93] the applicant was born out of wedlock in The Bahamas of a Bahamian father and non-Bahamian mother. When she was seven years old, her father attended The Bahamian Passport Office in Nassau and presented a completed application with supporting documents including the applicant's birth certificate. Her application for a Bahamian passport was rejected on the basis of the 'policy of The Bahamas Passport Office' not to issue a passport to a child, born in The Bahamas out of wedlock to a Bahamian father but a non-Bahamian mother. The question before the Hall CJ was the interpretation of the word 'parents' in article 6 of The Bahamas Constitution 1973. That article provides that every person born in The Bahamas, after 9 July 1973 shall become a citizen of The Bahamas at the date of his birth if at that date either of his parents is a citizen of The Bahamas. There was no definition of 'parent' in the Constitution. Nonetheless, the Court held that the father of the child born out of wedlock was not a parent within the meaning of the enabling provision. He said, 'I am unable to see how any other interpretation of the word "parent" is possible, nor am I able to accept the reliance on the provisions of the Births and Deaths Registration Act.'[94] This is in a country where the overwhelming majority of children are born out of wedlock!

It is interesting to surmise how Georges JA would have dealt with these cases, whether his realist activism could have saved the day for these litigants. Perhaps, this is what he would have reminded us in his unusual eloquence in the Bahamian case of *Smith v Commissioner of Police* that he could 'see no reason why the courts and common sense should in any way stand in possible antithesis the one to the other. To the extent that their paths diverge the law is likely to have been led astray.'[95] Common sense is a discourse based on values, evaluation of outcomes – of policy. Unless this kind of common sense discourse, as distinct from the inaccessible and highfaluting legalism that the ordinary person cannot

---

91. Ibid.
92. Ibid.
93. (2 January 2007) BS 2007 SC 28 (Bah).
94. Ibid 11.
95. (1984) 50 WIR 1 (PC Bah).

hope to understand is taken to Commonwealth Caribbean, I have argued elsewhere, 'The structure of the legal system will be geared towards the maintenance of the status quo and not towards an ability to articulate the internal values of the society which it serves.' I maintain that 'the doctrine of "reception" and precedent and the retention of appeals to the Judicial Committee of the Privy Council in England, reinforced by the structure of legal education, and the control of law reform by the dominant cultural minority' legitimises, reinforces and maintains 'the sectional prejudice of the law.'[96]

5. The Caribbean Court of Justice

One of the ingredients for the emergence of a Caribbean jurisprudence postulated by Patchett is the existence of a common court of appeal. The institution of the Caribbean Court of Justice, inaugurated in 2005 to serve as the final court of appeal for all Commonwealth Caribbean states replacing the Privy Council, is a move to this end. Unfortunately, only three states have so far subscribed to its appellate jurisdiction: Barbados, Belize and Guyana. Much has been written and said regarding the good reasons why such a court is needed, yet Mr Justice Duke Pollard, who recently retired from the Court laments that, 'Paradoxically, the most formidable and persistent detractors of the CCJ are to be found among the regional legal fraternity many of whom have expressed themselves to be comfortable about retaining the existing relationship with the JCPC—the retentionist.'[97] Needless to say there is nothing 'paradoxical' about this position. Indeed, the unacceptable position would be that the lawyers all want it and the political directorate and the populace do not. That the retentionists are lawyers means that they are not persuaded by the arguments made in favour of the court and new or additional arguments must be put forward.

Being of recent vintage there is a risk of unfairness in evaluating the judgments so far rendered by the court as an indication of its views with regard to the thesis of this chapter. That is, whether it subscribes to the formalist precedent-reliant approach to judicial decision-making or to a more robust realism.[98] Nonetheless, there are sufficient cases upon

---

96. L. Jackson, 'Family Law in the Commonwealth Caribbean: The Challenge for Validity and Authenticity' (DJur Thesis, York University 1988) 36.

97. D. Pollard, 'The Caribbean Court of Justice ('the CCJ'): Who Stands to Gain' (15th Public Lecture of Management Institute for National Development (MIND) in Jamaica 13 March 2008). <http://www.caribbeancourtofjustice.org/papers_addresses.html> accessed 6 December 2009.

98. Two other sources may also be useful in assessing the approach of the court. First is the prior opinions of the members of the court who were formerly members of Caribbean courts of appeal for individual jurisdictions, Second, the members of the CCJ have engaged in a great deal of extra-judicial statements which may be culled to understand individual positions.

which some comment may be made which would help to point to some general direction, to warn of danger or merely to complete this analysis.

A. *AG v Joseph*

By far the most extensive early decision of the CCJ in its appellate jurisdiction was rendered in the case of *AG v* Joseph.[99] As judicial opinions rendered by common law courts, it is a scrumptious and satisfying decision in which most principles, at least in the main judgment jointly issued by the President and Saunders J, with whom the other judges generally agreed, are evaluated and reinvestigated and tested by Huhn's five types of legal argument. Moreover, precedent, generously enriching the decision, was not allowed to shoulder the burden of justification for the result arrived at as is the normal method of Commonwealth Caribbean judicial decision-making. However, it is with the rules regarding precedent that *Joseph* provides a bit of concern.

In the case, the court felt it had to make a ruling how it would treat past decisions of the Privy Council. Several decisions of the Board were in issue, the main ones being *Pratt v AG*[100]and *Lewis v AG*.[101] In preparation for this review, the court quite early in its opinion made it clear how the rules of precedent would operate in its decision making. De la Bastide P and Saunders J said:

> The main purpose in establishing this court is to promote the development of a Caribbean jurisprudence, a goal which Caribbean courts are best equipped to pursue. In the promotion of such a jurisprudence, we shall naturally consider very carefully and respectfully the opinions of the final courts of other Commonwealth countries and particularly, the judgments of the JCPC which determine the law for those Caribbean states that accept the Judicial Committee as their final appellate court.[102]

In regard to the doctrine of precedent the statement is incomplete and unsatisfactory. First, the judges said that the CCJ would treat the previous decisions of the Privy Council as persuasive only. Second, they said that decisions of the Privy Council while it was still the final court of appeal for Barbados from other Caribbean countries on comparable written law, by which it is supposed it is meant statute law, in the absence of material difference, continue to be binding on Barbados courts unless overruled by the CCJ. Several other aspects of precedent were not

99. [2006] CCJ 3 (AJ), (2006) 69 WIR 104 (Bdos).
100. [1994] AC 1 (PC Ja).
101. [2001] 2 AC 50 (PC Ja).
102. *Joseph* (n 99) 18.

addressed by the Court that sees its institution as fostering Caribbean jurisprudence. Are the courts served by the CCJ bound by previous decisions of the Privy Council on the common law? Are the courts served by the CCJ bound by House of Lords decisions in its status, accepted by the Privy Council, as the final arbiter of the common law and similar statutes? Are the open reception provisions found in several statutes in the Commonwealth Caribbean served by the CCJ still open thereby permitting the continued reception of the laws of England, which only the CCJ can refuse to follow?

It seems clear that if the courts are bound by Privy Council interpretation of statute law *in pari materia*, then they must be bound by decisions given in relation to the common law. If this is correct, it seems that by virtue of this conclusion then the answer to the second question is obvious. Since the Privy Council is of the view that the House of Lords decides the common law, and the Privy Council decisions are binding, then this will be 'a conduit to channel English law into the English speaking territories'[103] through binding precedent on courts in the Commonwealth Caribbean that are under the jurisdiction of the CCJ. The answer to the third question also follows. The open reception provisions will continue to import House of Lords and English Court of Appeals decisions into the law of the Commonwealth Caribbean even with the advent of the CCJ. The sad fact is that this was accepted in the Court of Appeal of Barbados without any reason being given, and the CCJ failed to weigh the merits of such a far-reaching conclusion.

If the CCJ is true to its commitment to the development of Caribbean jurisprudence, it must, as a concomitant of that goal unshackle all the courts of the Commonwealth Caribbean from bondage to English jurisprudence. The dictum of the CCJ is too eerily similar to the dictum in the maligned case of *Robins v National Trust Co.*[104] We must cease being 'colonial courts.' We are no longer spouting 'English law' and the strictures laid down by the CCJ both expressly and inferentially on the very Caribbean jurisprudence it means to foster is neither indicated nor required. The release of the CCJ of its shackles from the binding precedents of the Privy Council and leaving the courts from which appeals come to it shackled, is tantamount to granting the Caribbean jurisprudence half freedom to develop.[105] The paradigm shift would not

---

103. White 'Jettison' (n 4) 20.

104. (n 5).

105. The Dutch West India Company often gave half-freedom to elderly blacks. This practice benefited the company for whom older slaves were a liability rather than an asset. Additionally, half-free people were required to pay annual tributes to the company. Because half-freedom could not be inherited, the children of manumitted slaves remained bound to the master.

have been made. The manner in which the CCJ has 'hedged in' the courts under its appellate jurisdiction, reserving only to itself changes in the law as laid down by English courts, forecloses any opportunity for these courts to contribute to the development of Caribbean jurisprudence.

Compelling arguments for a reversal of this decision either by the court itself or through national legislation can be made. The argument turns on its head the very argument that the proponents of the CCJ, including the CCJ judges themselves, make in relation to the competence of the judges who sit in the Caribbean. The restriction of the courts in the Commonwealth Caribbean has long been assailed as a lack of trust in the legal acumen and judicial responsibility of our judges. Saunders J, writing extra-judicially, instanced this precise point. He referred to the case of *Toussaint v AG*[106] which he claims media reports hailed as seminal and yet the very same issues had been subject to 'a masterly analysis in *Boodram v AG* by then Hamel-Smith J of the Trinidad and Tobago High Court as long ago as 1989.'[107] Of course, the reports are replete with these instances and one merely have to look at the numerous occasions in which the court at first instance got it right and the intermediate court got it wrong, or instances in which it is only decades later that the correct law recognized by a single judge and initially rejected is embraced.

There is no reason to believe that, like the CCJ, the Caribbean courts will act other than with due caution and care in reinvestigating common law principles and statutory interpretation settled in England against the background of decisions from other jurisdictions and the local circumstances. Indeed, there are two points at which these courts are in a better position than the CCJ to do so. Where there is an allegation that the local circumstances required a re-evaluation of the principles, evidence can be lead for the evaluation to be made. Additionally, lawyers will be on notice to move beyond the strictures of precedent from other sources and prepare their cases utilizing a broader range of legal argumentation.[108] It moreover saves money and judicial time by not requiring cases to be remitted for factual inquiry that cannot be undertaken at the level of the final court.

In order to move steadfastly to the goal of creating a jurisprudence that may be called Caribbean, all the resources must be utilized. To stifle, especially, the intermediate courts of appeal from engaging in

---

106. [2007] UKPC 48, (2007) 70 WIR 167 (PC St V-G).
107. A. Saunders, 'The Caribbean Court of Justice and the Legal Profession: Promoting our Caribbrisprudence' (Address to the OECS Bar Association in Grenada 21 September 2007) <http:// www.caribbeancourtofjustice.org/papers_addresses.html> accessed 6 December 2009, 15.
108. Especially policy arguments and arguments based on tradition which require the court to make factual determinations. See Huhn (n 24) 64.

an analysis and reinvestigation of the previous holdings of the Privy Council both of the common law and interpretation of statutes, as well as preventing the lawyers appearing before those courts from preparing their case in a way to provide the court with necessary research and argumentation is to choose to hear out of one ear, although endowed with two. The fallacy under which it is too often tempted to fall prey is that the law is clear, or in the words of Professor Levi, 'that the legal process is the application of known rules to diverse facts.'[109] He continues to point out that 'The problem for law is: When will it be just to treat different cases as though they were the same?' This is where all the players in the judicial process have a role and it is negating progress in the emergence of the new Caribbean legal order to suppress the contribution of any section.

It must also be remembered that the process of two levels of appeals has as its salutary advantage a refinement of the arguments, allowing the final court 'the opportunity for detached reflection.'[110] It allows the final court of appeal to clarify the issues and retract those that are mere puff. In this regard, Saunders J rightly admits, extra-judicially, that, 'The quality of any judgment is necessarily dependent upon the nature of the submissions of counsel.'[111] 'If the Privy Council judgments are of a superior standard, it is generally because the calibre of the submissions placed before their Lordships is usually higher than those made before the judges below.'[112]

6. Conclusion

For us to speak of Caribbean jurisprudence in any sense of the term in the near future there must be a move away from the heavy reliance on precedents and a more self-conscious exploration of the other theories of argumentation accepted by the legal culture. Only in this way can we contribute anything of value to common law jurisprudence. My limited review of the work of Chief Justice Wooding and Justice Georges indicates not only that it can be done but also that it is the only way. There are other judges in the Caribbean who are exhibiting this kind of courage and skill and it is for the academy to provide the intense critique

---

109. Levi (n 18) 3.
110. A. Smith, *Glanville Williams: Learning the Law* (13th edn, Sweet & Maxwell, London 2006) 9.
111. A. Saunders, 'Promoting our Caribbrisprudence' (n 107) 13.
112. Ibid. This is only a half-truth, of course, since many more factors go into a judicial opinion of superior standard, including the ability of the judge to both understand the arguments that are being made and to accurately synthesize the law using a broad range of argumentation, the judge's facility with language and the resources of time and manpower available to the judge to undertake independent research, in chamber dialogue, honing and editing the opinion.

that would encourage as well as assist in knowing where we are and where we are going.

In the meantime, the conclusion is that this at least a modified realist approach is one that must become the approach of choice at all levels of the adjudicative process, from the Supreme Court, intermediate courts of appeal through to the final court. Additionally, the way we teach the law must change to reflect this fact and instil in our students the skill to comfortably navigate their way through any source of legal argument that supports their conclusion and to be able to identify and articulate the weakness of the contrary positions. This involves moving away from a knowledge-based system of legal education in which the main skill is finding similarities and differences in facts under the umbrella of the doctrine of precedents. In going forward, the CCJ, as a critical component, but merely one component, of the move towards a Caribbean jurisprudence must release itself from past thinking and unshackle the resources of the Caribbean legal mind to assist in this endeavour. It means that the precepts of the doctrine of precedent that allow English law to flood into the jurisdiction without evaluation or reinvestigation must be modified. Most of all, we must be able to embrace the uncertainty of principles underlying legal rules with a sense of confidence that the resources of legal argument are not limited to finding cases that are on all fours. Caribbean jurisprudence? It isn't easy, to end as we began, in answer to Dorcas White.

Corporate Governance: One Size Fits All?

Suzanne Goldson

1. Introduction

The Commonwealth Caribbean as a whole has concentrated on an increased application of corporate governance principles since the 1980s and 1990s with the introduction of a modern corporate legislative regime emphasizing accountability, transparency and increased shareholder participation. In an effort to modernize and simplify corporate law and to encourage good corporate governance practices, most of the Caribbean has adopted legislation from Canada and emphasized adopting the corporate governance practices of the developed markets. In 1982, Barbados led the way in enacting a Canadian modelled Companies Act, followed by Guyana, Dominica and, later, Trinidad and Tobago, Antigua and Barbuda, St Lucia, St Kitts and Nevis, and Jamaica.[1] The latter two territories have a hybrid model based on older UK Companies Acts and the Canadian Business Corporations Act 1985.

The financial sector collapse of the late 1990s in Jamaica, which involved the failure of a number of indigenous banks and insurance companies, heightened the debate there and precipitated a slew of legislation to combat one of the perceived causes, which had been identified as poor corporate governance.[2] As a result, although Jamaica is one of the last Commonwealth Caribbean countries to adopt the more modern corporate law model, it has led the way in enacting stringent financial legislation and the introduction of the Financial Services Commission, which is a relatively new oversight body that supervises and regulates the securities industry, the insurance industry and the private pensions industry. Jamaica's central bank, the Bank of Jamaica, regulates the banks, and

---

1. Barbados Companies Act 1982 Cap 308, Guyana Companies Act 1991, Dominica Companies Act 1994, Trinidad and Tobago Companies Act 1995 Cap 81:01, Antigua and Barbuda Companies Act 1995, St Lucia Companies Act 1996, St Kitts-Nevis Companies Act 1996, Jamaica Companies Act 2004. Hereafter, these statutes are referred to by the abbreviated name of the jurisdiction.
2. The failed Jamaican banks included Century National Bank, Eagle Merchant Bank of Jamaica, Blaise Trust Company and Merchant Bank, Mutual Security Bank, Jamaica Mutual Life Assurance Society, Workers Savings and Loan Bank, Citizens Bank, Island Victoria Bank, Island Life Merchant Bank and Corporate Merchant Bank.

the Jamaica Stock Exchange regulates those companies which trade on the local stock market. Other Commonwealth Caribbean territories have increased their oversight of the financial sector through their central banks[3] and securities exchange commissions, which, between them, regulate financial institutions, insurance companies and the securities market.[4] Jamaica has also led the way in corporate governance by the introduction of the Private Sector Organization of Jamaica draft Corporate Governance Code ('PSOJ Draft Code') which is similar to the United Kingdom Combined Code on Corporate Governance 2003. Following on the heels of the PSOJ Draft Code, a proposed Caribbean Code of Corporate Governance in Securities Markets was introduced by the Caribbean Corporate Governance Forum in 2003. Subsequently, the Caribbean Corporate Governance Principles were recommended in 2005. Both the Code and Principles have yet to be implemented.

Generally speaking, the Enron debacle of 2001 in the United States, pressures from the international community and general winds of globalization, have forced the Commonwealth Caribbean nations to stand up and take note and to put in place preventative legislative measures and codes in accordance with OECD and World Bank principles. The greatest challenge to the Caribbean Commonwealth will be the current domino effect of the collapse of the United States financial markets and economy. Initial indications are that the ball was dropped in the oversight of corporate governance of the financial sectors in the United States and worldwide. A tightening of the financial legislative framework in the United States suggests that, perhaps, the models adopted in the form of 'Sarbanes-Oxley' have not been as effective as originally thought.

One of the main aims of the proposed Caribbean company law harmonization of the 1970s and 1980s was to introduce a corporate law regime to which North American investment would be more easily attracted. At the same time, the region expanded its offshore banking facilities to the same end. In the enthusiasm to adopt these laws, it is not clear whether there was due consideration to the corporate governance implications. Was any corporate governance philosophy entertained and, if so, did they assume that the corporate culture of the Commonwealth Caribbean is homogeneous? It is not. Since the enactment of 'new' Canadian companies' legislation in the late 1970s which the Caribbean modelled, Canada has faced a number of challenges in the interpretation and application of some of its provisions on corporate governance.

---

3. See Central Bank of Trinidad and Tobago, 'Corporate Governance Guidelines' (May 2006); Central Bank of Barbados, 'Corporate Governance Guidelines' (October 2006).
4. See T&T Securities and Exchange Commission 1995, Bdos Securities Commission 2003.

This chapter, while highlighting the obvious developments in the area of corporate governance in the region at the private sector level, will also explore the challenges which the region faces in attempting to fit models from the developed markets into their emerging markets. It is clear that the models developed by the 'First-World' may not always be appropriate for smaller territories which are not considered to be truly 'First-World,' but which at the same time are also not truly 'Third-World,' based on their level of sophistication and economic maturity from a global perspective.[5] Interestingly, the World Bank Data and Statistics as at July 2009 categorized Jamaica, St Kitts and Nevis, St Lucia, and St Vincent and the Grenadines as Upper Middle-Income Economies and Antigua and Barbuda, The Bahamas and Barbados as High Income Economies.[6]

2. International Corporate Governance Scandals

The now iconic Enron scandal has informed many of the initiatives in the Commonwealth Caribbean towards an increased vigilance of corporate governance standards for publicly trading companies. Enron was one of the largest companies in the United States and it collapsed in 2001 due to widespread fraud, resulting in losses in jobs, pensions and investments. Before Enron, however, the debate began in earnest in the United Kingdom after the Mirror Group fiasco in 1991 when it was found that hundreds of millions of pounds were missing from the pension funds of two publicly listed companies. The principal, Robert Maxwell, died (allegedly committing suicide, among other theories) in the wake of his fraud trial. The deficiencies in the corporate governance structure of the company included too much control by the chairman who was also the chief executive officer, ineffective non-executive directors who may not have been truly independent, weak audit functions, and the failure of the pension fund regulators to effectively investigate the Maxwell Pension Fund.[7] The Mirror Group collapse was followed in the United Kingdom by the Bank of Credit and Commerce International and the Polly Peck collapses of 1992.

These cases precipitated a number of reports and corporate governance codes in the United Kingdom. Since then, many reports and codes have been introduced under a 'comply or explain' requirement, which

---

5.   See S. Jain, *Market Evolution in Developing Countries: The Unfolding of the Indian Market* (International Business Press, Binghamton 1993).

6.   World Bank, 'Country Classifications' <http://data.worldbank.org/about/country-classifications> accessed 4 August 2010.

7.   C. Carmichael-Jones, *Corporate Governance* (Vogon International, Oxfordshire 2005).

states that companies should comply with the code or explain why they have not. Consequences of non-compliance without explanation range from board intervention to stock exchange de-listing. More recently, the United Kingdom has also introduced the Directors Remuneration Regulations 2002 and brought into force a new Companies Act 2006, which will reflect a more radical and aggressive approach to corporate governance. The provisions relating to directors and officers[8] and those relating to shareholder actions[9] which came into force in October 2007, reflect a more modern approach to corporate governance with an emphasis on accountability, transparency and, to some extent, corporate social responsibility.

The Enron scandal in 2001 involved one of the 10 largest companies in the United States. Kenneth Lay, the founder of Enron, who is now deceased, and Jeffrey Skilling, the then Chief Executive Officer, along with Enron's auditors, Arthur Andersen, were held responsible for what resulted in a catastrophic collapse of Enron, leaving thousands of employees losing their jobs as well as their retirement savings, shareholders losing their over US$50 billion in investment, and creditors whistling for their money. Kenneth Lay and Jeffrey Skilling faced charges of securities fraud, wire fraud, money laundering, insider trading, mail fraud and conspiracy to falsely inflate Enron's profits for personal gain. Arthur Andersen was convicted of obstructing justice for illegally shredding documents relating to the Enron investigation, but this was recently overturned by the United States Supreme Court on the basis that the judge's instructions to the jury were faulty.[10] Nevertheless, Arthur Andersen still faced and continues to face many lawsuits by shareholders of the company.

The collapse of other large United States public companies followed: Tyco (2002), Adelphia (2002) and Worldcom (2002) and were attributed mainly to fraudulent accounting practices and generally poor corporate governance. The collapse of the European company, Parmalat in 2003 also affected thousands of American investors with losses of over US$1 billion due to fraud. This fraud inflicted a further blow to investor confidence, which was, by then, quite fragile.

It has been widely accepted that certain weaknesses in corporate governance were at the heart of many of the collapses: failure of the directors' fiduciary duties, failure of the directors' duty of care and skill, fraudulent accounting practices, poor risk management, conflicts of

---

8.   UK Companies Act 2006 c 46 ss 154–259.
9.   Ibid ss 260–69.
10. *Arthur Anderson LLP v United States* 544 US 696 (2005).

interest and excessive board compensation. The knee-jerk reaction in the United States was to enact the Sarbanes-Oxley Act.[11] This law increases the criminal and civil liabilities of directors, chief executive officers and chief financial officer; restricts the services of external auditors and the scope for conflicts of interest; and sets up the Public Company Accounting Oversight Commission to oversee the accounting profession.[12] The Sarbanes-Oxley Act reflects a legislative rather than 'persuasive' approach to corporate governance. The latter relies on moral suasion. More recently, the collapse, or near-collapse, of some of the largest banks and corporations in the United States and the United Kingdom highlights the weaknesses in the very models which the Commonwealth Caribbean territories hope to follow. The weaknesses that have been identified relate to poor risk-management and weak enforcement.

3. Caribbean Corporate Governance Legislation: Borrowed Laws

The Commonwealth Caribbean has fulfilled a number of corporate governance imperatives through companies' legislation and much of it is a carbon copy of Canadian company law. These provisions also largely capture the spirit and intent behind the Organisation for Economic Co-operation and Development (OECD) Principles of Corporate Governance and the World Bank Principles of Corporate Governance.[13] These legislative provisions vary from territory to territory and in regards to directors and officers, include an increase in their duties and responsibilities,[14] the introduction of a duty to have regard to the interest of shareholders, employees and the community in which the company operates,[15] prohibition of certain loans to shareholders, directors, officers or employees of the company,[16] stringent disclosure requirements involving salaries, pensions, loans, interests in contracts, shareholding and service contracts,[17] prohibition of a director from voting on contracts

---

11. United States Sarbanes-Oxley Act 2002, Public Law 107–204.
12. Ibid ss101–9.
13. OECD Steering Group on Corporate Governance, *OECD Principles of Corporate Governance* (Paris France 2004) <http:www.oecd.org/dataoecd/32/18/31557724.pdf> accessed 7 December 2009.
14. A&B s 97(1), Bdos s 95(1), Dom s 97(1), Guy s 96(1) , Ja s 174(1), St Luc s 97(1), St K-N s 74(1), T&T s 99(1).
15. A&B s 97(2), Dom s 97(2), Ja s 174 (4), St Luc s 97(2), T&T s 99(2). Bar s 95(2) and Guy s 96(2) use the word 'must' is used instead of 'shall.' St Kitts-Nevis does not have this provision. It has been argued that this puts the directors in the invidious position of having to take into account the interests of other groups while at the same time ensuring that it is in the context of their duty to the company. S. Ffolkes-Goldson, 'The Commonwealth Caribbean: The Reform of The Law Relating to the Duties of Directors' (2003) 24(12) Co Law 378, 380–81.
16. For example, Bdos s 94, T&T s 98, Ja s 184.
17. For example, Bdos ss 89–92, T&T ss 93–96, Ja ss 186–98.

in which he has an interest,[18] and the introduction of the concept of 'shadow directors.'[19]

There are stricter rules regarding the role of the company secretary,[20] on the preparation of accounts and the information required,[21] and on the appointment and role of auditors.[22] Tools of redress for 'Claimants,' which can include current and former shareholders, current and former directors and current and former debenture-holders, and in some cases, any other person the court thinks fit, are available under the derivative action or oppression remedy.[23]

Mainly in securities, pensions and insurance legislation, there are now provisions for a 'fit and proper' test for dealers in securities or investment advisers,[24] criminal and civil liability for insider dealing,[25] audit committees for certain types of companies and, in some cases, a requirement for a conduct review committee,[26] protection of whistle-blowers in prescribed circumstances,[27] and the appointment of actuaries in certain types of companies and rules regarding his or her conduct and responsibilities.[28]

Although the general goal of good governance involving greater transparency, accountability and shareholder empowerment are already well accepted in the region, the Commonwealth Caribbean as a whole tends to have a number of challenges to adherence to what appears to be prescribed corporate governance principles which have emerged mainly from the developed markets.[29] Even without the traditional box-ticking, the prescribed methods found in many principles embodied in the various codes, legislation and Stock Exchange Rules of developed economies, do not always accord with the corporate culture of the Commonwealth Caribbean.

The various codes, principles and legislation of the developed markets modelled in the Caribbean do not always take into account the predominance of closely-held companies, few listings of public companies on the local stock exchanges, the limited investment in shares by local and foreign investors, limited desire for shareholder involvement by the

---

18. For example, Bdos s 89, T&T s 93, Ja sch 1 s 90.
19. Ja s 2.
20. For example, T&T s 63, Ja s 173.
21. For example, Bdos ss 147–52, T&T ss 151-56, Ja ss 144–53.
22. For example, Bdos ss 153–67, T&T ss 158-74, Ja ss 154–59.
23. A&B ss 239, 241, Bdos ss 226, 228, Guy ss 222, 224, Dom ss 239, 241, Ja ss 212, 213A, St K-N s 141(1) , St Luc ss 239, 241, T&T ss 240, 242 .
24. For example, Jamaica Securities Act 1993 s 59.
25. For example, Bdos ss 308–11, T&T ss 303-306, Ja Securities Act 1993 s 51.
26. T&T s 157, Ja Securities Act 1993 s 59.
27. Jamaica Insurance Act 2001 s 44.
28. Ibid.
29. For example, UK Combined Code on Corporate Governance 2003, US Sarbanes-Oxley Act 2002.

local shareholders; the limited involvement of institutional investors, the slow and limited supply of market information, and the predominance of debt financing as against equity financing. Moreover, in the context of the global financial meltdown, Commonwealth Caribbean territories and other smaller emerging economies, as opposed to larger emerging economies such as China, India and Brazil, are faced with the challenge of the cost of assessing risk, the difficulty in accessing such information and the cost of enforcement of legislation and regulations. The adoption of the Canadian model for Caribbean corporate governance legislation and the United Kingdom Combined Code in the form of the PSOJ Draft Code have been problematic at best and ill-suited at worst for the corporate culture of the Commonwealth Caribbean region and by extension, the developing world.

4. Interpretation of 'Borrowed' Legislation: Director's Duties

Interpretation of the provisions of 'borrowed' legislation can give rise to unfair and unexpected results. The purposive approach to statutory interpretation mandates that legislation be interpreted in light of the purpose behind the legislation.[30] Conventional legal wisdom suggests that copied legislation be interpreted in the light of precedent from the foreign jurisdiction from which it was copied.[31] Imputing the treatment and interpretations of the foreign statute to the Caribbean model presents a problem because the foreign precedent is based on the corporate culture of that jurisdiction. This may, however, be cured by what has come to be known as the 'local circumstances rule,' which is an exception to the rule that previous interpretations of the statute are binding where a statute is identical or *in pari materia* to a statute in the UK, in circumstances where it would produce an irrational result and therefore could not have been the legislative intent.[32]

An example of the possible difficulties of interpretation can be found in the provisions relating to the duties of directors and officers. In the main, most Commonwealth Caribbean territories have copied the provision from the Canadian Business Corporations Act 1985 (now revised) which states:

> Every director and officer of a company, in exercising his powers and discharging his duties shall-

---

30. *Pepper v Hart* [1993] AC 573 (HL), *Re Rizzo v Rizzo Shoes Ltd* [1998] 1 SCR 27 (SC Can).

31. R. Antoine, *Commonwealth Caribbean Law and Legal Systems* (2nd edn, Routledge-Cavendish, London 2008) 277. See also *Pollock v Manitoba* 272 DLR (4th) 142 (CA Man).

32. *Carreras Group Ltd v Stamp Commissioner* [2004] UKPC 16, (2004) 64 WIR 228 (PC Ja), *Re First Virginia Reinsurance Ltd* [1996] CILR 52 (SC Ber).

    e.   act honestly and in good faith with a view to the best interests of the company and

    f.   exercise the care, diligence and skill that a reasonably prudent person would exercise in comparable circumstances.[33]

Here, the Commonwealth Caribbean has an opportunity to either apply the purposive approach to statutory interpretation or some other approach.

A. Duty to Act Honestly and in Good Faith: Primary or Improper Purpose?

The courts in Canada have grappled with whether or not the phrase 'act honestly and in good faith with a view to the best interests of the company' codifies the common law fiduciary duty of not making a secret profit, not having a conflict of duty and interest, and acting bona fide in the best interest of the company without having an improper purpose. The debate in Canada surrounds the question as to whether the true test is one of an 'improper' purpose or that of a 'primary' purpose. Academic opinion supports a 'primary' purpose doctrine.[34] If a director acts in good faith, but his purpose is improper, he may run afoul of his fiduciary duty, unless, his primary purpose is not an improper purpose.

These questions have not been analysed seriously in Caribbean courts. Is the correct approach to interpret the provision in accordance with Canadian judicial decisions and discard the apparent intention of Parliament in the given Commonwealth Caribbean territory? A second option is to look to the intention of Parliament of the given Commonwealth Caribbean and a third option is to attempt to discern a broad Caribbean jurisprudence to guide the matter. It is difficult to discern a Commonwealth Caribbean jurisprudence on the interpretation of the fiduciary duty of directors, and in most instances the section was simply copied from the Canadian legislation. It must be therefore, that the legislature intended for the Canadian cases to form a precedent for interpretation in the Commonwealth Caribbean.

B. Duty of Care and Skill: Objective or Subjective?

The issue becomes even more problematic under an examination of the duty of care and skill. There is no doubt that the intention of Parliament in Canada and in the Commonwealth Caribbean was to raise the standard

---

33. Canada Business Corporations Act RSC 1985 c C-44 (as amended by SC 2001) s 122.

34. B. Welling, *Corporate Law in Canada: The Governing Principles* (Butterworths, Toronto 1991) 336–48.

of care, diligence and skill at common law. The question arises as to whether the test is objective, subjective or mixed objective/subjective. The objective approach is the more onerous one, where a director or officer is judged on the standard of what a reasonable person would have done in his circumstances. The combination of objective/subjective is the former objective interpretation, but also takes into account the specific director whose actions are called into question and his circumstances. The subjective test is entirely based on the individual director and that director's abilities. After much debate, the Supreme Court of Canada recently held that it is a purely objective test.[35] Does this mean that the Caribbean territories which have copied this provision are saddled with this precedent? I would hope not, but given that the words are also copied verbatim from the Canadian legislation in most Commonwealth Caribbean territories, the risk is that it will be so interpreted.

Jamaica, perhaps, in anticipation of a restrictive interpretation of the provision, took the step of including a due diligence defence so as to retain some element of subjectivity. The Jamaican provision may introduce different challenges but at least this will reflect its own jurisprudence and not that of another jurisdiction which may not prove suitable for the region.

C. The United States' 'Business Judgment Rule'

Another question that arises from this is whether the intention of the legislature in the various Commonwealth Caribbean territories was to take into account what is known as the United States' 'Business Judgment Rule.' The 'Business Judgment Rule' is the rule that creates a presumption that directors are not liable for a breach of care, diligence and skill for a decision, provided that, there was no conflict of the director's duty and interest, the director was informed and reasonably believed the decision was appropriate at the time it was made, and that the director had a rational belief that it was in the best interest of the company.

There is much debate in the wider Commonwealth, namely the United Kingdom, Canada and Australia, as to whether this formulation forms part of their law or whether they have their own style of the

---

35. *Peoples Department Stores (Trustee of) v Wise* (2004) 244 DLR (4th) 564 (SCC Can). I have argued that the objective test runs counter to the intention of the Canadian Parliament and academic opinion. See S. Ffolkes-Goldson 'Directors Duty to Creditors on or Near Insolvency and Directors Duty of Care in the Commonwealth Caribbean: Should The Peoples' Decision be Adopted?' (2006) 6 UCLJ 61, JA VanDuzer, *Law of Partnerships and Corporations* (2nd edn, Irwin Law Inc, Ottawa 2003), 2. See also M. O'Brien, 'The Duty of Care in Tax and Corporate Law' (2003) 36 UBCL Rev 673.

Rule. The conventional view is that there is a Commonwealth Business Judgment Doctrine where it is accepted that a businessman's foresight is not to be substituted with his hindsight.

In Australia, before the enactment of a provision introducing Australia's own style of the Business Judgment Rule,[36] Parliament introduced amendments to encourage the development of an Australian Business Judgment Rule in the courts. This is significant as the acceptance of this Rule at common law and the new provisions on directors' duties of care and skill, suggest that it must be taken into account when assessing the liability of a director for breach of his duty. In fact, it has been suggested in the Jamaican *Eagle* case,[37] that the Jamaican courts have accepted this as a part of the law, although that the judge misapplied it to the concept of a fiduciary duty.

There is no mention of contemplating to incorporate the Business Judgment Rule in the Draft Report of the Joint Select Committee of Parliament in Jamaica on the Companies Bill 2001.[38] Perhaps the inclusion of a due diligence defence in Jamaica is an indication of the enactment of Jamaica's own Business Judgment Rule. This begs the question as to whether the other Caribbean territories have left it to their own courts to develop. If this is the case, this is a dangerous line to follow, especially if not contemplated when copying/enacting legislation. The Commonwealth Caribbean territories may yet find a result that was not intended by the legislature if the legislation does not make it clear whether there is such a rule.

In the recent *BCE* case,[39] the Supreme Court of Canada accepted that the American-style Business Judgment Rule forms part of the Canadian corporate law jurisprudence.[40] This may well mean now that there is Canadian precedent for the adoption of the Rule in the Commonwealth Caribbean. One however must bear in mind that most Caribbean territories adopted the Canadian corporate model prior to the 2004 amendments to the CBCA, which forms the basis for the adoption of the American-style Business Judgment Rule in Canada.

---

36. Australia Corporations Act 2001 (Cth) s 180(2).
37. *Eagle Merchant Bank of Jamaica Ltd v Chen Young* (19 May 2003) JM 2003 SC 26 (Ja).
38. Joint Select Committee, 'Draft Report of the Joint Select Committee on the Companies Bill' (Parliament of Jamaica, August 2000).
39. *BCE Inc v 1976 Debentureholders* [2008] SCC 69 (SC Can).
40. Ibid 40.

D. Duty on Directors to Take into Account the Interests of Employees and Shareholders

The corporate governance provisions in Caribbean statutes also generally include a duty for directors to take into account the interests of employees and shareholders of the company when determining the best interest of the company.[41] The problem is that oftentimes the interests of the company and other stakeholders conflict. This requirement has caused some difficulty in the United Kingdom. The debate there centres on the delicate balancing act required of directors to avoid breach of their overriding duty to the company.[42] Although proponents of the stakeholder theory of corporate governance, which is the theory which sees the governance of companies in the context of a wider group of persons beyond shareholders to include creditors, employees and the community in which the company operates, welcome such provisions. Detractors cite the general view that directors cannot know whose interest to serve if their responsibility is other than making maximum profits for stockholders.[43] How the Commonwealth Caribbean territories will resolve this inevitable dilemma remains to be seen. The goals of United Kingdom legislation, whether leaning in favour of a stakeholder theory or not, should not be that of the Caribbean, if the region's corporate reality is taken into account. The approach, of necessity and good sense, must be aligned with the reality of the region.

In developing the jurisprudence of the Commonwealth Caribbean, many territories have adopted provisions promoting stakeholder interests. The region now has to decide whether the stakeholder theory is to be widely or expressly adopted by the courts or through legislation. This, of course, must bear in mind that to redefine directors' responsibilities in these terms may well lead, '…to a lack of accountability on the part of the directors to anyone since there would be no clear yardstick with which to judge their performance.'[44]

In the *BCE* case, the Supreme Court of Canada stated that where the interests of the shareholders and other stakeholders conflict, the director's duty is to the corporation. This clear statement of the law puts to bed, any notion that directors have been given an impossible task of balancing competing interests, at least in Canada.[45]

---

41. Ibid 15.
42. G. Proctor and L. Miles, *Corporate Governance* (Cavendish Publishing, London 2002) 54.
43. M. Freidman, 'The Social Responsibility of Business is to Increase Its Profits' *New York Times Magazine* (New York 13 September 1970) cited in J. Dine, *The Governance of Corporate Groups* (Cambridge, CUP 2000) 9.
44. Proctor and Miles (n 42) 10. See also UK Committee on Corporate Governance, *Final Report* (Gee Publishing, London 1998) 1.17.
45. *BCE* (n 39) 37.

E. Complainants' Remedies

Another concern for the Caribbean is that of the breadth of the complainant's remedies. Most Commonwealth Caribbean territories have copied the Canadian provisions on derivative actions and the oppression remedy. These provisions allow directors or officers, former directors or former officers, shareholders, former shareholders, debenture-holders and former debenture-holders, the Registrar and 'any other person who, in the discretion of the court, is a proper person to make an application to bring an action' against the directors once it is brought in good faith, is in the best interest of the company and reasonable notice of the action is given to the directors of the company.[46]

It is significant that in interpreting this provision, courts in Barbados, and Trinidad and Tobago have given the phrase 'any other person who, in the discretion of the court, is a proper person to make an application' an extremely liberal interpretation, beyond, it appears, that which was contemplated in Canada. In the Barbadian case of *Canwest International Inc. v Atlantic Television Ltd*,[47] parties to a pre-incorporation contract with a company were treated as 'complainants' based on the '...broad power to do justice and equity in the circumstances of the particular case.'[48] In the Trinidad and Tobago case of *Five Star Medical and Ambulance Services Ltd v Telecommunications Services of Trinidad and Tobago Ltd*,[49] the court adopted the very wide discretion to determine who in the circumstances of the particular case is a proper person to be elevated to the status of the 'complainant' for the purpose of section 242 of the Trinidad and Tobago Companies Act.

In the *BCE* case, a group of Bell Canada Enterprises (BCE) bondholders vigorously contested a plan for the acquisition of BCE on the basis that the leveraged buyout would increase BCE's indebtedness, thereby reducing the resale value of the bonds on the securities market. The case involved an action based on the oppression remedy, whereby the bondholders insisted that the directors acted in a manner that at the very least, unfairly disregarded their interests. It was established that there is need for a plaintiff to firstly establish the reasonable expectation asserted and then to establish that the reasonable expectation asserted was violated by, either, oppression, unfair prejudice or unfair disregard

---

46. Bdos ss 226 , 228, Guy ss 222, 224, Dom ss 239, 241, T&T ss 240, 242, A&B ss 239, 241, St Luc ss 239, 241, Ja ss 212, 213A, St K-N s 141(1) .
47. (1994) 48 WIR 40 (HC Bdos).
48. Ibid 46. Williams CJ citing with approval McDonald J in *Edmonton Place Ltd v 315888 Atlanta Ltd* (1988) 40 BLR 28, 62 (Alta QB Can).
49. TT 2002 HC 64, 28 May 2002 (T&T).

of a relevant interest. The plaintiffs, in this case, not having established the reasonable expectation of the preservation of the investment grade status of their debentures by the directors, lost their appeal.[50]

Various criteria were used in the case to ascertain whether the bondholders had a reasonable expectation, some of which involved the adoption of American case law. Whether this is the way in which the Commonwealth Caribbean courts will decide cases involving the oppression remedy remains to be seen. Thus far, however, cases from Barbados and Trinidad and Tobago on the oppression remedy have not made it clear that 'reasonable expectation' need first be established. The variations on the oppression remedy and the definition of 'complainant' in the Caribbean will surely challenge any cohesive corporate jurisprudence regarding stakeholder rights.

5. Transplanting Foreign Corporate Governance Codes

Jamaica's Draft PSOJ Code is modelled on the United Kingdom Combined Code 2003 which also gives rise to concerns of suitability for the region.

A. Ratio of Executive and 'Independent' Directors

The recommendation in the various codes of corporate governance, that board composition should reflect a certain ratio of executive to non-executive 'independent' directors may be difficult to prescribe in the Caribbean as this largely depends on the size and type of company.[51] Many of the large companies in the region started out as family-owned companies which were enlarged to include peers of the families. The directorship of many of these companies reflect that reality and, therefore, the balancing of the board of directors to include truly independent, non-executive directors may be difficult, especially in small societies.

B. Interlocking Directorships

These arguments dovetail with the recommendations against interlocking directorships, a strong feature of Caribbean corporate boards. The general school of thought in the Commonwealth Caribbean is that interlocking directorships are inevitable due to the lack of

---

50. *BCE* (n 39) 100.
51. UK Combined Code on Corporate Governance s A.3.2, PSOJ Draft Code on Corporate Governance s A 3:4, 2006 , Canada National Policy 58–201 Corporate Governance Guidelines 2005 s 3.1, Institute of Directors in Southern Africa, 'King Code of Governance for South Africa 2009' (King III) (RSA 2009), principle [2.18].

a sufficient pool of directors. The reality, however, may be that those directorships represent an 'old-boys' network,'[52] similar to that of the traditional United Kingdom boards which reflected class and old money without the attendant degree of responsibility and liability.[53] The aggressive drive in the United Kingdom, Canada and the United States to dismantle interlocking directorships in order to decrease the appearance of conflict and increase independence, mainly, if not always for the sake of minority shareholders and other stakeholders, has been by way of proposals and guidelines, limiting interlocking directorships and the number of directorships any one individual can hold and, indirectly, by the provisions designed to increase the duty of care and skill of that of the director and the attendant liabilities.[54]

If Commonwealth Caribbean territories adopt these guidelines and provisions, they need to appreciate the possible results of the adoption of those rules or legislative provisions which directly or indirectly impact on interlocking directorships. The result here would not reflect the corporate reality of the region.

C. Splitting CEO and Chairman

The further recommendations in many corporate governance codes, that the roles of CEO and Chairman be split, although theoretically sound, is of no real moment in the Commonwealth Caribbean where many of the best companies in the region have the same person fulfilling both roles or the roles are filled by close relatives. In any event, the smaller the society, the less relevant this recommendation, as the position of Chairman is still susceptible to abuse by the control he or she may have over the CEO.[55] The UK Combined Code recommendation that institutional shareholders should become more involved in the process of accountability and transparency in the companies in which they invest, does not accord with the business culture in the region.[56] Institutional shareholders are largely uninvolved in the region, with the focus being on financial targets.[57]

---

52. D. Skinner, 'Unlocking the interlocks: Common Law Fiduciary Duties and the Phenomenon of Interlocking Corporate Directorates in the Commonwealth Caribbean' (1994) 3 J Trans L & Pol 53, Report of the Pujo Committtee, 'The Concentration of Control of Money and Credit' (US 62d Congress 3rd Session House Report No 1593, 1913), chapter III.
53. *Re Cardiff Savings Bank* [1892] 2 Ch 100 (Ch Eng).
54. UK Combined Code 2003 [A:3–A:4].
55. V. Kerr, 'Effective Corporate Governance' (Centre for Corporate Governance and Competitive Strategy, Jamaica 2005) 83.
56. UK Combined Code s E.
57. Kerr (n 55) 172–73.

D. Shareholder Empowerment

Shareholder empowerment as recommended by corporate governance codes has been achieved in the region through legislation.[58] However, as observed in the United Kingdom in the Hampel Report the position at the time in the United Kingdom was that, private individuals owned only about 20 per cent of the shares in listed companies directly. It was further noted that only a minority of private shareholders take an active interest in the companies in which they invest.[59] The position in the Commonwealth Caribbean is even less. The investment market has been described as 'small, young, illiquid and lacking in variety, thus individual investors are by extension generally immature in character and almost invariably subscribe to a "buy and hold" investment strategy that does not call for active involvement.'[60]

E. Audit Requirements

Audit requirements under the Combined Code, although many have been adopted under the various companies legislation in the Commonwealth Caribbean, oftentimes introduce a great cost to even what may be considered a large company in the region. Even though there exists in the various territories Institutes of Chartered Accountants as well as a regional Institute of Chartered Accountants, there is no effective oversight or regulatory body for the accounting profession comparable to the Public Company Accounting Oversight Board introduced under the Sarbanes-Oxley Act. This would involve added expense and bureaucracy for the small territories of the region. One solution to minimize expenses would be to pool resources to enable companies within the region to comply with any added audit requirements.

The broader issue, relating to groups of companies, is also an area of concern when assessing the relative strengths and weaknesses of adoption of codes of corporate governance and legislation from developed markets.

---

58. A&B ss 239, 241, Bdos ss 226, 228, Dom ss 239, 241, Guy ss 222, 224, Ja ss 212, 213A, St Luc ss 239, 241, T&T ss 240, 242.
59. The Committee on Corporate Governance (Hampel Committee), *Committee on Corporate Governance: Final Report* (The Committee on Corporate Governance and Gee Publishing Ltd, London 1998) 5.23.
60. R. Dathorne, 'The Current and Future Status of Corporate Governance in the Caribbean and the Impact of Relevant Codes on the Rights of Institutional and Individual Shareholders' (LLM Research Paper, University of the West Indies 2006).

Groups Within the Domestic Market

Within the domestic market, the challenges for corporate governance involve reconciling the *Saloman v Saloman*[61] principle of the separate legal entity doctrine and the perception of groups – parent and subsidiaries – as a single economic unit with direction and control from the parent company, interlocking directorships and nominee directors.[62] Parent companies are separate in law from their subsidiaries. The courts are loathe to lift the veil of incorporation for reasons other than fraud.

The prevalence of nominee directors and interlocking directorships between parent companies and subsidiaries for the purpose of control suggests a breach in established corporate governance principles. Indeed, interlocking directorships are a feature of Caribbean companies and many indigenous companies in the Commonwealth Caribbean have emerged from the private family company, which in turn, have expanded to become groups of companies.

Transnational Groups

Transnational groups have to consider domestic law as it relates to corporate governance, Private International Law rules as well as the interpretation and enforcement of treaties such as the Caribbean Community Revised Treaty of Chagauramus 2001, the basis for the Caribbean Single Market and Economy (CSME), which allows for freedom of movement of individuals and companies within the region

Many Commonwealth Caribbean countries depend on foreign companies, which are transnational in nature, for development of their resources, telecommunications and energy. The countries affected by transnational groups of companies, therefore, have little control over the corporate governance practices of the transnational and can hardly rely on the standards set by the country of the parent company.

> If a company chooses to arrange the affairs of its group in such a way that the business carried on in a particular foreign country, is the business of the subsidiary and not its own, it is, in our judgment, entitled to do so. Neither in this class of case nor in any other class of case is it open to this court to disregard the principle of *Salomon v Salomon* [1897] AC 22 merely because it considers it just so to do.[63]

Further, there is now an aggressive takeover of companies within economically weaker Caribbean countries by companies in the

---

61. [1897] AC 22 (HL).
62. Dine (n 43) 47, 48, 50.
63. *Adams v Cape Industries plc* [1990] BCLC 479 (HL) 513.

48

economically stronger Caribbean countries. These factors no doubt, multiply the issues relating to corporate governance in the context of groups of companies. It is difficult, in these circumstances, to establish a coherent and consistent approach to corporate governance.

> Transnational companies are out of control. Although critics of this assumption will point to the programme of 'sustainable development' referred to in many corporate codes of conduct and individual good practice, together with environmental auditing and international codes of conduct such as the OECD Guidelines on Multinational Enterprises (OECD), 1992) there is nevertheless a significant problem that will inevitably be compounded by the addiction to 'growth'. The political and economic poser of many transnationals dwarfs the traditional regulator, the nation state, makes the idea of shareholder control laughable, and leaves us groping for alternative control mechanisms.[64]

6. Conclusion

There is no doubt that corporate governance is a business imperative, and in the wake of globalization coupled with the lessons learned from the unfortunate 'greed is good' campaign of the 1980s, to the Maxwell debacle of the '90s along with the various financial crashes, to the Enron debacle, the Commonwealth Caribbean should not be complacent in its efforts to ensure that corporate governance initiatives are a priority.

The Commonwealth Caribbean territories should understand the importance of the way in which effective corporate governance is achieved in the region. In order to ensure that good governance is a part of the Commonwealth Caribbean culture, it is imperative that the many models, whether by way of code, principles or legislation, emerging from the developed markets, are compatible with the economic and social reality of the region. The delicate balancing act that may be required will involve a commitment by territories in the Commonwealth Caribbean to individually and collectively consider the impact of the models proposed by the developed markets on the long-term goals and sustainable development of the region. This, of course, presumes that the goals of the individual territories are consistent with those of the region as a whole. The reality is that, in the context of the Commonwealth Caribbean, ironically, 'no man is an island.'

The added complication of interpretation of copied legislation, in the absence of a clear local legislative intent, has developed in an ad hoc

---

64. Dine (n 43) 174–75.

way by extra-judicial means. It appears that much of the Commonwealth Caribbean corporate law jurisprudence emerges from the world of practice and from the office of the Registrar of Companies. Anecdotally, practitioners seek advice on interpretation in these informal ways and the agreement as to particular interpretation becomes a part of the jurisprudence. This ad hoc approach may lead to inconsistencies within the Commonwealth Caribbean region. However, while not ideal, the ad hoc approach is an effective way in which the corporate culture of the territory or region may be incorporated into the law and applied.

Corporate governance codes and legislation should not be seen as a panacea for all the corporate evils that exist whether in developed or emerging markets. Sound corporate governance practices are founded on a culture of ethical corporate behaviour, which cannot be legislated.

Expanding the Purview of Accountability in Employment by the State

Rose-Marie Antoine

1. The Changing Paradigm of Employment in the Public Sector – An Impetus for a New Approach

In recent years, labour law has faced many challenges, not least of which is the much talked about process of globalization, which has resulted in different types of trade relations and attitudes toward work. Market-centred strategies have also been at the front of these new initiatives and indeed in new visions of development. Out of this emerged a workforce with enhanced mobility but at the same time, more informal. Such informalization or casualization meant that de-regulation was increased, given that the regulatory field of labour law depends ultimately on formal structures of work. Workers were thus rendered more vulnerable. Further, the welfare state and a labour movement which emphasized workers rights have slowly been undermined by this new economy. As such, the tools which labour law traditionally employed to find balance in the labour environment have become less effective.

The need to confront these new work paradigms by putting forward labour law models which are more sensitively attuned to the new labour environment was the subject of another paper by the writer in this Faculty Workshop Series.[1] The need to rethink labour law is not, however, restricted to the private employment sphere. In the public sector, market forces' ideals have also impacted the sacrosanct public service, resulting in increased privatization of the sector and employment arrangements modelled on contracts of employment typical of the private sector. These have been established in the name of commercial and administrative expediency. Indeed, a hybrid sector has now been created in which there are 'new blends of public and private power.'[2]

---

1. R-M. B. Antoine, 'Rethinking Labour Law in the New Caribbean Economy,' paper presented at the UWI Faculty of Law Workshop Series. This was a working paper initiated as part in a series of the McGill Labour and Development Group of which the writer is a member. The paper is soon to be published by McGill University, Canada. The paper focused on the limited scope of the contract of employment model for contemporary modes of work.
2. A. Aman, 'Globalizations, Democracy, and the Need for a New Administrative Law' (2003) 10 Indiana J Glob Leg Stud 125, 129.

The important issues surrounding employment by the state also include the question of employment in statutory, public, or private state-owned authorities. This is a subject which is relatively undeveloped in Commonwealth Caribbean jurisprudence. Where the courts have addressed the issue, the answers have not been consistent. Further, it involves the interlinking of public law and private employment law. As with traditional models of labour law in the private domain, the orthodox principles of public service law do not sit easily with this new labour environment. It is therefore necessary to posit new ideas which can adequately address these contemporary arrangements.

The framers of Commonwealth Caribbean Constitutions envisaged a sphere of protection against arbitrariness and in particular, political interference, for those employed by the state. This protection was secured through the mechanism of independent, constitutionally-enshrined Public Service Commissions with responsibility for appointments, discipline and the dismissal of employees. However, only the persons identified as public servants and certain other specifically named public officials were granted this specific constitutional protection.

The courts recognized the largesse of the constitutional protection and in time, formulated appropriate new principles for democratic governance. In *Thomas v AG*,[3] for example, the well established principle of dismissal at pleasure of the Crown or state was rejected by the Privy Council, because of the constitutional protection of public servants enshrined under the then new Trinidad and Tobago constitution.

Persons employed by the state, but who fall outside of the rather strict definition of a 'public servant,' or other specifically named public officials, are not mentioned in these constitutional provisions and are therefore not directly protected under the purview of constitutional law or public service commission regulations. One can speculate that one reason for this exclusion was that, at the time, the Commonwealth Caribbean had not yet witnessed the burgeoning of state sector institutions involved in the operation of governance that we see in contemporary times. Nevertheless, today, a large body of persons are employed by such public authorities.

The argument may be posited that the framers of the constitution adopted a paternalistic attitude toward the former colonial young nations and put excessively bureaucratic and limiting institutions and mechanisms in place to counter legitimate state power because they doubted, unjustly, the capacity of these new executive authorities to

---

3. [1982] AC 113 (PC T&T).

govern themselves in a democratic fashion. As these states have matured since independence, these burdensome bureaucracies serve only to fetter the legislative exercise of state power and moreover, constrain the efficiency of the public sector. Private contracts and models of operation enable state authorities to be run much more efficiently and with greater flexibility, in accordance with established market principles.

While this is a legitimate argument, it ignores the reality of the labour law environment as a whole. Labour law has moved steadily away from a 'hands off,' ad hoc notion of employment at will, to an approach centred on checks and balances, curtailing the use of arbitrary power by the employer and imposing expanding social and rights obligations upon him or her. Such ideas are readily seen, for example, in the development of unfair dismissal law, redundancy protection and the doctrine of implied terms, the latter of which today has grown to include even issues of anti-discrimination.

It is therefore somewhat incongruous that at the point at which private labour law is becoming more interventionist, the public sphere should be embracing private law arrangements without the responsibilities attached to them.

The recent trend of the increasing privatization of hitherto public law functions adds another dimension to this complex issue. Cases such as *Perch*,[4] which examined the legal implications for employees who were previously public servants and were metamorphosed into employees in a private postal corporation, thereby losing their constitutional protection, examine one aspect of this pervading problem. A common thread, however, is the large body of employees left totally unprotected by law. This occurs where employment decisions made by the state as employer are determined to fall within the purview of private employment law and that law is in itself inadequate to offer appropriate causes of action and remedies. The lacuna in the law underscores the need for the issue to be resolved jurisprudentially.

The broader question arises as to whether such persons, whom we may label as 'private, public sector employees,' are to be treated under ordinary principles of private employment law (i.e., the pure contract of employment approach). Alternatively, should these employees be viewed more broadly within the lens of public law, since they do, in fact, perform important public law functions? With the development of administrative law and the tendency of the courts to include more and more functions and functionaries within judicial review principles,

---

4. *Perch v AG* [2003] UKPC 17 (T&T).

good arguments can be made for the latter approach. Such a treatment will place employees of public authorities on a more equal footing with public servants. A powerful justification for this approach is that private, public sector employees are equally subject to political arbitrariness and interference. Yet, their terms and conditions of service are not governed by the constitution.

More broadly, the general principle that the exercise of public power, in all its forms, must be accountable to the public, should not be overlooked. Indeed, as other writers suggest, there is a 'democracy deficit'[5] in the way in which employment in the public sector is today organized.

The desire to impose adequate checks and balances on state power, in the face of its ever-increasing power over the citizenry, has been a forceful impetus for the expansion of the principles of judicial review of administrative action. Where that power involves the state's own employees, the motive can be no less justified.

In South Africa, constitutional reform ensued in order to enshrine the protection of employees of the state, without having to go the longwinded route of judicial review. The decision of *Chirwa v Transnet Ltd*, explained this rationale of the law:

> As pointed out earlier, the line of cases which hold the power to dismiss amounts to administrative action rely on *Zenzile*. This case and its progeny must be understood in the light of our history. Historically, recourse was had to administrative law in order to protect employees who did not enjoy the protection that private sector employees enjoyed. Since the advent of the new constitutional order, all that has changed. Section 23 of the Constitution guarantees to every employee, including public sector employees, the right to fair labour practices. The LRA, the Employment Equity Act and the Basic Conditions of Employment Act ('BCEA') have codified labour and employment rights. The purpose of the LRA and the BCEA is to give effect to and regulate the fundamental right to fair labour practices conferred by section 23 of the Constitution. Both the LRA and the BCEA, enacted to give effect to section 23, now govern the public sector employees, except those who are specifically excluded from its provisions. Labour and employment rights such as the right to a fair hearing, substantive fairness and remedies for non-compliance are now codified in the LRA. It is no longer necessary, therefore, to treat public sector employees differently and subject them to the protection of administrative law.[6]

This is a recognition of the principle of democratic governance in which government is made accountable, a principle which the Commonwealth Caribbean will do well to emulate.

---

5. Aman (n 2).
6. [2007] ZACC 23 (CC SA) [148] (footnotes omitted).

2. Common Law Developments – Walsh and its Progeny

Unquestionably, the trend under the common law, particularly with respect to judicial review of administrative action, has been to utilize the inherent supervisory jurisdiction of the courts to protect what is seen as the ever increasing power of the state over the interests and rights of ordinary citizens. Common law courts have recognized that while legal relationships governing the state and its 'private' employees may be identified as existing under a contract of employment, they have considered that such employment, in certain circumstances, can have significant public law elements which must also be incorporated into the contract. Accordingly, English and other Commonwealth courts have opened doorways for decisions where the state as employer may be reviewed under public law principles. This is in certain strict circumstances.

However, the jurisprudence has been far from uniform. Indeed, the law governing the dichotomy between public and private law in relation to contracts of employment has been marked by confounding tests and inconsistencies. Yet, upon close examination, they mirror the developments in relation to the expanding purview of judicial review. It is suggested that the tensions that exist, particularly in the Commonwealth Caribbean, stem mainly from the failure of the courts to fully appreciate these innovations as applied to employment law.

Moreover, some of these seeming contradictions in the case-law may be resolved if the courts are mindful of the additional constitutional umbrella of Commonwealth Caribbean jurisdictions. This should at least cause us to pause in adopting such English decisions wholesale. Instead, we should focus on a creative constitutional approach which emphasizes more, and not less accountability. The issue is one ripe for a mature reflection by our own judges and jurists, within the broader context of creating an indigenous common law jurisprudence which is more relevant to our needs.[7]

In one of the earliest cases on the subject, a UK court, in the case of *Ex p Walsh*,[8] identified the existence of public law principles applicable to employment. The court held that where the terms of employment by a public body were controlled by statute, its employees might have rights both in public and private law to enforce those terms, but a distinction

---

7. An enduring and powerful ethic for West Indian jurists. See R-M. B. Antoine *Commonwealth Caribbean Law and Legal Systems* (Routledge-Cavendish London 2008), for a discussion of this phenomenon.
8. *Regina v East Berkshire Health Authority, ex p Walsh* [1985] QB 152 (CA), 162[A–C], 165[D–G], 166[A–C], 172[C]–173[B], 179[B–C], 181[C–F], 181[H]–182[B] (*Walsh*).

had to be made between an infringement of statutory provisions giving rise to public law rights and those that arose solely from a breach of the contract of employment. To avoid a finding that his application was a misuse of the procedure for judicial review under RSC, Ord 53, an applicant for judicial review had to show that a public law right which he enjoyed had been infringed.[9] The court stated:

> The ordinary employer is free to act in breach of his contracts of employment and if he does so his employee will acquire certain private law rights and remedies in damages for wrongful dismissal, compensation for unfair dismissal, an order for reinstatement or re-engagement and so on. Parliament can underpin the position of public authority employees by directly restricting the freedom of the public authority to dismiss, thus giving the employee 'public law' rights and at least making him a potential candidate for administrative law remedies. Alternatively it can require the authority to contract with its employees on specified terms with a view to the employee acquiring 'private law' rights under the terms of the contract of employment. If the authority fails or refuses to thus create 'private law' rights for the employee, the employee will have 'public law' rights to compel compliance, the remedy being mandamus requiring the authority so to contract or a declaration that the employee has those rights. If, however, the authority gives the employee the required contractual protection, a breach of that contract is not a matter of 'public law' and gives rise to no administrative law remedies. [10]

It is apparent that from as early as the *Walsh* case certain presumptions were made by the courts. First, that the applicant has a remedy or right in private employment law to fall back on, and secondly, that there is available an established judicial review mechanism, such as the Order 53 mechanism in the UK, which emphasizes a dichotomy between public law and private law causes of action.

A number of rationales have been put forward by the courts to explain their willingness to clothe decisions relating to contractual employment by the state with public law principles and protections. These will be considered in turn.

3. Where the Power to Dismiss or Discipline Resides in Statute

Perhaps the most consistent context for asserting judicial review protection for contracts in the public sector is the existence of the 'statutory underpinnings' of the power to dismiss or discipline. Where

---

9.   Ibid 173[A–B].
10. Ibid 165[D–H].

such power is located under statute as opposed to existing solely within the boundaries of the contract itself, decisions involving the exercise of that power will be amenable to judicial review. This is a principle which has been applied far and wide.

The suggestion that judicial review would be granted if there is a 'statutory underpinning' to the employment relationship, is seen in the early decisions of the UK Courts. In *Ex p Walsh*,[11] for example, Lord Donaldson MR, after reviewing several cases emphasized that 'it is the existence of these statutory provisions which injects the element of public law necessary...to attract the remedies of administrative law.' A 'sufficient statutory underpinning' has been found in several cases,[12] but was denied in other cases.[13]

Interestingly, in South Africa, the necessary protection has been enshrined in the constitution. In *Awumey v Fort Cox Agricultural College*, relying on the earlier judgment of *Zenzile*, it was said:

> ...the College and its Board of Governors is a statutory institution which derives not only its power to contract from the enacting statute, but also its power to dismiss. That being the position, such power has to be exercised regularly and in accordance with the principles of natural justice, including the principle of *audi alteram partem* (see *Administrator, Transvaal and Others v Zenzile and Others* 1991 (1) SA 21 (A) and *Administrator, Natal and Another v Sibiya and Another* 1992 (4) SA 532...Accordingly, I find that there was a duty on the Interim Board to afford the applicant a hearing before his services were terminated and that its failure to do so resulted in an infringement of his right to procedurally fair administrative action, as entrenched in section 33 of the Constitution and given effect to in the Promotion of Administrative Justice Act.[14]

4. Whither a Public Law Element in the Absence of Statute?

The existence of statutory underpinnings is not the only basis for locating judicial review. It is important to note that even in the absence of a statutory underpinning for the exercise of a power, judicial review may ensue if the exercise of the power has a significant impact on the public so that it is in the public's interest that the courts supervise such power.

---

11. Ibid 164[C].
12. For example, *R v Home Secretary, ex p Benwell* [1985] QB 554 (QB); *R v Home Secretary, ex p Attard* (1990) 2 Admin LR 641 (CA).
13. For example, *R v Derbyshire CC, ex p Noble* [1990] ICR 808 (CA); *R v Crown Prosecution Services, ex p Hogg* [1994] 6 Admin LR 778 (CA), *R v Lord Chancellor's Department, ex p Nangle* [1992] 1 All ER 897 (QB).
14. (2003) 8 BCLR 861 (Ck SA).

The courts have considered the nature of the power exercised and the impact of that power. In the context of the Commonwealth Caribbean, this is a powerful rationale for intervention since many of the statutory and privatized bodies perform functions which have significant impact on the lives of the public, not least because, given the sizes of the various populations, there is often a monopoly of the particular industry.

It is only where the power to dismiss resides solely in contract, and where a private remedy exists, that the court will not grant judicial review. For example, in *McClaren v Home Office,* Woolf LJ noted that '[a]s long as the "tribunal" or other body has a sufficient public law element which it almost invariably will if the employer is the Crown and it is not domestic or, wholly informal, its proceedings and determination can be an appropriate subject for judicial review.'[15]

Further, in *Becker v Duggan,* the court said:

> In ascertaining whether or not there is the necessary public law element present, two approaches have emerged, the first being to identify the source of the power exercised and the second emerging in later cases is to focus on the nature of the power. Until the English case of *Reg. v Take-over Panel ex p. Datafin Plc.* [1987] Q.B. 815 the availability of the remedy depended upon the source of the power being either of a statutory nature or of being derived from the common law. Clearly excluded were decision-making powers based on a contract or consent between the decision maker and the person affected. This excluded the affairs of clubs and private associations from the purview of judicial review...Where the duty being carried out by a decision making authority, as occurs in this case, is of a nature which might ordinarily be seen as coming within the public domain, that decision can only be excluded from the reach of the jurisdiction in judicial review if it can be shown that it solely and exclusively derived from an individual contract made in private law.[16]

---

15. [1990] ICR 824 (CA) 836–7 (*McClaren*).
16. [2005] IEHC 376 (HC Ireland) [54]. The court also noted that a 'private company selected to run a prison, for example, although motivated by considerations of commercial profit should be regarded, at least in relation to some of its activities, as subject to public law because of the nature of the function it is performing. This is because the prisoners, for whose custody and care it is responsible, are in the prison in consequence of an order of the court, and the purpose and nature of their detention is a matter of public concern and interest.' Ibid. See also, *Police and Prisons Civil Rights Union v Minister of Correctional Services* (2006) 8 BCLR 971 [54] (HC SA), where the court quoted extensively from English authorities, saying: '...the public character of the Department and the pre-eminence of the public interest in the proper administration of prisons and the attainment of the purposes specified in section 2 of the Correctional Services Act all strengthen my view that the powers that are sought to be reviewed in this matter are public powers as envisaged by the common law, the Constitution and the PAJA.' This follows Craig's view that if a power is derived from statute, the body exercising that power is 'presumptively public.' See Craig, 'What is Public Power?' in Corder and Maluwa (eds), *Administrative Justice in Southern Africa* (University of Cape Town Department of Public Law, Cape Town 1997) 25, 27.

5. The Presumption Toward Procedural Fairness

A significant consequence of identifying a decision as one with a public law element is to require the decision maker to exercise his or her discretion in accordance with the well established rules of natural justice or procedural fairness. While a court may not be prepared to inquire into the substance of an employment decision, such as the decision to dismiss, it will mandate, at minimum, procedural safeguards before such dismissal. This has been the thrust of landmark cases from Canada. The case of *Knight*,[17] for example, emphasizes the reason for the court's intervention and its impact.

In *Knight*, the respondent director of education for the appellant Board was dismissed with three months notice. He challenged the decision for wrongful and unlawful dismissal, alleging the absence of procedural fairness. Speaking for the majority, L'Heureaux-Dube J noted that:

> the duty to act fairly does not depend on doctrines of employment law, but stems from the fact that the employer is a public body whose powers are derived from statute, powers that must be exercised according to the rules of administrative law.[18]

After exhaustive review of precedents from Canada and England, L'Heureaux-Dube J concluded that there is 'a general right to procedural fairness' autonomous of the operation of any statute resting on a public body in an employer/employee relationship.[19] Further, a public employee not protected by contract is entitled to a general duty of fairness.[20]

What, then, is encompassed in the principle of procedural fairness in relation to employment? In *Hall v University of New South Wales*, McClellan J stated that:

> A statutory body which makes a decision adversely, directly and personally affecting a person's rights, interests or legitimate expectations must ensure that the procedures utilized in making the decision are fair.[21]

His Lordship cited with approval the definition of the term by Mason J in *Kioa v West:*

> The expression 'procedural fairness' more aptly conveys the notion of a flexible obligation to adopt fair procedures which are appropriate

---

17. *Knight v Board of Education of Indian Head School Division No 19* [1990] 1 SCR 653 (SC Can) (*Knight*).
18. Ibid 26.
19. Ibid 37.
20. Ibid 49.
21. [2003] NSWC 669 (SC Australia) [66] (*Hall*).

and adapted to the circumstances of the particular case. The statutory power must be exercised fairly, i.e., in accordance with procedures that are fair to the individual considered in the light of the statutory requirements, the interests of the individual and the interests and purposes, whether public or private, which the statute seeks to advance or protect or permits to be taken into account as legitimate considerations.[22]

A fundamental element of procedural fairness is the hearing rule or 'the right to be heard'; as McClellan J said, the elements of 'the right will vary in particular cases.'[23] This view, we have seen, was echoed by L'Heureux-Dube J in *Knight*.[24]

Binnie J in *New Brunswick (Board of Management) v Dunsmuir*, reminds us further that:

...a fair procedure is said to be the handmaiden of justice. Accordingly, procedural limits are placed on administrative bodies by statute and the common law. These include the requirements of "procedural fairness," which will vary with the type of decision maker and the type of decision under review. On such matters, as well, the courts have the final say. The need for such procedural safeguards is obvious. Nobody should have his or her rights, interests or privileges adversely dealt with by an unjust process.[25]

6. Legitimate Expectation to be Heard

A legitimate expectation to be heard may also form part of the general obligation toward procedural fairness, where there was an established practice of a hearing before an employment decision such as a dismissal, or where an undertaking was made.

The concept of 'legitimate expectation' is now well established both in the context of reasonableness and in the context of natural justice.[26] According to Wade, '[t]he doctrine of legitimate expectation thus extends the procedural protection that would otherwise be applicable; it enhances but does not replace the duty to act fairly.'[27]

---

22. Ibid 67 (citing: *Kioa v West* (1985) 159 CLR 550, 585 (Mason J)).
23. Ibid 68.
24. *Knight* (n 17).
25. [2008] 1 SCR 190 (SC Can) [129] (*Dunsmuir*). These may include a requirement for the giving of reasons. See, e.g., *Lonrho plc v Secretary of State for Trade and Industry* [1989] 2 All ER 609 (HL) 620.
26. See H.W.R. Wade and C.F. Forsyth, *Administrative Law* (9th edn, OUP, Oxford 2004) 500.
27. Ibid 501–2. See also *Francois v Attorney General* [2002] 5 LRC 699, 717 [H–I], 2, at page 249 for a statement of the principle.

7. Importing a Public Law Element into the Contract on Grounds of Public Policy

The courts have also identified public policy as a compelling reason for incorporating public law principles into a contract of employment where a statutory authority is the employer. In the public policy cases, the dicta goes beyond mere procedural fairness and suggests broader notions of the legitimate use of state power. Such a rationale is more in keeping with the constitutional safeguards in relation to state power envisaged by the founding fathers.

In *Knight*, for example, it was stated:

> The conclusion that the respondent's employment could be legally terminated without a showing of just cause does not necessarily entail that the procedure involved can be arbitrary. There may be a general right to procedural fairness, autonomous of the operation of any statute, depending on consideration of three factors which have been held by this court to be determinative of the existence of such a right: *Cardinal v. Kent Inst.*, supra. If consideration of these factors in the context of the present appeal leads to the conclusion that the respondent was entitled to procedural fairness, the Education Act and, in this case, the terms of the contract of employment must then be considered to determine whether this entitlement is either limited or excluded entirely. It should be noted at this point that the duty to act fairly does not depend on doctrines of employment law, but stems from the fact that the employer is a public body whose powers are derived from statute, powers that must be exercised according to the rules of administrative law. It is in that context that the employee-employer relationship between the respondent and the appellant board must be examined, with the result that the analysis must go beyond the contract of employment to encompass arguments of public policy.[28]

The public policy context is explained further in *Martin v Vancouver (City)*, a judgment from the British Columbia Court of Appeal, relying on the earlier landmark case of *Knight*. Here, it was stated:

> Justice L'Heureux-Dubé's comments (at 668) that 'the duty to act fairly does not depend on doctrines of employment law, but stems from the fact that the employer is a public body whose powers are derived from statute, powers that must be exercised according to the rules of administrative law', and (at 669) that 'the analysis must encompass arguments of public policy', have resonance in this case.

---

28. *Knight* (n 17) 26.

She explained further (at 675):

> There is also a wider public policy argument militating in favour of the imposition of a duty to act fairly on administrative bodies making decisions similar to the one impugned in the case at bar. The powers exercised by the appellant Board are delegated statutory powers which, as much as the statutory powers exercised directly by the government, should be put only to legitimate use. As opposed to the employment cases dealing with 'pure master and servant' relationships, where no delegated statutory powers are involved, the public has an interest in the proper use of delegated power by administrative bodies.[29]

8. Protection of Livelihood and Other Significant Impacts on Individual Rights

In administrative law, courts have been particularly eager to intervene into contracts of employment involving statutory authorities where important interests such as a person's livelihood, whether in employment, trade, or the application of a license, are involved. Both the common law and statute have recognized the importance of protecting this right to a livelihood, and have imposed procedural and in some cases, substantive restraints on the deprivation of such livelihood or job.[30] This important rationale, seen in *Knight*,[31] was endorsed in *Martin* where the Court of Appeal stated:

> ...not every decision by a public body to terminate the appointment of the holder of a public office is subject to the duty of procedural fairness. Justice L'Heureux-Dubé set out (at 669) three factors for consideration in determining the existence of a duty to act fairly: the nature of the decision to be made by the administrative body, the relationship existing between that body and the individual, and the effect of that decision on the individual's rights.

In essence, the majority in *Knight* found that, where a public body decides to terminate the employment of an individual, there is a general duty to act fairly if the decision is administrative and specific (as opposed to legislative and general) and final (as opposed to preliminary) (at 670), the person dismissed holds an office at pleasure or from which he may be dismissed only for cause (at 676), *and the decision has a significant impact on the individual* (at 677).[32]

---

29. [2008] 8 WWR 387 (BCCA Can) [73] (*Martin*).
30. This mirrors the growth of the employer's duty of mutual trust and confidence as an implied term and the statutory right to be given a reason and a hearing before a dismissal in unfair dismissal law.
31. *Knight* (n 17).
32. *Martin* (n 29) 74–75 (emphasis added).

9. A Unique Contract

The courts have also recognized that the contract of employment is a 'unique' contract. This is the reason for implying duties of 'good faith.'[33]

10. Restriction of Judicial Review where an Alternative Remedy Exists and the Public/Private Law Dichotomy

Despite the several avenues available for courts to intervene in the contract of employment to locate protective principles of public law, they have not always done so. However, in those cases where the courts have sought to restrict the purview of judicial review of the actions of public authorities in employment cases, the intention has not been to reverse the trend of increased protection of the citizen's interests, but rather to enlarge the same. In such cases, the denial of judicial review was because the person suffering an adverse consequence of a decision relating to their employment could be directed to an alternative means of redress in private law, one which would more easily afford them a remedy. This, for example, was because the courts recognized the harshness of the public law concept of dismissal at pleasure. By redirecting an application for redress to the private law avenue, the person applying for relief could rely on the now well developed remedies in private employment law, which prevent employers from dismissing employees without a fair and valid reason and without a fair hearing, or adherence to general natural justice principles. Thus, where courts have refused to apply public law, it was because adequate, or superior protective mechanisms could be located under private employment law.

British courts were also responding to a vacuum in their own law – the absence of a written constitution and clearly enunciated principles of judicial review which placed corresponding duties on the state. The development of the public law/private law divide allowed the British courts to grant justice without disturbing important constitutional principles. Indeed, a contradictory principle of constitutional supremacy exists in the Commonwealth Caribbean. This was why in one stroke, and without committing constitutional heresy, dismissal at pleasure could be abolished. However, the underlying reasons for the failure to apply principles of judicial review and the idea of the public/private law dichotomy, have not always been appreciated by West Indian courts. The jurisprudence has therefore been inconsistent.

This notion that a court will not exercise its discretion in public law where an adequate remedy in private law exists is seen in the judgment of May LJ, in *Ex p Walsh*, where it was noted:

---

33. See *Wallace v United Grain Growers Ltd* [1997] 3 SCR 701 (SC Can).

> ... over the last decade Parliament has enacted a body of employment protection legislation, now consolidated in the Employment Protection (Consolidation) Act 1978. This has created a new cause of action and consequent remedies for employees who have been 'unfairly' dismissed. An unfair dismissal under the statute is by no means simultaneously a wrongful dismissal at common law. This new cause of action, however, and the statutory remedies that go with it, are not enforceable by ordinary action, nor indeed by judicial review: they are only available to an employee upon a successful application to an industrial tribunal.
>
> Upon a successful application to an industrial tribunal alleging unfair dismissal, the tribunal may in its discretion order the reinstatement of the employee...[or]...the employee is entitled to compensation under sections 71 to 76 of the Act of 1978, which will in most cases well exceed any damages to which the employee might have been entitled for wrongful dismissal at common law.
>
> For all these reasons I think that earlier decisions in this general field must now be read in the light of the employment protection legislation to which I have referred.[34]

In fact, this distinction was noted by the Supreme Court of Canada. Speaking for the majority in the case of *Dunsmuir*, Bastarache and LeBel JJ in upholding the dismissal of an employee of a Provincial Government pursuant to a contract of employment pointed out that:

> It is important to note as well that the appellant, as a public employee employed under a contract of employment, also had access to all of the same statutory and common law protections that surround private sector employment. He was protected from dismissal on the basis of a prohibited ground of discrimination under the *Human Rights Act*, R.S.N.B. 1973, c. H-11. His employer was bound to respect the norms laid down by the *Employment Standards Act*, S.N.B. 1982, c. E-7.2. As has already been mentioned, if his dismissal had been in bad faith or he had been subject to unfair dealing, it would have been open to him to argue for an extension of the notice pursuant to the principles laid down in *Wallace*. In short, the appellant was not without legal protection or remedies in the face of his dismissal.[35]

Instructively, in several instances, courts in the United Kingdom have been persuaded that a remedy in private law is more adequate or suitable because of the availability of alternative domestic remedies. The point is made by Woolf LJ in *McClaren v Home Office*, in respect of the

---

34. *Walsh* (n 8) 167[G]–168[A], 168[A–C], 169[G].
35. *Dunsmuir* (n 25) 111.

decision in *Reg v Civil Service Appeal Board ex p Bruce*.[36] According to his Lordship,

> If there had not been available the more effective alternative remedy before an industrial tribunal, the Divisional Court would have regarded the decision of the Civil Service Appeal Board in that case as reviewable upon judicial review. The decision of this court which has just been given in *Reg v Secretary of State for the Home Department, Ex parte Attard*, The Times, 14 March 1990 is another example of the same situation. There what was being considered by this court were the powers of a prison governor in connection with disciplinary proceedings in respect of prison officers. The prison governor's disciplinary powers in relation to prisoners are reviewable only on judicial review (see *Leech v Deputy Governor of Parkhurst Prison* [1988] C 533 and they can also be reviewed on judicial review where they affect a prison officer on the application of that officer.[37]

The case of *Re Aitken's Application* also underlined the point about the unavailability of a remedy as a basis for granting judicial review:

> [In *R v Secretary of State for the Home Dept, ex p Benwell* [1985] QB 554] a prison officer had been dismissed for disobeying orders contrary to the code of discipline for prison officers. In holding that the applicant was entitled to apply for judicial review Hodgson J was clearly influenced by two factors which he considered distinguished the case from the line of authority which preceded it. Firstly, the code of discipline under which Benwell had been dismissed had not been incorporated into his contract of employment. Therefore, in dismissing him, the Home Office was performing its duties under the statutory provisions by which it was empowered to order dismissal. Secondly, the applicant had no private law rights which could be enforced in civil proceedings nor could he have recourse to an industrial tribunal to claim that he had been unfairly dismissed.[38]

The conclusion to be drawn is that the courts will place limits on their authority in public law where contracts of employment between employees and state employers are concerned, because of the acknowledgement of the public/private law divide and the existence of adequate private law remedies.

It should be noted from the outset, however, that Commonwealth Caribbean courts have never fully developed the public/private law doctrine as exhibited in the UK courts, perhaps because Order 53

---

36. [1988] 3 All ER 686 (DC).
37. *McClaren* (n 15) 836–37.
38. [1995] NI 49 (QB) 7 (of LexisNexis printout) (*Re Aitken's*).

mechanisms were not enacted throughout the region. It is questionable to what extent a clear public/private law dichotomy for such hybrid cases exists in the region. Indeed, recent cases which concern judicial review of constitutional human rights suggest that earlier restrictions on redress for violations of rights where private law remedies exist, are now increasingly being relaxed.

11. Understanding Dunsmuir and the True Impact of the Public/Private Law Divide

As demonstrated earlier, the success of the public/private law dichotomy approach is dependent on the existence of an appropriate private law remedy. In a recent case, *Dunsmuir*,[39] the Supreme Court of Canada, in seeking to simplify the discussion on the public law/private law divide and to clarify the *locus classicus, Knight*, emphasized this aspect of the law.

In *Dunsmuir*, the issue was whether the Appellant who held an office 'at pleasure' in the civil service of New Brunswick had the right to procedural fairness in the employer's decision to terminate him. Bastarache and LaBell JJ, speaking for the majority, distinguished *Knight* in the following terms:

> While the majority opinion in *Knight* properly recognized the important place of a general duty of fairness in administrative law, in our opinion, it incorrectly analyzed the effects of a contract of employment on such a duty. The majority in *Knight* proceeded on the premise that a duty of fairness based on public law applied unless expressly excluded by the employment contract or the statute (p.681), without consideration of the terms of the contract with regard to fairness issues.[40]

The Court concluded: 'where a dismissal decision is properly within the public authority's powers and is taken pursuant to a contract of employment, there is no compelling public law purpose for imposing a duty of fairness.'[41] Further, a 'public authority which dismisses an employee pursuant to a contract of employment should not be subject to any additional duty of fairness.'[42]

At first glance, the conclusions of the Court support the contention that no rationale exists for public law principles to apply. However, there is an

---

39. *Dunsmuir* (n 25).
40. Ibid 81.
41. Ibid 106.
42. Ibid 113.

important qualification by their Lordships: 'where a public employee is protected from wrongful dismissal by contract, his or her remedy should be in private law not in public law.'[43] This conclusion echoes the dictum of Lord Donaldson MR who, as we saw earlier, emphasized that a contract that gives 'the required contractual protection' fails to be determined in private law.[44] Clearly, if there is no protection in the contract itself or there is no protection from statute, if the public employee can be dismissed at pleasure then the public employee is entitled to a general duty of procedural fairness. Justice L'Heureux-Dube's reasoning in *Knight* is instructive:

> The justification for granting to the holder of an office at pleasure the right to procedural fairness is that, whether or not just cause is necessary to terminate the employment, fairness dictates that the administrative body making the decision be cognizant of all relevant circumstances surrounding the employment and its termination: *Nicholson*, supra, p. 328, per Laskin C.J.C. One person capable of providing the administrative body with important insights into the situation is the office-holder himself.[45]

Since *Dunsmuir*, it is instructive that other courts have been anxious to explain that the basic principles on the rationales for intervention by way of public law as enumerated in *Knight* remain, and it is only where an applicant is *protected* by a private law remedy that the court will not exercise its public law jurisdiction. For example, the decision in *Dunsmuir* and its impact on *Knight* was quickly interpreted by the Court of Appeal of British Columbia in *Martin*.[46] The issue in this case was whether the Vancouver City Council acted within its statutory authority, in good faith, and in accordance with the principles of procedural fairness in rescinding the appointment of all of the members of a Board (described as 'the Board of Variance') without notice, a hearing or cause. The Court upheld the dismissal, but not before pronouncing on the requirement of procedural fairness. Levine JA reasoned:

> In *Knight*, L'Heureux-Dubé J., for the majority of the Supreme Court of Canada, concluded that there is a general duty of procedural fairness, 'autonomous of the operation of any statute' (at 668), resting on a public body in an employer-employee relationship. In *Dunsmuir*, the Supreme Court of Canada determined that the *Knight* analysis does not apply where the employment relationship

---

43. Ibid 114.
44. *Walsh* (n 8) 165[F–G].
45. *Knight* (n 17) 35.
46. *Martin* (n 29).

at issue is governed by contract. Justice Bastarache, for the majority, said (at para. 114): 'Where a public employee is protected from wrongful dismissal by contract, his or her remedy should be in private law, not in public law.' On my reading of *Dunsmuir*, the procedural fairness principles articulated in *Knight* continue to apply to non-contractual employment relationships and to public appointments from which the holder may be dismissed without cause: see para. 115. Thus, the Knight analysis continues to be applicable in this case.

Justice L'Heureux-Dubé's conclusion in *Knight*, as qualified by *Dunsmuir*, that public employees not protected by contract are entitled to a general duty of procedural fairness is compelling. It goes against the judicial grain to deny even minimal procedural fairness — notice and the opportunity to be heard — to a person whose position is rescinded without cause. Justice L'Heureux-Dubé's reasoning (at 674) is persuasive:

> The justification for granting to the holder of an office at pleasure the right to procedural fairness is that, whether or not just cause is necessary to terminate the employment, fairness dictates that the administrative body making the decision be cognizant of all relevant circumstances surrounding the employment and its termination (Nicholson, supra, at p. 328, per Laskin C.J.) One person capable of providing the administrative body with important insights into the situation is the office holder himself.

Justice L'Heureux-Dubé's comments (at 668) that 'the duty to act fairly does not depend on doctrines of employment law, but stems from the fact that the employer is a public body whose powers are derived from statute, powers that must be exercised according to the rules of administrative law', and (at 669) that 'the analysis must encompass arguments of public policy', have resonance in this case.[47]

The court in *Martin*, relying on *Knight*, emphasized that the duty of procedural fairness in relation to public employees, was 'autonomous of the operation of any statute.'[48]

Both *Knight* and *Martin*, therefore, confirm that not every decision by a public body to terminate the appointment of the holder of a public office is subject to procedural fairness. In *Knight,* Justice L'Heureux-Dubé identified three factors to be considered in determining the existence of a duty to act fairly: (i) the nature of the decision to be made by the administrative body,[49] (ii) the relationship between the administrative

---

47. Ibid 71–73.
48. Ibid 71.
49. *Knight* (n 17) 29–31.

body and the individual,[50] and (iii) the effect of the decision on the individual's rights.[51]

In *Martin*, the fact that the employees were mere part-time volunteers and could not therefore be said to have been deprived of their livelihood, nor that the decision made was personal or 'specific' to them, distinguished the case from *Knight* and the court denied a public law remedy. However, the actual result in the case should in no way detract from the general principles toward judicial review contained therein.

12. Where a Private Law Remedy Exceeds the Public Law Remedy

A point that can easily be missed is that a court may insist upon a private law remedy, not in order to diminish the state's accountability, but to enhance it. For example, this may occur where the law permits the state much leeway in employment decisions where dismissal at the pleasure of the Crown/state obtains. In such cases, the court may impose a private law remedy in order to frustrate the latitude of the state and thereby protect the employment interests of the employee. This was the situation in the case of *Wells v Newfoundland*.[52] In *Wells*, the Supreme Court of Canada treated the contract as a private one in order to impute responsibilities of the state toward its employees, despite legislation which abolished his office and sought to deny him compensation. The salient point is not where the contract is located, but the accountability of the state. The court said:

> The respondent held a senior public position of quasi-judicial responsibility. No misbehaviour was alleged against him, but his position was eliminated. In the private sector, this would clearly constitute a breach of the respondent's contract of employment, and he would be entitled to damages. His status as an employee of the Crown, in the circumstances, should not be different. The law regarding senior civil servants accords with contemporary understanding of the state's role and obligations in its dealings with employees. The most plausible interpretation of the respondent's terms of employment is that while his position, and the authority flowing from it, could be eliminated, he could not be deprived of the benefits of the job except by virtue of age or bad behaviour. ...In a nation governed by the rule of law, it is assumed that the government will honour its obligations unless it explicitly exercises its power not to.[53]

---

50. Ibid 32–38.
51. Ibid 39–40.
52. [1999] 3 SCR 199 (SC Can) (*Wells*).
53. Ibid headnote.

The reasoning in *Wells* was followed closely by the recently constituted Caribbean Court of Justice in *Edwards v AG and the Public Service Commission.*[54] In *Edwards*, counsel for the appellant contended that since an order on the constitutional motion in the second action would make a dismissal by the state a nullity, the appellant would be entitled to be treated as if he continued to be employed up to the normal retirement date of 31 July 1990 – with the result that the appellant could properly claim all his superannuation benefits as if he had worked until retirement. The CCJ referenced the private/public law dichotomy in coming to its decision:

> We are conscious of the dual dimension of the public employment relationship i.e. the public law and the private law elements. The notion taken from public law that a dismissal may be a nullity presents problems in terms of the relief appropriate in a case where a considerable period of time numbered in years has passed since dismissal during which the employee has performed no services for the employer. One possible approach is to say that the consequences of such nullity must vary 'according to the facts of the particular case', including whether the employee remained ready, willing and able to work for the employer notwithstanding the termination and sought relief in the courts expeditiously: see the approach taken by Lord Bingham of Cornhill in *McLaughlin v H.E. the Governor of the Cayman Islands*. However, it may be more appropriate to treat the State as any private employer, as this Court indicated obiter in *Brent Griffith v Guyana Revenue Authority*. In this way, a court might focus on the private law contractual obligation; see also the approach of the Canadian Supreme Court in *Her Majesty the Queen in Right of Newfoundland v Andrew Wells*. We need not consider the merits of these contrasting approaches.[55]

A salient point to note is that because the doctrine of dismissal at pleasure has been abolished in the Commonwealth Caribbean, the rationale behind the *Wells* line of cases is entirely absent. As such, the imposition of a private law remedy will rarely be a better option, a point which seems to have been missed by the CCJ.

13. Where No Equivalent Private Law Remedies in Contract or Common Law

From the exposition of the cases above, it is clear that courts outside of the region have chosen not to proceed along the *Walsh* route only

---

54. [2008] CCJ 10 (AJ) (Guy) (*Edwards*).
55. Ibid 15 (citing *McLaughlin* [2007] UKPC 50 at [14], [16], [17], *Brent* [2006] CCJ 2 (AJ), *Wells* [1999] 3 SCR 199).

where alternative or adequate, private law remedies are available. This, however, has not always been the experience in the Commonwealth Caribbean. Indeed, in some Commonwealth Caribbean countries, the common law presumption of employment at will still obtains and no safeguard has been established for termination of employment. This is the case, for example, in St Lucia and Barbados. It is therefore incongruous to transplant this progressive jurisprudence to jurisdictions such as ours where such alternative private law remedies are absent.

St Lucia, Jamaica and Barbados, for example, have no requisite statutory provisions against unfair dismissals. Unfair dismissal legislation is an important development in employment law which imports standards of both substantive and procedural fairness in the employment relationship. The employer is required to give a valid reason before it can legitimately dismiss an employee. Further, an employer must afford a hearing to an employee before such employee is dismissed.[56]

Similarly, common law developments on procedural fairness in dismissals based on the mutual duty of trust and confidence implied into the contract are not evident in the Commonwealth Caribbean. Elsewhere, such duties have grown up alongside statutory remedies for unlawful dismissal, either in individual employment law or employment law relating to industrial relations and the union. In Trinidad and Tobago, the jurisprudence of the specialized Industrial Relations Court – in particular, its reliance on 'good industrial relations practice' – has resulted in notions of fairness being imported into the common law. Similarly, in Jamaica, judicial developments have focused on contemporary labour law 'ameliorating' the harsh position of the common law with regard to employment relationships.[57] In the absence of such judicial or statutory developments, however, an employer under common law principles of contract can still dismiss employees without a reason and without procedural fairness without violating mutual trust and confidence.

14. Effect of the Presumption that Ordinary Legislation does not Bind the Crown or State

In addition, in many cases, ordinary legislation, such as protective employment legislation, does not bind the Crown. For example, in the case of St Lucia, this glaring absence of a remedy in private employment law is even more catastrophic since the only legislation which seeks to

---

56. Note, however, that in St Lucia, the Equality of Opportunity and Treatment in Employment and Occupation Act 2001 will make dismissals due to any stated ground of discrimination unlawful.
57. *Jamaica Flour Mills Limited v Industrial Disputes Tribunal* [2005] UKPC 16 (Ja).

regulate contracts of service in general, the Contracts of Service Act 1970, specifically excludes the Crown in its purview. Thus, even when the Labour Code, which was passed by Parliament in 2006, finally comes into being, with its new provisions for remedies in unfair dismissal, the Crown will be excluded. Such exclusions generally proceed on the assumption that persons employed in the public sector already have well articulated principles of law under the Constitution and under the common law to protect their own interests. This means that should the courts fail to apply broad principles of fairness derived in public law to situations such as these, employees in statutory authorities will be left in 'no man's land.' They will be denied the benefit of protections found under the Public Service Commission's rules and the Constitution and they will also be denied the protections found under private statutes on employment.

As demonstrated above, the courts have found various ways to identify public law remedies where none was forthcoming in private law, including the argument of public policy and the public interest. These rationales spurned the development of the law on the importation of public law elements into the contract of employment, or alternatively, to deny such incorporation where a sufficient remedy did in fact exist under the contract.

Persons employed by the state should not be denied these fundamental principles of fairness derived by the courts in their inherent supervisory jurisdiction to protect citizens against the ever-increasing and potentially arbitrary power. To do otherwise will perpetuate an injustice which was never intended, either by the framers of our constitutions, the policymakers, or even the founding fathers of administrative law.

15. Caribbean Responses to Contracts of Employment of the State

A number of courts in the Commonwealth Caribbean have considered the question whether decisions relating to contracts of employment where the state or Crown is the employer are reviewable. The decisions have not always been consistent and often the dicta have been sparse.

In *Romain v Water and Sewerage Authority*,[58] for example, Ramlogan J held that the Water and Sewerage Authority of Trinidad and Tobago in terminating the employment of the applicant without a hearing, was not performing a public function even if statutory regulations which were abolished in 1980 applied by agreement. The failure to find a ground for judicial review is perhaps explained by the fact that an agreement to

---

58. (17 Jan 1997) TT 1997 HC 13 (HC T&T).

apply a previous statute is not to be equivalent to a statute in existence.

In contrast, in the later case of *Singh v Agricultural Development Bank*,[59] Tiwary-Reddy J held that a statutory Board which terminated the employment contract of the applicant allegedly for failing to implement a Board decision, 'was exercising a public law function.'

Given the rapid developments in administrative law and the expanding purview of judicial review, it is understandable that a case decided some seven years later than *Singh* could treat the issue of the capacity of the courts to intervene in cases with a public law flavour more liberally. This was after the developments in administrative law which examined judicial review not only from the perspective of the source of the power, but also the nature of the decision and its impact on the public.[60]

In the Organisation of Eastern Caribbean States (OECS) jurisdiction, in the case of *British Virgin Islands Electricity Corporation v Virgin Islands Electricity Corporation Appeal Tribunal*, Rawlins J, as he then was, held, *inter alia*, that a statutory tribunal established by the BVI Electrical Corporation Act was a public body amenable to Judicial Review. Referring to the Corporation, he said:

> Now the corporation, a public body and a creature of statute, stands to be adversely affected by the decision of the Tribunal. That decision is of a public nature. The Corporation has the required nexus for the purposes of *locus standi* under Part 56.2 of the Rules. It is a body that has sufficient interest in the subject matter of the application for judicial review under Part 56.2(2)(e) of the Rules. It is a statutory body within whose statutory remit the subject matter of this case falls.[61]

However, in another case involving the same applicant, *Turnbull v Abraham*, Hariprashad-Charles J declared:

> Further, I take comfort from the judgment of Rawlins J in Turnbull No.1 [supra]. In that case, Mr. Turnbull (the present applicant) was offered the position of General Manager of the Corporation on an acting basis for a period of one year. The Corporation decided to revert him to his substantive post of Deputy General Manager. Mr. Turnbull appealed the decision and the External Appeal Tribunal heard the appeal. The majority was of the view that Mr. Turnbull had been dismissed from the position of General Manager and that the dismissal was procedurally incorrect. No preliminary objection was taken. Rawlins J. (as he then was) held that locus standi was not in issue. The Corporation, a public body and a creature

---

59. (24 Mar 2004) TT 2004 HC 26, 114 (HC T&T).
60. See Wade and Forsyth (n 26).
61. (28 Feb 2003) VG 2003 HC 5 (St V-G) [14].

of statute, stands to be adversely affected by the decision of the External Appeal Tribunal. The decision is of a public nature and as such, it was amenable to judicial review.

While it is true that in Turnbull No. 1, the Corporation had no other way of addressing the issue, it is mind-boggling to see how in that case, the Court decided that the External Appeal Tribunal was amenable to judicial review and in the present case, this Court should find that the same tribunal is not. However, the dissimilarity between Turnbull No. 1 and the present case lies in the fact that the applicant here, has the alternative remedy of suing for damages in private law.[62]

Two points emerge from these cases. Firstly, Judicial Review may be denied if alternative domestic remedies are available and are adequate. Secondly, if there is no contractual protection, then administrative law remedies may be invoked. The critical question becomes this: where an employee of a public authority is not protected from unfair dismissal by a contract, where does the remedy lie, in private law or public law? The response should be – in public law.

16. Conclusion – Interpreting the Abolition of Dismissal at Pleasure and Avoiding 'Contracting Out' Obligations by the State

This chapter has highlighted emerging jurisprudential principles to address employment by the state outside of the public servant context. It argues for more consistent, interventionist approaches by the courts to protect employees of the state who remain vulnerable to the exercise of increasing state power.

The question may be asked, what is the real impact of the abolition of the dismissal at pleasure restrictions, particularly when juxtaposed with the expanded purview of judicial review by the courts in their jurisdiction to curtail arbitrary conduct by the state? The 'public element'/'nature of the power' cases emphasize the priority placed on the burgeoning power of the state and the use of regulatory power in general in ways which impact adversely on the citizen.

The use of a regulatory power which has significant impact on the citizenry is no less destructive when such citizens are employed by the state. If anything, given the concerns expressed by the constitutional arrangements to fit what was then the predominant state employment context, the public service, one can legitimately argue that there is even

---

62. (5 Oct 2007) VG 2007 HC 30 (St V-G) [36–37].

more justification for courts to intervene where employment is concerned. The historical and constitutional context of the regulation of state power as exercised toward its employees, favours more, and not less review.

The fact that employment by the state outside of the constitutional borders which regulate the public service is fast increasing, is cause for even greater concern. Indeed, if non-public servant state employees are allowed to languish in no-man's-land, it encourages a situation whereby the state can deliberately 'opt out' of its constitutional obligations by continually decreasing the public service as it enlarges the number and type of positions created by ordinary, private contracts outside of the purview of service commissions. This is similar to the 'contracting out' phenomena emerging in the private sector, through which private sector employers plot to evade their legal obligations,[63] and is no less undesirable.

---

63. See Antoine (n 1).

More Questions Than Answers? Caribbean Jurisprudence on the Duty of *Uberrimae Fides*

Lesley A. Walcott[1]

1. Introduction

My colleagues have made important contributions on a myriad of issues relating to administrative law, public international law, employment law and intellectual property, contributions which cover a broad range of topics deepening our understanding of Caribbean law. This chapter relates to insurance – specifically the operation of the fundamental doctrine of *uberrimae fidei*, or utmost good faith, as manifested in Caribbean jurisprudence.

In evaluating Caribbean jurisprudence, it must be acknowledged that the doctrine of *uberrimae fidei* today bears little resemblance to that contemplated in 1766.[2] Today, over-refinement of the doctrine in the United Kingdom has filtered through to the Caribbean adding to its complexity and increasing the burden placed on the insured. Despite the oft-stated mutuality of the duty,[3] in reality, it is its imposition on the insured, rather than the insurer which has contributed to the volume of case law on point. Regional jurisprudence, while enlightening on the parameters of the duty of utmost good faith, must be assessed against the constant thread running throughout the discussion, namely, the pervasive tension between the insured and the insurer. Certainly in an environment devoid of statutory/self-regulatory assistance,[4] the common law assumes a larger significance, demanding further scrutiny. Overall, regional jurisprudence depicts a robust enthusiasm for the seminal House of Lords decision of *Pan Atlantic Insurance Co Ltd v Pine Top Insurance*

---

1. This chapter is a condensed version of a paper delivered on 3 April 2008 at the UWI Faculty of Law's Commercial Workshop Series.
2. *Carter v Boehm* (1766) 97 ER 1162, (1766) 3 Burr 1905 (KB). See further R.A. Hasson, 'The Doctrine of *Uberrimae Fides* in Insurance Law – A Critical Evaluation' [1969] MLR 615.
3. *La Banque Financiere de la Cite SA v Westgate Insurance Co Ltd* [1991] 2 AC 249 (HL).
4. In the Caribbean there is no comprehensive control of policy terms. Section 155 of the St Lucia Insurance Act Cap 12:08 [2001 Rev], simply provides that all policies must be in clearly legible letters. Most regional Insurance Acts contain a provision relating to the misstatement of age. See, for example, Barbados Insurance Act 1996–32 s 109; Guyana Insurance Act 1998–20 s 132; Jamaica Insurance Act 2001–26 s 93; Trinidad and Tobago Insurance Act Cap 84:01 s 122(4). The position in the Caribbean is in stark contrast to that obtaining elsewhere. See further, *infra* at n 25.

Co Ltd.[5] The danger with this however is that there is a tendency to neatly present this decision as the 'solution' and to ignore many of the underlying questions.

2. Statutory Assistance on the Doctrine of Utmost Good Faith?

It is perhaps useful to commence discussion with an inquiry into whether there exists any statutory assistance on the doctrine of utmost good faith. The statutory origins of Anglo-West Indian insurance law lie in the United Kingdom's Life Assurance Act of 1774,[6] the Gaming Act of 1845,[7] the Married Women's Property Act 1882[8] and the Marine Insurance Act 1906.[9] This eighteenth and nineteenth century United Kingdom legislation represents the foundation of Caribbean insurance law and the extent to which it continues to be relevant today, is dependent on whether the jurisdiction has embraced the Caribbean Law Institute (CLI) initiative.[10] The CLI Insurance Bill has been implemented in Barbados,[11] Guyana,[12] Jamaica,[13] and in St Vincent and the Grenadines[14] and, perhaps prompted by the current economic crises, more recently in St Kitts and Nevis[15] and the Commonwealth of The Bahamas.[16] Representing the stimulus for the emancipation of insurance law from its colonial roots towards a more indigenous regime, the CLI model has two notable features. One is its distinct financial rationale so that in territories which have enacted the model bill, insurers are subject, *inter alia,* to increased financial obligations relating to stipulated deposits,[17] statutory funds,[18] and share capital,[19] while additionally, the regulator's

---

5. [1995] 1 AC 501 (HL).
6. 14 Geo 3 c 48.
7. 8 & 9 Vict c 109.
8. 45 & 46 Vict c 75.
9. 28 Geo 3 c 56.
10. In April 1989, the CLI produced a Survey Report on the Status of Insurance Law in the Commonwealth Caribbean. This report identifies a number of areas where existing law in the Commonwealth Caribbean could be harmonized and modernized. As a consequence, in November 1990, the CLI established an Insurance Law Advisory Committee. The result was the Caribbean Law Institute Model Insurance Bill 1993, the Caribbean Law Institute Model Motor Vehicles Insurance Bill of 1993, the Insurance Association of the Caribbean Revision 2000 (CLI/CLIC 2000), and the Insurance Association of the Caribbean Revision 2000 (IAC Revision 2000).
11. Barbados Insurance Act (n 4).
12. Guyana Insurance Act (n 4).
13. Jamaica Insurance Act (n 4).
14. St Vincent and The Grenadines Insurance Act 2003-45.
15. Saint Christopher and Nevis Insurance Act 2009-8.
16. Bahamas Insurance Act Cap 347.
17. Trinidad and Tobago Insurance Act (n 4) s 21; Barbados Insurance Act (n 4) s 9; Guyana Insurance Act (n 4) s 40.
18. Barbados Insurance Act (n 4) s 25; Guyana Insurance Act (n 4) s 46.
19. For example, s 12 of the St Lucia Insurance Act (n 4) stipulates that the share capital for long term insurance is $1 million dollars for a local company and $2 million dollars for a foreign company.

powers have been significantly enhanced.[20] The critical underlying objective of the reform is solvency, namely, to ensure the insurer's ability to satisfy his obligations when they become due. Coupled with stringent monetary controls, the Insurance model contains an acute social purpose rendering the legislation culturally relevant by recognizing spousal relationships for the purposes of insurable interest[21] and the status of the beneficiary.[22]

As laudable as the briefly highlighted reform measures may be, regional insurance legislation is silent on the issue of utmost good faith.[23] Consequently, apart from ancillary rehabilitation of offenders legislation discussed below,[24] statutory assistance must be gathered from residual marine insurance legislation. In this regard, overall there is a conspicuous underutilization and/or appreciation for the Marine Insurance Act of 1906[25] and or its regional equivalent.[26] The claim that regional jurisprudence fails to acknowledge the importance of the Marine Insurance Act, can only be supported if there is an acceptance that the Act is critical to an understanding of insurance law and more

---

20. For example, modern insurance statutes bestow on regulators the power to search and seize. See, e.g., Barbados Insurance Act (n 4) s 53, Jamaica Insurance Act (n 4) s 49.

21. See s 127(1)(b) of the Barbados Insurance Act (n 4), which recognizes insurable interest of 'a spouse in the life of his or her spouse.'

22. The CLI Insurance Committee made a number of recommendations, including: (1) that there should be a statutory provision conferring a right of action on the named beneficiary to recover the proceeds of a life policy effected in his favour; (2) that the statutory framework should reflect a policy that, if he so desires, the insured could irrevocably designate a person as beneficiary and render the policy immune from creditors and unilateral action altering the designation; and (3) that the new framework should recognize that beneficiaries other than what is called the irrevocable beneficiary could be changed at any time during the lifetime of the policy holder in order to give flexibility to designations. See, e.g., ss 116–18 of the Barbados Insurance Act (n 4); Jamaica Insurance Act (n 4) s 98.

23. This stands in sharp contrast to the position adopted elsewhere. In the United Kingdom, the doctrine has been the subject of intense discussion. See, for instance, A. Hamilton QC, *Insurance Contract Law Reform: Recommendations to the Law Commission, Report of the Sub-Committee of the British Insurance Law Association* (BILA Secretariat, London 2002) <http://www.bila.org.uk/pdfs/Insurance_Law_Reform_Report.pdf> accessed 6 Aug 2010; Law Commission, 'Insurance Law: Non Disclosure and Breach of Warranty' (Law Com No 104 Cm 8064, 1980). In the United Kingdom, the Insurance Companies Amendment Act 1973 c 58 was amended by the Insurance Companies Amendment Act 1974 c 49, the Insurance Companies Act 1981 c 81 and the Insurance Companies Act 1982 c 50. Reform was instituted to accommodate the EC Directive, First Non-Life Directive Regarding the Freedom of Establishment in Non-Life Insurance, Dir 73/239 (23 Jul 1973) OJ L228/3. See the Financial Services and Markets Act 2000 (Regulated Activities) Order 2001 (SI 2001/544) art 10.

24. It should be noted, however, that misrepresentation legislation operates in two jurisdictions: Antigua and Barbuda Misrepresentation Act 1992-7; Trinidad and Tobago Misrepresentation Act 1983-12.

25. Marine Insurance Act 1906 (n 9).

26. Anguilla Marine Insurance Act RSA 2000 CM 25; British Virgin Islands Marine Insurance Ordinance Cap 257 [1961 Rev]; Cayman Islands Marine Insurance Act 1959 Cap 711 [1961 Rev]; Grenada Marine Insurance Act Cap 182; St Kitts and Nevis Marine Insurance Act 1959 Cap 711; St Lucia Marine Insurance Act 1959 Cap 711; St Vincent and The Grenadines Marine Insurance Act Cap 105 [1990 Rev]; Turks and Caicos Marine Insurance Act 1959 Cap 711.

specifically the doctrine of *uberrimae fidei*. Marine insurance legislation, as evidenced by the common law is often the source of debate and contention.[27] The Act is of broad application for notwithstanding its title, it extends beyond the boundaries of marine insurance[28] there being no difference between marine and non-marine insurance in this respect.[29] Apart from providing the foundation for an analysis of the duty of utmost good faith, it illuminates on several other aspects of insurance and hence represents more than a convenient starting point as borne out in subsequent discussion. While the precise origin of the seemingly unlimited requirement of 'utmost good faith' derived from the idea of *uberrimae fidei*, in the side note, remains a mystery,[30] the Act, constitutes the driving force behind the broad formulation of the duty that exists at common law today.

The utility of the marine insurance legislation was recognized by Justice Kissoon, in *Ali (Somat) v Hand-in-Hand Mutual Fire & Life Insurance Co Ltd*,[31] who set out in some detail the corresponding provisions in the United Kingdom equivalent. Here, the Court of Appeal used the Act as the framework to answer inquiries into materiality, the nature of the duty of utmost good faith and the effect of breach. Moreover, perhaps as noted, since regional case law exhibits an unmistaken reverence for the seminal House of Lords decision of *Pan Atlantic Insurance Co Ltd v Pine Top Insurance Co Ltd*,[32] a decision which, *inter alia,* relied heavily on the Marine Insurance Act, then perhaps albeit by a somewhat circuitous route, there is tacit acceptance of its relevance to the region. In a climate where insurance legislation is either ignored and/or is of little utility to the question of *uberrimae fidei* as in the case of CLI driven reform, it is easy to understand why a great deal of reliance must be placed on the common law.

---

27. See (n 89) and accompanying text.
28. *Lindenau v Desborough* (1828)108 ER 1160, (1828) 8 Barn & C 586 (KB); *Manifest Shipping Co Ltd v Uni-Polaris Shipping Co Ltd* [2001] UKHL 1, [2003] 1 AC 469 ('*The Star Sea*').
29. *PCW Syndicates v PCW Reinsurers* [1996] 1 WLR 1136 (CA).
30. As Lord Clyde observes in *The Star Sea* (n 28), the concept of *uberrimae fides* does not appear to have been derived from civil law and has been regarded unnecessary in civilian systems. See further M.A. Millner, 'Fraudulent Non-Disclosure' (1957) 76 SALJ 177; *Mutual and Federal Insurance Co Ltd v Oudtshoorn Municipality* 1985 (1) SA 419 (SC App Div SA) (suggesting that the concept should be jettisoned); *Blackstone's Commentaries*, vol II, chap 30 (4th edn, 1876) 412–13 (the very essence of contracts of marine insurance 'consists in observing the purest good faith and integrity'). But in *Carter v Boehm* (n 2), 1910, Lord Mansfield refers simply to 'good faith.'
31. (2007) 71 WIR 227 (CA Guy) (*Somat Ali*).
32. *Pan Atlantic* (n 5). There are, however, post-*Pan Atlantic* decisions where no reference was made. See *Jawahir v NEM (West Indies) Insurance Limited* [1996] ECLR 200 (HC St Luc); *Feannny v Globe Ins Co WI Ltd* (1997) 34 JLR 347 (SC Ja); *Browne v Anjo Ins Company Ltd* [1999] ECLR 423 (HC A&B); *St Jean and Ettiene v SAG Motors Co Ltd* [1999] ECLR 266 (HC Dom); *Simon v The Caribbean Home Insurance Co Ltd Ltd* [1999] ECLR 315 (HC Gren).

3. The Relevance of Regional Rehabilitation Legislation

Rehabilitation of offenders' legislation exists in The Bahamas,[33] Barbados,[34] the Cayman Islands[35] and Guyana.[36] Generally treated and regarded as simply being reflective of criminal law reform, the relationship between rehabilitation of offenders' legislation and insurance, at best, can be described as an uneasy one.

The relevance of this reform measure to insurance was recently reinforced by the decision of *Somat Ali*.[37] Justice Kissoon in the Court of Appeal, briefly and albeit *obiter,* in commenting on the objective of the legislation as expressed in subsections 7(1) and 7(2)(b) of the Guyana Act,[38] noted that disclosures by a proper person or any other person on his behalf 'cannot be used as a moral hazard by the insurers to increase his premium or if the spent conviction is not disclosed, that the insurers cannot avoid a policy for non-disclosure.' This reference, *en passant*, by Justice Kissoon was no doubt triggered by the discussion in the High Court.[39] But unfortunately, although the rationale of the legislation was highlighted, the decision does not resolve the question of the application of the legislation to what might be inelegantly described as non/quasi-criminal offences or to offences under securities law for example. Turning to rules of statutory interpretation for guidance, if the ordinary natural rule of construction is applied, surely the legislation is predicated on there being a 'conviction.' In accordance with the Oxford dictionary, the term conviction is 'the act or process of proving or finding guilty.' Logically, therefore, the expression 'conviction' narrows the reach of the legislation.

In addition to the restrictive ambit and reach of the legislation, even with respect to offences which fall squarely within the Act, a further limitation exists due to the residual discretion that is provided for in the legislation. In essence, a dichotomy exists in that, while on the one hand, it is clear that legislators regard rehabilitation with a certain degree of seriousness[40] (for instance under section 24 of the Barbados Act, the consequences for breach of which are severe – ranging from a

---

33. Rehabilitation of Offenders Act 1991-11.
34. Criminal Records (Rehabilitation of Offenders) Act 1997-6.
35. Rehabilitation of Offenders Law 1985-20.
36. Rehabilitation of Offenders Act 1994-6.
37. *Somat Ali* (n 31).
38. Cap 11:07.
39. (2001) 65 WIR 186 (HC T&T).
40. S 23(4) of the Barbados Criminal Records (Rehabilitation of Offenders) Act (n 34) states: 'Any insurance company registered in Barbados which knowingly attempts to avoid a policy of insurance made with the company because of non-disclosure of a spent or expunged conviction is guilty of an offence.'

fine of \$10,000 to imprisonment for a term of 2 years), the legislation simultaneously bestows a residual discretion upon the court to permit evidence of a spent conviction. This discretion can be seen in section 7(3) of the Barbados Act which provides:

> Nothing in section 6 shall affect the determination of any issue, or prevent the admission or requirement of any evidence, relating to a person's previous convictions or to circumstances ancillary thereto.

The section then goes on to identify circumstances where disclosure can take place. Subsections (3)(a)–(c) do not appear to pertain to insurance, relating as they do to criminal or disciplinary proceedings and proceedings relating to guardianship, marriage, or custody. Section 7(3) (d), however, seemingly does. It states:

> (3) Nothing in section 6 shall affect the determination of any issue, or prevent the admission or requirement of any evidence, relating to a person's previous convictions or to circumstances ancillary thereto(d) in any proceedings in which he is a party or witness, if, on the occasion when the issue or the admission or requirement of the evidence falls to be determined, he consents to the determination of the issue or, as the case may be, the admission or requirement of the evidence notwithstanding the provisions of section 6.

The thrust of the section is the purpose for which the disclosure is made, to wit, 'the determination of any issue....' While in that regard, the language of this section is deliberately vague and imprecise, it is predicated on the consent, in this case, the insured's consent. However, when the section is read in light of section 7(1)(d), the scope of the Act is restricted even further.

> Section 7(1), according to the short title, operates as a 'limitation on rehabilitation under this Act.' Section 7(1)(d) excludes from rehabilitation 'any civil or criminal proceedings where justice cannot be done without admitting or requiring evidence relating to a person's spent convictions.'[41] The presence of the rubric 'where justice cannot be done,' imports notions of equity,[42] broadening the ambit of courts' discretion to permit evidence in the 'interests of justice.'

Unfortunately, while this discretion imports flexibility, the nature and import of the judicial discretion remain a mystery. One thing is certain, that as far as the utility of the legislation is concerned, the

---

41. Barbados Criminal Records (Rehabilitation of Offenders) Act (n 34).
42. See further H.G. Hanbury and R.H. Maudsley, *Modern Equity* (13th edn, Stevens & Sons, London 1989).

discretion operates as a caveat on the extent to which a conviction can be considered as having been extinguished; a fact that inures for the benefit of the insurer. For the insured, the utility of the legislation given the inordinate burden placed on the insured to disclose matters pertaining to the moral hazard must be appreciated.[43] But the restrictive nature of the statute, in light of the residual discretion, means that there is doubt as to whether prior convictions will truly be considered to have been 'spent.' With respect to the common law, prior to the *Somat Ali* decision, reliance had to be placed on *Reynolds v Phoenix Assurance Co Ltd*,[44] an English decision of only marginal assistance since Justice Forbes in considering the UK equivalent,[45] confined his judgment to the narrow point that since the legislation did not exist when the offence was committed in 1961, the Act did not apply.

In sum, rehabilitation legislation is indeed relevant to insurance law and accordingly cannot be viewed as simply an ad hoc ancillary reform measure. To the insured policyholder, the legislation mitigates in some way the burdensome duty to disclose prior convictions once those convictions are marginal and not of a heinous character. But there is uncertainty as to when and in precisely what manner the legislation operates which weakens the level of protection afforded the insured policyholder.

4. The Moral Hazard: Consideration of Outstanding Criminal Charges, Acquittals, Suspicions and/or Rumours of Criminality

There are myriad considerations within the concept of moral hazard that pose considerable difficulty for jurists. But before exploring the ambit of the moral hazard, it is important to understand that section 21(2) of the Barbados Marine Insurance Act indicates that there is a clear correlation between materiality, the quantum of the premium to be charged and risk-assessment. By addressing the function of materiality, the section thereby intimates the type of factors which will be considered material. In this regard, the common law groups material facts into two main categories: the 'physical hazard,' the physical condition of the life or property being insured, and the 'moral hazard,' the factors concerning the character of the insured – the desirability of the assured as a person

---

43. Indeed, the introduction of the inducement test by the House of Lords in *Pan Atlantic* was motivated at least in part by the desire to place a heavier burden on insurers seeking to avoid a policy for non-disclosure.
44. [1978] 2 Lloyd's Rep 440 (QB).
45. Rehabilitation of Offenders Act 1974 c 53.

with whom the insurer's would want to contract.[46] It is important to appreciate that both 'hazards' may be subject to an express warranty, in which case there is no dispute as to the materiality of the information, as materiality is presumed.

Undoubtedly, the presence of the express term, as was the case in *Bowe v British Fidelity Assurance Limited*[47] and *Alleyne v Colonial Fire and General Insurance Company Limited*,[48] has a bearing on the judicial response. In the Barbadian decision of *Joseph v Clico International General Insurance Co Ltd*,[49] in response to the question whether the appellant was insured with any other company, the insured responded 'no' when in fact there was a pre-existing mortgage and insurance on the property. Chief Justice Sir David Simmons, in upholding the decision of Madam Justice Kentish in the High Court, referred to the basis of contract clause as the 'critical element' making the truth of the statement, a condition precedent to the liability of the insurer, so that the insurer was held entitled to avoid the contract on the basis of non-disclosure. In that regard, it must be noted that while facts as to the moral hazard are less likely to be subject to express questions, they can be. Moreover, notwithstanding the importance of basis of contract clauses, as acknowledged by Justice Moore-Bick in *James v CGU Insurance Plc*,[50] by their very nature many matters which insurers would regard as relevant to the moral hazard are unlikely to be the subject of questions in the proposal form and are equally unlikely to be volunteered by the insured. In any event, the duty of disclosure exists independently of any that may be spelt out in the policy documents. Consequently, the following additional questions may be posed: (i) whether the moral hazard extends beyond criminal activity to bankruptcy or financial mis-dealings; (ii) to what extent are the courts prepared to consider outstanding criminal history, criminal charges and acquittals;[51] (iii) what is the relevance of allegations or circumstances which raise suspicion of involvement in criminal activity; and (iv) what is the relevance of allegations or circumstances that affect the risk insured? Although the answers to these questions illuminate the scope and ambit of the moral hazard, compounding the difficulty is the fact that moral hazard can surface in a variety of situations, sometimes with no clear distinct line of demarcation separating one moral hazard from another.

---

46. *Locker & Woolf Limited v Western Australian Insurance Co Ltd* [1936] 1 KB 408 (CA); *Insurance Corporation of the Channel Islands v Royal Hotel No 2* [1998] Lloyd's Rep IR 151 (DC) ('*Royal Hotel*'). See, however, the decisions of *Sharp v Sphere Drake Insurance Co Ltd* [1992] 2 Lloyd's Rep 501 (QB Com Ct) ('*The Moonacre*'); *Inversiones Manria SA v Sphere Drake Insurance Co Plc* [1989] 1 Lloyd's Rep 69 (QB) ('*The Dora*') (the material fact did not fall within the ordinary classification).
47. (unrep) 15 July 2003, No 372 of 1997 (SC Bah).
48. (unrep) 23 Nov 2005, No 58 of 2004 (CA T&T).
49. (2006) 71 WIR 31 (CA Bdos).
50. [2002] Lloyd's Rep IR 206 (QB Com Ct) (*James*).
51. *The Dora* (n 46); *Brotherton v Aseguradoa Colseguros SA* [2003] EWCA Civ 705 (CA) ('*Brotherton*').

This blurring of the lines is apparent in the 'distinction' between bankruptcy, financial insecurity and general dishonesty. At the crux of the dilemma is whether the moral hazard extends beyond criminal activity to bankruptcy and/or financial mis-dealings. Generally, it is accepted that an allegation of general dishonesty is a material fact that must be disclosed. Thus, in *CTI v Oceanus*[52] at first instance, the Court stated that an insurer is entitled to know all facts which throw doubt on the business integrity of the assured at the time the insurance is placed. Similarly, in *Insurance Corporation of the Channel Islands Ltd v Royal Hotel No 2*,[53] Mance J held that it was a material fact that the insured, a director who was also the company secretary, had prepared false invoices in order to give the banker a more favourable impression of the company's profitability, even though the documents had no connection to the policy being effected. Arguably, as financial insecurity ultimately impacts on an insured's ability to pay the premiums, it provocatively may be argued to fall within section 21(2) of the Barbados Marine Insurance Act, as a factor which may 'influence the judgment of a prudent insurer in fixing the premium.'[54] This view must be countered, however, given that the fixing of the premium by underwriters correlates to the risk insured and not to the insured's ability to pay. The relevance of the insured's financial position can thus be seen in *James v CGU Insurance*[55] where the financial circumstances of the insured who was engaged in disputes with both Inland Revenue and Customs was found to be a material fact falling within the moral hazard. Of interest is the reference by the Court to United Kingdom Statements of General Insurance Practice and the code of practice on the type of matters that insurers regard as material – auxiliary mechanisms that are not available in the Caribbean.[56] The issue

---

52. [1982] 2 Lloyd's Rep 178 (QB) (Lloyd J), rev'd [1984] 1 Lloyd's Rep 476 (CA).
53. *Royal Hotel* (n 46). See also *James* (n 50); *Schoolman v Hall* [1951] 2 Lloyd's Rep 139 (CA).
54. *North Star Shipping Ltd v Sphere Drake Insurance Plc* [2005] EWHC 665 (Com Ct).
55. *James* (n 50).
56. See, e.g., Australian Law Reform Commission, *Insurance Contracts*, Report No 20 (Australian Government Publishing Service, Canberra 1982) Chapter 6 ('Non-Disclosure and Misrepresentation') <http://www.austlii.edu.au/au/other/alrc/publications/reports/20/20.pdf> accessed 6 Aug 2010; Australian Insurance Contracts Act 1984, 'Insured's duty of disclosure'; *Statement of Long Term Insurance Practice* (Association of British Insurers, London 1986). See also Insurance Law Reform, 'The Consumer Case for a Review of Insurance Law' (NCC, London 1997); 1993 Dir 93/13 *European Directive on Unfair Terms In Consumer Contracts* [1993] OJ L 95/29; 2002 Dir 2002/56 *Concerning the Marketing of Consumer Financial Services and Amending Council Directive* 90/619/EEC and Directives 97/7/EC and 98/27 EC [2002] OJ L 271/16. In the United States, consider *Holtzclaw v Bankers Mutual Insurance Co* 48 Ala App 570, 266 So 2d 780 (1972), *Napeir v Allstate Insurance Co* 961 F 2d 168, 170 (1992). It is noted that the position adopted by the various states differ. In some states, the duty is confined to marine policies so that in other areas proof of intent to conceal is required. In others, the insurer's right to avoid a policy for non-disclosure or misrepresentation is restricted by requiring proof of intentional concealment or misrepresentation of a material fact. Alabama is a more 'insurer-friendly state' and permits avoidance where the non-disclosure/misrepresentation is such as to increase the risk of loss.

also arose in *Galle Gowns Ltd v Licenses and General Insurance Ltd.*[57] Here, the facts surrounded a fire insurance policy where the chairman of the plaintiff company had a history of financial difficulties, including two adjudications of bankruptcy under an assumed name. In respect to the first bankruptcy, he had not obtained a discharge until 11 years after and in the case of the second, not until five years later. Additionally, according to the facts, two previous companies of which he was a director had gone into liquidation and he had been found guilty of breach of trust and misfeasance for which he was fined. The insurer was thus entitled to avoid liability due to non-disclosure. It seems clear therefore that the answer to at least one of the questions is 'yes' – the moral hazard does indeed embrace financial impecuniosities on the part of the insured.

The boundaries of moral hazard were tested in the leading decision of *Somat Ali*,[58] arising out of the jurisdiction of Guyana. The facts which were relatively uncomplicated, surrounded a policy of indemnity effected by the insured on 30 June 1994, on his dwelling house, factory and fibreglass moulds with the appellant insurance company. The initial cover was for a period of one month but subsequent to a request for additional insurance and a visit by agents of the insurer, additional coverage was agreed. On 31 July 1994, the respondent's house and factory were completely destroyed by fire. Upon an action for indemnity in the amount of $132 million, at first instance, Madam Justice Bernard ruled in favour of the insured, dismissing a counterclaim by the insurer that the policy was void. The insurer appealed to the Court of Appeal on the ground that the policy was void for material non-disclosure in that the insured had failed to disclose that at the time of effecting the contract the insured was declared bankrupt in Canada. The Court of Appeal while accepting the lower court's position on the parameters of the moral hazard, ruled in favour of the insurer on the ground that the insured had failed to comply with the condition precedent for additional coverage.

The findings of the lower court merit further scrutiny. There, Madam Justice Bernard acknowledged that 'any fact which influences the moral hazard assumed by the insurer and exposes him to the dishonesty of the insured' must be disclosed regardless of whether that fact involves criminality or just deceptive conduct. Nevertheless a measure of judicial restraint was exercised as the learned judge was loath to expand the moral hazard beyond accepted boundaries to embrace financial difficulty.

---

57. (1933) L1 L Rep 186 (KB) (*Galle Gowns*).
58. *Somat Ali* (n 31).

This is evident in the following extract:

> [M]ost of the cases in which materiality of a non-disclosed fact
> has been discussed, involve non-disclosure of previous criminal
> convictions for dishonesty although, as mentioned earlier, non-
> disclosure is not confined to this. I have not personally been able to
> discover any case and none was cited to me where failure to disclose
> prior bankruptcy when applying for coverage for fire insurance or
> non-marine insurance was held to be a material fact, or where such
> failure entitled the insurer to avoid.[59]

The Court of Appeal accepted that there was no duty on the respondent
to disclose his past bankruptcy and past financial history as those matters
were not material for the insurer to know and in any event, the failure of
the insurer to make due inquiry particularly having been put on alert as
to the insured's 'cash flow' problems amounted to waiver by the company
of the information sought.[60] Legal practitioners are cautioned, however,
as the result in *Somat Ali* cannot be relied upon as definitive on the
relevance of financial difficulty. Instead, relevance hinges on the *degree*
of financial difficulty. This is supported by the New Zealand decision of
*Quinby Enterprises Ltd (in liquidation) v General Accident Fire and Life
Assurance Corp plc,*[61] cited in *Somat Ali,* where the insured had a large
unsecured debt and had previous convictions in relation to fraudulent
financial transactions which 'cumulatively mean[t] that there should
have been disclosure to the insurer of Quinby's precarious financial
position.'[62] The Court held that the non-disclosure rendered the policy
void.[63] The *Somat Ali* decision is therefore justified given that the facts
are distinguishable from the *Quinby* decision.

With respect to the question raised, one can conclude as follows:
(i) that bankruptcy/financial difficulty is clearly not within the ambit
of rehabilitation legislation, (ii) bankruptcy/financial difficulties are,
however, relevant to the moral hazard despite the stance adopted by
Somat Ali, since bankruptcy/financial difficulties speak to the insured's
financial integrity.[64]

---

59. (2001) 65 WIR 186 (HC Guy) 196.
60. The Court of Appeal held that there was no completed contract for the additional coverage as this
    was predicated on the condition that the insured supply a list of items by 2 August 1994. This
    condition was not satisfied.
61. [1995] 1 NZLR 736 (HC NZ).
62. *Quinby* (n 61) 746 (Barker J).
63. An interesting argument advanced by the insured was that the insurer acted in breach of the
    Fair Trading Act 1986 by giving the insured the impression that all he had to do was answer the
    questions as set out. The Court ruled that the Fair Trading Act did not limit or affect the operation
    of any other statute, to wit, the Marine Insurance Act 1906.
64. *Woolcott v Sun Alliance* [1978] 1 All ER 1253(QB); *Galle Gowns* (n 57); *Quinby* (n 61).

As to the question, to what extent are the courts prepared to consider outstanding criminal history, criminal charges and acquittals, it is clear, that the insured's criminal history is similarly relevant to the moral hazard. Simply put, a conviction is a conviction and hence, unless rehabilitation legislation operates in the particular jurisdiction, a conviction goes to the moral hazard and therefore must be disclosed.[65] Thus, offences from a 'dim and distant' past have been found to be material.[66] While a close connection between the conviction and the insurance being effected is relevant,[67] it is not conclusive. In *Lambert v Cooperative Insurance Society Ltd*[68] two convictions for handling stolen goods were held to be material to a home insurance policy and in *Cleland v London General Insurance Co Ltd*[69] it was held that the insured's failure to disclose a conviction for breaking and entering should have been disclosed to effect motor insurance.[70]

The question remains, however, as to what extent are the courts prepared to consider outstanding criminal charges and acquittals?[71] If one looks to the common law for answers, material charges must be disclosed to the insurer even if the insured knows that the charges are unfounded.[72] This is in accordance with the decision of *March Cabaret Club & Casino v London Assurance*,[73] and the judgment of Justice May. There are two aspects of the *March Cabaret* case that reflect the nuances of modern commerce and which compound the difficulty relating to utmost good faith. Firstly, there were no questions on the proposal relating to moral hazard and secondly, the contract of insurance was renewed prior to the date of conviction.[74] This position, that material charges must be disclosed to the insurer even if the insured knows that the charges are unfounded was approved by Coleman J in the Court of Appeal in *Brotherton v Aseguradora Colseguros SA No 2*.[75] In *Brotherton*,

---

65. *Regina Fur Co v Bossom* [1957] 2 Lloyd's Rep 466 (CA); *Roselodge Ltd v Castle* [1966] 2 Lloyd's Rep 113 (QB).

66. *Schoolman v Hall* [1951] 1 Lloyd's Rep 139 (CA); *Regina Fur Co* (n 65); *Roselodge* (n 65); *The Dora* (n 46); *Brotherton* (n 51).

67. See with respect to motoring offences the decisions of *Bond v Commercial Union Assurance Co Ltd* (1930) 36 Ll LR 107 (DC); and *Jester-Barnes v Licences and General Insurance Co Ltd* (1934) 49 Ll LR 231 (KB).

68. [1975] 2 Lloyd's Rep 485 (CA).

69. (1935) 51 Ll LR 156 (CA).

70. *Woolcott* (n 64).

71. *The Dora* (n 46); *Brotherton* (n 51); *North Star Shipping Ltd v Sphere Drake Insurance plc* [2006] Lloyd's Rep IR 519 (CA); *Norwich Union Insurance Ltd v Meisels* [2007] Lloyd's Rep 139 (QB Com Ct).

72. *The Dora* (n 46).

73. [1975] 1 Lloyd's Rep 169 (QB).

74. The director was charged on June 14, committed to trial on November 28, and convicted on June 22. The insurance contract was renewed on June 20.

75. *Brotherton* (n 51). Note that Forbes J in the decision of *Reynolds v Phoenix Assurance Co* [1978] 2 Lloyd's Rep 440 (QB) 460 expressly refused to follow this reasoning.

the insured failed to disclose, at the time of effecting insurance, that he was under investigation for alleged fraudulent activity – an allegation that was subsequently proven false.

The danger for the insured is immediately apparent, a danger which is reinforced by the more recent decision of *Strive Shipping Corporation v Hellenic Mutual War Risks Association*.[76] Here the court considered that an outstanding charge on the date of the application for insurance was a material fact that must be disclosed. Furthermore, if the assured knows of facts which, when viewed objectively, suggest that circumstances might exist ('the suggested facts') which would increase the magnitude of the risk and, the known facts would have influenced the judgment of a prudent insurer, the known facts do not cease to be material because it may ultimately be demonstrated that the suggested facts did not exist. The upshot is that there has been a rapid development in the relevance of allegations and charges which is seemingly at odds with the presumption of innocence that operates in criminal law.

In disentangling the common law on the relevance of outstanding criminal charges and allegations of dishonesty, certain principles emerge: (i) if the insured has been charged with an offence and committed to trial, this is a material fact that must be disclosed in accordance with *March Caberet*; (ii) this position stands, even where the matter has come to trial and the insured has been acquitted and/or where the matter has not yet come to trial and the insured is aware that the charges are groundless; (iii) where the insured is of the view that the charges are groundless, in accordance with the decision of *Brotherton*, the insured is still required to make full disclosure, including his own assertions of innocence and put forward any exculpatory evidence (although the effectiveness of this mechanism was doubted in the decision of *The Dora*;[77] (iv) as to the corollary question of the relevance of allegations or circumstances which raise suspicion of involvement in criminal activity, it is not necessary for the assured to evaluate perfectly innocent facts in order to determine whether they might or might not be misconstrued by an underwriter for the duty to disclose does not involve such a rigorous approach.[78] Put another way, there is no duty on the insured to disclose matters which he knows have no bearing on his honesty and integrity even though a suspicious third party might take a different view.[79]

While these tentative conclusions may be proffered, an ancillary question remains relating to the relevance of rumours and the subject

---

76. [2002] 2 Lloyd's Rep 88 (QB Com Ct) (*The Grecia Express*).
77. *The Dora* (n 46).
78. See *Galle Gowns* (n 57).
79. Colinvaux's *Law of Insurance* (8th edn, Thomson Sweet & Maxwell, London 2009) 6–49.

matter insured. The relevance of 'rumours and rumours of war' was interestingly addressed in the Trinidad and Tobago case of *Solomon Ghany Oil & Engineering Ltd v NEM (West Indies) Insurance Ltd.*[80] In *Solomon Ghany*, decided before *Brotherton v Aseguradoa Colseguros SA*,[81] a threat to 'burn the place down' was considered material. Evidence of the actual insurer was used to assist in the determination of materiality. Justice Moosai stated:

> It would obviously have been material for a prudent insurer, in assessing the risk, to know that shortly before the contract, a threat had been made to burn down the building, and that threat had been reported to the police. I am therefore of the view that was a material fact which ought to have been disclosed by the plaintiff. And Cabral's evidence establishes that the fact that a threat had been made would also have influenced the insurance company whether or not to accept the risk. That was therefore a material fact, the non-disclosure or omission of which would have had an effect on the decision of the actual underwriter.[82]

Based on the foregoing, it does appear that a rumour relating to the subject matter insured may indeed go to the question of materiality. If one goes further, given that section 21(3)(b) of the Barbados Marine Insurance Act relinquishes an insured from disclosing 'a circumstance that is known, or presumed to be known and the insurer is presumed to know matters of common notoriety or knowledge,'[83] the question can be raised as to whether it can it be argued that widely published media reports amount to manifest knowledge and, therefore, fall within the rubric of 'circumstances that need not be disclosed'? In *Brotherton*, media reports circulating on the president of the bank's misconduct were found by Morrison J to be material. The answer to the question must, therefore, depend on the manner in which the matter of 'common notoriety' became public, for an unsubstantiated rumour cannot satisfy the test.

It is important to appreciate that at the core of understanding the breadth of the moral hazard is the nature of risk. 'Risk' is not simply the peril or possibility of loss or damage occurring within the scope of the policy, but it embraces all matters which would, if known, influence the judgment of a prudent underwriter. But for the insured, the range of the moral hazard is worrisome, particularly where the conditionality of insurance coverage is tied to financing.

---

80. (unrep) 19 May 2000, HCA No S 3114 of 1986 (HC T&T) (*Solomon Ghany*).
81. *Brotherton* (n 51).
82. *Solomon Ghany* (n 80) 30.
83. Marine Insurance Act (n 9) s 18(3)(b).

5. The Regional Influence of *Pan Atlantic Insurance Co Ltd v Pine Top Insurance Co Ltd*

The House of Lords' decision of *Pan Atlantic Insurance Co Ltd v Pine Top Insurance Co Ltd*[84] has had a fundamental effect on Caribbean jurisprudence in the region's acceptance of the broad test of materiality and in the recognition of inducement so that the non-disclosed material fact must be seen to have *induced* the underwriter to enter into a contract.

First it is perhaps trite to observe that regional jurisprudence accepts that materiality is an essential ingredient of the duty of utmost good faith. As Justice Hamel-Smith in the High Court decision of *Hosein & Co v Goodwill Life & General Insurance Co Ltd* opined: 'non-disclosure does not exist in isolation...the crucial qualification [on the duty of *uberrimae fidei*] is the right to avoid a contract on the basis of non-disclosure hinges on materiality.'[85] Indeed, the relevance of materiality is well settled; the test of materiality being a question of law, while the actual determination of the issue in any particular case involves the resolution of a question of fact.[86] Being a question of fact, it is generally a question solely for the trial judge or arbitrator and not subject to appeal, and, furthermore, strictly no decision is actually binding in a later case under the doctrine of precedent.[87] But as John Birds notes, 'much of the criticism of the wide ranging nature of the duty has been directed at the central question of the test for determining materiality.'[88] Disputes as to the test to be applied, stem from the phrase 'influence the judgment' in section 18 of the Marine Insurance Act of 1906. A narrow interpretation of the phrase 'would influence the judgment of a prudent insurer,' equates the meaning of the term 'judgment' with the final decision, i.e., 'would have a decisive influence in the determination of the premium.' The broader test on the other hand is that all that is required is that the prudent or reasonable insurer would have wished to know about the fact when reaching his decision.[89] The stringent approach – equating 'affecting' the mind with those considerations which will ultimately determine whether or not the insurer will accept insurance and if so at what premium and on what condition – was applied in the decisions of *Lambert v Cooperative Insurance Society Ltd*,[90] and *Barclays Holdings (Australia) Pty Ltd v*

---

84. *Pan Atlantic* (n 5).
85. [1990] 3 Carib Comm LR 163 (HC T&T).
86. Ibid 266.
87. See *Somat Ali* (n 31).
88. Birds' *Modern Insurance Law* (6th edn, Thomson Sweet & Maxwell, London 2004) 114.
89. *Container Transport International Inc v Oceanus Mutual Underwriting Association (Bermuda) Ltd No1* [1984] 1 Lloyd's Rep 467 (CA).
90. [1975] 2 Lloyd's Rep 485 (CA).

British National Insurance Co Ltd.[91] In the Caribbean, although the narrow test briefly made appearance with the judgment of Justice Hamel-Smith in *Hosein & Co v Goodwill Life & General Insurance Co Ltd,*[92] *Pan Atlantic* has firmly shut the door on this option as the House of Lords by a majority of three to two rejected the decisive influence test with the result that materiality does not depend on what the ordinary insured would or would not be expected to disclose, but on what a prudent underwriter would take into account when assessing the risks.[93]

The other aspect of the *Pan Atlantic* decision which certainly adds to the complexity of the doctrine is that the House of Lords, by a unanimous decision, held that there must be a causal connection between the non-disclosure and the making of the contract if the insurer is to be entitled to avoid the contract. In other words, the failure to disclose must have *induced* the insurer to enter the contract. Inducement, which has always been a requirement of misrepresentation in contract law, is, or rather *was* novel in relation to non-disclosure.[94] Lord Mustill, dismissive of the novelty stated '[i]f this requires the making of new law, so be it.' This position was endorsed by the subsequent decision of *St Paul Fire & Marine Insurance Co (UK) Ltd v McConnell Dowell Constructors Ltd.*[95] The House of Lords in *Pan Atlantic* then went on to forge a presumption of inducement which signifies for the insurer that he can simply now rely on the presumption of inducement, i.e., that the misrepresented or undisclosed fact was *an* inducement, not necessarily the inducement. As for the insured, the onus is on him to rebut such a presumption.

The presumption of a causative effect in the Caribbean[96] is confirmed by several cases including *Solomon Ghany,*[97] *Bowe,*[98] and *Alleyne.*[99] It is cautiously suggested that the test of inducement *may* be satisfied, as opposed to being presumed, where there is strong evidence of materiality

---

91. (1987) 8 NSWLR 514 (CA Australia).
92. *Hosein* (n 85). Justice Hamel-Smith, ibid 170 states: 'It would be unreasonable to expect an insured to know, in any detail, the kinds of considerations which would affect the business decisions of the insurer. The more stringent the test at least goes some way in protecting the insured against a *variety of prudent insurers.*' On the facts of the case, although the narrow test was applied limiting the ambit of materiality, the test was nevertheless satisfied.
93. See *Royal Hotel* (n 46) 157.
94. J. Birds and N. J. Hird, 'Misrepresentation and Non Disclosure in Insurance Law – Identical Twins or Separate Issues?' (1996) 59 MLR 285.
95. [1996] 1 All ER 96 (CA).
96. In a powerful dissenting judgment in *Pan Atlantic* (n 5), Lord Lloyd was of the view that the presumption of inducement was a 'myth long exploded.' He reasoned that for the purposes of section 18 of the Marine Insurance Act, the phrase 'influence' should be determined by the question whether or not the influence had a decisive effect in moving the underwriter to accept the risk.
97. *Solomon Ghany* (n 80).
98. *Bowe* (n 47).
99. *Alleyne* (n 48).

– for as is often stated, inducement cannot be inferred in law from proved materiality.

The question therefore becomes how strong must the evidence be? In *Insurance Corporation of the Channel Islands v Royal Hotel Ltd,*[100] the falsification of the hotel's occupancy rates to inflate the sums payable under a business' interruption policy, easily amounted to inducement. Similarly, in *Bowe,* the non-disclosure of the insured's chronic alcoholism easily satisfied the test; in *Joseph*, the insured's non-compliance with an express clause obviously rendered the question of materiality redundant. On the other side of the coin are instances where the actual insurer failed to establish inducement. So that in *Drake Insurance plc v Provident Insurance plc,*[101] a case of motor insurance, where it was common ground that the non-disclosure was objectively material due to an elaborate point system and the question hinged on inducement, the Court of Appeal found that the insurer had no right to avoid the policy as it had not been induced to enter into the contract by reason of the speeding conviction. Had the fact been disclosed on renewal, the insurer would have simply charged a higher premium. There is therefore great difficulty in strictly adhering to the stated distinction between materiality and inducement. According to the law, the insurer must establish on the balance of probabilities that he was induced. There is no presumption of law that an insurer or reinsurer is induced. In sum, the onus lies on he who alleges so that it is possible for the insured to assert that a non-disclosure of a material fact would have made no difference to the insurer.

The next question to be addressed is on which insurer's shoulders does the inducement test lie? Is it the reasonable insurer, the prudent insurer, or the actual insurer? While it is clear that the test is not to be satisfied by the reasonable insurer, the prudent insurer and the actual insurer are inextricably intertwined. According to *Pan Atlantic*, the non-disclosed fact must be material in the opinion of the *prudent* insurer but must have actually induced the *actual* insurer to enter into the contract. It seems, therefore, that with regard to materiality, an objective standard applies – the prudent insurer – while with inducement, a subjective test of the actual insurer applies. This distinction is not clearly upheld in Caribbean common law. In the complex marine insurance case, *Marc Rich & Co AG v Portman,*[102] the extremely poor claims record of the insured led to a presumption of inducement. Longmore J stated that the presumption of inducement can only operate where the actual underwriter cannot, for

100. [1998] Lloyd's Rep IR 151 (QB Com Ct).
101. [2003] EWCA Civ 1834, [2003] 1 All ER (D) 02 (QB Com Ct).
102. [1996] 1 Lloyd's Rep 430 (QB Com Ct).

very good reason, give evidence and there is no reason to suppose that he acted other than prudently for at the end of the day it is for the insurer to establish inducement (a position upheld by the Court of Appeal without any clarification of the issue). According to Clarke LJ in the subsequent decision of *Assicurazoni Generali Spa v Arab Insurance Group (BSC)*,[103] in order to be entitled to avoid a contract of insurance, an insurer must prove on the balance of probabilities that he was induced. There is no presumption of law that an insurer or reinsurer is induced to enter in the contract by a material non-disclosure or misrepresentation.

A sense of the regional approach can be gleaned from *Solomon Ghany*,[104] where Justice Moosai concluded at page 31:

> (i) That appears to me to satisfy the test of inducement as propounded in Pan Atlantic. (ii) Inducement cannot be inferred in law from proved materiality, although there may be cases where the materiality is so obvious as to justify an inference of fact that the representee was actually induced, but, even in such exceptional circumstances, the inference is only a prima facie one, and may be rebutted by counter-evidence. (iii) On the facts of the case, the materiality was so obvious as to justify an inference that the representee was actually induced entitling the defendant insurer to avoid the contract.

Although there is difficulty in understanding how an insurer can be induced to enter into a contract due to a circumstance of which he was unaware,[105] materiality does not automatically lead to a presumption of inducement but that the particular facts *may* give rise to such an inference.[106] The requirement of inducement prompts further inquiry since the House of Lords rejected the narrow test of materiality because it required reading more into the Marine Insurance Act than is apparent on its face but surely the majority by concluding 'that there is to be implied in the Act of 1906, a requirement that a material misrepresentation will only entitle the insurer to avoid the policy *if it induced the making of the contract*' amounts to the same offence given that there is no mention of 'inducement' in section 21(1).[107] Apart from the academic concern, unfortunately, the insured cannot take comfort in the view that, by attaching inducement to the requirement of *uberrimae*

---

103. [2003] 1 WLR 577 (CA).
104. *Solomon Ghany* (n 80).
105. Birds' *Modern Insurance* (n 88) 124.
106. N. J. Hird, 'Pan Atlantic – Yet More to Disclose?' [1995] JBL 608.
107. Birds' *Modern Insurance* (n 88) 122, notes that conceptually misrepresentation and non-disclosure are different creatures, certainly when they are innocent, and that it is difficult to see how someone can be 'induced' by something of which they were unaware.

fidei, an additional burden has been placed on the insurer since such hopes are effectively dashed due to the ease with which inducement, it being presumed, can be established.

6. The Duty of Utmost Good Faith – Temporal Application

An issue that has arisen is whether the requirement of utmost good faith applies throughout the contract of insurance. The debate stems from section 20 of the Barbados Marine Insurance Act, Cap 292, which provides:

> A contract of Marine Insurance is a contract based upon the utmost good faith; and if the utmost good faith be not observed by either party, the contract may be avoided by the other party.

The confusion arises because section 20 has no temporal restriction, whereas section 21 and 23 are clearly restricted to the pre-contractual stage. According to this section, the remedy for breach of *uberrimae fidei* is the option of avoidance i.e., from the beginning (*ab initio*), because the duty applies and operates up until the conclusion of the contract, although it remerges, of course, on renewal.[108] There has been an attempt however, to apply this somewhat draconian remedy, to situations where the breach of utmost good faith occurs during the existence of the contract. As discussed earlier the term 'utmost' was introduced by the Marine Insurance Act. Admittedly, according to the Oxford dictionary, the term means 'furthest, extreme or the greatest,' so that the section has been relied upon to canvass a continuing duty of utmost good faith. One argument is that, if section 20 is coloured by sections 21 and 23, it is superfluous and unnecessary so that the logical assumption is that its purpose is to impose a wider, continuing duty. The other argument is that the term 'utmost' must be read in light of section 21 and 23 to refer to the pre-contractual stage.

In accordance with *The Star Sea*, the idea of good faith in the context of insurance contracts reflects the degrees of openness required of the parties in the various stages of their relationship. It is not an absolute and there is a clear distinction to be made between the pre-contractual duty to disclose and any duty of disclosure which might exist after the contract has been made. So that it is not right to reason from the existence of an extensive pre-contractual duty positively to disclose all material facts, that the duty which exists at the post-contractual stage triggers a similarly extensive obligation. Rather, it is reasonable to expect a very

---

108. *Pim v Reid* (1843) 12 LJCP 299, 6 Man & G 1 (pre-SCJA).

high degree of openness at the stage of the formation of the contract, but there is no justification for requiring that degree necessarily to continue once the contract had been made.

From an academic standpoint, the dispute has been described as 'unquestionably one of the most academically challenging issues in insurance law.'[109] From a practical standpoint, the issue may arise in connection with some action or inaction on the part of the insured but also to the insurer's tardiness in paying claims.[110] At the crux of the dispute is whether:

    i.   a breach of the duty of utmost good faith, at the claims stage, entitles the insurer to avoid the entire contract *ab initio*;

    ii. the insurer can only repudiate as from the date of the breach of the duty; or

    iii. the insurer is restricted to merely repudiating the claim.[111]

Unfortunately, there is no Caribbean authority on point. If one looks to authority from the United Kingdom for guidance, there is dicta suggesting that fair dealing does not come to an end when the contract has been concluded,[112] and it appears that the strictness of the level of duty 'fluctuates depending on the stages of contract.'[113] The complexity can be seen in two Court of Appeal decisions, *K/S Merc-Scandia XXXXII v Lloyd's Underwriters (The Mercandian Continent)*[114] and *Agapitos v Agnew (The Aegeon)*.[115] The Queen's Bench Division first had to confront the decision of *Black King Shipping Corporation v Massie (The Litsion Pride)*.[116]

In the *Litsion Pride*,[117] the insurer was entitled to avoid the whole contract, *ab initio*. Here, a fraudulent claim was categorized as a breach of the duty of utmost good faith imposed on the insured by virtue of section 17 of the United Kingdom Marine Insurance Act (section 20 in

109. Birds' *Modern Insurance* (n 88), 128.

110. *The Star Sea* (n 28); *Black King Shipping v Massie* [1985] 1 Lloyd's Rep 437 (QB Com Ct) (*The Litsion Pride*). American case law is replete with references of the obligation of the insurer to the insured at the claims stage. See, for instance, *Maschke Estate v Gleeson* (1986) 54 OR (2d) 753 (Div Ct) 756, where Montgomery J states: 'A contract of insurance is one of *uberrimae fides*, the utmost good faith. This is not a situation where an insurer is indemnifying its assured and paying a third party. This is a case where the insurer is being asked to pay its own insured. The duty to act promptly and in good faith arises the day the insurer receives the claim. To find otherwise is to fail to understand the realities of the market place.'

111. An attempt to apply this recognition in Canada failed in the decision of *Fredrikson v Insurance Corp of British Columbia* (1990) 44 BCLR (2d) 303, [1990] 4 WWR 637 (BCSC Can).

112. See the judgment of Lord Hobhouse in *The Star Sea* (n 28). Lord Hobhouse went on to say that good faith has a different application and content in different situations.

113. Birds' *Modern Insurance* (n 88) 129.

114. [2001] 2 Lloyd's Rep 563 (CA Civ Div) (*Mercandian*).

115. [2002] 2 Lloyd's Rep 42 (CA Civ Div).

116. *Litsion* (n 110).

117. Ibid.

the Barbados Marine Insurance Act), and avoidance was construed to mean *ab initio*. To arrive at this conclusion, Mr Justice Hirst adopted the notion of culpability to the effect that a fraudulent claim could amount to a breach of duty under the Marine Insurance Act of 1906, entitling the insurer to avoid the contract *ab initio,* the implied term theory being adopted as the juristic basis for the duty of good faith. This statement compels further discussion but it appears that such an approach is also discernible in the Court of Appeal decision of *Joseph v Clico International General Insurance Company Limited.*[118] On this point, there is considerable uncertainty as to the juristic character of the requirement of utmost good faith. Unfortunately, the argument cannot be pursued here. Suffice it to say, there are three schools of thought: (i) that the nature of the duty is fiduciary in nature,[119] as postulated in the frequently-cited decision of *Joel v Law Union and Crown Insurance Co No 2;*[120] (ii) that it is an implied term of the contract; and (iii) that the duty is not an implied term but a condition precedent to the conclusion of the contract of insurance.[121] If one examines the marine insurance legislation, section 21(1) of the Barbados Marine Insurance Act contradicts the implied term theory. The section provides: '[the] assured must disclose to the insurer, *before* the contract is concluded....'

In *Joseph v Clico International*, there was a breach of an expressed term of the contract. Chief Justice Simmons, however, stated:

> In a contract of fire insurance, in addition to the express terms constituted through answers to specific questions in the proposal form, there is an implied term of the contract that the person seeking insurance must communicate all matters within his knowledge which are in fact material to the question of insurance and not merely those which he believes to be material.[122]

If this statement refers broadly to the duty of *uberrimae fidei*, then an obvious difficulty arises as to how can the requirement of *uberrimae*

---

118. *Joseph* (n 49). In *Joseph*, the Court of Appeal ruled that the failure of the insured to disclose a pre-existing mortgage and an insurance policy effected with another insurer entitled the insurer to avoid the policy for breach of warranty which was created by the basis of contract clause. Chief Justice Simmons states at page 51: 'In our judgement, Clico was entitled to forfeit all benefits under the policy. The requirement of utmost good faith continued after the policy had been issued and was still operative at the time when the claim came to be considered by Clico. Looking at the claim, there was material fraud which tainted the entire claim.'
119. *Merchants & Manufacturers Insurance Ltd Co v Hunt* [1941] 1 KB 295 (CA).
120. [1908] 2 KB 863 (CA).
121. *Zurich General Accident and Liability Insurance Co Ltd v Morrison* [1942] 2 KB 53, [1942] 1 All ER 529 (CA).
122. *Joseph* (n 49) 38.

fidei be an implied term of the contract?[123] Admittedly, the implied term of the contract theory would facilitate the operation of section 50(2) of the Marine Insurance Act of 1906.[124] As section 50(2) refers to 'defences arising out of the contract' it was argued in the *The Litsion Pride* that the provision would be ineffective if the duty of utmost good faith was based on a rule of law. But the implied term theory was disapproved in *The Star Sea*.[125] There, the House of Lords ruled that culpable non-disclosure was insufficient to attract the drastic consequence of avoidance contemplated in section 17 of the 1906 Marine Insurance Act. But their Lordships did not resolve the debate on the ambit and nature of the post-contractual duty of good faith – so that the issue continues to be litigated.

Subsequently, in *Agapitos v Agnew (The Aegeon) No 1*[126] the Court of Appeal, *inter alia*, considered whether and in what circumstances the common law rule of law and/or section 17 can apply in the event of the fraudulent devices being used to promote a claim, which (the claim) may be proved at trial to be in all respects valid and, if so, whether the application of the rule and the Marine Insurance Act ceases with the commencement of litigation. Mance LJ distinguished the decision of *The Star Sea* because the fraud in that case was directed at the third party claimant and hence it was considered as affording no guidance as to the appropriate approach to fraudulent devices. A distinction was made between 'fraudulent devices' and 'material fraud.' Material fraud, according to the learned judge, operated during the life of the contract and attracted severe consequences entitling the insurer to terminate the contract for breach as was the case in the *Mercandian Continent*.[127] Mance LJ tentatively concluded that the section 17 duty (section 20 in the Barbados Act) has no application to fraudulent claims. Rather, the common law fraudulent claim rule – that of forfeiture of the claim – should be applied in cases where fraudulent devices are used.

Unravelling the complicated common law principles is undoubtedly a tortuous process that is far from complete. Although public policy may justify the operation of good faith at the post-contractual stage – for, as Longmore LJ observed in the *Mercandian Continent*, post-formation duty is a 'necessary and beneficial discipline' to discourage deliberately exaggerated claims[128] – a forfeiture of all benefits due to public policy considerations is not the same as the remedy of avoidance of the contract,

---

123. Of course, these perspectives need not be mutually exclusive.
124. See s 54 of the Barbados Marine Insurance Act, Cap 292.
125. *The Star Sea* (n 28).
126. [2002] Lloyd's Rep IR 573 (CA).
127. *Mercandian* (n 114).
128. Ibid 11.

ab initio, as prescribed by section 20.[129] Further, a distinction must be drawn between material fraud and fraudulent devices. A fraudulent device is used to promote a fraudulent claim. In such circumstances, the insured believes he has suffered the loss claimed and seeks to embellish the facts and as such section 20 of the Barbados Marine Insurance Act has no application. In such circumstances, the insurer must therefore seek protection under the common law instead.

Before concluding, mention must be made of a feature of modern commerce where good faith arguably transcends the pre-contractual stage. Invariably, policies of insurance contain an express clause known as an 'increase of risk clause.' This type of clause, usually created by way of a promissory warranty, triggers a duty *analogous* to that of *uberrimae fidei*. In accordance with section 37 of the Barbados Marine Insurance Act:

> (1) A warranty...means a promissory warranty, that is to say, a warranty by which the assured undertakes that some particular thing will or will not be done, or that some condition will be fulfilled, or where he affirms or negatives the existence of a particular state of facts.

A promissory or continuing warranty places an obligation on the insured to keep the insurer abreast of material facts which may affect the risk. It is an absolute undertaking by the insured that certain facts or conditions pertaining to the risk shall continue, or that certain things will be done or omitted.[130] The implications of the insertion of such a clause can be seen in the decision of the House of Lords in *Dawson v Bonnin*[131] where it was held that the insurer was entitled to repudiate liability, since compliance with a warranty bearing on the risk is a condition precedent to the attaching of risk and when the answers are declared to be the 'basis of contract' exact fulfilment is foundational to its enforceability. Interestingly, although there is Caribbean authority surrounding the obligation created by such a clause, adjudication has been primarily on principles of construction. This can be seen for instance in *Solomon Ghany,*[132] where when the insurers argued, *inter*

---

129. Interestingly, similar sentiments were expressed by Chief Justice Simmons in *Joseph* (n 49) 51: 'Since the contract of insurance remained one of good faith, Mr Joseph, as the insured, was obliged to exercise such good faith when making the claim. The true facts were peculiarly within his knowledge and Clico, as insurer, depended on his exercise of good faith in order to assess his claim. An insurance Company must surely be able to trust an insured person to present a claim in good faith. Any fraud in making the claim strikes at the root of the insurance contract and entitles the insurer to be discharged from it.'
130. *Reid v Hardware Mutual Insurance Co* 252 SC 339, 166 SE 2d 317 (1969) (SC South Carolina).
131. [1922] 2 AC 413 (HL).
132. *Solomon Ghany* (n 80).

alia, that the insured was in contravention of clause 5(1) of the policy by storing on the premises a flammable oil, the decision of *Thomson v Equity Fire Insurance Co*[133] was cited and applied in order to determine whether diesel was 'stored' on the premises. The High Court of Trinidad and Tobago stated that in a contract of insurance the first relevant rule of construction is the literal meaning but the words of warranty must be restricted if they 'produce a result inconsistent with a reasonable and business like interpretation of such a warranty.' The court held that the phrase connoted a notion of warehousing or depositing for safe custody or keeping for stock in trade so that the small quantity, 'about a gallon or so, for washing rust off one's hands after handling the oilfield equipment,' did not amount to the storing of diesel oil.[134]

With respect to fire policies, clauses descriptive of the risk similarly give rise to analogous specific disclosure requirements. Generally, such terms relate to property being unoccupied for a specific period requiring the insured to provide a continuing warranty and to notify the insurer should the property become unoccupied. The operation of such a clause arose for consideration in the Privy Council decision of *Marzouca v Atlantic and British Commercial Insurance Company*[135] on appeal from Jamaica. Here, Lord Hodson stated that for the occupation to be effectual it must be actual, not constructive. It must involve the regular daily presence of someone in the building. If there is no one present for a continuous period of more than 30 days, there is a breach of condition.[136] In *Swaby v Prudential Assurance Co Ltd* the Court of Appeal of Jamaica in construing the term, ruled that the phrase 'become unoccupied' implied a change of status and did not cover instances where absence was merely temporary and there was a manifest intention to return.'[137]

It is clear that the terms of the insurance contract and the presence of promissory or continuing warranty place an obligation on the insured to keep the insurer abreast of material facts which may affect the risk. Moreover, clauses descriptive of the risk similarly give rise to a duty analogous to that of the duty of utmost good faith. The question remains, however, as to the extent of the duty of utmost good faith and whether it is capable of extending beyond the pre-contractual stage to the post-contractual stage. The law is far from settled. While the region must

---

133. [1910] AC 592 (PC Can).
134. The plaintiff lost on other grounds.
135. [1971] 1 Lloyd's Rep 449 (PC Ja) ('*Marzouca*'). See also *Weeks v Motor and General Insurance Co Ltd* (1969) 15 WIR 188 (HC Bdos).
136. *Marzouca* ibid 453–54.
137. (1964) 6 WIR 246 (CA Ja) 254 (Lewis JA).

understandably look to the common law for answers, regional marine insurance legislation can also be resorted to, to resolve many a thorny question.

7. Conclusion

One cannot resolve all of the questions raised in this chapter. Analysis reveals that Caribbean jurists are understandably constrained by the weight of persuasive English authority. But a number of questions remain, such as the relevance of rehabilitation of offenders legislation and the utility of marine insurance legislation. Further, what are the parameters of the moral hazard as it relates to outstanding criminal charges and acquittals, suspicions and or rumours of criminality? Does the moral hazard encompass bankruptcy/financial difficulty? Finally, is the duty of utmost good faith a continuing duty, and if so, what is the juristic character of the duty? As one examines the common law for answers to these questions, broadly the regional approach could be described as a functional one. The advantage with this is that it offers predictability by providing specific solutions to specific legal questions. The problem is, however, that the solution to the doctrine of utmost good faith is not necessarily effectively addressed by this method. A more conceptual approach, however, would offer adaptability and flexibility to embrace new legal questions.[138]

Confronted with this inordinate burden, perhaps one solution is for the industry to adopt self-regulatory mechanisms providing guidelines as to the kind of circumstances that are likely to be considered material, copies of proposal forms, standard answers to questions coupled with a warning of the severe ramifications of an insured being found to have breached his duty of *uberrimae fidei*. In the absence of such assistance, the unfortunate policyholder is confronted with a burdensome obligation which shows no signs of abating. Until that time comes, there are more questions than answers.

---

138. Brooke, 'Materiality in Insurance Contracts' [1985] LMCLQ 437; Steyn J, 'The Role of Good Faith and Fair Dealing in Contract Law: A Hairshirt Philosophy?' [1991] Denning LJ 131; Bennett, 'The Duty to Disclose in Insurance Law' [1993] LQR 513.

II.

THE CONFLUENCE OF INTERNATIONAL AND DOMESTIC LAW

The Use of International Law by Domestic Tribunals in the Caribbean in Death Penalty Cases

David S. Berry[1]

1. Introduction

International law has become increasingly relevant to decision-making in national courts. It provides judges with access to a vast body of information and legal material on almost every topic. International treaties mandate specific rules and standards in most areas of human activity, and the reports of related treaty-bodies illustrate concrete examples of international and national best practices. But national tribunals face several challenges with respect to the use of international law. They often lack familiarity with international legal sources, both in terms of how to access relevant rules and how to assess their value or weight. They also face questions regarding when it is appropriate to refer to rules of international law, and for what purposes. These latter questions are answered by a specific set of common law rules that are the focus of this chapter.

This chapter suggests that the traditional common law rules regarding use of international law within the domestic judicial forum are precise, comprehensive and comprehensible. Further, these same rules have been misunderstood (or at least misapplied), by some of the highest judges in the Commonwealth Caribbean. This is clearly demonstrated by the decisions of the Judicial Committee of the Privy Council (hereafter the 'Privy Council' or 'Board') in one of the most difficult areas of Caribbean domestic law – the application of the death penalty.

This chapter addresses this deficiency for the legal community of the Commonwealth Caribbean. It introduces theoretical frameworks for understanding the relationship of international law and municipal law as well as sets out the fundamental common law rules regarding use of international law by domestic courts. It then examines some of the more interesting examples of (mis)application of these rules by the Privy Council and the Caribbean Court of Justice. The decisions of these courts, all involving the death penalty, merit close critical scrutiny.

---

1. The views expressed herein are the author's and are not to be attributed to any state or other entity.

Most are problematic because they deviate from the common law rules regarding use of international law without providing any juridical foundation. Moreover, many, if not all, of the kinds of progressive developments sought by the Privy Council could have been achieved by using existing common law rights without infringing the rules regarding use of international law in domestic courts. This point is important. In an especially contentious area like capital punishment, courts must not only arrive at the right conclusion, they must do so convincingly, by applying impeccable legal analysis that will convince even the fiercest critics. To the extent that a tribunal does otherwise, it undermines the legitimacy of its own jurisprudence. For this reason, the final sections of the chapter demonstrate a number of ways in which international law can properly be used in domestic courts, including the Caribbean Court of Justice, in compliance with the common law rules.

2. Three Theoretical Frameworks

In order to understand the role of international law before a domestic tribunal the conceptual framework for the relationship of the two fields of law must be appreciated. In this regard, international legal writers usually mention at least two strongly opposing schools of thought, namely, the monist and dualist schools.[2]

Expressed in its simplest form, the *monist* view of the relationship of international law and municipal law is a holistic, unified one: international law and municipal law are seen as part of a single legal order. Most commonly, monist theories view international law as sitting at the apex of this order, being a superior set of legal norms from which national legal orders derive their validity. From this viewpoint, international law takes precedence over domestic law. The *dualist* view, in contrast, suggests that international law and municipal law are two competing legal orders with, most commonly, the municipal order taking priority. In some formulations, dualist theorists foresee the possibility of direct conflict between the two legal orders, envisaging, for example, cases in which a tribunal is forced to choose between applying a rule of international law or a rule of domestic law.

A third position is suggested by Sir Gerald Fitzmaurice, who views international law and municipal law as distinct legal orders, or different

---

2. See generally, Sir R. Jennings and Sir A. Watts, *Oppenheim's International Law* (9th edn, Longman, London 1996) 52–86; I. Brownlie, *Principles of Public International Law* (6th edn, OUP, Oxford 2003) 31–53; M. Shaw, *International Law* (4th edn, CUP, Cambridge 1997) 99–136; P. Malanczuk, *Akehurst's Modern Introduction to International Law* (7th edn, Routledge, London 1997) 63–74. For a Caribbean analysis see W. Anderson, 'Treaty Implementation in Caribbean Law and Practice' (1988) 8 Carib LR 185.

fields of law, which can never conflict.[3] For him, each body of law sets out rules applicable only in its own legal order – in the same manner that, for example, the laws of France and England are applicable in their distinct spheres of authority. As a result, there can never be a conflict between international law and domestic law *per se*; at most there can be a conflict of legal obligations on the part of the state.[4] The validity of any legal act must be assessed separately in accordance with the rules of the relevant sphere – either under the rules of domestic law or international law. If an action violates international law but conforms to domestic law, there is no conflict between the two fields of law. Each decides legality within its own sphere. Rather, the conflict is one of obligation because the same actor – the state – is required to uphold both sets of rules.

Nevertheless, the conflict between these *obligations* may be particularly acute for the state concerned. For example, as illustrated in the recent decision of the Privy Council in the case of *Boyce v R*, discussed below, domestic rules might uphold the legality of mandatory capital punishment, on the one hand, and international human rights treaty obligations might render such punishment illegal, on the other. But even in such a case, Fitzmaurice would argue there is no real conflict between the two legal systems *per se*, since each determines the validity of a legal action under its own rules. The same action can be lawful under domestic law and in contravention of an international treaty obligation.

Fitzmaurice's viewpoint about the relationship of international law and municipal law is most helpful for our purposes, because it reveals the way in which two different legal orders can coexist and have important consequences for the state, but remain distinct as a matter of law. Such a framework allows us to more clearly and rigorously examine questions regarding the use of international law in domestic courts.

3. The Common Law Rules

In traditional common law jurisprudence, a large degree of consensus has emerged about the rules regarding the use of both conventional and customary international law before domestic tribunals. This consensus was established in a long line of jurisprudence by the courts of the United Kingdom.

---

3. Sir G. Fitzmaurice, 'The General Principles of International Law Considered from the Standpoint of the Rule of Law' (1957-II) 92 Recueil des Cours de l'Académie de Droit International 5.
4. Ibid 79–80.

A. Customary International Law

From the end of the eighteenth century, customary international law has been considered part of the law of the land. William Blackstone, in his *Commentaries on the Laws of England*, wrote that the 'law of nations [customary international law] is here adopted in its full extent by the common law, and is held to be part of the law of the land.'[5]

However, several qualifications are necessary to Blackstone's broad, monist statement. Firstly, the existence of the customary rule relied upon must be strictly proved.[6] Secondly, the customary rule must be either universally recognized by states around the globe or accepted as a binding customary rule by the state concerned.[7] Thirdly, the applicability of rules of customary international law in the domestic legal order is subject to the overriding effect of statute law and, with one exception,[8] that of binding judicial precedent.[9] These latter limitations are fundamental. If an existing, unambiguous statute or binding judicial precedent is applicable, then the court must uphold that domestic law, regardless of whether it is compatible with the state's international legal obligations.[10] Finally, it is important to notice that when customary international law becomes part of the law of the land it *changes* and literally becomes domestic law, or the common law.

B. International Treaty Obligations

The second firmly accepted rule in this area is that international treaties have no binding force in domestic law without transformation.[11] Treaties do, of course, create binding obligations for States Parties at the *international level* once they have entered into force. However, in both the United Kingdom and Commonwealth Caribbean the general position

---

5. W. Morrison (ed), *Blackstone's Commentaries on the Laws of England* (Routledge-Cavendish, London 2001) vol 4, 53.
6. See e.g., *West Rand Central Gold Mining Company Ltd v R* [1905] 2 KB 391, 407 (Div Ct Eng).
7. As summarized by Jennings and Watts, in *Oppenheim's* (n 2) 56–57. See also *West Rand* (n 6) 407.
8. The exception is regarding domestic judicial precedent that relies upon a superseded rule of customary international law. In such a situation, the doctrine of *stare decisis* does not prevent a national court from applying the current, existing rule of international law. *Trendtex Trading Corporation v Central Bank of Nigeria* [1977] QB 529 (CA Eng).
9. As succinctly summarized by Professor Ian Brownlie, in *Principles* (n 2) 41, 'customary rules are to be considered part of the law of the land and enforced as such, with the qualification that they are incorporated only so far as is not inconsistent with Acts of Parliament or prior judicial decisions of final authority' [citations omitted]. *Cf.* Jennings and Watts, *Oppenheim's* (n 2) 56–57.
10. See e.g., *Mortensen v Peters* (1906) 8 F(J) 93, 14 SLT 227 (HC Justiciary Scot) 231–32.
11. *R v Lyons* [2003] 1 AC 976 (HL), *Higgs v Minister of National Security and Others* [2000] 2 AC 228 (PC Bah), *JH Rayner (Mincing Lane) Ltd v Department of Trade and Industry* (also called *Maclaine Watson & Co Ltd v International Tin Council*) [1990] 2 AC 418 (HL), *R v Secretary of State for the Home Department, ex parte Brind* [1991] 1 AC 696 (HL), *Salomon v Commissioners of Customs and Excise* [1967] 2 QB 116 (CA Eng).

is that the only way treaties can have binding legal force at the domestic level is by being incorporated – by being made part of that domestic law through, for example, an Act of Parliament. The latter statute fulfils the role of converting the international legal rights and obligations that the state has entered into at the international level into parallel domestic law obligations.

The act of converting an international treaty obligation into a domestic statutory one is most often called 'transformation' or 'incorporation.' Statutes that perform this role may do by *indirect* enactment of the treaty – by specifying that the entire treaty is, or sections of the treaty are, to have the force of law in the domestic legal system (and then in many cases attaching the relevant treaty text as a schedule to the act).[12] But they can also transform a treaty *directly*, by drafting a statute for the specific purpose of incorporating the international legal obligations within the precise language of domestic statutory provisions.[13] This latter approach is in many ways preferable, because it allows the international legal obligations to be tailored to the specific statutory language of domestic legislation; but it has the drawback of decreasing the potential for uniformity in the application of the treaty around the globe.[14]

Transformation is important because it ensures that Parliament remains the branch of government that makes law. Parliament creates legal rights and duties in domestic law through statutory enactment, not the executive or judiciary. Transformation also has the effect of making international law *into* domestic law: it completely changes its legal nature and ceases to be international law. As a result, domestic courts never actually apply international treaty law; they apply domestic legislation which contains rights and obligations that mirror those contained in the treaty.[15]

In sum, under the common law, treaties have no binding force in domestic law without transformation by Parliament; and even after transformation the binding right or obligation, strictly speaking, is one of domestic, not international, law.

C. Unincorporated Treaties

The final set of rules regarding the use of international law in the domestic forum is that regarding the effect of treaties which have *not*

---

12. FAR Bennion, *Bennion on Statutory Interpretation: A Code* (5th edn, Lexisnexis Reed Elsevier, London 2008) 684.
13. Ibid 683.
14. Ibid.
15. See *Lyons* (n 11) 992 [27] (Lord Hoffman).

been transformed, often referred to as 'unincorporated treaties.' Such unincorporated treaties have no binding force in domestic law, but in some cases may be used for the limited purpose of interpreting *unclear* domestic legislation.

This interpretive use is founded upon the rebuttable presumption that Parliament does not intend to legislate in violation of the state's international obligations.[16] This presumption is rebuttable and is subject to any available counter presumptions.[17] Further, the rebuttable presumption does not even arise unless the court has failed to determine the meaning of the legislation through the application of ordinary principles of statutory interpretation. Thus, if the law is clear, domestic courts must apply it regardless of whether this will entail the breach of an international treaty. This is because it is fully within the sovereign power of the state to both enter into, and breach, treaty obligations: 'the sovereign power of the Queen in Parliament extends to breaking treaties.'[18]

In this context, the requirement for lack of clarity of domestic legislation has emerged as a precise one under the common law. The question of whether a provision is 'unclear' or 'ambiguous' only arises where that provision can yield at least two meanings, one which conforms to, and one which conflicts with, the international legal obligation.[19]

If a domestic tribunal finds such an 'ambiguity,' the result is striking. The judge is empowered to look at the unincorporated treaty and in most cases, as a result of the presumption, will uphold the interpretation that complies with the international obligation. The presumption is so strong that it may even be applicable 'retroactively,' allowing a court to interpret a statute created long before the state became a party to the treaty, with the text of the later treaty. As stated by Lord Hoffman in *Boyce v R*:

> This principle is obviously at its strongest when it appears that the domestic law was passed to give effect to an international obligation or may otherwise be assumed to have been drafted with the treaty in mind. Its application to laws which existed before the treaty is more difficult to justify as an exercise in construction but their Lordships are willing to proceed on the hypothesis that the principle requires one to construe the Constitution and other contemporary legislation in the light of treaties which the government afterwards concluded.[20]

---

16. Ibid 27–28; see generally Bennion (n 12) 8, 17–24.
17. *Mortensen v Peters* (n 10) 233 (Lord Kyllachy).
18. *Salomon* (n 11) 143 (Lord Diplock).
19. Ibid 143–44 (Lord Diplock), *Ex parte Brind* (n 11) 747–48 (Lord Bridge).
20. *Boyce v R* [2004] UKPC 32, [2005] 1 AC 400 (Bdos) 416 [26].

Therefore, legislation enacted in the 1960s may be interpreted in the light of a treaty to which the state only became a party in the 1980s. Such a broad temporal application of the ambiguity rule may be justified by the 'always speaking' rule of statutory interpretation.[21]

This was the status of the common law rules regarding the use of international law before domestic tribunals for *both* the United Kingdom and the Commonwealth Caribbean until the early 1990s. From that period, however, the jurisprudence of the Privy Council started to diverge from that of the House of Lords in a series of death penalty cases. The fact that the House of Lords continued to apply the common law rules in their traditional form in the United Kingdom is noteworthy, especially considering that the same judges served on both judicial bodies.[22]

4. The Departures by the Privy Council and the Caribbean Court of Justice

A. Background: *Pratt v AG*

The first case, which foreshadows the wider path taken by the Judicial Committee of the Privy Council, is the 1993 decision in *Pratt v AG*.[23] In this case, the Board decided that a period of detention on death row longer than five years from the date of conviction could amount to cruel and inhuman treatment and punishment, requiring the commutation of a death sentence to life imprisonment. The facts of the case are well known. But what may be overlooked is that the Board included both domestic *and international procedures*, such as petitions to the Inter-American Commission on Human Rights ('Commission'), in determining what constitutes a reasonable period of time on death row. The Board held that *all* of these procedures, domestic and international, required completion within a period of roughly five years.[24]

This is striking because international procedures, such as petitions to the Commission, are the by-product of an unincorporated treaty and have no status or binding effect in the domestic law of Jamaica. Thus *Pratt* allowed international legal processes to have real and meaningful consequences under domestic law, without explaining why. The Board also opened up a new front in the death penalty battle – the international

---

21. See Bennion (n 12) 477 and generally, ibid Code s 288.
22. For an example of a recent, traditional application of the rules by the House of Lords see *Lyons* (n 11). Of course, the courts of the UK have substantially changed their practice with respect to the European Convention on Human Rights following the promulgation of the Human Rights Act 1998. The latter Act at least partially transformed the Convention into domestic law, changing its status from an unincorporated treaty to an incorporated one.
23. *Pratt v AG* [1994] 2 AC 1 (PC Ja).
24. Ibid 34–36.

legal front. This is because referring a case to an international legal body, such as the Commission, likely would extend a prisoner's detention under sentence of death beyond the five year limit, and therefore could represent the difference between life and death.

B. *Thomas v Baptiste*

In 1999, the Privy Council handed down its decision in the case of *Thomas v Baptiste*.[25] This case arose in response to instructions by the government of Trinidad and Tobago which imposed strict time limits for referral of petitions to international bodies like the Inter-American Commission on Human Rights. These instructions aimed to ensure that all appeals and international petition processes would be completed within the five-year period established by *Pratt*.[26] The Privy Council decided that the instructions of the government were unlawful. Although the state of Trinidad and Tobago had the right to impose some restrictions on the duration of time that petitioners could wait for completion of these international processes, the particular instructions given by the government were disproportionate and therefore impermissible.[27]

Of interest for present purposes are the passages of the judgment that deal with the question of *whether there is a right to conclude international petition processes in the first place*. The government submitted that there could be no such right on the part of the appellants under the laws of Trinidad and Tobago because these international petition processes were available only through an unincorporated treaty. The Board rejected these arguments and went to great lengths to articulate the basis for a right to conclude international petition processes. The Privy Council held that the right to due process, a right expressly protected by the Constitution of Trinidad and Tobago and by the common law, encompassed the right to conclude international petitions. Referring to the due process clause in the Constitution, Lord Millett held that it 'includes the right of a condemned man to be allowed to complete *any appellate or analogous legal process* that is capable of resulting in a reduction or commutation of his sentence before the process is rendered nugatory by executive action.'[28] Although the Privy Council formally endorsed the position that unincorporated treaties cannot give rise to rights or obligations under domestic law, nevertheless, their Lordships included *international*

---

25. *Thomas v Baptiste* [2000] 2 AC 1 (PC T&T).
26. Ibid 18–19.
27. Ibid 20–21.
28. Ibid 22.

petition processes under the due process protections available under the law of Trinidad and Tobago:

> It is the general right accorded to all litigants not to have the outcome of any pending appellate or other legal process pre-empted by executive action. This general right is not created by the [American] Convention; it is accorded by the common law and affirmed by section 4(a) of the Constitution. The applicants are not seeking to enforce the terms of an unincorporated treaty, but a provision of the domestic law of Trinidad and Tobago contained in the Constitution. By ratifying a treaty which provides for individual access to an international body, the government made that process for the time being part of the domestic criminal justice system and thereby temporarily at least extended the scope of the due process clause in the Constitution.[29]

In other words, the Board viewed the right to exhaust international processes as being one arising under the common law or domestic legal system, not under international law. Lord Millett justified this determination by referring to the way that the Inter-American Commission processes could, in relation to Trinidad and Tobago, result in a *binding* determination by the Inter-American Court of Human Rights.[30]

The difficulty with this decision, however, is that the Board nowhere explains how a non-binding Commission process that is initiated and concluded entirely under international law, and at no point is included under the laws of Trinidad and Tobago, can give rise to a legal right under domestic law. The Board's reference to the binding nature of the Inter-American Court judgments is also puzzling because such judgments bind the state *as a matter of international law only*. No decision of the Inter-American Court can have binding effect, or be enforceable, upon any individual in Trinidad and Tobago until that decision, as an international act, has first been transformed and made part of the law of the land.

Some of these difficulties are highlighted in the strong dissent of Lords Goff and Hobhouse, who point out that the only laws protected by the Constitution and common law are the laws of Trinidad and Tobago, not international law.[31] By requiring domestic organs to await the conclusion of international petition processes, their Lordships argue, the majority of the Board allows these international legal processes to have domestic effect without any act of incorporation by Parliament.

---

29. Ibid 23.
30. Ibid 24.
31. Ibid 31–32.

C. *Neville Lewis*

The Privy Council pushes this idea further in the 2000 Jamaican case of *Neville Lewis*.[32] This case is widely known in the Commonwealth Caribbean for its innovative interpretation of the meaning of the right of due process ('protection of the law') in relation to the Jamaican Privy Council (the mercy committee). However, attention is also merited for the way in which the case extends the Board's interpretation of the common law rules regarding use of unincorporated treaties. In *Lewis*, the Board held that when exercising the prerogative of mercy, the Jamaican Privy Council must provide a fair and proper process. This requirement for fair and proper process was grounded in no small part upon (1) Jamaica's status as a party to the American Convention on Human Rights and the (2) decisions of the Inter-American Court of Human Rights.[33] This is surprising because the American Convention was, and remains, an unincorporated treaty under the law of Jamaica. As a result, neither the American Convention nor the judgments of the Inter-American Court of Human Rights (to whose jurisdiction Jamaica had not consented), could have any binding force in Jamaican law.

Also striking is the way in which the provisions of the American Convention and the subsequent interpretative jurisprudence of the Inter-American Court are introduced into the judgment of the Board. They are introduced in passing, without comment, almost as a *non sequitur*. In a passage in which the Board discusses the proposition that a state's 'domestic legislation should as far as possible be interpreted so as to conform to the state's obligation under...a treaty,' the American Convention and its related jurisprudence is casually invoked.[34] The Board moves directly from consideration of a common law concept – the protection of the law or due process – to looking at death penalty jurisprudence under the American Convention on Human Rights, an unincorporated treaty.

Such a move, however, does not comply with the rules related to the use of unincorporated treaties. No statement is made by the Board about the lack of clarity of a particular legislative provision or legal concept, nor is there a discussion of the two necessary competing legal positions (one which conforms to the treaty obligation and one which does not). In fact, no reference is even made to the relevant provisions of the American Convention – articles 24 or 25 – which guarantee equal

---

32. *Lewis v AG* [2001] 2 AC 50 (PC Ja).
33. Ibid 78–79.
34. Ibid.

protection (including protection of the law) and judicial protection. Instead, the Board turns to article 4 of the American Convention, the provision guaranteeing the right to life, and the related jurisprudence. This is a telling analytical leap: from due process under the common law to the right to life under the American Convention.

In concluding its analysis, the Board decides that the Jamaican Privy Council is required to consider the reports of international human rights bodies (such as the Inter-American Commission on Human Rights), and if it does not accept such reports, to explain why it does not do so.[35] The Board bases its decision on the concept of 'protection of the law'/'due process' that is contained in section 13 of the Jamaican Constitution and in the common law. Following the Trinidadian decision of *Thomas v Baptiste*, the Board decided that due process rights can develop over time and come to include new processes, including international ones. But it goes even further here, determining that there is a right to conclude the processes of the Inter-American Commission, a body without the competence to make binding decisions which operates entirely under unincorporated treaties and which is not backed, in the case of Jamaica, by the Inter-American Court of Human Rights.

D. *Reyes, Fox* and *Hughes*

The next three cases, the trilogy of *Reyes*, *Fox* and *Hughes*, deal with the actual form of death sentence, namely, mandatory capital punishment.[36] What is interesting in the present context is how the Belizean case of *Reyes v R*, which sets out the *rationale* for finding mandatory capital punishment unconstitutional, bases its reasoning to a significant extent upon international human rights norms. In *Reyes*, although this point is *not made expressly*, the Board grounds its decision in part upon the understanding that certain international norms had been transformed into domestic law through the Constitution itself. This is an interesting idea and is pursued further below.

The central issue in *Reyes* was whether the mandatory death penalty for Class A murder amounted to inhuman or degrading punishment. The Board addressed this question in four stages. Firstly, the Board established that murder is an offence that varies widely in its culpability.[37] Secondly, the Board set out at length relevant international human

---

35. Ibid 79.
36. *Reyes v R* [2002] UKPC 11, [2002] 2 AC 235 (Bze); *R v Hughes* [2002] UKPC 12, [2002] 2 AC 259 (St Luc); *Fox v R* [2002] UKPC 13, [2002] 2 AC 284 (St K-N).
37. *Reyes* ibid 241–43, 10–16.

rights developments, both in terms of human rights declarations and treaties, which protect the individual from cruel and inhuman treatment and punishment.[38] Within this second stage, the Board also commented upon the facts that (1) Belize, when a dependent territory of the United Kingdom, was subject to the European Convention on Human Rights (from 1953–81), and (2) that in drafting the human rights provisions of Belize's Constitution 'heavy reliance was placed on the European Convention.'[39] Thirdly, the Board outlined the modern, generous and purposive approach to constitutional interpretation, an approach that requires the Court 'to consider the substance of the fundamental right at issue and ensure contemporary protection of that right in the light of evolving standards of decency that mark the progress of a maturing society.'[40] It is within this third stage, when deciding what contemporary protections are provided by Belize's human rights framework, that the Board returns to the effect of, *inter alia*, the European Convention upon Belize. Although noting that the Convention was never expressly incorporated into the laws of Belize, the Board suggests that the 'rights' available under it could not be diminished as a result of Belize's independence.[41]

This suggestion that Belize's independence Constitution was not meant to *diminish rights available during dependency* is striking for several reasons. It assumes, incorrectly, that European Convention rights were somehow available to the citizens of Belize prior to independence, even though the Convention had never been transformed into the laws of Belize or even transformed into the laws of the United Kingdom itself. Without such transformation the European Convention could have no legal effect in domestic law. Further, the Board suggests that such 'rights' somehow became part of the *permanent* law of Belize, so that even if a later government decided to sever its treaty obligations (which Belize in fact did upon independence), it would somehow remain subject to them as part of the domestic law. How such a situation could arise under either international law (which recognizes and allows for withdrawal from a treaty), or the doctrines of parliamentary or constitutional supremacy, is never explained.

In the fourth and final stage of the Board's reasoning, their Lordships examine the meaning of the phrase 'inhuman or degrading punishment or other treatment' under the Belize Constitution and in the

---

38. Ibid 244–45, 17–24.
39. Ibid 245, 23–24.
40. Ibid 246, 26.
41. Ibid 247, 28.

jurisprudence of both domestic and international tribunals. The latter jurisprudential references are all comparative in nature, with the Board analysing the reasoning of other authorities from across the globe for persuasiveness. None of these references are suggested to be binding and thus the Board's analysis here is fully compatible with the rules regarding use of international law by domestic tribunals.[42] However, it may be no coincidence that the final decision examined by the Board is one under the European Convention, the 1989 case of *Soering v UK*.[43] This latter decision provides the ultimate rhetorical link in the Board's judgment because it implicitly, and naturally, ties Belize's suggested pre-independence human rights status with the more recent jurisprudence of the European Convention.

In this way, the *Reyes* case is particularly fascinating in terms of its use of international law. Many of its premises are implicit, rather than explicit. The decision could be justified as falling entirely under the traditional rules regarding use of international law, where international legal materials are only used as persuasive, not binding authority. In fact, the *ratio* of the Board's decision can be said to rest upon its own interpretation of the *common law* meaning of the term 'inhuman or degrading punishment or other treatment.' However, the reference to Belize's European Convention obligations prior to, and possibly subsequent to, independence may challenge such an analysis.

E. *Boyce v R*

Moving forward to 2004, the Board returns to the death penalty and the role of international law in the trilogy of *Boyce v R, Matthew v State*, and *Watson v R*.[44] The majority decision in *Boyce and Joseph* is the leading one in the trilogy on the issue of the use of international law within the domestic sphere. The reasoning of this decision can be summarized very succinctly: (1) under Barbadian law the Constitution is supreme, (2) section 15(1) of the Barbados Constitution does not allow a person to be subject to an inhuman or degrading punishment, (3) but section 26 of the Constitution provides that no existing law shall be held to be inconsistent with, *inter alia*, section 15; therefore (4) since the mandatory death penalty is an existing law, it remains valid.[45]

---

42. Ibid 254, 40–41.
43. Ibid 256, 42 (referring to *Soering v UK* (1989) 11 EHRR 439 [ECtHR]).
44. *Boyce* (n 20); *Matthew v State* [2004] UKPC 33, [2005] 1 AC 433 (T&T); *Watson v R* [2004] UKPC 34, [2005] 1 AC 472 (Ja).
45. *Boyce* ibid 410–11.

However, in coming to this decision the Board also makes clear that *but for* the effect of its existing laws clause, Barbados's mandatory capital punishment would be unconstitutional as inhuman and degrading punishment as well as would likely violate its international human rights obligations.[46] Thus, we find juxtaposed in this case two clearly incompatible obligations, one constitutional and the other conventional. But since each exists in a different sphere of law – domestic law and international law – there is no conflict of law. The rules of each sphere determine legality and so in domestic law the mandatory form of capital punishment must remain lawful as an existing law.

Generally speaking, it can be argued that this decision reinstates the traditional view of the role of international law in the jurisprudence of the Privy Council. For instance, the Board, as it did in *Reyes*, refers to the fact that Barbados was subject to the European Convention on Human Rights prior to independence. However, unlike in *Reyes*, the majority draws a clear distinction between the role of the Convention at the international level and the role of the Constitution in domestic law. The Board held that the Convention was only binding upon the UK as a matter of international law, whereas the Constitution is supreme and binds the people of Barbados.[47] This is a clear rejection of the kinds of arguments about the role of the European Convention on Human Rights that were started in *Reyes*.

The majority judgment also contains an entire section on international law which deals with Barbados's ratification of various human rights treaties. This section is interesting both for the fact that it exists as a distinct, headed section, and for the fact that the Board is clearly sensitive to criticisms of the way in which international law has been used in previous Privy Council decisions. On the question of the use of international law within the domestic forum, the majority returns to the more traditional position on such matters, the one that has been fairly consistently followed in the House of Lords. Firstly, the Board establishes that 'the rights of the people of Barbados in domestic law derive solely from the Constitution.'[48] This implies a rejection of any kind of 'direct effectiveness' of international human rights treaties. Secondly, the Board held that the only relevance of unincorporated international

---

46. Ibid 416, 27. Note that Barbados's mandatory capital punishment, and s 26 of the Constitution, subsequently were held to be in violation of the American Convention on Human Rights: *Boyce v Barbados* (Preliminary Objections, Merits, Reparations and Costs), Inter-American Court of Human Rights, Judgment of November 20, 2007, Series C, No 169 <http://www.corteidh.or.cr/casos.cfm> accessed 23 April 2009.
47. *Boyce* (n 20) 413, 15.
48. Ibid 415.

law is for the purposes of assisting with the interpretation of legislation, including the Constitution, where a provision is ambiguous:

> The rights of the people of Barbados in domestic law derive solely from the Constitution. But international law can have a significant influence upon the interpretation of the Constitution because of the well established principle that the courts will so far as possible construe domestic law so as to avoid creating a breach of the State's international obligations. 'So far as possible' means that if the legislation is ambiguous ('in the sense that it is capable of a meaning which either conforms to or conflicts with the [treaty]')... the court will, other things being equal, choose the meaning which accords with the obligations imposed by the treaty.[49]

This is a clear restatement of the 'ambiguity test' found in the earlier case law and relied upon by the House of Lords.

A more general point is made about the use of non-national human rights jurisprudence. The Board states clearly that human rights norms, including human rights provisions of constitutions, must change and evolve to match the requirements of a just society at any given time.[50] This is often expressed by speaking of a constitution as a 'living tree' or 'living instrument.' However, the Board also makes it clear in *Boyce* that not all constitutional provisions change and evolve; some, like the existing laws clauses, do not change.[51] Because of this fundamental distinction, the majority is very critical of the liberal references to international law and general constitutional principles made by the appellants. Their Lordships go so far as to comment:

> The "living instrument" principle...is not a magic ingredient which can be stirred into a jurisprudential pot together with "international obligations", "generous construction" and other such phrases, sprinkled with a cherished aphorism or two and brewed up into a potion which will make the Constitution mean something which it obviously does not.[52]

> This statement appears to reflect disquiet with the way in which, perhaps particularly in death penalty cases, an exceptionally wide-ranging mix of international and comparative law authorities have been used in argument without clarity as to their purpose or potential role.

---

49. Ibid 415–16.
50. Ibid 416–17, 28.
51. Ibid 418, 31–33.
52. Ibid 424, 59.

F.　The Caribbean Court of Justice: *AG v Joseph*

A more recent case in the death penalty jurisprudence of the Commonwealth Caribbean has come not from the Privy Council, but rather from the Caribbean Court of Justice (CCJ). In 2006 the CCJ heard an appeal in the case of the *AG v Joseph* on the issue of whether the Barbados Privy Council (the mercy committee) was subject to judicial review as well as whether it was required to await the conclusion of international human rights petition processes, and to consider the reports of those bodies, before making its recommendation in relation to the exercise of the prerogative of mercy.[53] In their six concurring opinions, the judges of the CCJ upheld the right of the respondents to have their international petitions considered on the basis of the doctrine of legitimate expectation. Interestingly, in doing so, the Court rejected the justifications of *Thomas v Baptiste* and *Neville Lewis*, which anchored the right to await the conclusion of international petition processes on an expanded right to due process. In fact, several of the judges of the CCJ firmly criticized both the jurisprudence and the motivation of the Privy Council in the latter two cases.[54] Importantly, these criticisms were related to the Privy Council's application of the common law rules regarding the use of international law.[55]

But one of the judges, Wit J, went a step further than his colleagues. He did not simply criticize the decisions of the Privy Council and the delaying tactics of the Inter-American system;[56] he criticized the common law theory of dualism itself. Admitting that his legal training in a civil law system made the dualist system of the relationship of international law and municipal law seem strange to him, Wit J went so far as to argue against the entire doctrine. He pointed out that the supposed dichotomy between the legislature and the executive with regard to law-making is false. Parliament can make law directly for the people, but so too can the executive. As a result, it should not be impermissible for the executive to have law making powers in other areas, such as through treaties.[57] As a result, Wit J argued that unincorporated treaties may *create*, but not

---

53.　*AG v Joseph* [2006] CCJ 3 (AJ) (2006) 69 WIR 104 (Bdos). The same convicted killers, Lennox Boyce and Jeffrey Joseph, were involved in this case and the Privy Council decision of *Boyce v R* (n 20), one of the last cases heard by the Privy Council as Barbados's final court of appeal.

54.　Ibid (Pollard J) 51: 'a dramatic and remarkable reversal of historical understanding of dualism and the separation of powers principle'; ibid (Wit J) 10–11: *Neville Lewis* seen as 'an ingenious device to effectively dismantle the application of the death penalty even though that sentence is still on the books.'

55.　Ibid 76 (de la Bastide P and Saunders J).

56.　Hayton J, for example, indicated that improper motivations may be ascribed to the organs of the Inter-American system, which have used delays in their own legal processes as a mechanism to force states to commute death sentences: Ibid 10–11.

57.　Ibid (Wit J) 42.

infringe or diminish, rights.[58] This judgment is fascinating and sows the seeds for reconsideration of the relevance of the dualist doctrine in the Commonwealth Caribbean. However, for the present Wit J's approach did not attract the support of his colleagues on the bench.

Despite rejecting the Privy Council's approach, the CCJ obtained the same result by deciding that the doctrine of legitimate expectation grounds the right to exhaust international petition processes, and does so without violating the dualist perspective of the role of international law. Legitimate expectations are said to arise and to be justifiable in the case of the respondents as a result of several factors: (1) Barbados's ratification of the American Convention on Human Rights (making the state bound by Convention obligations as a matter of international law); (2) the positive statements made by the executive evincing an intention or desire to abide by that Convention, including statements made in Parliament; and (3) the practice of the Barbados government of giving an opportunity to condemned men to have their petitions to international human rights bodies processed before proceeding to execution.[59] These three factors lead de la Bastide P and Saunders J to conclude that the 'respondents had a legitimate expectation that the state would not execute them without first allowing them a reasonable time within which to complete the proceedings they had initiated under the ACHR by petition to the Commission.'[60] This result, they argue, upholds the doctrine of division of powers and enhances the protections afforded to human rights.[61] In this way the CCJ recognized, and attempted to avoid, the inconsistencies in the death penalty jurisprudence of the Privy Council regarding use of international law in domestic courts.

It may nevertheless be argued, however, that the decision of the CCJ falls prey to the same criticisms it makes of the jurisprudence of the Privy Council. Under a strict dualist understanding of the relationship of international law and municipal law, it is difficult to see how one could have a *legitimate* expectation about a process which is not part of the domestic legal system. As discussed earlier, international legal processes are binding in the international legal sphere but have no binding force or effect in domestic law. Under the constitutions and laws of the Commonwealth Caribbean 'law' is defined as the statutory and common law of that jurisdiction. 'International law' is not included in the term and, although there may be some room for manoeuvre in relation to

---

58. Ibid 43.
59. Ibid 118 (de la Bastide P and Saunders J).
60. Ibid.
61. Ibid 127.

customary international law, one would be hard put to consider any part of an unincorporated international treaty as being part of the domestic law *per se*. Further, it is assumed that a *legitimate* expectation must relate to processes established, or at least recognized, by domestic law. It would seem difficult to conceive of a legitimate expectation arising in relation to entirely non-legal processes.[62] It is to be seen if, or how, the CCJ will develop this doctrine of legitimate expectation in the future. However, for the present, the decision of the CCJ does little to resolve the difficulties created by the jurisprudence of the Privy Council.

5. Different Ways of Using International Law

The judicial challenges involved in stretching, perhaps even breaking, the common law rules related to use of international law in the domestic sphere are illustrated in the death penalty jurisprudence of the Commonwealth Caribbean. But was this inevitable? Could the courts have used international law in conformity with the common law rules to obtain similar results? To answer such a question, it will be useful to examine the different ways in which international law may be used in the domestic forum.

A. Comparative Uses of All Forms of International Law

Firstly, international law, like any non-national system of law, can be relied upon by a domestic court as non-binding, but perhaps persuasive, comparative authority. Judges may take judicial notice of the rules and principles of public international law, including those established by treaties to which their state is a party, even when they are not embodied in municipal law.[63] Further, as a result of the presumption that Parliament does not intend to violate its international legal obligations, judges are obliged to consider any relevant rule of public international law and permit the citation of any relevant treaty, including the 1969 Vienna Convention on the Law of Treaties.[64]

Such comparative uses of public international law cannot be said to be extraordinary. Just as a Commonwealth Caribbean judge can turn to an Australian precedent to help interpret or apply a rule or principle, so too

---

62. For other reasons, the Privy Council early on rejected the utility of this doctrine in relation to international petition processes. In the case of *Thomas v Baptiste* (n 25) at 25, Lord Millett expressly rejected legitimate expectation on the basis that it could only guarantee a process, not any substantive rights associated with that process.
63. Bennion (n 12) 823.
64. Ibid 688–90 and 824; Vienna Convention on the Law of Treaties (opened for signature 23 May 1969, entered into force 27 January 1980), 1155 UNTS 331 (VCLT).

can she or he look to an international legal norm or international judicial decision for guidance. The international source will not be binding, but it can assist the judge by providing a concrete example of legal analysis and legal practice on a particular issue. In this way, the courts in *Thomas v Baptiste* and *Neville Lewis*, for example, legitimately could have looked at Inter-American norms to help understand and elaborate common law concepts, such as the right of due process, in relation to domestic procedures – such as whether one has the right to make submissions to the mercy committee. In such a way, international legal norms may be used to provide indications of tendencies in general social (human) development – possibly evidencing the evolving standards of *international* society – as well as national social development.

But such a comparative or illustrative use of international law may only be helpful to clarify or develop an *existing* domestic legal concept, not to bridge the gap between domestic law and international law. In other words, international jurisprudence could help reveal the full meaning of a right, such as the right to due process; but contrary to *Thomas v Baptiste* and *Neville Lewis*, international law could not provide the link between a domestic law right (protection of the law) and a non-domestic process (an Inter-American petition). Only if one were to say that the international legal process somehow *became* a domestic law one, would it be possible to decide that other domestic processes must await its completion.

Nevertheless such comparative uses of international law can be important and *all* international norms can be used for such purposes. National judges equally could refer to various forms of international law: (1) binding treaty obligations; (2) 'incomplete' treaty obligations (i.e., where the state has yet to complete the final act required to formally consent to the treaty, and therefore is not yet fully bound);[65] (3) non-binding treaties, such as treaties concluded between third parties; (4) international judicial decisions; and (5) 'soft law', including non-binding international statements that may shed light on the meaning of a concept or rule. Equally, it is important to note that the *strength* of the international legal norm as evaluated by international law, either generally or as against the state itself, becomes irrelevant when the norm is merely being relied upon for comparative or illustrative purposes. A non-binding international norm may be equally helpful.

Interestingly, although the use of international law in this illustrative

---

65. For example, VCLT art 18 imposes an obligation upon states that merely *sign* a treaty (which is subject to ratification) not to defeat the object and purpose of the treaty prior to its entry into force for that state, or prior to its indicating an intention not to become a party to the treaty.

sense may not seem particularly potent, the hard-fought battles at the Privy Council on whether to include, or exclude, international law suggest otherwise. In fact, the pattern that arguably emerges from the jurisprudence of the Privy Council is one where if international law is invoked in a serious manner, it tends to be accepted and applied by the Board.

B. Customary Law as Part of the Law of the Land

Secondly, a domestic tribunal can refer to, and apply, customary international law so long as it is not contradicted by statutory or judicial authority. Customary international law in such cases *becomes* domestic law and therefore can be applied directly by a domestic court without statutory basis, in the same manner that a judge applies a rule of common law. Interestingly, as established in the *Trendtex* case, a national judge can even apply customary law that appears to conflict with a prior precedent, if that prior precedent itself adopted and relied upon a rule of customary international law that is no longer in existence.[66] In other words, domestic judges could use the development of customary international law as a basis for distinguishing prior domestic precedents.

C. As Domestic Statutory Law (Transformation)

Thirdly, international law may affect the domestic sphere when a treaty or customary obligation is transformed by statute. Technically speaking, the international legal obligation is replaced by the domestic law obligation in the incorporating statute, and therefore one might say that international law no longer plays a role here. But this process nevertheless allows a domestic judge to apply national law which closely parallels international law, thereby potentially upholding the state's international legal obligations.

Importantly, since the judge is applying a *domestic* statute, the rules of statutory interpretation apply and allow a variety of sources to be examined to ascertain the legislative intention.[67] One of these sources is the incorporated treaty itself. Francis A.R. Bennion argues that treaties can be looked to in interpreting legislation even where that legislation is unambiguous, and even where the treaty is not referred to in the text of the legislation.[68] He submits that judicial decisions 'suggesting that the court is entitled to consult a relevant treaty only where the

---

66. *Trendtex* (n 8).
67. On legislative intention see Bennion (n 12) Part VIII.
68. Ibid 685–86.

enactment is ambiguous can no longer be relied on...[and that the] true rule is that in this area, as in others, the court is to arrive at an informed interpretation.'[69] Bennion also states that it is permissible to make 'cautious reference' to the drafting records and other preparatory work related to a treaty (the *travaux préparatoires*) for the purposes of construing the treaty and any enactment based on it, although only where such material is 'both public and accessible and indisputably points to a definite legislative intention.'[70] In addition, a court is entitled to look at the decisions of foreign courts in order to ensure both the correct, and uniform international, interpretation of the treaty; for the same reasons a court also may refer to the writings of foreign jurists.[71]

On such grounds, a domestic court therefore may permissibly look to the following sources when interpreting domestic legislation: the treaty which it transforms, its *travaux préparatoires*, decisions of foreign courts and writings of foreign jurists which point to the correct interpretation of the treaty, and decisions of the organs of international organizations which are entrusted with the task of authoritatively interpreting the treaty (such as the Inter-American Commission on Human Rights and Inter-American Court of Human Rights).[72]

What may also prove interesting in this context is the question of the *manner* of transformation. It is easy to recognize express examples of statutory transformation, such as a 'Caribbean Court of Justice Act,' or a 'Revised Treaty of Chaguaramas Act.' But perhaps other, subtler forms of transformation may also exist. This is an area that will be examined below and which could be developed in Commonwealth Caribbean jurisprudence.

D. Interpretation of Ambiguous Domestic Law

Thirdly, it is clear that an unincorporated treaty may be used by courts for the purposes of interpreting ambiguous domestic law. If the domestic statute is ambiguous in the sense of being capable of being read so as to support, or contradict, the treaty obligation, then reference may be made to the unincorporated treaty for interpretive purposes. The 'ambiguity' could be in relation to a number of domestic legal sources including (1) a statute, (2) a constitutional provision, or (3) a common law rule.

What is interesting here is how *powerful* the interpretive process

---

69. Ibid 685 [citations omitted].
70. Ibid 687, citing: *Fothergill v Monarch Airlines Ltd* [1981] AC 251 (HL) 278 (Lord Wilberforce).
71. Ibid 691.
72. As illustrated by the Board in *Lewis* (n 32).

becomes in such circumstances. The presumption that domestic law should be interpreted so as to comply with international obligations, if not rebutted, has tended to work like a switch: once ambiguity is found, the court will interpret the law so as to conform to the treaty obligation. In other words, ambiguity is followed by conformity with the international rule.

6. Potential Use of International Law by Caribbean Courts

This chapter has illustrated that the common law rules regarding use of international law in the domestic forum are clear, comprehensive, and comprehensible. The unfortunate mischief that has arisen in our regional jurisprudence on the death penalty is that these rules have been stretched to the point of seeming incoherence. This is where advocates and judges of the Commonwealth Caribbean can serve a key role in both re-articulating these common law rules with clarity and precision as part of an indigenous jurisprudence and in developing and reapplying these rules in a manner that suits our regional reality. As seen in the brief discussion of the judgment of Wit J in the case of *AG v Joseph*, alternative visions can be found in our region regarding the role that international law can have in domestic legal systems.

Two further developments might lead to an expanded role for international law in our domestic legal systems. The first arises out of the very nature of the Caribbean Court of Justice. The CCJ, like all Commonwealth Caribbean courts, has the capacity to apply the common law rules regarding use of international law in its appellate jurisdiction. It has clear scope to further interpret and apply these rules in all of its appellate cases. But the Court also has a treaty-interpreting role under its original jurisdiction. This role is unlikely to require the Court to use these common law rules, precisely because it will be acting as an international, treaty-applying body. In such cases, the question will not be whether the Court can interpret and apply the relevant treaty, as it most certainly can, but whether there has been a breach of the international legal obligation.

But it must be remembered that the Court's original jurisdiction also encompasses referrals from national courts.[73] This referral process allows a national judge to ask, and to have answered by the CCJ, questions

---

73. See Revised Treaty of Chaguaramas Establishing the Caribbean Community Including the CARICOM Single Market and Economy (opened for signature 5 July 2001, entered into force 9 Feb 2006) <http://www.caricomlaw.org/doc.php?id=131> accessed 22 Apr 2009 (Revised Treaty) art 211(1)(c); Agreement Establishing the Caribbean Court of Justice (opened for signature 14 Feb 2001, entered into force 23 July 2002), <http://www.caricomlaw.org/doc.php?id=490> accessed 22 Apr 2009 (CCJ Agreement) art XII(1)(c).

related to the Revised Treaty; it also preserves the right of the national judge to ultimately decide the case. In this context, when answering a referral application from a national court, it is likely that the CCJ may wish to offer guidance to the national judge on not only the nature of the relevant obligation at the Community level (the referral question), but also on its status in the national law as an incorporated treaty obligation (whether fully, partially, or imperfectly incorporated). The Court may even wish to advise the national judge on the status of an unincorporated treaty obligation.[74] In addition, the judges of the CCJ should have a much greater understanding of the sources and rules of international law as a result of the requirements for the composition of the Court.[75] It is likely that this richer understanding of international law may influence all of the decisions of the Court.

Finally, *all* Commonwealth Caribbean judges have an opportunity to clarify or develop one area of the common law related to the use of international law in the domestic sphere, namely, understanding which statutes can 'transform' treaty obligations. It is well accepted that Parliament may make enactments which either directly or indirectly incorporate treaty obligations. But can pre-existing statutes also be read to perform a treaty-transformation role?

As a matter of statutory interpretation, it is well established that *ambiguous* pre-existing legislation, even if making no reference to the treaty and enacted before the state became a party to a treaty, may be interpreted in light of the treaty. Further, such eminent writers as Bennion have stated that treaties may be looked to generally for the purposes of statutory interpretation, even in cases where the legislation is clear.[76] Thus, it may be permissible to interpret any statute, whether ambiguous or clear, whether enacted subsequent to or prior to the state assuming treaty obligations, in light of the treaty.

But can we go further and argue that particular pre-existing statutes have actually become incorporating acts, thus giving rise to a stronger interpretive role for the treaty in question? Such an argument can be founded on direct and objectively verifiable state actions. States, both at the domestic level (in parliamentary debates) and at the international level (in official written or oral submissions to international treaty-monitoring bodies), frequently indicate that a particular treaty to which

---

74. If the approach of the European Court of Justice is taken, unincorporated treaties may be held to give rise to binding obligations as a matter of domestic law under the doctrine of direct effect. On 'direct effect' in the EU see, e.g., T.C. Hartley, *The Foundations of European Community Law* (6th edn, OUP, NY 2007) chapter 7.

75. See also CCJ Agreement ibid art IV(1), which requires the Court to include no less than three judges who 'shall possess expertise in international law including international trade law.'

76. Bennion (n 12) 685.

they are parties, although not incorporated by any specifically-enacted law, is nevertheless being implemented by means of a pre-existing statute. Before these treaty bodies, such statements are made in direct response to questions about the state's compliance with a particular treaty obligation and specify that a pre-existing national statute, or the Constitution itself, implements and fulfils the (otherwise unincorporated) treaty obligation. In such circumstances, the state may be estopped at the international level from subsequently denying the transforming role of the statute it relies upon. But what consequence might such action have for a domestic court? Can a national judge find a pre-existing statute to have become, through state action, an incorporating act? It would appear to be possible to make such a judicial determination simply by construing the *current* legislative intent for the statute, which in most cases will be 'always speaking,' when such statements have been made in Parliament. In such a case, Parliament itself will be aiding the court in establishing legislative intention. However, it will be more difficult to infer legislative intent from executive conduct before international treaty bodies. Allowing the executive to perform such a role would be inconsistent with the doctrine of separation of powers and the authority of Parliament to make domestic law. Nevertheless, it may be possible to ascribe such an incorporating role to a statute if the interpretive context as a whole supports such a position, since the crucial role of a judge when examining any statute is to 'arrive at an informed interpretation' of its meaning.[77] In any event, even if the statute cannot be read as an incorporating act, a judge will still be entitled to interpret it in light of the state's treaty obligations, under the general rules of statutory interpretation described above.

Why argue for such a broad approach to transformation? It would entitle a domestic judge to interpret all domestic laws which have been *relied upon by the state* to provide evidence of compliance with treaty obligations as transforming laws, and thus enable speedy and authoritative interpretive access to the treaty obligations those laws are supposed to transform. Importantly, this idea of broad transformation would not fall foul of the common law rules regarding reference to international law in domestic courts because it would maintain the distinction between the domestic and international spheres. Because the statute would be transforming an international obligation, it would make it part of domestic law, and therefore avoid the problems entailed in bringing international law in through the back door. The treaty would remain external to the domestic legal system and would not itself give rise

---

77. Ibid.

to binding rights or obligations at the national level. Rather, the scope of the *domestic* legislation which is deemed to implement international legal obligations is expanded. For this reason, such an approach is superior to that of legitimate expectation as set out in *AG v Joseph*,[78] since the doctrine of legitimate expectation has the effect of allowing an individual to use an *international* process, one not part of domestic law. In contrast, a broad view of transformation would change the nature of the international process into a domestic one, by transforming it.

Such an approach is not unfair to the states of the Commonwealth Caribbean. It simply takes states at their word: if they choose to implement an international legal obligation by means of a pre-existing statute *and communicate this to the world*, their own judges should be entitled to refer to the relevant treaty for the purposes of interpreting that same statute. In doing so a judge would help his or her state to uphold its international legal obligations, including its obligation to perform treaties to which it is a party in good faith, and to implement treaty obligations in its domestic law where required.[79] This latter rule of domestic implementation is frequently embodied in treaties,[80] and is complemented by the fundamental rule that a state cannot invoke provisions of its domestic law (or failure to enact such provisions) as an excuse for non-performance of its treaty obligations.[81]

7. Conclusion

In sum, a body of clear rules exists which allows, but also restricts, reference to international legal norms in domestic settings. Conformity with these common law rules has positive value because they are fundamental to a number of basic constitutional goods, from that of upholding parliamentary sovereignty, to checking executive excesses, to ensuring respect for the rule of law. But these rules should not constrain able advocates and members of the judiciary, who can and should actively refer to international legal sources both because they represent a vast repository of knowledge and good practices, and because ultimately doing so may help states comply with both their national and international legal obligations.

---

78. See n 52.
79. See VCLT (n 64) art 26; *Exchange of Greek and Turkish Populations Case* (Advisory Opinion) (1925) PCIJ Rep Series B No 10, 20.
80. See, for example, American Convention on Human Rights (opened for signature 22 Nov 1969, entered into force 18 July 1978) 1144 UNTS 143, art 2.
81. See VCLT (n 64) art 27.

Legitimate Expectations, International Treaties and the Caribbean Court of Justice

Eddy D. Ventose

1. Introduction

The decision of the recently-established Caribbean Court of Justice (CCJ) in *AG v Joseph and Boyce*[1] has been hailed as revolutionary by legal practitioners and academic lawyers. And in many respects it is. It has clearly given public lawyers much food for thought and it will take some time before the full ramifications for constitutional, human rights, and administrative law areas are fully explored.[2] The focus of this chapter is the exploration of the CCJ's approach to legitimate expectations. Notwithstanding that the discussion of legitimate expectations was *obiter*, the decision still indicates the approach the CCJ might take if the issue arises directly for consideration in the near future.[3] Although the CCJ did not engage in any rigorous analysis of the issues that lie at the heart of legal protection for substantive legitimate expectations, its approach seems to be in accordance with the evolving approach to legitimate expectations in England and elsewhere. And, even if it is accepted that the boundaries of substantive legitimate expectations are still being drawn, as will be seen in due course, the CCJ's approach

---

1. [2006] CCJ 3, (2006) 69 WIR 104 (Bdos). See also D. Pollard, 'Unincorporated Treaties and Small States' (2007) 33 Comm LB 389; P. Sales, 'International Law in Domestic Courts: A Developing Framework' (2008) 124 LQR 288; and M. Taggart, 'Legitimate Expectations and Treaties in the High Court of Australia' (1996) 112 LQR 50.

2. See A. Fiadjoe, 'A Pandora's Box in Commonwealth Caribbean Public Law: The CCJ's Approach to the Doctrine of Legitimate Expectations' UWI Faculty of Law Faculty Workshop Series Paper (28 November 2007); D. McKoy, 'Identifying the Chi in Commonwealth Caribbean Law: The Contribution of the Common Law and Human Rights Law to Constitutional Interpretation' UWI Faculty of Law Faculty Workshop Series Paper (18 October 2007), and T. Robinson, 'Our Inherent Constitution,' Chapter 11.

3. The CCJ accepted (n 1) 15 that over five years had elapsed since the appellants' conviction and sentence and that the Crown accepted that commutation of sentence was the logical consequence following *Pratt v AG* [1994] 2 AC 1 (PC Ja). The appellants succeeded on that basis alone. However, the CCJ went on to state at page 16 that although it was now possible to dispose of this appeal without deciding whether it was lawful for the respondents to be executed before the Barbados Privy Council received and considered the decision of the Inter-American body, it believed that the parties were entitled to receive its views on the issue because, first, the issue was examined by the lower courts and answered differently by Greenidge J and the Court of Appeal (*Joseph v AG* (2005) 68 WIR 123 (CA)); and, secondly, the issue was identified by the parties as one of the major issues raised by the appeal to the CCJ.

is forward thinking since it anticipated subsequent developments in England.

This chapter is an examination of the treatment by the CCJ of the doctrine of legitimate expectations, in particular, the standard of review the courts must deploy when faced with a substantive, as opposed to a procedural, legitimate expectation.[4] Before the CCJ explored that issue, it delineated its view on the role of legitimate expectations and unincorporated treaties, accepting that such treaties do create legitimate expectations – a notion that has been rejected in most Commonwealth countries. In any event, the result in the decision is almost inevitable, in light of the issues that the court dealt with. This chapter, first, examines how the Judicial Committee of the Privy Council (Privy Council) has dealt with the issue of legitimate expectations and international treaties; and, second, critically examines the standard of review articulated by the CCJ in *Joseph* to determine when a legitimate expectation can prevail over any compelling state interest advanced. It will also outline the central arguments accepted by the CCJ in relation to unincorporated treaties and legitimate expectations.

2. The Privy Council's Approach

In recent years, the issue of whether a state had to await the decision of any international human rights body before it can lawfully execute a condemned prisoner was one that has been explored by the Privy Council in a myriad of decisions. The law was in a state of confusion and has only recently given a hint of certainty by some rather dubious legal reasoning. In light of the subject matter at issue – the lawfulness of the execution of the condemned person – it is hardly surprising that the CCJ in *Joseph and Boyce* came to the conclusion that it did. It traversed the much-trodden terrain of decisions of the Privy Council relating to the question of whether the state must await the conclusion of any relevant international proceedings before it can lawfully execute the condemned man.[5]

A. *Fisher v Minister of Public Safety and Immigration No 2*

One of the first decisions where the issue of legitimate expectation was canvassed is *Fisher v Minister of Public Safety and Immigration No 2*.[6]

---

4. P. Craig, 'Substantive Legitimate Expectations in Domestic and Community Law' (1996) 55 CLJ 291.
5. D. O'Brien and V. Carter, 'Constitutional Rights, Legitimate Expectations and the Death Penalty' (2000) PL 573.
6. (1998) 52 WIR 27 (PC Bah).

In that decision, the appellant initially argued that he had a legitimate expectation that he would not be executed while his petition to the Inter-American Commission on Human Rights (IACHR) was outstanding.[7] However, by the time the matter came before the Privy Council, counsel for the appellant argued against his client's execution on the grounds that: (a) the government having given an undertaking through counsel that it would abide by the IACHR Regulations, (b) the appellant had a legitimate expectation that the government would allow a reasonable time for the completion of the process, and (c) a reasonable time in the circumstances was not less than 18 months commencing on 16 December 1997.[8]

At the outset, the Board observed that '[t]he fact that a petition is pending might give rise to an argument in public law based on legitimate expectation which their Lordships consider and reject hereafter.'[9] The Privy Council dealt with the issue in the following manner:

> The first of the public law grounds is that the appellant had a legitimate expectation that he would not be executed so long as his petition was outstanding. But legitimate expectations do not create binding rules of law. As Mason C.J. made clear at page 291 *a decision-maker can act inconsistently with a legitimate expectation which he has created, provided he gives adequate notice of his intention to do so, and provided he gives those who are affected an opportunity to state their case. Procedural fairness requires of him no more than that.* Even if therefore the appellant had a legitimate expectation that he would not be executed while his petition was pending his expectation could not survive the Government's letters of 2nd and 30th January 1998 in which it informed the appellant's solicitors in unequivocal terms that it would wait no longer than 15th February 1998.[10]

The Privy Council held, correctly, that there was no implication by virtue of the right to life that the executive would wait for any reasonable period before the appellant's international petitions were completed; for that to happen, the treaty had to be incorporated into domestic law.[11] That much is trite law. However, it must be remembered that *Fisher No 2* pre-dated the evolved thinking of legitimate expectations. To suggest now that the only way a substantive legitimate expectation can be protected is procedurally to overlook over 10 years of refinement

---

7.   Ibid 32.
8.   Ibid 33.
9.   Ibid 35.
10. Ibid 36 (emphasis added).
11. Ibid 37.

and development of the concept. As we will see shortly, the courts have specifically jettisoned such notions. Specifically, the statement of the Privy Council that 'Legitimate expectations do not create binding rules of law'[12] is clearly now incorrect in light of the modern approach to legitimate expectations. In their dissent, Lords Slynn and Hope accepted that the statements by the government had:

> ...provided Fisher with a legitimate expectation that, if the IACHR were to recommend against the carrying out of the death sentence, their views would be considered before the final decision is taken as to whether or not he is to be executed. But any such recommendation would plainly be pointless if he were to be executed before the recommendation was made and communicated to the Government.[13]

However, their Lordships noted that:

> We fully accept that a change of policy might be announced to prevent legitimate expectations arising in the future, but we do not read the judgment as saying that once a procedure like the present has actually begun that a Government can by a unilateral announcement terminate legitimate expectations already created.[14]

The minority decided that a legitimate expectation existed but that it could be defeated by a clear change in policy by the government. Implicit in their argument was that where such a change of policy is effected, it would defeat any expectations going forward, but would not affect those expectations already created. The minority accepted the argument of counsel for the appellant that 'as a matter of *good administration* the law required his legitimate expectation to be respected, and that he should not be executed until the decision of the IACHR is received, and that to do otherwise would be a wholly unreasonable exercise of the power or discretion.'[15]

This statement anticipates the current view relating to what lies at the heart of the concept of legitimate expectations; good administration requires public authorities to act fairly towards members of the public, in particular, those whose legitimate expectations are frustrated by changes in policy and retraction of promises made. The interest by applicants in pushing the argument relating to legitimate expectations continued unabated, focusing now on establishing the expectation from statements made by the executive rather than locating it merely in ratification of the relevant treaty.

---

12. Ibid 36.
13. Ibid 42.
14. Ibid 45 (emphasis added).
15. Ibid (emphasis added).

B. *Thomas v Baptiste*

Unsurprisingly therefore, the issue arose again for consideration in *Thomas v Baptiste*.[16] In that decision, the law took a turn for the worse, in my view, with a differently constituted Board, holding that the 'due process' clause in the Constitution of Trinidad and Tobago extends to the appellate process as well as the trial itself and includes 'the right of a condemned man to be allowed to complete any appellate process or analogous legal process that is capable of resulting in a reduction or commutation of his sentence before the process is rendered nugatory by executive action'.[17] The illogicality and plain result-oriented decision of the majority was laid bare by the minority who argued that due process could not, bar incorporation, extend to international law and that the terms of international treaties could not extend the due process clause which was only concerned with municipal law, and not international law.[18]

Notwithstanding the criticisms that can be made of the reasoning of the Privy Council in *Thomas*, their arguments relating to legitimate expectations could hardly be regarded as authoritative, because the issue as the Board saw it was whether 'the Government's *ratification* of the Convention gave rise to a legitimate expectation on the part of the appellants that they would not be executed before their petitions to the IACHR were finally determined.'[19] In other words, the appellants contended that ratification alone gave rise to this legitimate expectation. The state, however, claimed that (a) 'ratification is a private process which is not attended by public notice and that the ratification of the Convention was a transaction between the Government of Trinidad and Tobago and the Organisation of American States';[20] and (b) '[t]here was no public statement that the Government had ratified the Convention and the appellants were not informed of the fact.'[21] They also submitted that ratification of an unincorporated treaty: (a) 'is incapable of raising a legitimate expectation that the Government will comply with the provisions of the treaty';[22] or (b) 'raises at best a legitimate expectation that the Government will introduce appropriate legislative measures to give effect to the treaty.'[23]

---

16. (1999) 54 WIR 387 (PC T&T).
17. Ibid 421.
18. Ibid 432.
19. Ibid 424.
20. Ibid.
21. Ibid.
22. Ibid.
23. Ibid.

These actions, even when taken together, hardly amounted to an unequivocal statement by the state that it would abide by its international treaty obligations in relation to the condemned men. It was, therefore, hardly surprising that that view was rejected by the majority of the Board, because if it were accepted it would mean that that reasoning would, in principle, also be applicable to other international treaties – a conclusion the Privy Council would not countenance. In rejecting the arguments, the Privy Council stated that:

> In their Lordships' view, however, the appellants' arguments based on legitimate expectation face an insurmountable obstacle. Even if a legitimate expectation founded on the provisions of an unincorporated treaty may give procedural protection, it cannot by itself, that is to say unsupported by other constitutional safeguards, give substantive protection, for this would be tantamount to the indirect enforcement of the treaty...In this sense legitimate expectations do not create binding rules of law...*The result is that a decision-maker is free to act inconsistently with the expectation in any particular case provided that he acts fairly towards those likely to be affected.* But mere procedural protection would not avail the present appellants. Any legitimate expectation that their execution would be delayed until their petitions were heard, however long it might take, cannot have survived the publication of the Instructions...*The question is not whether their legitimate expectations were lawfully disappointed, but whether they were in fact disappointed.*[24]

Lords Goff and Hobhouse, who dissented, merely noted that they 'also agree that the doctrine of legitimate expectation is of no assistance to the appellants on the fact of the present cases.'[25] Importantly, the minority pointed out that they 'accept that treaty obligations assumed by the executive are capable of giving rise to legitimate expectations which the executive will not under the municipal law be at liberty to disregard'.[26] However, they noted that 'in the present case there was not at the material time any legitimate expectation' and that on this point, they agreed 'with what is said in the judgment of the majority.'[27] The minority further observed that:

> The rights which are protected are those set out in the Constitution,

---

24. Ibid (emphasis added).

25. Ibid 429.

26. Citing *Minister for Immigration and Ethnic Affairs v Teoh* [1995] 183 CLR 273 (HC Aus); *R v Secretary of State for the Home Department, ex p Ahmed* [1998] INLR 570 (CA Eng); and *Fisher No 2* (n 6).

27. *Thomas v Baptiste* (1999) 54 WIR 387 (PC T&T) 429.

including those previously existing in the law of the Republic. This does not include (without more) expectations raised by treaties entered into by the executive which have not been incorporated into the law of the Republic, *though in such cases the municipal law doctrine of legitimate expectation may, where appropriate, be invoked by individual citizens.*[28]

Soon thereafter, in the light of day, the *Thomas* line of reasoning became exposed. However, Lord Millet, although not overruling *Thomas*, shook the very foundations of that decision by declaring in *Briggs v Baptiste*[29] that *Thomas* 'did not overturn the constitutional principle that international conventions do not alter domestic law except to the extent that they are incorporated into domestic law by legislation.'[30] But, it was clear to legal practitioners and academic lawyers that that was exactly what *Thomas* sought unashamedly to achieve. The majority in *Lewis*[31] also pointed out that *Thomas* 'did not decide that the recommendations of the commission are directly enforceable in domestic law (which are not binding even in international law) or the orders of the Inter-American Court are directly enforceable in domestic law.'[32] There was no mention of legitimate expectations.

So although the Privy Council, sitting on an appeal from The Bahamas, in *Higgs v Minister of National Security*[33] thought *Fisher No 2* indistinguishable from the instant case, it simply noted that the Privy Council in *Thomas* did not cast doubt on the correctness of *Fisher No 2*.[34] Since The Bahamas did not have a 'due process' clause, or an analogous clause like 'protection of the law,' as was the case in *Lewis* in Jamaica, the Board in *Higgs and Mitchell* held that the Privy Council in *Thomas* 'did not regard the common law concept as having the power (absent specific language in the Constitution) to incorporate procedures having an existence only under international law into the domestic criminal justice system.'[35] Therefore, the Privy Council held that unincorporated treaties have no effect upon the rights and duties of citizens at common law or by statute, and that:

They may have an indirect effect upon the construction of statutes as a result of the presumption that Parliament does not intend to pass

---

28. Ibid (emphasis added).
29. (1999) 55 WIR 460 (PC T&T).
30. Ibid 472.
31. [2001] 2 AC 50 (PC Ja).
32. Ibid.
33. (1999) 55 WIR 10 (PC Bah).
34. Ibid 22.
35. Ibid.

legislation which would put the Crown in breach of its international obligations. *Or the existence of a treaty may give rise to a legitimate expectation on the part of citizens that the government, in its acts affecting them, will observe the terms of the treaty.*[36]

The Privy Council, citing *Teoh*, observed that:

In this respect there is nothing special about a treaty. Such legitimate expectations may arise from any course of conduct which the executive has made it known that it will follow. And, as the High Court of Australia made clear in *Teoh's* case, *the legal effect of creating such a legitimate expectation is purely procedural. The executive cannot depart from the expected course of conduct unless it has given notice that intends to do so and has given the person affected an opportunity to make representations.*[37]

What decision the Privy Council would make in relation to this issue was certainly as predictable as a coin toss.

C. *Lewis v AG*

Notwithstanding the doubts expressed in *Briggs*, and *Higgs and Mitchell* about the reasoning of the Privy Council in *Thomas*, the Board was so confident with its reasoning in *Thomas* that it extended it, in *Lewis v AG*,[38] to the 'protection of the law' clause in the Constitution of Jamaica 1962. In relation to legitimate expectations, the Privy Council observed that:

Moreover since legitimate expectations did not create rules of law *the government could act inconsistently with those expectations so long as it gave those affected an opportunity to put their case.* Since the appellant was given notice that the government would not wait beyond the fixed date for the Commission to report they could no longer have a legitimate expectation that the government would wait for that report. The government had in all the circumstances of that case acted reasonably.[39]

The Privy Council also pointed out that:

Nor can there be any question of the prisoners having had a legitimate expectation (as the term is now understood in administrative law) that the state would await a response to their petitions. All the

---

36. Ibid 17 (emphasis added).
37. Ibid (emphasis added).
38. (2000) 57 WIR 275 (PC Ja). See also D. O'Brien, 'Due Process: Philosopher's Stone or Fool's Gold' (2001) 117 LQR 220.
39. Ibid 301 (emphasis added).

petitions were presented after the Government had issued the Instructions and *a legitimate expectation can hardly arise in the face of a clear existing contrary statement of policy.*[40]

Commonwealth Caribbean law was in a complete state of disarray, with both appellants and states seeking to advance their arguments before differently constituted Boards more sympathetic to their points of view. The dissents of yesterday became the majority decisions of today – a concept that cannot but bring a high degree of uncertainty to Commonwealth Caribbean constitutional and human rights law.

3. The CCJ Decision

It was against this tumultuous background that the decision of the CCJ in *AG v Joseph*[41] came to be decided. De la Bastide P and Saunders J gave the leading judgment of the Court.[42] They accepted that the law in this area is unsettled and still evolving,[43] and that there is a huge divergence of opinion and approach between different courts, but also between judges of the same court.[44] Punishment by death, we are told, is 'punishment in a class of its own, warranting special procedures before it is carried out.'[45] The court alluded to four approaches represented in the case law. The first, as espoused by the House of Lords in *ex p Brind*, was that such conventions do not create binding rules of law.[46] Second, execution of the condemned person before exhaustion of his international petitions was 'cruel and inhumane punishment'.[47] Third, there is the approach adopted by *Thomas* and *Lewis*, which, the CCJ made clear when it stated, 'we have expressed our disagreement.'[48] The fourth one, relating the use of legitimate expectations, clearly piqued the interest of de la Bastide P and Saunders J.[49]

Commonwealth Caribbean courts have not grappled with the central issues which lie at the heart of legitimate expectations, in particular, legal protection for substantive legitimate expectations.[50] However, it

---

40. Ibid 307 (emphasis added).
41. [2006] CCJ 3, (2006) 69 WIR 104 (Bdos).
42. The joint judgment was the longest, running some 144 paragraphs.
43. *Joseph* (n 1) 103.
44. Ibid.
45. Ibid 108.
46. Ibid 111.
47. Ibid 112.
48. Ibid 113.
49. Ibid 114.
50. A clear example of this is the Barbados case of *Leacock v AG* (2005) 68 WIR 181 (HC Bdos). See also, A. Fiadjoe, *Commonwealth Caribbean Public Law* (3rd edn, Routledge-Cavendish, London 2007) 275.

has raised its ugly head in the context of death penalty litigation in the Commonwealth Caribbean, and there has been a dearth of decisions by the Privy Council making reference to this public law concept to give life to appellants' argument that the state is obliged to await the conclusion of the international legal process they had initiated before it can lawfully execute them. These decisions have not dealt with the issue of, first, the method by which such legitimate expectations are actually created; second, where they are created, whether they lead to only procedural as opposed to substantive legitimate expectations; and, third, what test should the courts use in determining whether to give effect to a substantive legitimate expectations.

The decision in *Joseph* will be analysed to also understand whether, first, the CCJ was at all cognizant of the implications of its recognition of substantive legitimate expectations and, second, the test used by the CCJ was one which could properly guide the courts going forward in relation to substantive legitimate expectations. For present purposes, the conceptual difficultly raised by the subject matter of the legitimate expectation in *Joseph and Boyce* has been put aside – an unincorporated treaty – and focus will be placed on those aspects of the decision that have far-reaching implications for Commonwealth Caribbean public law.

4. Creating the Legitimate Expectation

A. The CCJ's View

It is not surprising that the CCJ found that a legitimate expectation existed on the facts, as presented to them. The case for such a finding was *a fortiori*. First, there was ratification by the Barbados Government of the American Convention on Human Rights. This was not, however, enough to found a legitimate expectation, in my view. More was needed. The CCJ cited the decision of the Australian High Court in *Teoh*, but it did not opine on the question of whether ratification alone could give rise to a legitimate expectation, and, given the nature of the reasoning of the CCJ, it did not rely on that case for its decision in relation to legitimate expectations. Second, there were positive statements from the executive that they would abide by the treaty in relation to such condemned prisoners.[51] Third, there was previous practice by the Barbados government to allow those prisoners to have their petitions heard and adjudicated upon before execution.[52] Fourth, Parliament,

---

51. *Joseph* (n 1) 118.
52. Ibid.

in amending the Constitution, impliedly recognized that it was the practice and indeed the obligation of the state to await the Commission's process, at least for some period of time.[53] Therefore, the conclusion that 'the respondents had a legitimate expectation that the state would not execute them without first allowing them a reasonable time within which to complete the [international human rights] proceedings they had initiated' seems irresistible.[54]

One of the major criticisms that can be made of this aspect of the decision was that the CCJ did not hear any arguments from either side on the use of legitimate expectations in this context. If that was done, the arguments for and against such an approach might have been canvassed before the court. Indeed, the conceptual difficulty noted below would have been fully argued to assist the CCJ making its decision. However, we are left in the dark as to how to interpret and make sense of the decision. Importantly, the fundamental issues concerning the application of legitimate expectations, in particular, substantive legitimate expectations, in this context were simply not addressed. The CCJ merely relied on the reasoning in decisions relating to substantive legitimate expectations in England as the basis upon which to found the legitimate expectation in its decision. That, in my view is entirely sensible, but these decisions, for example *ex p Hamble Fisheries*[55] and *ex p Coughlan*,[56] can only go so far, because the central issue raised in *Joseph* was simply not addressed by the courts in those cases – indeed they could not have been, in light of the nature of the expectations created therein. Specifically, the CCJ itself noted that it was 'not specifically directed to the *evidence* on which any such expectation might be grounded. Nor were we addressed on the principles that would govern it.'[57] This is quite a startling admission. There is no question, in light of the subject matter at issue, the fundamental questions raised, and the fact that a decision on this point was not necessary, that the CCJ ought to have exercised judicial restraint and should not have addressed this issue as comprehensively as it did in its judgment. But it did, and we are left to make sense of the decision and its far-reaching implications.

B. Justifications

I have little difficulty with the conclusion of the CCJ in *Joseph and*

---

53. Ibid 116.
54. Ibid 118.
55. [1995] 2 All ER 714 (CA Eng.).
56. [2001] QB 213.
57. *Joseph* (n 1) 77 (emphasis added).

Boyce for the following reasons: first, the class of individuals affected by that decision is a narrow one indeed – condemned prisoners – there was no intention on the part of the CCJ to extend that principle beyond the parameters of the decision. Second, that conclusion does not involve important policymaking decisions. In other words, it does not risk assuming the mantle of the executive or the legislator. Third, the conclusion of the CCJ was simply that the condemned prisoners had a legitimate expectation that the state would wait for reasonable period for completion of the international proceedings before it could lawfully execute them. Fourth, the court did not conclude that the content of the international rights instruments could *generally* form part of domestic law – this was not *as such* the subject matter of the legitimate expectation, for if it were, and the court had held that the international treaty was incorporated into domestic law for all and sundry, via the legitimate expectation route, then, I would imagine, the decision would, of course, be quite problematic. In other words, the effect of the decision is simply that, *in relation to the appellants*, the content of the international treaty must have some force in domestic law via the legitimate expectation which had arisen. Since the decision of the CCJ rests solely on timing (i.e., the substantive expectation to the procedure under the relevant treaty), little can be extrapolated from the decision, even if the CCJ might have endorsed decisions such as *Teoh* where the legitimate expectation was only of a procedural benefit. In *Joseph*, the legitimate expectation was 'procedural' (in the sense outlined above) and, as such, can hardly be said to involve macro-political considerations, which the courts should properly avoid adjudicating on. Therefore, the decision is almost an inevitable one when the subject matter of the expectation and the consequences for the condemned prisoner is concerned. So far, the result seems unassailable, if it is accepted that it does not create any general binding principle of law, but is clearly a result driven solely by the facts presented.

C. Conceptual Difficulties

Legitimate expectations can arise in a myriad of circumstances, in particular the three classes identified by the recent decision of the Court of Appeal in *ex p Murphy*,[58] namely, first, if the public authority has distinctly promised to consult those affected or potentially affected, then ordinarily it must consult (the paradigm case of procedural expectation). Second, if the public authority has distinctly promised to preserve existing policy for a specific person or group who would be substantially affected by the change, then ordinarily it must keep its promise (substantive

---

58. [2008] EWCA Civ 755 (CA Eng).

expectation). Third, if, without any promise, the public authority has established a policy distinctly and substantially affecting a specific person or group who in the circumstances was in reason entitled to rely on its continuance and did so, then ordinarily it must consult before effecting any change (the secondary case of procedural expectation).

The first point to note about legitimate expectations is that they give legal force to what are 'non-rights'. So, a 'change in policy' or an 'express promise to preserve an existing policy' falls in that category. They are transformed into a legally enforceable right if they give rise to a legitimate expectation, which occurs broadly where the authority has 'distinctly promised to consult' or 'distinctly promised to preserve existing policy' in relation to those affected (or those potentially or substantially affected) or has 'established a policy distinctly and substantially affecting a specific person or group.' So, in *Joseph*, there was a clear promise to preserve an existing policy, and a potential change in policy by the executive, to a 'specific group or person' – the condemned men. The case for finding a legitimate expectation on the facts was a compelling one. It cannot be correct to suggest that a legitimate expectation cannot arise in relation to a process which originates from an international treaty. Before the court pronounces on the 'change in policy' or the 'express promise made,' the applicant has no legal right. The legitimate expectation is the route by which the 'non-right' is clothed with legality. When that is accomplished – by establishing that a legitimate expectation has arisen – then that 'non-right' becomes a 'legal right' which the court will give effect to. In this case, it is the legitimate expectation that gives the international process legal validity in domestic law *in relation to the appellants* – for if it were already 'recognized by law' or a 'process recognized by law' then surely there would be no need to have recourse to legitimate expectations!

It is a constitutional principle that unincorporated treaties have no binding force in domestic law unless they are incorporated into domestic law through legislation. Constitutional principles do not exist in a vacuum, so any attempt at delineating the boundaries of a principle without regard to the basis for that principle is bound to be problematic. In *ex parte Brind*, it was noted that:

> it is a *constitutional principle* that a treaty obligation, undertaken by the Crown as a matter of prerogative power, can only be woven into the domestic law if Parliament so decrees. It follows that the court cannot itself purport to incorporate an *obligation* since it would be arrogating to itself the exercise of an authority only vested in the legislature.[59]

---

59. [1991] AC 696 (HL) 709 (emphasis added).

The limitation on the courts' power is in relation to obligation, but legitimate expectations are clearly recognized principles of domestic public law. That their content in the exceptional case is derived in part from a treaty obligation is beside the point. As a result, the constitutional principle enunciated above cannot, and should not, be applied without exception, for it would be contrary to the rule of law that the executive can act arbitrarily or abuse its powers, while the courts remain powerless. The question of what process can be recognized as legal in any legal system is a question of national law. One cannot but agree that under our Constitutions law is defined as common law and statute. So, if the courts say that a particular international process has domestic effect (by whatever means), it makes that process part of the common law of that jurisdiction.

The courts are very cognizant of their role under the constitution and that only parliament has the power to legislate, but, when faced with deliberate and calculated actions by the executive to frustrate the legitimate expectations of a specific group of persons, should the courts be impotent to act to ensure that there is no abuse of power? Surely not! The concept of substantive legitimate expectations was born out of the struggle the courts had in deciding the circumstances in which a public authority should be bound by its promise made to, or previous practice in relation to, a specific group or persons. The courts are now unanimous in their view that that would be where reneging on that promise or changing the policy by the public authority amounts to an abuse of power.[60] If the courts were able to overcome arguments that accepting substantive legitimate expectations amounted to usurping the executive function, why should it shirk when the argument is made that it would be assuming the legislative function? We all now know that executive power is subject to judicial review, not only administrative powers.[61] The separation of powers doctrine requires the courts to be restrained, but when confronted with such a blatant abuse of power by the executive, it should not allow the executive to simply hide behind the curtain of parliamentary sovereignty!

Given the narrow nature of the doctrine, the same way that substantive legitimate expectations do not run the risk that the court is assuming the role of the decision maker, its application to international treaties (in the *specific* manner outlined above) would hardly generally result in the court assuming the role of the legislator. As a result of the decision

---

60. *Ex p Coughlan* [2001] QB 213 (CA Eng).
61. *CO Williams Construction Ltd v Blackman* [1995] 1 WLR 102 (PC Bdos).

of the CCJ in *Joseph*, the constitutional principle relating to the effect of international treaties and domestic law must yield to any *legitimate* expectation found to exist. Proving such an expectation is not as easy as it might appear.

To reiterate, the CCJ in *Joseph* noted the following factors which contributed to the establishment of the legitimate expectation: (a) ratification (which clearly was not of itself sufficient to found a legitimate expectation – properly understood); (b) positive statements by the state to abide by the Convention; (c) an established practice by the state of allowing condemned persons to allow their petitions to be processed before execution; and (d) Parliament in making that amendment impliedly recognized that it was the practice and indeed the obligation of the state to await the Commission's process, at least for some period of time. In this respect, the question always is 'to what has the public authority, whether by practice or by promise, committed itself?'[62] The government of Barbados specifically committed itself not to execute the condemned men before the final determination of their cases before international bodies. Therefore, the substantive legitimate expectation was to the procedure that ought to be followed in the case of the condemned persons *viz.* the state has to await the completion of the international processes before it could lawfully execute them. This meant that in relation to those condemned persons, the treaty must have legal effect in domestic law, for clearly the process that the state must await completion originates from the treaty obligation.

For the following reasons, the decision of the CCJ in *Joseph* will not result in the 'wholesale enforcement of unincorporated treaties': (a) the need to find, *inter alia*, a 'distinct promise to consult' or 'distinct promise to preserve existing policy' or 'established policy' in order to establish the legitimacy of the expectation; and (b) that expectation must be made specifically to those affected (or those potentially or substantially affected) or a distinct group of persons. These factors narrow the scope of the doctrine, as it necessarily should be – in this case, to the treaty obligations in relation to the condemned prisoners, and in circumstances in which the expectation arose were quite limited. The CCJ also referred to other reasons, including: (a) the desirability of giving the condemned person every opportunity to secure the commutation of his sentence; (b) the direct access which the treaty affords him to the international law process; (c) the disproportion between giving effect to the state's interest in avoiding delay even for a limited period in the carrying out of a death sentence; and (d) the finality of an execution.

---

62. *Ex p Bibi* [2002] 1 WLR 237 (CA Eng).

5. Substantive Legitimate Expectations

The CCJ began its discussion of legal protection for the legitimate expectations by asking 'whether, and if so to what extent, the legitimate expectation of the respondent should produce a substantive benefit?'[63] The issue of whether the court should give effect to a substantive legitimate expectation, the court observed, 'is still a matter of ongoing judicial debate,' citing *ex p Hamble Fisheries*.[64] If that issue was discussed in the context of the approaches of final courts of different jurisdictions, then that remark would be unassailable, but it is clearly understood that ever since *ex p Coughlan* the debate relating to whether the English common law should recognize substantive legitimate expectations had ended in favour of allowing such expectations. The CCJ correctly referenced *ex p Coughlan*, noting that the legitimate expectation therein was 'rooted in an express promise, repeatedly made to a select, identifiable group of persons, that had the character of a contract' and that 'unwarranted frustration of the legitimate expectation [was equated] with an abuse of power and the case was treated almost like an estoppel in private law, justifying a standard of review by the courts that was higher than would normally be the case.'[65]

The review of the authorities dealing with the question of the standard of review was scant indeed, with the court referring to only two other decisions, one being that of Simmons CJ in *Leacock v AG*.[66] There was no question that the decision of the CCJ was rooted in substantive legitimate expectations, contrary to the view that '[t]he CCJ perhaps confused the question of whether such an expectation was substantive or procedural.'[67] This, however, does not detract from the real issue being raised. The issue raised in this decision concerned whether the appellants had a substantive right that the state would not execute them pending the determination of their petitions before the international human rights bodies. This clearly is a substantive legitimate expectation. It was not rooted in any expectation that they would be allowed a right to be heard or make representations before they are executed. The CCJ can be faulted for not being as rigorous as one might have expected, since the court was accepting that substantive legitimate expectations form part of Barbados law. However, the court was very cognizant of its role in

---

63. *Joseph* (n 1) 119.
64. Ibid.
65. Ibid.
66. (2005) 68 WIR 181 (HC Bdos).
67. R. Antoine, *Commonwealth Caribbean Law and Legal Systems* (2nd edn, Routledge-Cavendish, London 2008) 224.

relation to substantive legitimate expectations and how it was to resolve the legal and policy implications of accepting that doctrine.

6. The Role of the Court

Lord Bingham in *ex p Coughlan* observed that 'the courts' role in relation to the third category is *still controversial*; but, as we hope to show, it is now clarified by authority.'[68] Notwithstanding the CCJ's very limited review of the case law relating to substantive legitimate expectations, it was able confidently to assert that:

> In matters such as these, *courts must carry out a balancing exercise*. The court must weigh the competing interests of the individual, who has placed legitimate trust in the State consistently to adhere to its declared policy, and that of the public authority, which seeks to pursue its policy objectives through some new measure. The court must make an assessment of how to strike the balance or be prepared to review the fairness of any such assessment if it had been made previously by the public authority. [69]

The CCJ then proceeded to apply that test to the factual matrix before it. It noted that, on the one hand, there was the legitimate expectation of the condemned men that they 'will be permitted a reasonable time to pursue their petitions with the Commission with the consequence that any report resulting from the Inter-American process will be available for consideration by the Barbados Privy Council';[70] whereas, on the other, 'there is whatever the state may advance as an overriding interest in refusing to await completion of the international process before carrying out the death sentence.'[71]

The CCJ noted that apart from the time constraints of the *Pratt*[72] time limit, the Barbados government claimed 'no overriding interest in putting the condemned men to death without allowing their legitimate expectation to be fulfilled.'[73] It therefore concluded that:

> In our view, to deny the substantive benefit promised by the creation of the legitimate expectation here would not be proportionate having regard to the distress and possible detriment that will be unfairly occasioned to men who hope to be allowed a reasonable time to pursue their petitions and receive a favourable report from the international body. *The substantive benefit the condemned men*

---

68. *Ex p Coughlan* (n 60) 59 (emphasis added).
69. *Joseph* (n 1) 124 (emphasis added).
70. Ibid 125.
71. Ibid.
72. *Pratt v AG* (n 3).
73. *Joseph* (n 1).

legitimately expect is actually as to the procedure that should be followed before their sentences are executed. It does not extend to requiring the BPC to abide by the recommendations in the report.[74]

The CCJ agreed that the substantive legitimate expectation that the condemned person had was to the procedure that they expected to be followed in their case, and presumably in for all persons on death row whose cases were before an international body. The CCJ recognized that the state had no compelling interest, apart from abiding by the *Pratt* guideline, which, it noted, was never meant to be applied as rigidly as it seems to have been applied by Caribbean courts and administrators of justice alike.[75] Since the legitimate expectation was to a substantive right (although, exceptionally, it was to a procedure under the relevant treaty) where broader political issues and considerations would hardly militate against giving effect to it, the decision of the CCJ in *Joseph* does not risk fettering the discretion of the executive or assuming the mantle of the decision maker.

7. Setting Limits

The CCJ anticipated some of the arguments that might be made against the use of legitimate expectations in this context. As a result, it cautioned that any '*protracted delay* on the part of the international body in disposing of the proceedings initiated before it by a condemned person, *would justify the State, notwithstanding the existence of the condemned man's legitimate expectation, proceedings to carry out an execution before completion of the international process.*'[76] In light of the agenda of these human rights bodies to abolish the death penalty throughout their member states, they could very well, in light of the CCJ's judgment, prolong their processes to extend the period of the condemned person on death row, with the result that the *Pratt*[77] time limit would be breached, resulting in commutation of the death sentence to life imprisonment. This qualification by the CCJ preserves the right of the state to act as it so desires, despite the legitimate expectation, when there is an inexcusable and protracted delay in determining such cases before those international bodies. The rationale for this, the CCJ noted, was grounded in either the legitimate expectation itself, meaning that it would last so long as there was no undue delay from the international bodies, or that the legitimate

---

74. Ibid (emphasis added).
75. Ibid.
76. Ibid 126 (emphasis added).
77. *Pratt v AG* (n 3).

expectation may properly be thwarted by 'an overriding public interest in support of which the state may justifiably modify its compliance with the treaty.'[78]

The CCJ, therefore, concluded that the reading of the death warrants to the respondents breached their legitimate expectations and it also 'constituted a breach of [their] right to the protection of the law.'[79] In one sentence, the CCJ unwittingly gave constitutional status to a concept that had only just breathed life less than eight years prior, and whose boundaries are still being delineated. That newly-found constitutional principle 'can only be defeated by some overriding interest of the State.'[80] If the state 'imposes reasonable time limits within which a condemned man' may appeal to such international bodies, then it cannot be said that in so doing the state has not shown a good faith intention to abide by its treaty obligations.[81] Even if such a right to petition such bodies exists, the state 'cannot reasonably be expected to delay indefinitely the carrying out of a sentence, even a sentence of death, lawfully passed by its domestic courts pending the completion of a petition by an international body.'[82] This was stressed repeatedly by the CCJ, indicating that although its conclusion mirrors that of *Lewis* 'save that the obligation of the State to await the outcome of the international process is not in our judgment open-ended,' it followed a different route.[83]

8. Conclusion

The CCJ's decision in *Joseph and Boyce* attempted to emancipate Commonwealth Caribbean jurisprudence from the strained legal analysis of the Privy Council in *Thomas* and *Lewis*. The CCJ jettisoned the notion that the due process clause or the protection of the law clause applied to any legal process, including rights under international human rights treaties, thereby extending the criminal justice system of Commonwealth Caribbean states to the effect that a condemned prisoner would not be executed until the completion of all these processes. The route by which the CCJ achieved this death-knell is troublesome, for it seemingly runs counter to the constitutional principle that international treaties do not form part of the domestic legal process until they have been incorporated by the legislature. This was the same objection that plagued the reasoning of the Privy Council in *Thomas* and *Lewis* – although not the

---

78. *Joseph* (n1) 126.
79. Ibid 128.
80. Ibid 130.
81. Ibid.
82. Ibid.
83. Ibid 132.

only one. As argued above, the rule of law dictates that the courts, as guardians of the Constitution and the rights of citizens, should not be impotent to provide a remedy where there has been an abuse of power by the executive. Where the executive has distinctly promised to preserve existing policy (that condemned prisoners will not be executed before the final determination of the international process) for a specific person or group (condemned prisoners) who would be substantially affected by the change (suffer death), then ordinarily it must keep its promise. This is the substantive legitimate expectation – to frustrate that expectation where there is no significant public interest consideration militating against it is an abuse of power. The CCJ's decision in *Joseph* clearly shows that the courts will not countenance such, and where appropriate will not hesitate to act.

Human Trafficking Legislation in the Commonwealth Caribbean: Effective or Effected?

Kamille Adair

1. Introduction

Human Trafficking, contrary to appearances, is not a 'new' global phenomenon. But the issue has increasingly impinged on the conscience of governments and policymakers for various reasons. Smuggling in human beings has expanded from '[a] small-scale cross border activity affecting a handful of countries' into a global multimillion-dollar activity.[1] Although information concerning the actual number of persons affected by trafficking is far from certain, it is estimated that approximately 800,000 people are smuggled across borders annually, with about 80 per cent of transnational victims being women and girls and up to 50 per cent being minors.[2]

Human trafficking now occupies a place of high priority on political agendas throughout the region and attempts have been made by Caribbean governments in recent years to combat smuggling in persons within and across national borders. This has resulted in the introduction of anti-trafficking legislation within the last 10 years addressing human trafficking as a transnational crime in three Caribbean jurisdictions. Leading the way in 2003, Belize enacted its Trafficking in Persons (Prohibition) Act 2003-18. The Guyana Combating of Trafficking in Persons Act 2005-2 followed two years later, and finally, another two years later, Jamaica enacted its Trafficking in Persons (Prevention, Suppression and Punishment) Act 2007-1. These statutes outlaw human trafficking, impose stringent sanctions for committing or participating in the crime, and provide extensive protection for and assistance to the victims of trafficking.

The sudden introduction of these statutes in Belize, Guyana and Jamaica is less a response to the problem of human trafficking and more a reaction to external pressures. The exercise of United States hegemony,

---

1. J. Bhabba, 'Trafficking, Smuggling and Human Rights,' Migration Information Source Homepage <http://www.migrationinformation.org/Feature/display.cfm?ID=294> accessed 29 Jul 2010.
2. US Department of State, *Trafficking in Persons Report 2008* (Washington DC 2008), 7 <http://www.state.gov/g/tip/rls/tiprpt/> accessed 30 Jul 2010.

through its blacklisting and sanctioning process under the US Victims of Trafficking and Violence Protection Act 2000,[3] is the single most powerful stimulant in effecting the introduction of statutory regimes against human trafficking in the region. To satisfy the United States' minimum requirements, the Acts transplanted the Palermo Protocol on the Prevention, Suppression and Punishment of Trafficking in Persons and the Convention against Transnational Crime, both adopted in 2000.[4] There was no meaningful assessment of the phenomenon of human trafficking in the Caribbean, an essential prerequisite for good law-making. Further, the interaction between the domestic legislative process and international standards in these countries resulted in statutes that are not tailored for the Caribbean region. Rather, they embody carbon copies of the international standards, with their peculiarities and deficiencies.

2. The Impact of the United States' Minimum Standards and Tier System

Through domestic legislation and national policy, the United States exerted severe pressure on the three Caribbean countries to enact anti-trafficking in persons legislation. However, the Victims of Trafficking and Violence Protection Act (TVPA) 2000 did not itself provide a model for lawmaking. The TVPA states that it 'is the policy of the United States not to provide non-humanitarian, non-trade-related foreign assistance to any government that: (1) does not comply with Minimum Standards for the elimination of trafficking; and (2) is not making significant efforts to bring itself into compliance with such standards.'[5]

A. The Minimum Standards

The Minimum Standards for countries of origin, transit or destination, or OTD Countries as they are called in the Act, are outlined in section 108 of the TVPA. Section 108(a) provides that:

1. The government of the country should prohibit severe forms of trafficking in persons and punish acts of such trafficking.

---

3. United States Victims of Trafficking and Violence Protection Act of 2000, 22 USCA §7101(2000), Pub L 106-386, Div A, § 102, Oct 28, 2000, 114 Stat 1466 ('TVPA').
4. Protocol to Prevent, Suppress and Punish Trafficking in Persons, Especially Women and Children, Supplementing the United Nations Convention Against Transnational Organized Crime (adopted 15 Nov 2000, entered into force 25 Dec 2003) 2237 UNTS 319 ('Palermo Protocol'), United Nations Convention Against Transnational Organized Crime (adopted 15 Nov 2000, entered into force 29 Sep 2003) 2225 UNTS 209.
5. TVPA (n 3) s 110.

2. For the knowing commission of any act of sex trafficking involving force, fraud, coercion, or in which the victim of sex trafficking is a child incapable of giving meaningful consent, or of trafficking which includes rape or kidnapping or which causes a death, the government of the country should prescribe punishment commensurate with that for grave crimes, such as forcible sexual assault.

3. For the knowing commission of any act of a severe form of trafficking in persons, the government of the country should prescribe punishment that is sufficiently stringent to deter and that adequately reflects the heinous nature of the offense.

4. The government of the country should make serious and sustained efforts to eliminate severe forms of trafficking in persons

In understanding the reasons for the introduction of anti-trafficking legislations in all three jurisdictions, the 'collateral consequences' rationale for state compliance with international obligations put forward by Oona Hathaway is relevant.[6] Put simply, developing states were obliged to support the international fight against human trafficking because of the assertion of political and economic pressure by the United States under the mandate of its domestic legislation – the TVPA.[7]

B. The Tier System

The United States Department of State produces an Annual Trafficking in Persons (TIP) Report, categorizing countries in four tiers based on their compliance with United States' Minimum Standards for the elimination of trafficking in persons. Non-compliant states receive a negative 'tier 3' rating while more compliant states are dispersed between the Tier 2 watchlist, Tier 2 and Tier 1.[8] The Tier 1 listing is the most favourable and includes countries whose governments fully comply with the Act's Minimum Standards. The Tier 2 designation is for countries whose governments have not fully complied with the Act's Minimum Standards but are making significant efforts to bring themselves into compliance with those standards. Countries are placed on the Tier 2 watchlist if, in addition to this, (a) the absolute number of victims of severe forms of trafficking is very significant or is increasing significantly, or (b) there is a failure to provide evidence of increasing

---

6. O. Hathaway, 'Why Do States Commit to Human Rights Treaties?' (2007) 51 J Conflict Resol 588.

7. K. Bravo, 'Exploring the Analogy Between Modern Trafficking in Humans and the Trans-Atlantic Slave Trade' (2007) 25 Boston U Intl LJ 207, 228.

8. See, e.g., C. Ribando Seelke, 'Trafficking in Persons in Latin America and the Caribbean,' CRS Report for Congress (16 Oct 2009) RL3320, 9 <http://assets.opencrs.com/rpts/RL33200_20091016.pdf> accessed 29 Jul 2010.

efforts to combat severe forms of trafficking in persons from the previous year, or (c) the determination that the country or territory is making significant efforts to bring themselves into compliance with Minimum Standards was based on commitments by the country to take additional future steps over the next year. The lowest level, Tier 3, is a designation for countries whose governments do not fully comply with the Minimum Standards and are not making significant efforts to do so.

Countries placed in the lowest tier are threatened with economic sanctions in the form of withheld non-humanitarian, non-trade-related assistance from the United States.[9] This reinforces the economic stronghold of the United States over smaller developing countries, like those of the Caribbean, which are heavily dependent on United States economic aid.

C. Caribbean Governments Respond to Tier 3 Listings

Belize, Guyana and Jamaica reacted swiftly to the threats of economic sanctions and the United States blacklisting through Tier 3 listings. Belize was so listed in 2003 but jumped quickly to the Tier 2 watchlist after enacting their Act later that same year.[10] They were commended by United States President George Bush for 'swift and positive action' following the report.[11] Similar tier progression resulted for Guyana in 2005 and Jamaica in 2007 after the passing of legislation specific to human trafficking.[12] The Jamaica Act outlines as its objects the Minimum Standards prescribed by the TVPA.[13] All three statutes adopt the largely law enforcement framework outlined in the Minimum Standards, placing emphasis on the prosecution and punishment of offenders in contrast to safeguarding the human rights of the victims.

Critics have noted that prior to the blacklisting, little or no effort was made by the governments of Belize, Guyana and Jamaica to alleviate the problem of human trafficking.[14] During the debates on the legislation in Jamaica, Opposition Member of Parliament Olivia Grange expressed

---

9. Panos Productions, 'Human Trafficking in the Caribbean: The Experience of Seven Countries' <http://www.panosinst.org/productions/> accessed 17 December 2008.
10. US Department of State, *Trafficking in Persons Report 2003* (Washington DC 2003) <http://www.state.gov/g/tip/rls/tiprpt/> accessed 5 Aug 2010.
11. President GW Bush, Presidential Determination 2003-35 (9 Sep 2003) <http://www.state.gov/g/tip/rls/rpt/25017.htm#belize> accessed 17 December 2008.
12. US Department of State, *Trafficking in Persons Report 2005* (Washington DC 2005), *Trafficking in Persons Report 2007* (Washington DC 2007) <http://www.state.gov/g/tip/rls/tiprpt/> accessed 30 Jul 2010.
13. Jamaica Trafficking in Persons (Prevention, Suppression and Punishment) Act 2007-1 s 3.
14. A. Novelo, 'Belize Gets Cracking on Human Trafficking' *The Reporter*, 4 Aug 2006. D. Roper, 'Who Are These Victims of Human Trafficking?' *Jamaica Observer*, 5 Mar 2006.

concern that it took the government five years to 'move from the position where we recognize that human trafficking especially as it affects women and children exists' by signing the United Nations Protocol to enacting legislation.[15] Like many others, she attributed the speed with which the Act was introduced solely to the US tier assessments.[16] She also questioned why the government was enacting legislation covering only one of the protocols, the human trafficking protocol, and not the other two dealing with migrant smuggling and trafficking in firearms.[17]

Dr Peter Phillips, then minister of national security, rejected the claim that the legislation was in response to 'any pressure or desire to please any other country.' He said, 'We do it and we bring it because the protection of the people of Jamaica warrants this legislation coming here.'[18] He justified the interest of the United States in the anti-trafficking campaigns of other countries as a manifestation of 'international cooperation,' which was necessary to successfully confront human trafficking in its international context.[19] Despite these protestations, other Caribbean government officials readily confirmed that legislation was prompted by tier placements.[20] Some government officials have expressed immense delight at an improved tier placement[21] or great distress at a slip in ranking.[22] The Minister of Foreign Affairs of Belize, Godfrey Smith, who was charged with leading the debate on the Bill through Parliament, acknowledged plainly that the tier ranking was the sole motivating factor for the speedy drafting of the legislation. He said:

> The impetus for the legislation was simple. The US government, based on flimsy data, placed Belize in the bottom-most category of countries that were taking measures to combat trafficking in persons. This happened without any notice to the government and we were shocked at it. Even the then US Ambassador to Belize at

15. Jamaica Hansard HR vol 32(2) 650, 656–57 (21 Nov 2006).

16. Ibid 657.

17. Ibid.

18. Ibid 678.

19. Ibid.

20. See Gerald Westby Commissioner of Police of Belize quoted in 'Belize Gets Cracking on Human Trafficking' (n 14), Audrey Sewell, Director of the Justice Training Institute of Jamaica, quoted in Jamaica Information Service, 'Justice Training Institute Conducts Anti-Human Trafficking Seminars' (Kingston 2 Jul 2008) <http://www.jis.gov.jm/justice/html/20080702t100000-0500_15854_ jis_justice_training_institute_conducts_anti_human_trafficking_seminars.asp> accessed 30 Jul 2010.

21. Senator Colin Campbell, then Information and Development Minister quoted in Jamaica Information Service, 'Jamaica Making Some Progress in Combating Human Trafficking – Campbell' (Kingston 7 Jun 2006) <http://www.jis.gov.jm/development/html/20060606T100000-0500_9035_ JIS_JAMAICA_MAKING_SOME_PROGRESS_IN_COMBATING_HUMAN_TRAFFICKING___ CAMPBELL.asp> accessed 30 Jul 2010.

22. 'Guyana Shouldn't Be on US Trafficking-In-Persons Radar – Manickchand' *Stabroeck News*, 6 June 2008.

the time expressed surprise. If we did nothing, it meant that Belize stood to be affected by the withholding of different forms of aid to Belize by the US. We therefore quickly drafted legislation and set up a national committee to address the issue. We took it through all three readings of parliament without objection from the Opposition. Some months later we were upgraded to category 2.[23]

3. Incorporation of the Palermo Protocol

Although the provisions of the TVPA and the anti-trafficking statutes of the Caribbean region are similar in some of their provisions, the precise form of the TVPA was not adopted in the Caribbean. The TVPA does not set out a comprehensive legislative regime that can be easily transplanted because it includes amendments to existing United States legislation. It devotes much of its attention to laying down the minimum requirements demanded of other countries and the sanctions for non-compliance. The Palermo Protocol 2000, which was ratified by all three Caribbean countries, provided a recent and more comprehensive framework for satisfying the United States' Minimum Standards.[24] The three Caribbean territories transplanted it with its peculiarities and its deficiencies.

A. Why States Comply with Treaty Obligations

Oona Hathaway offers two central dynamics that influence state decisions to commit to or comply with human rights treaties: domestic legal enforcement and collateral consequences.[25] The first examines how the treaty will be enforced against the government within the state itself. Hathaway highlights the absence of an international enforcing body for most human rights treaties making domestic legal enforcement the determinative factor. Where powerful extra-governmental actors can hold the government accountable to its international obligations, there tends to be a higher level of commitment.[26] One expects these forces to exist to a greater extent in democratic states.[27]

---

23. Statement by Godfrey Smith (Personal email correspondence 20 October 2008).
24. All three states are Parties to the Palermo Protocol (n 4). Belize and Guyana acceded to the Protocol on 26 September 2003 and 14 September 2004, respectively. Jamaica ratified the Protocol on 29 September 2003 after signing the instrument in February 2002. In order to become Parties to the Protocol, states must first be Party to the UN Convention against Transnational Crime, ibid. Belize and Guyana became Parties to this Convention on the same day as their accession to the Protocol. Jamaica signed the instrument on 16 September 2001 and subsequently ratified on the same day as its ratification of the Protocol.
25. Hathaway (n 6).
26. Ibid 593.
27. Ibid.

The second, collateral consequences, arises from the reaction of domestic or transnational actors to the state's decision to commit to a treaty and may prove to be equally, if not more, vital in influencing state compliance than the scope for legal enforcement.[28] On the domestic level, the existence of a vast number of human rights pressure and advocacy groups, particularly non-governmental organizations (NGOs), increases the probability of a state complying with international treaty obligations.[29] Collateral consequences can also originate from transnational actors whose reaction to a state's compliance is of particular concern to the state.[30] Collateral consequences, Hathaway highlights, may also take the form of the withholding of foreign aid, a decision by investors to invest or to withhold funds, or even through negative publicity that shapes the way a country is viewed by the international community, which brings with it far-reaching consequences of its own.[31] The rate of ratification of a treaty within a region may also prompt a state's decision to commit to such a treaty as a means of securing smooth relations with neighbouring states by demonstrating its commitment to shared norms.[32]

The Convention against Transnational Organized Crime and the Palermo Protocol on trafficking are not governed by an international enforcement mechanism. Using Hathaway's model to rationalize not only ratification but compliance with these treaty obligations, there is no indication that private entities, NGOs or human rights advocacy groups attempted to hold governments of Belize, Guyana and Jamaica accountable to these international obligations. In Jamaica for example, the five-year lapse between signing the Protocol in February of 2002 and the introduction of the Act in February 2007 is indicative of a lack of pressure on the government to provide for domestic legal enforcement of its international obligations under the Protocol.

B. Functional Legal Transplantation

It is not doubted that human trafficking is an issue affecting Caribbean territories and as such, legislative intervention is welcomed.[33]

---

28. Ibid 596.
29. Ibid.
30. Ibid.
31. Ibid.
32. Ibid 597.
33. This is clearly indicated in the study of the International Organization of Migration, *Exploratory Assessment of Trafficking in Persons in the Caribbean* (Washington DC June 2005) 1–2 <http://www.oas.org/atip/Caribbean%20Research%202005.pdf> accessed 30 Jul 2010. Although unable to definitively establish precise scope of the problem, the study states that 'trafficking in persons does exist at some level in all of the countries included in this research.'

Legal drafters are expected to take into account the state's international obligations with a view to ensuring there will be no conflict between the two. Consequently, international law not only informs domestic legislation but often serves as a catalyst for drafters to expedite the legislative process.[34] It has been argued that countries 'cannot claim good records in areas such as international human rights, protection of the environment and anti-corruption efforts without importing some foreign or international models.'[35] Therefore, it is expected that in order to meet international commitments and coexist with international neighbours, domestic lawmaking must necessarily include some transplantation. The Palermo Protocol represents the international standard for the combating of human trafficking. Domestic legislation must have reference to the Protocol. The question is whether the Caribbean was well served by wholesale transplantation of the Protocol in domestic legislation.

Using Jonathan Miller's typology of legal transplants, Caribbean human trafficking statutes could be described as 'externally-dictated transplants.'[36] Miller indicates that the externally-dictated transplant will operate irrespective of how efficient the transplant proves to be in the recipient country as long as the external pressure or incentives outweigh the inefficiency.[37] It has been suggested that any of these transplants can be successful regardless of its origin, if it is functional and able to serve the receiving legal system well.[38] The success of the transplant depends on an assessment of the social and political context into which it is placed and its ability to conform to its new environment. Even an externally-dictated transplant may prove effective if it is suited to the social demands of the recipient state and is, in that regard, functional.[39]

Functionalism, however, demands an assessment of the extant circumstances in the recipient state.[40] Legislation that targets a particular societal issue should be preceded by an assessment of the nature and scope of that issue. It is only through this systematic evaluation that provision can be made to effectively tackle the problem.[41] There is no evidence of a proper evaluation process in the three Caribbean territories before the introduction of the respective anti-trafficking statutes. As a result, they do not reflect a response tailored to the needs of these

---

34. H. Xanthaki, 'Legal Transplants in Legislation: Defusing the Trap' (2008) 57 ICLQ 659, 659.
35. J. Miller, 'A Typology of Legal Transplants: Using Sociology, Legal History and Argentine Examples to Explain the Transplant Process' (2003) 51 Am J Comp L 839, 839.
36. Ibid 843–67.
37. Ibid 868.
38. Xanthaki (n 34) 662.
39. Ibid.
40. Ibid.
41. V. Crabbe, *Legislative Drafting* (Cavendish Publishing, London 1993) 8.

particular countries. The Acts were developed substantially, if not entirely, on what the legislators perceived the expectations of the TIP Office to be. The three governments failed to conduct their own, context-specific assessment of the issue in its Caribbean and local reality and as such, these acts have not proved, and possibly will not prove, to be an effective means of combating human trafficking in the Caribbean.

4. Defining Exploitation

A. The Consent Debate and the Palermo Protocol

During the negotiation of the Palermo Protocol there was much debate concerning whether the offence of trafficking could be established irrespective of the victim's consent. This debate was based solely on the consideration of whether a woman could consent to prostitution or other sexual exploitation. Although the concept of trafficking has been expanded beyond that of the sexual exploitation of women, the debate continues to permeate modern discourse on human trafficking. This focus diverts much-needed attention from other areas of the trafficking dilemma. The differences of opinion concerning the issue of consent which clouded the drafting process of the Palermo Protocol, greatly affected the definition of trafficking which emerged.

There are two dominant feminist positions on the issue of consent. There are those who articulate that there can never be consent to prostitution.[42] Others argue that prostitution is a legitimate activity which an individual, a woman, may opt to engage in for her own purposes.[43] The anti-choice feminists argue that prostitution is inherently exploitative and as such cannot be consented to. This position of the radical feminist Left-lobby groups in the United States was very instrumental in the formulation of the TVPA 2000.[44] In their estimation, all movement and migration having a nexus to paid sexual labour constitute trafficking

---

42. This position is supported by several scholars. See K. Miriam, 'Stopping the Traffic in Women: Power, Agency and Abolition in Feminist Debates over Sex-Trafficking' (2005) 36 J Social Phil 1. NGOs have also backed this position. The Coalition Against Trafficking in Women is one of the most avid supporters of this position.

43. The Global Alliance Against Traffic in Women, an alliance of over 90 non-governmental organizations supported this position along with the Human Rights Caucus. Members of the Human Rights Caucus included the following NGOs: International Human Rights Law Group (United States), Foundation Against Trafficking in Women (Netherlands), Global Alliance Against Traffic in Women (Thailand), Asian Women's Human Rights Council (Philippines, India), La Strada (Poland, Ukraine, Czech Republic), Fundación Esperanza (Colombia, Netherlands, Spain), Ban Ying (Germany), Foundation for Women (Thailand), and KOK-German NGO Network against Trafficking in Women.

44. J. Berman, 'The Left, The Right, and the Prostitute: The Making of US Anti-trafficking in Persons Policy' (2006) 14 Tul J Intl & Comp L 269, 272.

in women.[45] There exists no distinction between forced and voluntary movement for sex work. They say that prostitution constitutes a form of trafficking as it enforces the subordination of women by men and male dominance.[46] The central premise of this argument is that 'men create the demand; women are the supply.'[47] As Kathy Miriam puts it, '[t]he "sex work" model of agency occludes the reality that it is men's demand that makes prostitution intelligible and legitimate as a means of survival for women in the first place.'[48] The conclusion is that prostitution is inherently exploitative, whether as an act of violence against women's bodies, or as a practice which, by commercializing women's bodies and sexuality reinforces 'traditional hierarchical power structures premised on male dominance.'[49]

The pro-choice/pro-prostitution position suggests that women should be allowed to choose to engage in prostitution for various reasons. Miriam identified two variations in the pro-sex-work caucus which she gave the sobriquets the 'economist' and 'expressivist' models of agency. The economist approach advances that women engage in prostitution as a means of gainful employment as it provides a source of income for themselves and their families. Such a position is advanced by the Global Alliance Against Traffic in Women (GAATW), which highlights the fact that many women engage in prostitution because of a desire for a better life, their situation of poverty and the substantial profits that can be made from the trade. Kamala Kempadoo advances support for this position arguing that sexuality may be viewed as an 'economic resource which may be self-activated and used to benefit the individual or family.'[50] She reiterated that:

> ... a woman (or) man may opt – in the face of very limited alternatives and opportunities for economic participation – for sex work as an income-generating strategy. Prostitution may then become work that women and men consciously decide to take up. The righteous call to end the traffic of women collides with a reality that makes sex work a viable alternative for economic advancement.[51]

---

45. Ibid 270.
46. J. Halley et al., 'From the International to the Local in Feminist Legal Responses to Rape, Prostitution/Sex Work, and Sex Trafficking: Four Studies in Contemporary Governance Feminism' (2006) 29 Harv JL & Gender 335, 349.
47. Miriam (n 42). She extracted the phrase from the title of an article written by D. Hughes, 'Men Create the Demand, Women Are the Supply,' Lecture on Sexual Exploitation, Queen Sophia Center, Valencia Spain (Nov 2000) <http://www.uri.edu/artsci/wms/hughes/demand.htm> accessed 30 Jul 2010.
48. Miriam ibid 9.
49. J. Chuang, 'Redirecting the Debate over Trafficking in Women: Definitions, Paradigms and Contexts' (1998) 11 Harv Hum Rts J 65, 85–86.
50. K. Kempadoo, 'The War on Human Trafficking in the Caribbean' (2007) 49 Race & Class 79, 83.
51. Ibid 83–84.

The 'expressivist' approach is that a woman's ability to consent to prostitution secures for her autonomy and an exercise of her fundamental rights and freedoms. This approach defends for women the right to self-determination, the right to work, and the right to self-expression. It equates a woman's choice to engage in prostitution as a form of self-actualization. Pro-choice feminists advocate that the act of prostitution is not inherently exploitative as is suggested by the abolitionists. It is the general contempt of the profession that invites exploitation and abuse within the sex industry. Pro-choice advocates call on governments to regulate the sex industry and safeguard labour rights for sex workers through decriminalization and unionization of sex-work-labour.

Although there is no express condemnation or criminalization of prostitution in the anti-trafficking statutes of Belize, Guyana and Jamaica, they serve, like the traditional sexual offences provisions and minor offences regarding prostitution under vagrancy laws, to amplify the stigma attached to the practice, without complete criminalization.[52] In Belize and Guyana, sexual offences are dealt with in omnibus criminal codes which entail provisions specifically criminalizing the procuring of *females* for prostitution or the frequenting of a brothel within or without these countries.[53] This is also the position in Jamaica under the Offences Against the Person Act, as amended by the Sexual Offences Act 2009-12.[54]

Anti-trafficking statutes in all three jurisdictions define exploitation to include exploitation of the prostitution of another and engaging in any form of sexual exploitation.[55] The Belize and Guyana statutes expressly provide that commercial sexual exploitation includes, but is not limited to pimping, pandering or procuring prostitution, or profiting from sexual prostitution, maintaining a brothel and engaging in child pornography.[56] The Belize Act goes further to enumerate engaging in striptease dances where females and males dance nude or in a state of semi-nudity as a form of commercial sexual exploitation.[57] This approach has not been

---

52. See, e.g., Belize Criminal Code 1981 Cap 101, Guyana Criminal Law (Offences) Act 1893 Cap 8:01, Jamaica Sexual Offences Act 2009-12, Jamaica Offences Against the Person Act 1864, Jamaica Town and Communities Act 1843, Guyana Summary Jurisdiction (Offences) Act 1894 Cap 8:02, Belize Summary Jurisdiction (Offences) Act 1953 Cap 98.
53. Belize Criminal Code (n 52) s 49, Guyana Criminal Law Act (n 52) s 73.
54. Jamaica OAPA (n 52) s 58.
55. Belize Trafficking in Persons (Prohibition) Act 2003-18 s 2(e) ('Belize Act'), (f), Guyana Combating of Trafficking in Persons Act 2005-2 s 2(e) ('Guyana Act'), Jamaica Trafficking in Persons (Prevention, Suppression and Punishment) Act 2007-1 s 2 ('Jamaica Act').
56. Belize Act ibid s 2(f), Guyana Act ibid s 2(e)(vi).
57. Belize Act ibid s 2(f). It is to be noted that these acts are not covered by the sexual offences provisions under the Belize Criminal Code.

adopted in the Guyana and Jamaica Acts. Discussions surrounding the introduction of the Jamaica Trafficking in Persons Act suggest that exotic dancing was not intended to be a profession falling within the statute. During the discussions, Mr Horace Dalley, then minister of health, stressed the distinction between prostitution and exotic dancing, stating that an individual who is 'trained in artistic skills' may 'wish to ply their trade as a dancer.' Persons 'who have people dancing' were not to be equated with traffickers in his estimation.[58]

There is no enumeration of what specific activities amount to prostitution-related exploitation in the Jamaican Act but it is expected that the non-exhaustive lists produced in the Guyana and Belize statutes will influence the interpretation of the Jamaican provision. This is particularly so considering that third party involvement in prostitution is criminalized to the same extent in all three countries. In any event, the Jamaican Act uniquely provides a definition for the term 'exploitation of the prostitution of a person' as a form of exploitation which would subsume the activities listed in the Guyanese and Belizean statutory sections. It provides:

> "exploitation of the prostitution of a person" means the deriving by one person of monetary or other benefit through the provision of sexual services for money or other benefit by another person.[59]

Defining 'exploitation' to include these prostitution-related activities clearly indicates a belief that these activities are inherently exploitative. Additionally, the Belize and Guyana anti-trafficking statutes create a separate criminal offence relating to the transportation of any person for the purpose of exploiting that person's prostitution.[60] The wording of these provisions suggests that the legislatures of these Caribbean territories favour the position adopted by the anti-prostitution feminists. This articulation, however, is not supported by the sexual offences legislation in these countries, which adopt a partial criminalization regime, a policy which has not changed in over a hundred years since the introduction of prostitution-related offences.

Anti-choice feminists, honourable as their intentions might be, present a fundamentally flawed argument as to the best solution to the international human rights issue of trafficking – that trafficking is to include all forms of recruitment and transportation for prostitution regardless of consent. Such a position fails to acknowledge that

---

58. Jamaica Hansard HR vol 32(2) 673 (21 Nov 2006).
59. Jamaica Act (n 55) s 2.
60. Belize Act ibid s 5, Guyana Act ibid s 5.

prostitution is, and has always been, a viable economic resort for both men and women in various societies. Caribbean societies, which hold respect for the fundamental rights and freedoms of all human beings, should consider the more progressive position of the pro-choice activists which encourages an address of the social and economic factors which may prompt persons to engage in prostitution without obliterating the practice as a viable alternative for economic advancement as well as an avenue for self-expression and determination.

During the preparatory stages of the Palermo Protocol states and non-governmental organizations (NGOs) were divided on the question of whether a person could properly consent to the process of trafficking as well as to prostitution and sex work as the purposes of their recruitment. No resolution could be achieved. Consequently, the Protocol itself reflects an 'ambiguous compromise' between both sides of the debate, a cause for the debate to continue.[61] This is in stark contrast to the Convention of 1949 which explicitly provided that consent was of no bearing in establishing the offence of trafficking.[62] The final draft of the 2000 Protocol adopted neither of the two extremes, expressly rejecting the notion that the offence of trafficking included all acts taking place irrespective of consent, yet providing that consent becomes irrelevant where any of the exploitative means listed in Article 3(a) have been employed.[63]

This precise formulation has been adopted in the anti-trafficking statutes of Belize and Guyana.[64] The Guyana Act for instance, provides that in a prosecution for trafficking 'the alleged consent of a person to the intended or realized exploitation is irrelevant once any of the means or circumstances set forth in section 2(k) is established.' Consent then, becomes irrelevant only in certain circumstances. These 'certain circumstances,' however, are far from certainly defined in the Protocol. The means described in Article 3(a) of the Protocol, as well as in the anti-trafficking statutes of Belize and Guyana, are:

a.   the threat or use of force or other forms of coercion;
b.   abduction;
c.   fraud;
d.   deception;
e.   the abuse of power or of a position of vulnerability; and
f.   the giving or receiving of payments or benefits to achieve the consent of a person having control over another person.

---

61. K. Abramson, 'Beyond Consent, Toward Safeguarding Human Rights: Implementing the United Nations Trafficking Protocol' (2003) 44 Harv Intl LJ 473, 475.
62. Convention for the Suppression of the Traffic in Persons and of the Exploitation of the Prostitution of Others (opened for signature 21 Mar 1950, entered into force 25 Jul 1951) 96 UNTS 271 art I.
63. Palermo Protocol (n 4) art 3(b).
64. Belize Act (n 55) s 8(1), Guyana Act ibid s 9(1).

The consent provision in the Jamaican Act is more akin to the 1949 Convention formulation. Section 4 of the Act provides that it is not 'a defence for a person who commits the offence of trafficking in persons that the offence was committed with the victim's consent.'[65] This provision, unlike its Belizean and Guyanese counterparts, makes no reference to the exploitative means or circumstances outlined in the 'trafficking of persons' definition. This gives the appearance that Jamaica has adopted the protectionist approach to trafficking, rendering consent immaterial in all instances of trafficking. Closer scrutiny, however, reveals that the cumulative effect of section 4 of the Act is the same as in Belize and Guyana.

The immateriality of consent under the Jamaican Act does not form part of the definition of trafficking as it does in the 1949 Convention. In order for trafficking to be established under the Jamaican Act, precisely the same conditions as exist in Belize and Guyana must be satisfied. The effect of section 4(4) under the Act is that *once* these conditions have been met, the offence of trafficking *is* established and consent may not be raised as a defence. The consent provisions of Belize and Guyana, although differently phrased, have the exact effect. It could be discerned with sufficient certainty when there has been a threat or use of force, abduction, fraud, deception or even the bribery of a person having control of another. In such circumstances, consent becomes immaterial.

However, uncertainty lies with the exact scope of 'the abuse of power or of a position of vulnerability' mechanism. This particular category could encompass a wide range of activities and is open to varied interpretation. The limits are further obscured when one regards the *travaux préparatoires* to the Protocol which states that this reference is understood as encompassing any situation in which the supposed victim has no real option rather than to submit to the abuse involved.[66] As with the Protocol, the *travaux préparatoires* fail to enumerate what may amount to such a situation.

The anti-trafficking legislations of Belize and Guyana attempt to clarify this ambiguity by providing a definition for the term 'abuse of a position of vulnerability.'[67] No such attempt has been made in the Jamaican statute. These provisions reveal very little as they adopt the formless definition embodied in the *travaux préparatoires* to the Protocol. However, they do provide a non-exhaustive list of what actions

---

65. Jamaica Act ibid s 4(4).
66. UNGA, 'Interpretative Notes for the Official Records (*Travaux Préparatoires*) of the Negotiation of the United Nations Convention against Transnational Organized Crime and the Protocols Thereto' (3 Nov 2000) UN Doc A/55/383/Add 1.
67. Belize Act (n 55) s 2, Guyana Act ibid s 2(a).

may satisfy the category. For example, the Belize Trafficking in Persons Prohibition Act includes:

> ...taking advantage of the vulnerabilities of the abused person resulting from his having entered Belize illegally or without proper immigration documents, or resulting from the abused person's pregnancy, diseased condition (physical or mental) or disability of the person, or the addiction of the person to alcohol or any illegal drugs, or reduced capacity to form judgements by virtue of being a child....[68]

The Belizean and Guyanese legislators failed to effectively utilize the opportunity afforded to them to clarify the circumstances in which the offence of trafficking is established. The provisions in these statutes, consequently, reflect an unsatisfactory state of the law. The Jamaican legislator completely failed to address this issue.

The question then arises as to whether consent provisions have a place in the anti-trafficking legislations of the region at all. Presently, the consent provisions included in Caribbean anti-trafficking statutes serve only to declare something already understood – that once there has been the use of fraud, force or other similar mechanism there cannot be genuine consent. The inclusion of consent provisions in the Acts of Belize, Guyana and Jamaica, however, cloud these statutes with the consent debate which is a foreign element in the region. This debate is primarily one that occurs on the political stage of the United States between varying feminist groups and lobbyists. The emergence of Governance Feminism has impacted the shaping of the US anti-trafficking policy as well as the international standard regarding combating human trafficking. The phenomenon has been described as an important element of governance involving the 'installation of feminists and feminist ideas in the actual legal-institutional power.'[69] Thomas defined the concept as 'feminism that seeks not only to analyze and critique the problem, but to *devise, pursue and achieve reform to address the problem in the real world*.'[70]

There existed a general discontent with the state of the law both in the United States and globally as it related to human trafficking and in particular the sex trafficking of women and being true to the essence of Governance Feminism, feminist groups sought not only to critique but to provide solutions and to influence the reform process. The TVPA had its genesis in an anti-trafficking bill drafted by Congressman Chris Smith

---

68. Belize Act ibid s 2.
69. Halley and others (n 46) 340.
70. Ibid 348.

who was lobbied by a coalition of Evangelical Christians and abolitionist feminists. The draft was focused entirely on sex trafficking and prostitution, being expanded subsequently to address all forms of forced labour within the scope of human trafficking.[71] This coalition also had an impact on the structure of the United States Department of State Office to Monitor and Combat Trafficking in Persons. Caribbean legislatures have readily conformed to a regime without evaluating the underpinnings and making an assessment of the Caribbean reality. Feminist discourse on the area in the region is scant; Kempadoo is perhaps one of the very few who articulates what she believes the Caribbean response should be. Her approach is in stark contrast to the US approach and would have been a proper starting point for moulding the Caribbean anti-trafficking legal order.

Kara Abramson highlighted an important submission of the Human Rights Caucus in her article.[72] The organization suggested that the best approach to safeguard the ability to consent would be to eliminate it as an issue in anti-trafficking discourse. It is argued that if trafficking is to be unequivocally defined as an exploitative activity, then no trafficked person could be deemed to have 'consented to their plight' and consequently there would no longer be a need to include a provision in anti-trafficking instruments heralding the immateriality of consent.[73] If this approach is to be adopted, the inclusion of a consent provision in anti-trafficking legislation would become redundant, as it perhaps already is under the statutes of Belize, Guyana and Jamaica.

The adoption of the GAATW distinction between the offences of recruitment and subjecting a person to forced-labour/slavery-like conditions may prove a valid solution for anti-trafficking in the region.[74] It would be very useful in providing a more effective framework for identifying the elements of the offence of trafficking and therefore, where there is a lack of genuine consent in a particular situation. Coercion, deception and abuse may exist at both or any one of these planes in any given case. An individual may have consented to being recruited and transported for the purpose of prostitution without an intention to be subjected to the forced labour/slavery-like conditions she is compelled to endure. Current definitions of trafficking collapse the two dimensions into one making it very difficult to determine whether consent was

---

71. Berman (n 44) 283.
72. Abramson (n 61) 485.
73. Human Rights Caucus, 'Recommendations and Commentary on the Draft Protocol to Prevent, Suppress, and Punish Trafficking in Persons, Especially Women and Children, Supplementing the United Nations Convention Against Transnational Organized Crime' (1999) Recommendation 7.
74. The GAATW definition is discussed below, text to (n 92).

given at all. As Janice Chuang pointed out, a woman might deliberately and without any form of coercion, deception or abuse, choose to use a trafficker as her avenue for migration.[75]

There also persists a less politically and morally charged debate as to whether there may be consent to trafficking itself, that is, the recruitment and transportation processes.[76] Those who contend that trafficking itself may be established irrespective of consent fail to justify why the person who consents to being trafficked should be offered the protection of a state while the undocumented migrant is to be abhorred and punished; the two are, after all, the same individual in different disguises. In such a situation, the GAATW approach provides an effective framework for protecting as wide a cross-section of 'real' victims as possible, as the person who consents to being trafficked would not be categorized as a victim in that regard but may still be afforded protection should he/she in fact become subjected to forced labour to which no consent was given, as would the illegal migrant who suffers a similar fate.

The normative debate concerning whether women should be allowed to consent to prostitution has proved to be more of a distraction in the efforts to combat human trafficking than an aid in their advancement. As Chuang correctly points out, treating consent as an immaterial consideration and deeming it impossible creates the risk of dismissing the fact that some women actually do choose to engage in trafficking and prostitution but do not assent to the exploitative conditions that sometime accompany their course of work.[77] Efforts should be centralized on creating a system for combating human trafficking in the region that provides recourse for as many victims as possible.

5. Deficiencies with the Definition of Trafficking and the Assistance and Protection Provisions

A. The Definition Provisions

The anti-trafficking statutes of the region should provide a complete framework for prosecuting all persons involved in the criminal activity as well as provide protection for as wide a cross section of victims as possible. Currently, under the Acts, the categorization of 'victim' is limited to the individual who experiences the chain process of recruitment, transportation and receipt as a result of force, coercion, abduction, fraud or the abuse of power or a position of vulnerability. However, the 'victim'

---

75. Chuang (n 49) 89.
76. Ibid 87–90 for a brief discussion of the debate concerning consent to trafficking.
77. Ibid 86.

is not solely the individual who is forced *into* a particular course of labour, but also the individual who is coerced and exploited *in* his or her selected course of work, whether it be in the sex industry or otherwise. This deficiency is reflected in the definition of the offence of trafficking employed in the Acts of the region and the related offences subsumed under the 'Criminal Offences and Related Provisions.'

The Belizean and Guyanese Acts adopt the exact formulation of the definition of 'trafficking in persons' laid down in the Palermo Protocol.[78] This includes the 'recruitment, transportation, transfer, harbouring or receipt of persons, by means of the threat or use of force or other forms of coercion, of abduction, of fraud, of deception, of the abuse of power or of a position of vulnerability or of the giving or receiving of payments or benefits to achieve the consent of a person having control over another person, for the purpose of exploitation.'[79] The Jamaican legislature outlined this provision in more specific terms, providing that the offence includes:

a. recruiting, transporting, transferring, harbouring or receiving another person *within Jamaica*
b. recruiting, transporting or transferring another person *from Jamaica to another country*; or
c. recruiting, transporting, transferring, or receiving another person *from another country into Jamaica,*

by threat or use of force or other form of coercion, abduction, deception or fraud, the abuse of power or position of vulnerability or the giving or receiving of a benefit to obtain the consent of a person having control of another.[80]

The definition of trafficking outlined in the Convention for the Suppression of the Traffic in Persons and of the Exploitation of the Prostitution of Others prohibited the trafficking of persons for the purpose of prostitution and sexual exploitation.[81] This Convention was the most comprehensive treaty addressing the issue of trafficking at that time. It took an anti-prostitution and law enforcement approach and was the first international instrument on trafficking which included provisions directly related to implementation, although these were very weak.[82] Several criticisms have been offered against the 1949 Convention. The Global Alliance Against Traffic in Women, a coalition of

---

78. Belize Act (n 55) s 2, Guyana Act ibid s 2 (k).
79. Palermo Protocol (n 4) art 3(a).
80. Jamaica Act (n 55) s 4.
81. Convention for the Suppression of the Traffic in Persons (n 62).
82. E. Bruch, 'Models Wanted: The Search for an Effective Response to Human Trafficking' (2004) 40 Stan J Intl L 1, 10.

non-governmental organizations promoting the elimination of trafficking in women, argues that the Convention fails to take into consideration the fact that exploitative purposes go beyond sexual exploitation and prostitution of women.[83] Additionally, as the offences covered under the Convention are limited to the recruitment and transportation of victims only, several other and equally exploitative acts and actors, such as the individual who receives and holds the victim in exploitative and slavery-like labour conditions would go unpunished, leaving a section of victims without restitution.[84] The first of these criticisms has been remedied by the Palermo Protocol and the anti-trafficking legislations in the region.

As the illicit traffic in humans progressed, there came a realization that exploitation was not limited to any particular sex nor was it solely characterized by sexual exploitation and prostitution.[85] The surfacing of new manifestations of trafficking, for example, trafficking for domestic or industrialized labour or for commercial marriage, prompted the broadening of the trafficking definition to include trafficking for any form of forced labour or slavery-like practices. Although there remains some emphasis on the exploitation of the prostitution of others and commercial sexual exploitation, this broadened concept of trafficking has been echoed in the anti-trafficking statutes of Belize, Guyana and Jamaica.[86]

The Palermo Protocol, however, was unsuccessful in fully addressing the second of the criticisms raised above. It failed to advance the scope of offences subsumed by its provisions to include not only the recruitment and transporting of individuals, as was the emphasis under the 1949 Convention, but also the exploitative end purposes of trafficking, which is not limited to sexual exploitation but includes domestic work, sweatshop labour, migrant labour, or any other work in the informal economy. The anti-trafficking statutes of Belize, Guyana and Jamaica, which embody almost precise carbon copies of the Protocol, all reflect this deficiency. The definition of trafficking under these statutes, as well as the Palermo Protocol, has been expanded beyond the recruitment and transfer of individuals to include the transport, harbouring or receipt of individuals.[87] This expansion allows for persons involved at any stage of the trafficking process to face sanctions for their illegal activity – those at the beginning of the chain, who provide or sell the trafficked person,

---

83. Global Alliance Against Traffic in Women, *Human Rights and Trafficking in Persons: A Handbook* (Global Alliance Against Traffic in Women, Bangkok 2000) <http://gaatw.org/books_pdf/Human%20 Rights%20and%20Trafficking%20in%20Person.pdf> accessed 3 Aug 2010 ('GAATW Handbook').

84. This criticism is offered by several human rights and feminist groups including the GAATW.

85. Chuang (n 49) 80.

86. Belize Act (n 55) s 2, Guyana Act ibid s 2(e), Jamaica Act ibid s 2.

87. Belize Act ibid s 2, Guyana Act ibid s 2(k), Jamaica Act ibid s 4. See also Palermo Protocol (n 4) art 3(a).

and those at the end of the chain, who receive or purchase the trafficked person, hold the trafficked person in forced labour and profit from that labour.[88]

Despite this advancement, there still exists an ineffective standard for criminalizing all exploitative activities. The recruitment and transportation process is currently criminalized under the statutes. However, no provision has been made to specifically criminalize the act of subjecting an individual to forced labour or slavery-like conditions. There is also no such provision under the various criminal codes or offences against the person legislation in the region. Forced labour practices are not dealt with in a single comprehensive statute in any of these territories but may appear as minor offences under various labour laws.[89] Consequently, no protection is made available to the 'undocumented migrant' who is not 'trafficked' in the traditional sense of the word, but who becomes a victim of exploitation by his/her own actions subsequent to arrival in the country of destination, for example, the unassuming migrant woman who voluntarily employs herself in the services of a massage parlour and is then forced to engage in sexual activity.

Under the anti-trafficking Acts of Belize, Guyana and Jamaica, the offence of trafficking in persons involves the recruitment, transportation, transfer, harbouring or receipt of a person by manipulative means.[90] These definitions victimize the individual caught in the chain of trafficking – the individual who is recruited, transported and finally received – and criminalizes the activities of offenders who play a part in beginning, perpetuating or completing this chain. The definition of trafficking laid down in the Protocol, and adopted in the Caribbean statutes, has been so interpreted by the UN Special Rapporteur on Violence Against Women:

> ... the definition covers all persons involved in the trafficking chain: those at the beginning of the chain, who provide or sell the trafficked person, and those at the end of the chain, who receive or purchase the trafficked person, hold the trafficked person in forced labour and profit from that labour. Criminalizing the activities of all parties involved throughout the process of trafficking would facilitate efforts to both prevent trafficking and punish traffickers.[91]

88. GAATW Handbook (n 83).
89. For example, Belize Labour Act 2000, Cap 297 s 158.
90. Belize Act (n 55) s 2, Guyana Act ibid s 2(k), Jamaica Act ibid s 4.
91. UNCHR, 'Integration of the Human Rights of Women and the Gender Perspective: Violence Against Women,' Report of the Special Rapporteur on Violence Against Women, Its Causes and Consequences, R Coomaraswamy (29 Feb 2000) UN Doc E/CN.4/2000/68 [14].

But the question remains – what provision is made for the person who becomes a victim of exploitation but who has not been a link in the chain of events? It is accepted that the exploitative end purposes to which a person may be subjected may not be properly categorized as 'trafficking' in the general understanding of the term, however, it would be a great addition to the statutes to provide for the offence of exploitation in and of itself, independently from the chain process of recruitment, transportation and receipt. No such provision exists in the anti-trafficking statutes of Belize, Guyana and Jamaica.

The GAATW had suggested that the prohibited offences under the 1949 Convention, and by extension, domestic legislation, should be expanded to reflect a bifurcation of the act of recruitment from the exploitative end purposes of trafficking, the former being defined as 'trafficking' and the latter as 'forced labour and slavery like practices.' The GAATW defines trafficking in this context as 'all acts involved in the recruitment and/or transportation of a person within and across national borders for work or services by means of violence or threat of violence, abuse of authority or dominant position, debt bondage, deception or other forms of coercion.'[92] Forced labour and slavery-like practices are defined as: 'The extraction of work or services from any person or the appropriation of the legal identity and/or physical person of any person by means of violence or threat of violence, abuse of authority or dominant position, debt-bondage, deception or other forms of coercion.'[93]

This separation can play a definitive role in the formulation of strategies to effectively combat human trafficking on all planes and to provide remedies and protections to the victims of these abusive practices. Chuang, who favours the GAATW approach, states that such a division would prove useful in securing protection for a wider cross section of victims as it is not all 'trafficking' victims that are subjected to forced labour/slavery-like practices, and not all women subjected to forced labour/slavery-like practices that are also victims of trafficking.[94] This distinction recognizes 'that one practice may be an act of choice, while the other act, an imposition of force, deceit, or abuse.'[95] For example, a woman may unreservedly choose to migrate illegally into a country by her own resources, but find herself being exploited in a forced labour or slavery-like practice as a consequence of her attempt to

---

92. Global Alliance Against Traffic in Women and the Foundation for Women in cooperation with the Foundation Against Trafficking in Women, 'Standard Minimum Rules for the Treatment of Victims of Trafficking in Persons, Forced Labour and Slavery-like Practices' (April 1997).
93. Ibid.
94. Chuang (n 49) 82.
95. Ibid.

find gainful employment. In such circumstances, the GAATW approach would improve anti-trafficking statutes, providing for a more inclusive framework for possible victims. The legislatures of Belize, Guyana and Jamaica, in their attempt to swiftly appease the government of the United States and keep open the coffers, failed to recognize and remedy the lacuna that exists in the international standard by charting a new course in their respective domestic legislations.

This is not to advance the perception that the undocumented migrant is wholly unaccounted for in the anti-trafficking statutes of the region. The statutes of Belize and Guyana explicitly provide for the protection of illegal migrants from internal trafficking. Under the definition sections of both statutes, it is an offence to recruit, transport, transfer, harbour or receive a person by means of the abuse of a position of vulnerability, for the means of exploitation.[96] These Acts expressly define the 'abuse of a position of vulnerability' to include taking advantage of the vulnerabilities resulting from a person having entered the country illegally or without proper documentation.[97] Under the Jamaica anti-trafficking Act, however, there is no definition given as to what amounts to an 'abuse of a position of vulnerability.' However, the inclusion of this ground of abuse under the definition section should also be given a similar interpretation not only in light of the regional statutes that precede it, but also the international standard which exists under the Palermo Protocol. The *travaux préparatoires* of the Protocol indicate that the reference to the abuse of a position of vulnerability is to be understood to refer to any situation in which the person involved has no real acceptable alternative but to submit to the abuse involved.[98]

It is possible to see the analytical importance of drawing a distinction between the act of 'trafficking' and the forced labour/slavery-like practice in human trafficking discourse. Chuang points out that in so doing one is better able to understand the different dimensions to the trafficking problem and consequently prescribe policies, strategies and solutions that will specifically target one area or the other.[99] This formulation would be better suited to the issue of human trafficking in its Caribbean context as the countries of the region generally attract voluntary immigrants seeking to participate in the sex tourism industry or who are simply in transit to the Global North.

Additionally, this would have the added benefit of shifting anti-trafficking campaigns away from restricting immigration in the interest

---

96. Belize Act (n 55) s 2, Guyana Act ibid s 2(k).
97. Belize Act ibid s 2, Guyana Act ibid s 2(a).
98. UNGA, 'Interpretative Notes' (n 66).
99. Chuang (n 49) 82.

of the state, a factor which plays a significant part in mobilizing efforts against trafficking, to a greater focus on protecting the human rights of the individual victim. This of course calls Caribbean governments to a higher standard than that which exists internationally, and admittedly it may not be a standard considered worthy of pursuing so long as there is no desire in the region to lead the progression of human rights protection worldwide rather than follow the standards prescribed and promulgated by developed states in an attempt to secure their own interests.

As Chuang highlights, the problem of forced labour/slavery-like practices, as an issue particularly domestic in character, may have less political ramifications for a state than the issue of trafficking. As such, it is suspected that states may overlook the former of the two evils.[100] Here, she emphasizes, is where the anti-trafficking movement and non-governmental organizations would have to be particularly instrumental in lobbying on behalf of victims of forced labour/slavery-like practices as a distinct class of victims equally in need of protection.

B. The Assistance and Protection Provisions

The United States TVPA in section 108 prescribes the Minimum Standards to be adopted by countries receiving security and financial assistance. Subsection 2 mandates that states provide protection for victims of severe forms of trafficking in persons. The anti-trafficking statutes of Belize, Guyana and Jamaica, which all had their genesis after the Palermo Protocol came into force, have supplemented the skeletal framework laid down in the TVPA with the comprehensive protections under the Protocol. There is an emphasis, however, on the repatriation of victims to their 'home' or the place they first suffered abuse.

Although the matter of repatriation is not dealt with particularly in the TVPA, it is understood from the Act that victims are to be returned to their place of origin. This is evident on a careful construction of the Act: continued presence is dependent on a number of factors and conditions which must be met by the applicant, including proof of extreme hardship should he/she be removed from the United States.[101] Article 8 of the Palermo Protocol mandates that states facilitate and accept, with due regard for the safety of victims, the return of such persons without undue or unreasonable delay.[102] The Protocol specifies that this return should preferably be voluntary but does not mandate this.[103]

---

100. Ibid 83.
101. TVPA (n 3) sec 107 (2) (E).
102. Palermo Protocol (n 4) art 8(1).
103. Ibid art 8(2).

Under the Acts of Belize, Guyana and Jamaica, the relevant authorities are mandated to establish a system to effect the safe return of victims to their country of citizenship or permanent residency.[104] As is the position in the Protocol, such a provision is not optional and is considered the first option in relation to a victim of trafficking.

The Belizean and Guyanese Acts, however, make additional provisions in relation to repatriation. In reaching a decision as to whether to return a victim to his or her country of origin, the relevant authorities must consider the right of the victim to apply for temporary or permanent residency status, or even citizenship in the case of Belize.[105] No such provision is made under the Trafficking in Persons Act of Jamaica. Factors to be taken into consideration in relation to repatriation there add nothing to the chances of the victim to remain in the country but serve only to ensure that the process is as expedient as is possible.[106] The Minister, under the Jamaican Act, must first take into consideration the safety of the victim while in Jamaica. This suggests that if the victim is likely to be harmed due to reprisal attacks in Jamaica, repatriation is to be done more swiftly. The safe return of the victim without undue delay is also a relevant consideration. Finally, the wish of the victim as to the choice of country to which he is to be *sent* is the final consideration. The only choice the victim has is in relation to where he is to be sent, not whether he is to stay or go.

Returning a victim to place of origin serves only to put that person at risk of 'revictimization,' especially where the economic and social conditions of the country influenced the initial victimization. The Jamaican Act provides no different treatment than that afforded to illegal immigrants under Caribbean immigration laws, under which prohibited immigrants are ineligible for the grant of immigrant status.[107]

The United States Act authorizes the continued presence of a victim if he or she may be a potential witness in effectuating prosecution of a trafficking offender.[108] Certification must be awarded for continued presence and this certification is effective only for so long as the 'Attorney General determines that the continued presence of such person is necessary to effectuate prosecution of traffickers in persons.'[109] Under the Palermo Protocol, State Parties are to consider adopting legislative

---

104. Belize Act (n 55) s 16 (1), Guyana Act ibid s 22(1), Jamaica Act ibid s 12(1).
105. Belize Act ibid s 16 (2), Guyana Act ibid s 22(2).
106. Jamaica Act ibid s 12(2).
107. Belize Immigration Act, Cap 156 s 5, Guyana Immigration Act, Cap 14:02, Jamaica Immigration Restriction (Commonwealth Citizens) Act 1973 s 4.
108. TVPA (n 3) sec 107(1)(E)(i) & (2)(C).
109. Ibid sec 107(1)(E)(ii).

or other appropriate measures permitting victims to remain in their respective territories temporarily or permanently.[110] Although this is merely a consideration that states ought to take, the legislators of Belize, Guyana and Jamaica have enacted provisions providing for some variation of legal status for victims.

Under section 13(2) of the Belize Act, a victim may apply for permanent residency status or citizenship of Belize. In the interim, the Department of Immigration and Nationality Services is to issue temporary residency permits or other authorized permits allowing the victim and any dependent children accompanying him/her to remain in Belize during the criminal proceedings against the traffickers.[111] This provision, however, is conditional on the willingness of the victim to assist in the investigation or prosecution of the trafficker(s) on request. A similar position is adopted under the Guyana Act.[112]

Jamaica, on the contrary, has adopted a much more restrictive approach to the legal status of trafficking victims in the territory. No provision is made for a victim to apply for residency or citizenship in Jamaica and authorization granted for temporary stay in the island shall only be for the duration necessary to carry out the:

a. process of identifying the victim or verifying his identity and nationality;
b. activities necessary to find accommodation for and other assistance to the victim;
c. criminal prosecution against the persons who have committed or facilitated the commission of the offence of the trafficking in persons;
d. investigations necessary to prosecute the offence of trafficking in persons or facilitating the offence and other legal and administrative activities.[113]

Additionally, the Minister may cancel at any time the visas or other documents permitting the victim to remain in Jamaica, where he considers it justified in the particular circumstances.[114] This provision gives the Minister great latitude as it specifies no circumstances that would warrant such a revocation. The provision is also open to abuse as it allows for the Minister to make a unilateral decision concerning the cancellation of authorization documents.

---

110. Palermo Protocol (n 4) art 7.
111. Belize Act (n 55) s 14.
112. Guyana Act ibid s 19(1).
113. Jamaica Act ibid s 13(1).
114. Ibid s 13(2).

From the preceding paragraphs it is evident that the Jamaican Act is particularly deficient as to provisions regarding the legal status of victims, whether temporary or permanent. Although additional options are available in Belize and Guyana, it must be noted that they are discretionary in nature; therefore, their extensive potential may not translate into benefits in practice.

6. Conclusion

The anti-trafficking Acts of Belize, Guyana and Jamaica reflect mostly a reaction to external pressure and therefore do not represent a thought-through and effective response to the issue of trafficking of humans in its Caribbean context. Transplanting existing international conventions and standards without an assessment of the implications on the domestic level may prove to be problematic. The anti-trafficking statutes of the Caribbean, as they are presently, have incorporated wholesale the United States policy and the general international standard with its shortfalls and misguided policy. It would be prudent for the rest of the region, and even these three countries, to conduct an assessment of the human trafficking reality in the Caribbean before attempting to develop a campaign to combat the phenomenon. If that approach is adopted, legislation can be specifically tailored to meet the specific needs of the Caribbean and there will be no need for untimely revision.

There is clearly a more functional mode of facilitating an interaction between international conventions and standards and domestic law than the latter being cloned from the former. International treaties and standards often embody compromises between many different states, including between the various views expressed during their negotiations. These instruments embody standards that can offer guidance to a state in enacting its own legislation but should not be, in all cases, accepted by a state without reservations or modifications. International conventions and standards often conform to the specifications of world powers and First World, developed countries. Caribbean countries should be more proactive in advocating for provisions that are more advantageous for developing states. This, however, cannot be done without an assessment of the relevant issue in its Caribbean context. It is only when the Caribbean realities are understood that effective bargaining can take place on the international level. Caribbean governments should also be ready to express reservations to international provisions which have negative implications for the states they are called to govern. Caribbean countries must develop an attitude of prescribing for our particular needs while continuing to meet international obligations.

A major inadequacy of the US TVPA and the international predecessors to anti-trafficking statutes is the law enforcement regime that is created without sufficient regard to human rights or labour rights standards. This is despite the fact that human rights activists have played a pivotal role in the negotiation of these instruments. Regretfully, Caribbean legislatures have adopted precisely the approach that will prove inadequate to combat human trafficking in the most comprehensive way. The *modus operandi* suggested by Professor Elizabeth Bruch is one which would undoubtedly create a better mechanism for successfully tackling the international plague of human trafficking. She suggests that the best solution would be to draw on the strengths of three approaches in formulating a system to combat trafficking.[115] The *law enforcement* approach provides the advantage of prosecuting offenders and therefore deterring the commission of the crime and bringing justice to victims of the crime. In employing this approach without regard for the human rights of the victims however, there is a failure to recognize a victim as a rights holder and the provision of protection hinges on how 'innocent' or 'not' an individual is perceived to be.[116] Incorporating a *human rights* approach would have the benefit of guaranteeing protection to all individuals in need of it, without discrimination on the basis of that individual's choice of activities, for example prostitution. Adopting elements of the *labour rights* approach would enhance anti-trafficking campaigns by extending protection to individuals in their course of work. Such an approach would complement the GAATW bifurcation of the offence of 'trafficking' from that of exploiting an individual in 'forced labour or slavery-like conditions.' The exploitative employer is just as criminally motivated as the individual who recruits by force, to ultimately benefit the former, and should be similarly dealt with by the law.

The most important point to note is that all anti-trafficking campaigns will come to nought unless greater emphasis is placed on addressing the surrounding circumstances that operate as catalysts in the increase of human trafficking. Anti-trafficking legislation in its nakedness will do little to remedy the situation. The decrepit state of the economy, rampant poverty, social and gender inequalities, and high levels of unemployment amongst the youth are all factors which must be tackled if legislation is to have any impact in stemming the tide of human trafficking. Ironically, in their attempt to satisfy the Minimum Standards prescribed by the United States, Caribbean legislatures have failed to copy perhaps the most important provision made in the US TVPA – section 106. This section

---

115. Bruch (n 82) 15.
116. Ibid 32.

provides for the prevention of trafficking through economic alternatives and opportunities for potential victims. Offering skills training, job counselling, programmes to promote women's participation in economic decision making and to keep children in school are the provisions that should have been adopted from the TVPA.

It is not just the threat, coercion or violence of another – the trafficker – that forces an individual into a state of victimization. The prevailing economic and social conditions left unremedied by the governments of Caribbean nations exert even more force than any individual could. In that sense, Caribbean governments are just as guilty in creating and perpetuating the cycle of human trafficking. For human trafficking to be successfully combated, we must hack at the root of the tree and not merely at its branches.

III.

THE HABITS OF CONSTITUTIONALISM

The Common Law and the Litigation of Fundamental Rights and Freedoms Before the Privy Council

Margaret Demerieux[1]

1. Setting for the Adjudication

In keeping with post-war constitution-making throughout the world, Commonwealth Caribbean Constitutions all contain a Bill of Rights as a chapter headed 'Fundamental Rights and Freedoms.'[2] The proclamation of these Bills was a declaration that certain values and concepts were the basis of the constitutional order and also of the relation between the individual and the state. The provisions of the Bills of Rights were both statements of enforceable rights in law, and statements of constitutional norms. The Bills in all cases save that of Trinidad and Tobago, are derived from the European Convention for the Protection of Human Rights and Fundamental Freedoms (ECHR). It fell therefore to the Privy Council, from the promulgation in 1962 of the constitutions of Jamaica and Trinidad and Tobago, to interpret the Bills and determine their law and their application – to be the *final arbiter of the meaning and effect of Bills of Rights* newly set into a long established common law system. This task, crucially, was set by the Privy Council well before the advent in the United Kingdom of a supposed 'common law of human rights.'[3] This task arose too, before it was *denied* in the United Kingdom that the common law conceptions of fundamental liberties operated to produce *merely residuary entitlements* and before it was asserted that the common law did not diverge either from the European Convention or from United

---

1. This chapter is published posthumously with the permission of the executor of the Demerieux estate.
2. The first of these chapters (hereinafter referred to as 'Bill(s) of Rights') in a Commonwealth Caribbean constitution, occurred in the 1961 Constitution of Guyana, a pre-independence document. States in Association with the United Kingdom, before achieving independence in the late 1970s and 1980s, had constitutions with Bills. Certain other states as, for example, The Bahamas before independence, and currently dependencies of the United Kingdom, had or have had extended to them the European Convention for the Protection of Human Rights and Fundamental Freedoms (ECHR).
3. See M. Hunt, *Using Human Rights Law in English Courts* (Hart Publishing, Oxford 1997), especially chapter 5.

States Bill of Rights understandings, at least in relation to free speech.[4]

In addition, at the time of promulgation of the West Indian Bills of Rights, international and regional human rights regimes were in their infancy (as for the European system), or non-existent (as for the current 'world system' and the Inter-American regime). The United Kingdom had permitted individual petitions under the ECHR in 1966, about one year before the Privy Council decided its first West Indian Bill of Rights case – *DPP v Nasralla*.[5]

What then was the response of that Court, one whose power to determine whether official action and legislation was compatible or not with a Bill of Rights provision was undisputed? Up until the very end of the period stated, a reaching for existing law and in particular the common law (as the Privy Council determined it to be at the time of promulgation of the constitutions), had been its dominant response. One moreover, with the purpose to give a restricted content or effect to the right litigated. The Court had consistently declined to admit the contribution of the Bill of Rights to the law and constitution of Commonwealth Caribbean states. While there had been the occasional ingenuous use of the common law to support a litigant's view of his entitlement under the Constitution, the Court had not accepted what should logically have been the presumed premise of the 'enactment' of a Bill of Rights, namely that the freedoms of the common law were not automatically to be seen as coextensive with the newly stated fundamental rights and freedoms.

The frequent pointing to the established common law as the source of certain liberties also made newer perspectives on the rights and freedoms and the emergence of a rights jurisprudence more difficult.[6] An observation made in 1990, in the context of the United Kingdom, would have applied equally to the Judicial Committee at the period of the 1960s when it began adjudication of the Bills: 'The common law, in its concern with remedies adopts a very technical approach to fundamental

---

4. See the observation of Lord Goff in *AG v Guardian Newspapers No 2* [1990] 1 AC 109 (HL) ('*Spycatcher No 2*') at 283, cited in the text to note 39. *Derbyshire CC v Times Newspapers* [1993] AC 534 (HL) declared the similarity of the common law of England to that of the regimes mentioned in the text. One strongly suspects that these developments, and certainly the decisions in *Derbyshire* and *Spycatcher No 2*, were a response to litigation against the United Kingdom under the ECHR – especially that in *Sunday Times v United Kingdom* (A/30) (1979–80) 2 EHRR 245 (ECtHR), which declared the House of Lords decision in *AG v Times Newspapers* [1974] AC 273 to have been an infringement of Article 10 of the ECHR. The latter decision is the 'classical location' of the traditional common law's response to an assertion of free speech in the way it approaches the restraint on what is not a fundamental right. The restraint in that case was the common law of contempt.

5. [1967] 2 AC 238 (PC Ja).

6. More recently, in *AG v Williams* [1998] AC 351 (PC Ja) 354–55, the Court stated: 'The fundamental human right to protection against unlawful searches and seizure is part of the English common law. ... From the common law this right passed into the Fourth Amendment to the Constitution of the United States and into the constitutions of the countries throughout the world.'

questions and human rights are not yet an important part of the English legal culture or constitution.'[7]

With or without the assistance of devices set out in some of the constitutions, as for example a special savings clause,[8] the Privy Council has sought to justify or perhaps even *legitimate* its *interpretation* of *the Bills* and its decisions thereunder by reference to existing law and in particular the Court's understanding in a specific case of an area of the common law – even in the face of the actual statement of the right in the Constitution – so as to deny claims presented to the court. Accordingly, in the earliest Bill of Rights litigation before it, *DPP v Nasralla,* the Privy Council observed:

> All the judges below have treated [section 20(8) of the Constitution] as declaring or intended to declare the common law on the subject. Their Lordships agree...The laws in force are not to be subjected to scrutiny in order to see whether or not they conform to the precise terms of the protective provisions.[9]

Similarly, in *King v Queen,*[10] the Privy Council asserted:

> This constitutional right may or may not be enshrined in a written constitution, but it seems to their Lordships that it matters not whether it depends on such enshrinement or simply upon the common law as it would do in this country. In either event the discretion of the court must be exercised and has not been taken away by the declaration of the right in written form.

Nearly 30 years later, in considering the relation of a speedy trial to a fair trial, in a Bill of Rights which did not confer expressly a right to be tried within a reasonable time, it was said:

> [T]he opening words of section 4 indicate that the rights in question are rights which existed at the coming into force of the Constitution. The present Constitution is that of 1976, but the relevant wording in the original independence Constitution of 1962 was identical. It follows that the rights in question are rights which were enjoyed at common law before the Constitution of 1962 came into force.[11]

---

7. D. Feldman, 'Public Law Values in the House of Lords' (1990) 106 LQR 246, 262.
8. This clause, to be distinguished from the general savings clause, protects existing law from being challenged and struck down as derogating from the rights conferred in the Bill of Rights. It is now to be found in four states of the region which sent appeals to the Privy Council – Jamaica, Trinidad and Tobago, Barbados and The Bahamas. The Belize clause was spent after five years from the promulgation of that state's Constitution.
9. *Nasralla* (n 5) 247–48.
10. [1969] 1 AC 304 (PC Ja) 319. The case was concerned with the admissibility of illegally obtained evidence.
11. *DPP v Tokai* [1996] AC 856 (PC T&T) 862.

A number of cases have asserted either that sections of the Bill of Rights do no more than 'codify in writing the requirements of the common law,'[12] or that a section of the Bill of Rights makes no difference (as was asserted in *France v Simmonds*),[13] in relation to defamation and free expression. Given that the dominant approach had been to assert existing law and common law rules so as to deny claims under the Bills of Rights, the most celebrated cases have been those which appear to 'set aside' the common law rule, or better, which do not allow common law rules to obstruct the development of a Bill of Rights jurisprudence. These cases form a 'counter-current' to the *Nasralla* line.

2. West Indian Bills and Existing Law

In the context of litigation and judicial determinations, the single most crucial issue raised by the enactment of a Bill of Rights is the impact of existing law, and more particularly the common law, on the assertion of the conferred rights. For, depending on the understanding given to rights stated in a Bill, and not discounting the fact that existing law as the common law can help to elucidate the meaning of a newly conferred right, it is quite conceivable that many well established rules of law could be 'invalidated' on the enactment of a Bill of Rights. The Privy Council observed in *Maharaj v AG No 2*,[14] that in view of the breadth of language used to describe the fundamental rights and freedoms, detailed examination of all the laws in force at promulgation of the Constitution (including the common law so far as it had not been superseded by written law) might have revealed provisions which could plausibly be argued contravened one or other of the rights recognized in the constitution. Conversely, the possible impact of the newly created rights on the ordinary law is also implicated, but the issue stated above is most often at the root of litigation in which it is claimed that a right has been infringed.

The fact that the common law itself is the source of many of the basic liberties, some now dubbed 'rights,' has obscured, or perhaps has made untenable for some, the notion of any conflict or incongruity between that law and enacted fundamental right and freedoms. But in addition to any substantive discontinuity between elements of an enacted rights regime and the body of rules constituting the common law, incongruities may relate, for example, to the fact that a Bill could include rights arguably unknown to the common law – as would be the case where, however formulated, a right to privacy is conferred. Lord Diplock had occasion to

---

12. *Vincent v Queen* [1993] 1 WLR 862 (PC Ja) 867.
13. (1990) 38 WIR 172 (PC St K-N).
14. [1979] AC 385 (PC T&T) 395–96.

point this out in *Maharaj No 2* in relation to rights stated in the Constitution of Trinidad and Tobago, namely, that of a parent or guardian to a free choice in the matter of education for his child or ward, and the right to join political parties and to express political views. Again, the common law understanding may not be coextensive with the actual formulation of the rights in a Bill. This was exemplified in *Nasralla,* considered below, in which the clear words of the statement of the right went beyond the understanding of the common law in the relevant area, as stated by the Privy Council in that case. It also illustrated uncertainty and obscurity in the common law itself.

A significant divergence between common law understandings of fundamental rights occurs where, as for all of the West Indian Bills, the enacting document creates *a cause of action* for breach or threatened breach of one of the conferred rights. This feature is hardly known to the common law. The breach of (what would now be) a right could form the basis of an appeal as for example, where procedural rights in a criminal trial are infringed making the trial unfair; or could result in the discharge of an injunction prohibiting publication of some 'speech' where freedom of expression was invoked. In neither case would an *independent action arise* on an allegation of deprivation of right.

Looking at the relation between the common law and enacted fundamental rights, two Privy Council decisions in the sphere of personal liberty, being cases in which the court declined to 'apply' the common law to defeat a claim under a Bill of Rights, are illustrative. The entitlement to personal liberty, well established in the common law, is expressed as a 'right' not to be deprived of liberty without the observance of certain procedures. In the Trinidad and Tobago chapter on fundamental rights and freedoms, the individual is accorded the right not to be deprived of liberty 'except by due process of law.' So in the *Maharaj No 2* scenario, in which a barrister was sent to prison for seven days for contempt, the summary procedure in committal for contempt was well known and accepted in the common law with the 'judicial officer,' in familiar parlance, being 'judge and jury.' On the facts however, the Privy Council found a denial of natural justice in the lack of opportunity to be heard before committal. *Maharaj No 2* was an action for redress under the Bill of Rights for deprivation of liberty without due process. Two 'common law-existing law' issues were engaged, namely, the law of contempt and judicial immunity. The constitution concerned contained a special savings clause preserving the legality of existing law *against* the assertion of a conferred right. Inevitably, the saved common law was held aloft by the defence. The Privy Council majority, in a judgment delivered by Lord

Diplock could countenance the appellant's claim for redress without disparaging the common law.

The character of contempt proceedings and its existence in common law notwithstanding, it was not existing law that the rules of natural justice could be breached. Moreover, the savings clause did not operate to render action *not lawful* at the promulgation of the constitution, lawful thereafter. The task of the court to *prevent the common law* from blocking the action was more onerous in relation to judicial immunity, and the resolution of the problem involved a clarification of the character of the 'new' action for breach of a fundamental right. The action, it was affirmed, was one in *public law and against the state,* not the judicial officer. While the mere invocation of 'public law' did not *per se* explain the action, it at least made it clear that the judge was not himself being sued in a civil action.[15] It may be that the majority view left unrebutted an argument that judicial immunity in principle forbade any form of recourse to a court to challenge the 'doings' of a judge and arguably, *more so,* a 'public law action.'[16]

Lord Diplock also had to deal with anxieties about actions for judicial error, but pointed out that the action could only arise for 'errors' that were 'procedural,' since 'no human right or fundamental freedom recognised by Chapter I of the Constitution is contravened by a judgment or order that is wrong and liable to be set aside on appeal for an error of fact or substantive law, even where the error has resulted in a person's serving a sentence of imprisonment. The remedy for errors of these kinds is to appeal to a higher court. Where there is no higher court to appeal to then none can say that there was error.'[17]

---

15. Indeed, Lord Diplock's observation went solely to stating that the action was 'public' rather than to showing that a public law action was not inconsistent with judicial immunity. He said, ibid at 396–97: 'The chapter is concerned with public law, not private law... [A]s regards infringements by one private individual of rights of another private individual, section 1 implicitly acknowledges that the existing law of torts provides a sufficient accommodation between their conflicting rights and freedoms to satisfy the requirements of the new Constitution as respects the rights specifically conferred to.'

16. Lord Hailsham's cogent dissent saw the section on redress as purely procedural and therefore (one must assume) as insufficient to 'override' the existing law on judicial immunity. This depends on a view of that law as being itself *substantive,* and on the perception that the 'new' public law action for redress was effectively a procedure to challenge judicial action, prohibited by the common law. See ibid 407.

17. Ibid 399. Unhappily, the observation did for a while (in Trinidad and Tobago at least) give rise to a number of actions under the constitution claiming procedural error and the consequent right to redress, thus bringing to pass Lord Hailsham's prophecy, that a new and probably unattractive branch of jurisprudence was almost certain to arise based on the distinction between those judicial errors which do and those which do not, constitute a deprivation of due process of law. Ibid 406. Two of these actions, did reach the Privy Council. See *Nannan v State* [1986] AC 360 (PC T&T) and *Chokolingo v AG* [1981] 1 WLR 106 (PC T&T).

The jurisdiction of Trinidad and Tobago also provided the next major case in which the Privy Council ensured that arguments based on the common law did not defeat the assertion of a fundamental right. In *Thornhill v AG*,[18] the Privy Council was invited to say that the alleged *non existence* in common law of a right to counsel on arrest, negated a claim to such access in the face of the clear statement of the right in the Constitution. In addition, the common law understanding that police officers acted on their own account, and were not agents of the state, was raised. The first argument derived from the fact that the Constitution concerned, as for all the West Indian Constitutions, had declared that the rights therein stated had existed previously and were to continue to exist. There was no written law conferring an entitlement to access to counsel on detention and, as apparently accepted by the Court of Appeal, the common law knew of no such entitlement. It was, therefore, reasoned that the drafters of the Constitution had erred in including such a right in the Constitution.

The Privy Council taking a pragmatic view and not, as the Court of Appeal had done, dredging the ancient common law to see whether or not it had granted access to counsel on arrest, affirmed the statement of right in the Constitution, and that it had in fact been enjoyed, whether or not *de jure* or as a result of a settled executive practice to allow such access. There was, therefore, no need to decide the common law position at all. Moreover, the special savings clause could not render unlawful a practice which was not unlawful and which had subsequently been set out in the constitution as a right. The de facto right had been converted into *a de jure right*. The established fact that in Trinidad and Tobago persons arrested and detained by the police had been accorded access to counsel, and that the judiciary of the state had adopted in identical terms principles set out in Appendix A to the English Judges Rules [1964], determined the issue in the appellant's favour.[19] On the common law arguments as to the status of police officers, the Privy Council perceived that to exclude the activities of the police would be to insulate from the commands of the Bills a large area of official conduct impinging on the rights declared. It said: 'Indeed, the very nature of the executive function which it is

---

18. [1981] AC 61 (PC T&T).
19. The third of these principles is set out for its historical (in a comparative sense) interest. It reads: 'That every person at any stage of an investigation should be able to communicate and to consult privately with a solicitor. This is so even if he is in custody, provided that in such a case no unreasonable delay or hindrances is caused to the processes of investigation or the administration of justice by his doing so.' Section 5(2)(c) of the Trinidad and Tobago Constitution states the right of 'a person who has been arrested or detained...to retain and instruct without delay a legal adviser of his own choice and to hold communication with him.'

the duty of police officers to perform is likely in practice to involve the commonest risk of contravention of an individual's rights under section 1(a) and (b) through overzealousness in carrying out those duties.'[20] On the issue of the 'status' of the police officer in rights litigation (as for judges), the Privy Council through Lord Diplock must have realized that to exclude the activities of the 'personages' concerned – judicial officers and police officers – would have been to create too large a hole in the fabric of the rights structure. But it is some interest that whereas in *Thornhill* a concept of the common law had to be declared abolished, in *Maharaj* it was merely inapplicable.

A comparison of *Maharaj* and *Thornhill* shows up the subtleties of the interaction between the common law and enacted fundamental rights. In the first case, Lord Diplock, by focusing on the fact that at common law there could be no deprivation of liberty on an infringement of natural justice (translating into the constitutional right not to be deprived of liberty without due process), rather than on the non-existence in common law of a remedy for 'judicial error,' could declare:

> So to understand the legal nature of the various rights and freedoms that are described in the succeeding Section 1 paragraphs (a) to (k) in broad terms and in language more familiar to politics than to legal draftsmanship, it is necessary to examine the extent to which, in his exercise and enjoyment of rights and freedoms capable of falling within the broad descriptions in the section, the individual was entitled to protection or non-interference under the law as it existed immediately before the Constitution came into effect. That is the extent of the protection or freedom from interference by the law that section 2 provides shall not be abrogated, abridged or infringed by any future law....[21]

But in *Thornhill,* Lord Diplock, reasoning similarly that existing laws, as administered in practice, could be a relevant aid to the ascertainment of the kind of executive or judicial act intended to be prohibited by the 'wide and vague words' used in section 1, concluded:

> This external aid to construction is neither necessary nor permissible where the treatment complained of is of any of the kinds specifically described in...section 2...So there is no need to consider whether before the commencement of the Constitution a person arrested and detained by the police would have had at common law a legal

---

20. *Thornhill* (n 18) 74.
21. *Maharaj* (n 14) 395. Section 1, now section 4 of the Constitution once concerned, sets out the main civil and political rights, with a few new ones as referred to in the text, while section 2 now section 5, sets out 'procedural rights,' such as those included in the fair hearing/trial clauses of the other Commonwealth Caribbean states.

remedy if he had been prevented from exercising what is specifically described in section 2....[22]

The scope of the right could, therefore, be ascertained independently of the common law once it was set out unambiguously in the Constitution.

The reference to 'political language' in the paragraph cited from *Maharaj* gives a clue to one possible justification for judicial recourse to the common law. Such recourse can operate as a form of judicial disclaimer, as the interpretation of a right is given by the common law and can thus be seen to be free of subjective bias. For immediate purposes, however, the statements from the two cases are in a certain tension; albeit taken in isolation from each other, both are perfectly valid. In *Maharaj,* pre-existing and common law could be used to give content to the broadly stated rights in section one of the Constitution of Trinidad and Tobago which then established the extent of the protection given under section 2. That being the case, it is not clear that resort to the pre-existing law and common law becomes *impermissible* in a *Thornhill type scenario* though it might well be unnecessary. Again, as has been seen, *pre-existing practice* was a significant factor in the decision in *Thornhill*.

Many of the tensions or incongruities in the relation between rights and the rules of the common law arise from the obvious fact that the common law can determine both the existence and scope of a right as well as limit it or even negate it. The existence or not at common law of a *remedy*, in circumstances seen to constitute a breach of an enacted right, has grounded arguments (as seen above) for or against a right in the face of its inclusion in a constitutional document. *Maharaj* and *Thornhill* establish that the absence of a common law remedy cannot logically deny an enacted right, though the *existence* of such a remedy may well reinforce a right stated in a Bill.

The case of *Bell v DPP*[23] is one of those placed in the *Maharaj-Thornhill* line, as a case in which the Court did not endorse the use of the common law against the assertion of a constitutional right. In this case the Privy Council, happily, recognized a broadly stated entitlement to a 'fair trial within a reasonable time' as conferred by the Constitution, while using existing 'practice and procedure' to determine whether the applicant had been given a trial within a reasonable time. The respondent, premising himself on *Nasralla,* argued not only that there was no right at common law to a speedy trial, but in effect that delay was part of the legal culture and the 'practice' of the Jamaican court system. The Privy Council saw

---

22. *Thornhill* (n 18) 70.
23. [1985] 1 AC 937 (PC Ja).

very precisely that this argument was an attempt 'to whittle away the right of the applicant under the Constitution by reference to the common law in force before the Constitution.' The Court reasoned that if the speedy trial right did not exist at common law, the *setting out of a right* 'to a fair hearing within a reasonable time by an independent and impartial court established by law' in section 20(1) of the Constitution of Jamaica *was* sufficient to confer it.[24]

3. Common Law Dominance over the Bills of Rights

The three Privy Council decisions looked at so far are taken to be examples of cases in which that Court has not opposed the common law to rights enacted as law. But in the earliest litigation of a Bill of Rights clause from the Commonwealth Caribbean, the case of *DPP v Nasralla*,[25] the Privy Council gave its first statement on the relation between the Bills of Rights in the constitutions and the common law. This case has largely set the standard in this area, so that cases following it can be seen to form one current thought, and those in the *Maharaj-Thornhill* line another on the issue of 'the common law and the Bills of Rights.' Section 20(8) of the Constitution of Jamaica states:

> No person who shows that he has been tried by any competent court for a criminal offence and either convicted or acquitted shall again be tried for that offence, or for any other criminal offence of which he could have been convicted at the trial for that offence save upon the order of a superior court made in the course of appeal proceedings relating to the conviction or acquittal.

The applicant had been acquitted of murder, the jury being unable to agree a verdict of manslaughter. He was subsequently rearraigned for manslaughter. The Jamaica Court of Appeal was of the view that the fact that the jury could not agree on a verdict as regards manslaughter 'does not mean that the applicant was not in peril of conviction for manslaughter.'[26] In allowing the appeal of the Director of Public Prosecutions, the Privy Council in a judgment delivered by Lord Devlin responded to the statement by observing that while the word 'peril' had been used in its 'natural and ordinary' sense by the Court of Appeal it

---

24. Ibid 948–49.
25. *Nasralla* (n 5). This case became the precedent for a number of cases in which the Privy Council subjected its interpretation of Bill of Rights provisions to existing law, including the common law. In particular, cases brought by persons under the sentence of death challenging that sentence either under the right of life or punishment clauses of the constitutions, were premised on the *Nasralla* doctrine of the supremacy of 'the common law – existing law' over the statement of fundamental rights in the Constitutions.
26. Ibid 249.

was necessary 'if the *rule against double jeopardy and the principles of autrefois* were to produce the same result, the word "peril" must be given a more restricted meaning.'[27] The restriction was clearly placed on the words set out in the constitution.

It might have been thought that the *principle* involved was one of obviating *double jeopardy,* and that the *autrefois rule* or *group of rules* gave expression to the principles. In any event, the Privy Council was prepared to merge rule with principle, in fact to subject principle to rule, even on its view of what the principle and rule, respectively, were.[28] *Autrefois* required either an actual conviction or acquittal, therefore the Privy Council could conclude that at common law double jeopardy also required conviction or acquittal. The Director of Public Prosecutions, therefore, won the day in the face of section 20(8) which clearly sought to create a situation in which the accused was not exposed to the *risk or peril of being* tried again, once he had been so tried and 'could have been convicted' of *any other offence* at the trial.

The Privy Council effectively reconstructed the common law giving expression to the *concept* of double jeopardy stated as a fundamental right.[29] Of more immediate interest for the discussion here, was the general perspective on the Bill of Rights which led the Privy Council to believe that the common law (however eventually detailed) had to prevail over the actual statement of right in the Constitution. The Bill of Rights, Chapter III of the Constitution of Jamaica, begins its first section, section 13 with a declaration: 'whereas every person in Jamaica is entitled to the fundamental rights and freedoms of the individual... to each and all of the following [rights]....' The section continues with a statement of three groups of rights[30] and then further declares that the subsequent provisions of the chapter are to have effect 'for the purpose of protecting the aforesaid rights.' The detailing of rights begins with section 14 and starts in the now established fashion with the right to life or more precisely, the right not to be deprived of life. The redress clause in section 25 gives a right of redress in relation to the provisions of section 14–24.

---

27. Ibid (emphasis added).
28. The *autrefois* rules protect against double jeopardy. Another 'rule' developed at common law, which protected against double jeopardy was that of *issue estoppels* which is in fact a plea, where the circumstances did not quite fall within the *autrefois* rules. It should be noted that Lord Devlin had doubted the availability of *issue estoppel* in *Connelly v DPP* [1964] AC 1254 (HL). The plea was abolished in England in *DPP v Humphrys* [1977] AC 1 (HL).
29. *Richards v R* (1992) 41 WIR 263 (PC Ja) applied and possibly extended the holding in *Nasralla,* which was not referred to. Section 20(2) of the Constitution was of no avail, where the appellant had been 'discharged' following the entry of a *nolle prosequi* by the Director of Public Prosecutions.
30. These are (a) life, liberty, security of the person, the enjoyment of property and the protection of the law; (b) freedom of conscience, of expression and of peaceful assembly and association; and (c) respect for his private and family life.

Clearly, the recital with which section 13 begins is largely rhetorical in character and does not form part of the statement either of the 'group' of rights in section 13 or those specified in sections 14–24. Yet, it was from this recital that the Privy Council found not merely that the right already existed at common law in Jamaica, but that they were 'already secured' to individuals in the state *under that* law, which therefore defined the scope of the rights. The Court could then say:

> Whereas the general rule as is to be expected in a Constitution and as is here embodied in section 2, is that the provisions of the Constitution should prevail over other law, an exception is made in Chapter III. This chapter, as their Lordships have already noted proceeds upon the presumption that the fundamental rights which it covers are already secured to the people of Jamaica by existing law. The laws in force are not to be subjected to scrutiny in order to see whether or not they conform to the precise terms of the protective provisions.[31]

This, together with the actual method of ascertaining the common law in *Nasralla,* established that the meaning and scope of the rights are *exactly coextensive* with the common law rules in force on the promulgation of the Constitutions, and that a Bill of Rights claim will fail where it could not have been made at common law (and existing law) prior to the promulgation of the Bills.[32]

The use of the word 'exception' in the quoted statement invites comment. It is particularly unfortunate that the Privy Council should have suggested and indeed pronounced a chapter of a constitution, especially the Bill of Rights *not* to be part of the Supreme Law of the State, more so when this was unnecessary. The statement, moreover, creates a situation of great paradox, for apart from asserting the 'supremacy' of the common law, it suggests that there is a conflict or at least some opposition between that law and the statement of right. But as already seen, the informing principle of *Nasralla,* that the existing common law already secured the rights to Jamaica, implies that the common law was congruent with the statement of the rights in the Constitution. This conundrum is as unnecessary as it is foolish. The common law on a given subject and certainly the application of common law rules is ultimately that which the judiciary says it is. The interpretation of the rights as they are set out

---

31. *Nasralla* (n 5) 247–48 (emphasis added). Section 2 states that subject to the sections dealing with alteration to the Constitution and the general lawmaking power, if any other law is inconsistent with this Constitution, this Constitution shall prevail and the other law shall, to the extent of the inconsistencies, be void.
32. For the application of this reasoning see, e.g., *De Freitas v Benny* [1976] AC 239 (PC T&T); *Riley v AG* [1983] 1 AC 719 (PC Ja); *Thomas v Baptiste* [2000] 2 AC 1 (PC T&T).

in the constitutions is itself a matter for judges. This being the case and there being nothing in the special savings clauses to compel a court not to interpret the common law consistently with the unambiguous provisions of a Constitution, there should have been for *the most part little conflict* between the rights, the Bills and the common law.

The point just stated can be seen in the celebrated dissent of Lords Scarman and Brightman in *Riley v AG*.[33] They said:

> The contribution which the Constitution makes to the jurisprudence of Jamaica is that it offers to every person in Jamaica the protection of a written constitution in respect of the rights and freedoms recognised and acknowledged by the law; and *'law' means both the pre-existing law* so far as it remains in force...and the new law arising from the Constitution itself and from future enactment.[34]

The passage can be seen as a negation of a necessary antagonism between existing law as the common law and the constitution.[35] It is now also recognized in the context of the United Kingdom that common law adjudication can itself develop rights or recognize and create new ones, with or without the help of the ECHR as detailed below.

A final point of interest on *Nasralla* derives from an observation of Lord Devlin, in which he asserted that the object of the Bill of Rights provision was to ensure that no *future enactment* should in any matter which the Bill covered 'derogate from the rights which at the coming into force of the Constitution, the individual enjoyed.' This reflects not merely the view that the conferred freedoms were sufficiently protected by the law extant at the constitution, but constitutes a 'political perception' that Bills of Rights were necessary to preserve the newly independent inhabitants of the various Commonwealth Caribbean states from local regimes that could turn oppressive.[36] *Nasralla* and its view of existing law including the common law, taken with the limitations set out with the statement of rights in the Constitutions has been a dominant feature in the understanding and interpretation of the constitutionally enacted and entrenched Bills of Rights, until the mid-'90s.

The brief conclusion of this part of the discussion is that the two attitudes to the relation between the common law and enacted rights

---

33. *Riley* ibid.
34. Ibid 729 (emphasis added).
35. But the limitations in existing law and the common law had been noticed. However, the Constitution's introduction of a new judicial remedy negatives any presumption that the remedies available under the pre-existing law were necessarily sufficient, indeed, the enactment of new protections suggests that they needed strengthening.
36. One can compare the view which might have informed the remark, with the observations of Lord Diplock in *Thomas v AG* [1982] AC 113 (PC T&T) 123–24. These observations were cited in *AG v Lake* [1999] 1 WLR 68 (PC A&B).

described in the foregoing pages illustrate that the common law is *per se* not opposed to enacted rights, even where the latter include 'entitlements' and forms of recourse unknown to that law, and even given that the terms of 'enacted rights' may not coincide with specific common-law rules or any particular understanding thereof. It must be the case that the impact of the common law depends on judicial choice and the judicial determination to countenance, or not, Bill of Rights claims. The reason for a particular choice or set of choices in the specific context of Privy Council adjudication is considered in examining the devices used by the Privy Council in Bill of Rights litigation.

4. Defining Restraints on Fundamental Rights and Freedoms: The Common Law

A major area of interaction between common law rules and fundamental rights and freedoms as enforceable legal claims is the setting of the restraints and limits on the formulated rights.[37] The fact that the setting of these limits can well be seen as the actual defining of the rights brings up the matter of the content of specific rights and especially those constituting freedoms known to the law before enactment as rights. The issues, therefore, of limitations on rights and the defining content of these rights converge. The fundamental freedoms known to the common law have, no doubt due to the influence of Dicey, been seen as and indeed are residual in character.[38] This reflects the view that the content of a

---

37. The limitation sub clause to the right of freedom of expression in the St Christopher-Nevis Constitution (typifying those subclauses for the Bill of Rights other than that of Trinidad and Tobago) reads as follows:

> (2) Nothing contained in or done under the authority of any law shall be held to be inconsistent with or in contravention of this section to the extent that the law in question makes provision –
> > a) that is reasonably required in the interests of defence, public safety, public order, public morality or public health;
> > b) that is reasonably required for the purpose of protecting the reputations, rights and freedoms of other persons or the private lives of persons concerned in legal proceedings, preventing the disclosure of information received in confidence, maintaining the authority and independence of the courts of regulating telephoning, telegraphy, posts, wireless broadcasting or television; or
> > c) that imposes restrictions upon public officers that are reasonably required for the proper performance of their functions,'
> and except so far as that provision or, as the case may be, the thing done under the authority thereof is shown not to be reasonably justifiable in a democratic society.

> The concluding clause does not occur in the earlier constitutions including those of Jamaica and Barbados.

38. A.V. Dicey, *Introduction to the Study of the Law of the Constitution* (10th edn, Macmillan, London 1959). In fact, chapters VI and VII on 'freedom of discussion' and the 'right of public meeting' seem designed to illustrate the narrow scope at common law of these freedoms thus: 'Nor is the law of England specially favourable to free speech or to free writing, in the rules which it maintains in theory and often enforces in fact, as to the kind of statements which a man has a legal right to make'; ibid 240. Dicey could therefore assert: 'When once, however, the principles of the common law and the force of the enactments still contained in the statute-book are really appreciated, no one can maintain that the law of England recognizes anything like that natural right to free communication of thoughts and opinions which was proclaimed in France a little over a hundred years ago to be one of the most valuable Rights of Man.' Ibid 245–6.

'liberty' is 'freedom' – that which is left after the limitations on the liberty have been taken into account. Liberty of speech is apt for illustrative purposes as it is one of the more broadly stated freedoms. As a 'residual freedom,' the expression to which the individual was entitled would be such as was left after the application of the law relating, for example, to contempt of court, defamation, confidentiality, official secrecy and defence. These areas of law appear as limitations on stated rights in the constitutions of the Commonwealth Caribbean states with the exception of Trinidad and Tobago. At common law, the freedoms known to it *do not constitute rights* such as to require the state to justify 'exceptions' thereto. In broader theoretical terms and as Dicey puts it in relation to free speech, there did not exist in the common law 'anything like that natural right to free communication of thoughts and opinions' as in the French Declaration of the Rights of Man.[39]

But in more recent times, the residual character of freedoms at common law has been denied thus:

> [W]e in this country (where everybody is free to do anything, subject only to the provisions of the law) proceed upon an assumption of freedom of speech, and turn to our law to discover the established exceptions to it.[40]

According to Lord Goff this approach was opposed to that under the ECHR in which a right was stated and then qualified. It seems however, that under the ECHR and certainly as interpreted by its Court, there is under that Convention an actual right in the individual, albeit subsequently qualified; whilst at common law, free expression was the liberty to communicate matter not defamatory, not a threat to the defence of the realm, not a breach of confidence and not a contempt of court, amongst many other 'nots.' The liberty *did not precede* the setting of restraints on a freedom, but rather the restraining laws applied automatically, albeit not always in advance.

The residual nature of common law freedoms is best illustrated in the case of *AG v Times Newspapers*[41] and especially in the judgment of Lord Simon of Glaisdale which comprehensively explained the way in which the common law has traditionally dealt with the tension between the

---

39. Ibid.
40. *Spycatcher No 2* (n 4) 283 (Lord Goff).
41. *Times Newspapers* (n 4). It is to be noticed that the decision in this case represents the law of contempt for the Commonwealth Caribbean, as it is a determination of the common law by the most authoritative court on that law, in the absence of a Privy Council decision binding on West Indian jurisdictions, and containing a contrary exposition of the law. This is so in face of the fact that the constitutions of the region, with one exception, virtually reproduce the ECHR and specifically, Art 10 on free expression.

public interest representing the 'right' on one hand and the restraint on the other. 'Individual right' does not appear in the judgment and the 'interests' dealt with were those in 'freedom of discussion' in a democratic society and in the 'due administration of justice.' The two interests, 'which are apt to conflict, but should so far as possible be reconciled and otherwise be held in careful balance.'[42] The words quoted may well describe the task involved in interpreting the statement of rights in the West Indian Bills, which, save for one, follow the pattern provided in the ECHR, with a first subclause conferring a right and a second stating the restraints thereon. Lord Simon having stated his task in the words just quoted, describes the law of contempt repeatedly used the phrase 'an objective code,'[43] undoubtedly to mean 'the common law.' The significance of this becomes apparent when, in getting to the point of balance, he declared that it could not be struck anew on a case to case basis since, 'the law...and its application would tend to vary with the length of the particular judge's foot.'[44] Here is a major explanation of recourse to the common law in the adjudication of enacted rights. The judge can point to a body of law, extant law, to negative the argument that she has decided on the basis of her personal beliefs, political views and so forth. Such recourse may ultimately be used to refute the argument that human rights adjudication is premised on the predilections of the individual judge and is, therefore, undemocratic. What is then justified is not so much the actual restraint, but finding *it as, and in a pre-existent objective code,* the common law.

In *AG v Times Newspapers*, the common law was used to strike the balance, or indeed it could well be said, *constituted the balance between the two public interests* in tension. If the common law is seen to establish this balance, then it is the case that the restraining law must apply automatically and that the adjudicating court will not look to ascertain whether and to what extent the restraint is needed in the particular case before it. Whenever the circumstances fall within the ambit of the rule it will be applied. In this way, the right, or in the terms used in *Times Newspapers* the interest in free speech, being argued for falls away. It is outweighed by the restraining law. This was a major concern of the European Human Rights Court in the *Sunday Times* litigation engendered

---

42. Ibid 315.
43. Ibid 316 (where the phrase is used four times). The objective code becomes 'the relevant law as a continuing code' in a notable passage thus: 'society, through its political and legal institutions, has established the relevant law as a continuing code, and has further established special institutions (courts of law) to make the relevant decisions on the basis of such law. The public at large has delegated its decision-making in this sphere to its microcosm, the jury or judge.' Ibid 320.
44. Ibid 319.

by the House of Lords decision.[45] The House of Lords had asserted that 'the paramount public interest *pendente lite* is that the legal proceeding should progress without interference.'[46] This interest was that supported by the law of contempt. And since this law as it relates to publications of the kind involved only operated *pendente lite,* the court was applying it without taking into account free expression.

The question of permissible restraint on an enacted right (the application of the rules of the law restraining an enacted right), was before the Privy Council in *Francis v Chief of Police*[47] as the question as to the way in which the restraining second subclause of the freedom of expression right in the constitution of St Christopher-Nevis should be read. In this case, the restraining law was a piece of legislation. Lord Pearson asserted that there were two approaches. One was to read into the statement of right the restraints of the second subsection as inherent in the right concerned; the other was to take literally the conferment of the right in the first subsection and then to look to the second subsection to see whether the *prima facie* infringement was justified under it. It may be that this second mode of approach accords with the words of Lord Goff quoted earlier. In any event however, the question remained whether once the challenged law fell within a head of restraint stated in the second subsection, the alleged infringement of the right was 'justified.' The Privy Council in *Francis* appears to have decided, as the House of Lords was later to do in *Times Newspapers,* that this was indeed the case. In this way, the Privy Council could avoid an examination of the circumstances specific to the case and an assessment of the impact of the limiting law on the exercise of the freedom. This was the eschewing of the *case by case* striking of the balance, and 'the *application of an absolute rule* [even] though it may seem to be *unreasonable* if one looks only to the particular case,' as asserted in *Times Newspapers.*[48] An approach which is the antithesis of *Francis* is to be found in the Privy Council decision in *De Freitas v Benny.*[49]

---

45. *Sunday Times* (n 4). The European Court of Human Rights said at page 65: 'It is not sufficient that the interference involved belongs to that class of the exceptions listed in Article 10(2) which has been invoked; neither is it sufficient that the interference was imposed because its subject-matter fell within a particular category or was caught by a legal rule formulated in general or absolute terms: the Court has to be satisfied that the interference was necessary having regard to the facts and circumstances prevailing in the specific case before it.'

46. Ibid 32.

47. [1973] AC 761 (PC St K-N).

48. *Times Newspapers* (n 4) 323 (Lord Cross).

49. *De Freitas* (n 32).

5. Using Common Law Concepts in Support of Rights

In defining the scope of the conferred rights there have been a few indications of the way in which the common law can be used to buttress those rights and in particular rights of fair procedure. In two cases, the Privy Council was concerned with the question of the requirements of a fair hearing in multi-stage procedures, one set up in legislation and one in the Constitution itself. In *Rees v Crane*,[50] concerning the three stage procedures for the removal of judges, the respondent judge claimed that the denial of a hearing at the first or preliminary stage breached the right stated at section 4(b) of the Trinidad and Tobago Constitution to 'equality before the law and the protection of the law.' The whole of the judgment on this point, as indeed on others, was premised on the common law, and in particular the concept of natural justice, to find that the judge was indeed entitled to be heard at the preliminary stage.[51]

In *Huntley v AG*[52] the Court having found that the impugned procedure provided for in the challenged legislation did not implicate the fair trial right, nevertheless looked to the common law to see whether the appellant could claim to be heard at the first stage of a procedure relating to classification of murders as capital or non-capital for persons convicted before these categories had been introduced. The Court, citing *Wiseman v Borneman*,[53] declared that the common law could always be used to augment a statute. A fair extrapolation from this where legislation is being measured against the Constitution is that the common law can illuminate understandings both of legislation and the law of the Constitution. The common law is implicated in Bill of Rights litigation where a litigant takes one of its doctrines or creations to establish that his claim is to be brought within the protection of or meaning of a stated fundamental right.

The doctrine of legitimate expectation has been pleaded before the Privy Council by persons under sentence of death from The Bahamas and Trinidad and Tobago, to the effect that the appellants had a legitimate expectation not to be executed until their petitions before international and regional human rights entities had been determined. In *Fisher v Minister for Public Safety and Immigration No 2*,[54] the expectation just

---

50. [1994] 2 AC 173 (PC T&T).
51. Their Lordships, in ibid 192, assessed the total situation and circumstances declined to follow *Wiseman v Borneman* [1971] AC 297 (HL) and relied on a passage in *Furnell v Whangarei High Schools Board* [1973] AC 660 (PC NZ) 679, requiring courts to look at the specific circumstances of a case.
52. [1995] 2 AC 1 (PC Ja).
53. *Wiseman* (n 51). The Court, however, declined to follow the decision in this case, and declared that the absence of a provision for a hearing at the first stage of the procedure did not vitiate the legislation.
54. [2000] 1 AC 434 (PC Bah). But see the 2000 decision in *Lewis et al v AG* [2001] 2 AC 50 (PC Ja).

described was raised in the litigation of the right to life clause. The Court giving voice (as it appears to the writer) to the more restricted view of legitimate expectation, as to be found in the English decision of *Ex p Hargreaves*,[55] declared:

> [A] decision-maker can act inconsistently with a legitimate expectation which he has created, provided he gives adequate notice of his intention to do so, and provided he gives those who are affected an opportunity to state their case. Procedural fairness requires of him no more than that. Even if therefore the appellant had a legitimate expectation that he would not be executed while his petition was pending his expectation could not survive the government's letter of 2 and 30 January 1998 in which it informed the appellant's solicitors in unequivocal terms that it would wait no longer than 15 February 1998.[56]

Hargreaves has been seen to reflect the reluctance of English Courts to extend notions of 'proportionality and general fairness' outside the area of fundamental rights.[57] So that if indeed *Fisher No 2* does reflect that case, the legitimate expectation argument could not help the assertion of the fundamental right. In *Thomas v Baptiste*,[58] the appellants under sentence of death (as was Mr Fisher), were granted a stay pending hearing of their petitions before the Inter-American Commission on an argument based on the fact that the Trinidad and Tobago right to life clause declares that there is to be no deprivation of life 'without due process.' The Privy Council found *a common law right in individuals* not to have the result of proceedings pre-empted by executive action. 'Proceedings' were made to relate to 'due process' in the statement of the right.[59] While however, the common law enhanced the understanding or working out of the right on the specific facts, recourse to the common law did involve a *denial* that the constitutional right invoked could extend to 'rights' or claims arising subsequent to the promulgation of the Bills. The Privy Council *did not* extend the understanding of right to life clauses to include the making of petitions to international bodies by persons whose lives were subject to forfeiture by the state in *Thomas,* but was to do so in the decision in *Lewis.*[60]

---

55. [1997] 1 WLR 906 (CA Eng).
56. *Fisher* (n 54) 447.
57. S. Foster, 'Legitimate Expectations and Prisoner's Rights: The Right to Get What You Are Given,' (1997) 60 MLR 727, 734.
58. *Baptiste* (n 32).
59. The Privy Council could distinguish *Fisher No 2* on the basis that the right to life in the constitution of The Bahamas allowed forfeiture of life after sentence by a court and not, as in Trinidad and Tobago, after 'due process.'
60. *Lewis* (n 54).

Unhappily for any perception that a common law rule or principle can as such be deployed in the litigation of the Bill of Rights, *Fisher No 2* declared that 'public law points not arising out of or in connection with the Constitution should not normally be raised in a motion claiming constitutional relief.' It is difficult to justify this recommended exclusion of public law arguments on a constitutional action. This public law, surely the common law, is part of the law in light of which the Privy Council has interpreted the constitutions in the years since their promulgation. And, since we have it on the authority of Lord Diplock that the action for constitutional redress is one in public law, a supposed dichotomy between 'public law' and 'constitutional law' must in principle be unsound.

Judicial Independence as an Indispensable Feature of the Rule of Law and Democracy: Implications for the Commonwealth Caribbean

Arif Bulkan

1. Introduction

Although the Commonwealth Caribbean is notable among the countries of the former British Empire for the stability of its institutions and the levels of accountability in government, like every generalization this one too is subject to exceptions. In many, if not all of the territories, there have been occasions following political independence where constitutionalism has been threatened – sometimes dramatically as in Grenada and Guyana – but more often than not in quotidian and less obvious fashion, as newly independent governments have tested the limits of their power. Resulting tensions with educated and informed populations are most readily identifiable in litigation under the constitutional bills of rights, the outcome of which is obviously dependent on the degree to which judges are able and prepared to scrutinize both legislative and executive acts and thereby hold governments to account. The mechanisms by which judiciaries have been insulated against interference and how these actually operate in practice are therefore crucial, as they impact significantly on the ability and willingness of judges to fulfil this role, and, by extension, on the measure of constitutionalism that exists in a society.

A judiciary is, obviously, only as good as its individual members, but the general level of independence depends not only on the individual judges themselves, but also on the conditions under which they operate and the protection conferred on their offices. The latter factors have been described by Allen SJ as the 'institutional dimension' of judicial independence, as distinct from the individual dimension which relates to the integrity of the specific judge.[1] Both dimensions, however, are equally dependent on a number of key factors protected by Caribbean constitutions, which can be broadly categorized as (i) the procedures for

---

1. *R v Jones* (2007) 72 WIR 1 (SC Bah) 4 [10].

selecting judges, (ii) the conditions under which the judiciary operates, and (iii) the jurisdiction of the courts themselves.

But there is a broader and somewhat elusive issue, namely whether these written provisions comprise the total of the constitutional guarantee of judicial independence, or whether they are simply manifestations of a deeper, underlying philosophy or natural moral order. This chapter will show that the bare constitutional provisions have often not been enough to achieve their stated goals but have been subject to evasion and on occasion even subversion or outright manipulation. Reflecting on the constitutionalization of human rights norms in the Commonwealth, Professor Albert Fiadjoe unearths a gap between ethos and literalism, concluding that the 'mere re-statement or absence of human rights provisions is not really an adequate index or fair measure of the enjoyment of human rights.'[2] Another distinguished commentator, Professor Keith Patchett, has made similar observations, attributing the disconnect partly to the lack of autochthony in the norms that were formulated in the independence constitutions. In the process of constitution-making, Patchett argues, the drafters failed to consider whether the 'underlayer' necessary for the effective operation of these norms was present.[3]

An independent judiciary is key in the context of these realities, for though itself partly unaccountable, the judiciary is an acknowledged bulwark against executive excess and in this way can hold politicians to account. But as with the itemization of human rights norms and standards, there are limits to what the text itself can accomplish by way of securing an independent judiciary, as will be demonstrated below. It is here that the true potential of implicit constitutional norms is most evident, for where the text is lacking, resort to the constitution's underlying values can help to promote the independence of the judiciary – the latter being vital to secure the ultimate goals of democracy and adherence to the rule of law.

2. Procedures for Selecting Judges

Procedures for selecting judges are fairly standard across the region, with only minor variations among individual territories. Generally, appointments are made by the Head of State acting on advice, but it

---

2. A. Fiadjoe, 'Human Rights and Comparative Constitutions – A Non-Traditional View' (paper presented at a conference in Mahwah, New Jersey, USA, June 1990 on Human Rights and Comparative Constitutions).
3. K. Patchett, 'The Legal Inheritance of the Smaller Commonwealth States' (1989) 8 Commonwealth Jud J 16.

is in the source of that advice that the differences are to be found. In Barbados, all appointments to the Supreme Court are made on the recommendation of the Prime Minister after consultation with the Leader of the Opposition,[4] but in many of the other territories a distinction is made between the Chief Justice and the remaining judges on the Supreme Court or High Court. A typical approach is that followed in Jamaica, where the Chief Justice is appointed by the Governor General acting on the recommendation of the Prime Minister after consultation with the Leader of the Opposition,[5] while puisne judges are appointed by the Governor General on the advice of a Judicial Services Commission.[6]

Ultimately, the strategy was to minimize the role of the executive in the process, hence the requirement of consultation with the Leader of the Opposition as in Barbados, or more meaningfully as adopted elsewhere, the creation of a specific Commission to make recommendations. For countries with the latter approach, the composition of this Judicial Services Commission is therefore critical, given the integral role it plays in the process of appointments. While it is difficult to find a norm across the Caribbean, generally this Commission is composed of five to six members, chaired by the Chief Justice and for the remainder comprising one other Judge recommended by the Chief Justice, the Chairman of the Public Service Commission, and two or three members appointed by the Governor General on the Prime Minister's recommendation.[7] The success of these procedures in achieving their desired outcome depends heavily on the integrity of various office-holders, such as the Prime Minister, Chief Justice and various individuals appointed to the Commission.

A. Political Control of the Selection of the Head of the Judiciary

Nowhere in the Caribbean are the tensions between executive and judiciary better highlighted than in Guyana, where successive post-independence governments have displayed a shrewd appreciation of the crucial role of selection procedures for fashioning a compliant judiciary. When the remaining avenues of appeal to the Privy Council were abolished in 1973[8] and the Guyana Court of Appeal became the country's final appellate court, the Burnham regime (which had just

---

4. Barbados Constitution 1966 s 81(1).
5. Jamaica Constitution 1962 s 98(1).
6. Ibid s 98(2).
7. See ibid s 111.
8. Constitution (Amendment) Act 1973-19 s 4.

installed itself by a massively rigged election)[9] took the opportunity to create the position of Chancellor of the judiciary. On the surface, this was presented as mere nomenclature – instead of a President of the Court of Appeal (as in Jamaica), Guyana would have a Chancellor. The motive for the position, however, lay in a far more sinister and corrupt objective. At the time the Chief Justice was Sir Joseph Luckhoo, a Guyanese of East Indian descent and a jurist of unimpeachable character, on both counts unacceptable to the increasingly dictatorial Forbes Burnham. Burnham's solution was thus to create this new position of Chancellor as head of the judiciary, to which he appointed Sir Kenneth Stoby, then Chief Justice of Barbados. Through these machinations – all effected through superficially lawful procedures – Luckhoo CJ was effectively demoted while Burnham openly signalled the role he envisaged for the judiciary in the post-colonial era.

Almost 30 years later, and despite the return of free and fair elections or democracy in Guyana, a similar drama came to be played out once again. Upon the retirement of Cecil Kennard and his replacement by Madam Desiree Bernard as Chancellor of the judiciary, the next Judge in line for the position of Chief Justice was Madam Justice Claudette Singh, but she was passed over in favour of Justice Carl Singh. There are advantages to selecting only the best from an available list of candidates for promotion to a higher position, but given that the overlooked Judge had 14 years' experience while the favoured one possessed a mere six, such a move could be justified only by reason of uncommon brilliance in one or unacceptable incompetence in the other – neither of which seemed to be the case. Instead, the barely disguised facts revealed a rather more sordid explanation. Claudette Singh is of mixed ethnicity and immediately prior to this vacancy had ruled against the People's Progressive Party/Civic (PPP/C) government in a petition challenging the 1997 election.[10] In her decision, Claudette Singh invalidated the electoral results on certain procedural grounds, and though she applied the doctrine of necessity to validate all official acts in the intervening period, the result was a public humiliation for the PPP/C which had

---

9. It is widely acknowledged that in order to retain power, the PNC rigged successive elections in 1973, 1980 and 1985, as well as a referendum in 1978 by which the Republican Constitution was foisted on Guyana: P.C. Hintzen, 'Creoleness and Nationalism in Guyanese Anticolonialism and Postcolonial Formation' *Small Axe* 8 2004: 106, 118; A. Morrison, *Justice: The Struggle for Democracy in Guyana, 1952–1992* (Red Thread Women's Press, Georgetown 1998) 114–29; M. DeMerieux, *Fundamental Rights in Commonwealth Caribbean Constitutions* (Faculty of Law Library, Cave Hill 1992) 17–18. Note also Professor DeMerieux's tongue-in-cheek comment regarding the 1978 referendum: ibid 10.

10. *Perreira v Chief Election Officer* (unrep) 15 Jan 2001, No 36-P/1998 (HC Guy); see also *Singh v Perreira, Jagan v Perreira* (18 Nov 1998) GY 1998 CA 8 (Guy).

been in charge of the election as the incumbent government. For this, Claudette Singh incurred the lasting wrath of the PPP/C. By contrast, Carl Singh is of East Indian descent, and more importantly had by then also demonstrated his loyalty to the administration in a critical and extremely sensitive case.[11] Thus Claudette Singh was rejected for the very reason that Luckhoo CJ had been passed over 30 years before to head the Judiciary, that is, the unabashed preference of both regimes for 'one of their own.'

B. The Inefficacy of Consultation Requirements

These tribal politics are not confined to Guyana, and have been paralleled elsewhere in the Commonwealth Caribbean. In most countries, the degree of influence enjoyed by the executive is as a result of the inherent vagueness of the requirement of 'consultation' prior to making these appointments. As opposed to the requirement of 'consent,' consultation imposes a standard that can be easily met, and functions at best to give a superficial gloss on the selection process. It does not assure meaningful participation and still less does it ensure that input once received will be influential. In practice, even where there has been a failure to consult, Caribbean courts have been slow to acknowledge any irregularity in the process. In *Whitfield v AG*,[12] the issue under consideration was the validity of the extension of term granted to the incumbent Chief Justice of The Bahamas, who had reached the constitutional age for retirement. The Prime Minister had in fact raised this issue with the Leader of the Opposition before making the recommendation to the Governor General, but he did so in passing in a letter and only after he had already discussed the matter with the candidate himself and agreed that the latter's term would be extended. On a subsequent challenge brought by the Leader of the Opposition, the trial judge viewed the belated consultation as a mere matter of procedure, holding that there was no requirement for

---

11. Just prior to his meteoric elevation Carl Singh J ruled in the government's favour in *Chue v AG* (unrep) 27 Jan 2000, No 66-M/1998 (HC Guy), which involved a challenge to the Revenue Authority created by the government to consolidate the customs and excise and inland revenue departments and by which public servants were turned into mere employees. Carl Singh J upheld the validity of the newly created Authority despite very serious questions as to its legitimacy. This decision has not been favourably received by commentators. See, for example, S. Fraser, 'The Evolution of Constitutional Protection of Fundamental Rights in Guyana' (2001) 11 Carib LR 89, 103, and even though the applicants' appeal was dismissed by the Guyana Court of Appeal [see *Chue v AG* (2006) 72 WIR 213 (CA Guy)], the latter decision has also garnered trenchant criticism: L. Jackson, 'The Ideology of Judicial Decision-Making in the Commonwealth Caribbean: Interrogating the Doctrine of Separation of Powers.' Paper presented at the Faculty Workshop Series 2008–9, Conversations betwen the CCJ and the Faculty of Law UWI, Trinidad (November 2008, unpublished paper on file with author).

12. (1989) 44 WIR 1 (SC Bah).

such consultation to take place before the judge in question reached retirement age. This was possibly correct on one interpretation of an admittedly opaque provision, but there was more at stake here than mere chronology. To dismiss as *de minimis* the Prime Minister's failure to consult with the Leader of the Opposition prior to discussing the extension with (and giving his agreement to) the Chief Justice, as the trial judge did, demonstrates clearly how the requirement of consultation is a mere formality at best and farcical at worst.

In Belize, where the constitution actually specifies what consultation is to entail, being 'a genuine opportunity to present his or her view before the decision or action...is taken,'[13] such particularization was still not enough to restrain the executive. On the eve of national elections scheduled for 27 August 1998, the government hastily made several appointments to the judiciary, including that of Chief Justice, without consulting the Leader of the Opposition as constitutionally required. In fact, the Opposition Leader was contacted prior to the appointments, but even as the parties were exchanging correspondence as to a mutually convenient date to meet, a Chief Justice was sworn in on the day before the elections even though there had been no consultation. A constitutional challenge subsequently brought against the appointment of the Chief Justice succeeded on the ground that the procedure specified in the constitution had not been followed; thus, there was never a valid appointment to begin with.[14] Meerabux J had strong words for the Prime Minister's timing of the judicial appointments:

> Such a course of action is unheard of in a parliamentary democracy based on the Westminster model where the government of the day after the issue of the Writ of Elections acts merely in a caretaker capacity and refrains from taking any major decisions. To my mind, to appoint a Chief Justice substantively just a day before the general elections makes a mockery of parliamentary democracy.[15]

One is driven to conclude from these events that constitutional provisions by themselves are not sufficient to restrain an executive bent on creating a sympathetic judiciary, and certainly not any that require – as did Guyana's and many others in the Commonwealth Caribbean – mere 'consultation' with the Leader of the Opposition. Ultimately, consultation imposes the most minimal of requirements, one in which process defers to personality – that is to say, political nepotism in appointments can only be avoided if those holding the power are prepared

---

13. Belize Constitution 1981 s 97(1).
14. *Mohammed v AG* (unrep) 2 Feb 1999, No 73 of 1999 (HC Bze).
15. Ibid [as quoted in Sir Fred Phillips, *Commonwealth Caribbean Constitutional Law* (Cavendish Publishing Ltd, London 2002) 288].

to exercise it responsibly and honourably. The solution adopted by many of the Commonwealth Caribbean countries in vesting the responsibility for appointments in a Judicial Services Commission is also illusory, since members of the Commission are appointed by the Prime Minister and invariably end up being persons sympathetic to his or her cause and prepared to do his or her bidding.

C. Consent Requirements

In recognition of, and partly to address, these deficiencies, the relevant provisions of the Guyana Constitution governing appointments to the higher judiciary were amended in 2001. Whereas under the 1980 arrangements the appointment of the Chancellor and Chief Justice could be made by the President after consultation with the Minority Leader, under the new procedure the actual agreement of the Leader of the Opposition became necessary.[16] Requiring consent, however, is premised on the existence of a mature political climate, and the experience elsewhere in the Commonwealth Caribbean was not encouraging. In the OECS, the appointment of the Chief Justice of the Court of Appeal requires consensus from the member countries, a requirement that was to prove insuperable the last time that a vacancy arose in this office. A protracted impasse ensued because Brian Alleyne, the candidate next in line, was unpalatable to Grenada, one of the OECS member states. In one version of the events, the root of the candidate's unpopularity with the Grenada government lay in decisions rendered while he was a resident judge on that island – decisions no doubt adverse to the government. Despite overwhelming support from lawyers practising before the court as well as regional bar associations, the Grenada government remained intractable; Alleyne was never appointed as Chief Justice and retired as Acting Chief Justice.[17]

In Guyana, vacancies in the top judicial positions opened up for the first time after the 2001 constitutional amendments when Chancellor Desiree Bernard resigned in March 2005 to take up a seat on the Caribbean Court of Justice. Claudette Singh was by then the longest serving judge, but Carl Singh was now senior to her having previously been appointed Chief Justice. Like before, he remained the President's choice, but the Leader of the Opposition favoured Claudette Singh, and as it turned out no agreement could be reached. In this battle over the Singhs, the two functionaries responsible for making the decision

---

16. Guyana Constitution 1980, art 127(1) as amended by Act No 6 of 2001.
17. 'Brian Alleyne is Snubbed' *Grenada Today*, 10 February 2007 <http://www.belgrafix.com/gtoday/2007news/Feb/Feb10/Brian-Alleyne-is-snubbed.htm> accessed 27 Jul 2010.

obdurately stuck to their respective choices and at the time of writing – more than four years after the opening of the vacancy – the position of Chancellor remains substantively unfilled.

The pendulum, then, had swung to the other extreme in Guyana – from poor governance to none at all. As experience has shown both in the OECS and now Guyana, requiring consensus prior to making an appointment can be equally counter-productive, for in a politically immature society it is a recipe for paralysis. In the meantime, pursuant to his power in article 127(2) – which only requires 'meaningful consultation' with the Leader of the Opposition – the President appointed Carl Singh to act as Chancellor (thereby underscoring the meaninglessness of that requirement). One month later, the President announced publicly that he had established a search committee to identify a suitable candidate for the position of Chief Justice. This made it clear that Claudette Singh had no future in the Guyana judiciary; but personalities aside, this announcement of a search committee betrayed a flagrant disregard of the constitutional procedures. This was exposed by the Leader of the Opposition who claimed that the President refused to discuss the names of his candidate for Chief Justice or even to reveal the persons on the search committee. If true, this was not even 'consultation,' much less a process designed to achieve agreement as is constitutionally required.[18]

After more than a year of this impasse, with Carl Singh performing the functions of both Chancellor and Chief Justice, public interest litigation was initiated in which a determination was sought as to the constitutionality of one person simultaneously holding both offices, as well as a declaration that the appointment of Carl Singh CJ to act as Chancellor had become unconstitutional by his so continuing to act for more than a year. In a decision handed down one year later,[19] the trial judge held on the first point that the spirit and intent of the Constitution does not permit the simultaneous holding of the offices of Chancellor and Chief Justice. Thus, while performing the functions of Chancellor pursuant to article 127(2), Carl Singh could not at the same time function in his substantive role as Chief Justice. In arriving at this decision, Ramlal J approached the issue as a simple one of construction, examining a number of constitutional provisions. From article 123(1),

---

18. R. Corbin, 'PNCR Letter to Pres Jagdeo on the Issue of the Constitution of Guyana in Relation to The Judiciary,' People's National Congress Reform Press Release, 8 July 2007 <http://www. guyanapnc.org/MediaCentre/PressRelease/PNCR%20Letter%20to%20Pres.%20Jagdeo%20 on%20the%20Issue%20of%20the%20Constitution%20of%20Guyana%20in%20Relation%20to%20 The%20Judiciary.html> accessed 27 Jul 2010.

19. *Committee for the Defence of the Constitution v AG* (unrep) 16 Nov 2007, Civ Act No 993-S/A of 2006 (HC Guy).

which states that the Supreme Court 'shall' consist of a Court of Appeal and a High Court, and article 123(2) which states that 'each of those courts shall be a superior court of record,' Ramlal J deduced a clear intention to provide separate and distinct courts; while from article 124, which sets out the composition of the respective courts, he found that the offices of Chancellor and Chief Justice must be held by separate persons.

Ramlal J refused the second declaration, however, holding that once an appointment to any office was regularly made, it could not thereafter become unconstitutional merely by its holder performing functions outside of the statutory mandate. Somewhat obscurely he added that the functions can become unlawful, but not so the appointment itself.[20] Nonetheless, he did conclude that the 'spirit' of the Constitution did not envisage such long delays in filling these offices, and he held that the failure to appoint a substantive Chancellor for such a prolonged period constituted a violation of article 122A(1) of the Constitution by the President and the Leader of the Opposition. That provision reads:

> All courts and all persons presiding over the courts shall exercise their functions independently of the control and direction of any person or authority; and shall be free and independent from political, executive and any other form of direction and control.

Ramlal J rejected an argument based on the protracted length of time in which the relevant politicians had failed to come to an agreement. According to him, delay was irrelevant since neither the Constitution nor any other law laid down any time limit for the period of an acting appointment or within which agreement had to be reached on a successful candidate.[21] In so ruling, the judge adopted a very formalistic approach to the dilemma since the mere absence of a time limit in the Constitution for the making of a critical appointment could hardly be decisive. As Professor Simeon McIntosh has argued, constitutional provisions are not to be read univocally, that is to say provisions cannot be plucked out and interpreted in isolation.[22] This is entirely consistent with the fundamental nature of constitutions and the dynamic approach called for in their interpretation. The mere absence of a time limit in the text cannot be an insuperable obstacle. What the judge ought to have considered were factors such as the role of a constitution in establishing institutions of government, the central importance of the judiciary under Guyana's unique socialist constitution with its enlarged executive powers, and the

---

20. Ibid 27.
21. Ibid 28–9.
22. S. McIntosh, *Caribbean Constitutional Reform: Rethinking the West Indian Polity* (The Caribbean Law Publishing Co, Kingston 2002) 254.

general principle of judicial independence at the root of all the detailed provisions governing the appointment, conditions, and tenure of members of the judiciary. In other words, the court could have legitimately been guided by those implicit constitutional norms that promote the separation of powers and, by extension, judicial independence, in order to invalidate the acting appointment.

There is, besides, ample precedent elsewhere for looking beyond the bare text. In *Reference re Remuneration of Judges of the Provincial Court (PEI)*, the Supreme Court of Canada struck down several provincial measures reducing the salaries of provincial judges as unconstitutional on the ground that they violated the principle of judicial independence.[23] Various provisions in the text were invoked, but ultimately the majority affirmed that judicial independence is 'at root an unwritten constitutional principle, in the sense that it is exterior to the particular sections of the Constitution Acts.'[24] Similarly, in the Guyanese case, the trial judge could have legitimately found the situation complained of by the applicants – an acting appointment in the head of the judiciary for close to three years and continuing – to be unworkable, inimical to good governance and in violation of the fundamental constitutional norm of judicial independence.

D. Acting Appointments

One of the most effective guarantees of judicial independence is the fact that judicial appointments are made until retirement, a condition acknowledged by a high level colloquium of Commonwealth judges in 1998.[25] This permanency, save for specific situations in which removal may occur, insulates the office-holder from political pressure and any obligation – real or perceived – to please the executive. By contrast, an acting appointment places the judge in a perpetual state of probation, and demands strength of character in order to rule fearlessly. Hanging over the judge's head is the unspoken possibility that rulings adverse to the state would result in non-confirmation. As it has been succinctly put by the Lord Irvine, Lord Chancellor of Britain, 'If judges depend on the goodwill of the government for their continuing (and here I would add extended) employment, then they may find themselves unable to resist political or other improper interference in individual cases.'[26]

---

23. [1998] 1 SCR 3 (SC Can).
24. Ibid 83.
25. Reproduced in the Latimer House Guidelines. See J. Hatchard and P. Slinn (eds), *Parliamentary Supremacy and Judicial Independence: A Commonwealth Approach* (Cavendish, London 1999) 20.
26. Quoted in Hatchard, ibid 34.

Aside from these cases, the practice of long acting appointments in Guyana is not confined to situations of necessity such as this one where agreement could not be reached – a fact regarding which the trial judge could not have been unaware.[27] In 2007, when this decision was handed down, a staggering five out of a total complement of 11 puisne judges were holding acting appointments. Two of those judges had by then been acting in excess of five years, one of whom retired in 2008 without ever being confirmed. Acting appointments for protracted periods are generally inimical to fearless, independent performance. Further, as pointed out by Lord Irvine, by subjecting the judge to the pleasure of the executive for permanent employment, the judge's ability to render independent judgments is compromised. This is, therefore, unconstitutional since judicial independence is explicitly provided for in the Guyana constitution. Arguably, the position should be no different elsewhere in the Commonwealth Caribbean where the constitutions provide for this by implication.

Thus, despite the painstaking detail of Commonwealth Constitutions, those provisions standing alone have been of limited value across diverse jurisdictions in securing a neutral appointment process for judicial officers. The difficulties have been compounded in the more highly divided societies where to the prevailing political immaturity one can add other variables related to race and ethnicity. Appeals to implicit constitutional norms or the core values underpinning the constitutions may therefore have a valuable role to play in their interpretation, and ultimately in promoting certain key goals such as judicial independence.

3. Conditions of Service of the Judiciary

Once appointed, even judges chosen for their perceived sympathies may rise to the occasion and eschew partisan rulings. Such independence, however, is possible only where a Judge's tenure is secure, and Commonwealth Caribbean constitutions contain various safeguards to promote this objective. Thus, appointment to the higher judiciary (once confirmed, of course) is a lifetime one, relinquished in the normal course only upon attaining a specific retirement age.[28] The office itself is protected, in the sense that it cannot be abolished while it has a substantive holder.[29] Most crucially, judges' salaries are charged on

---

27. The practice is a significant problem in the public service and one that is consistently condemned by the unions. See 'Appoint Acting Public Servants to Posts – GPSU' *Stabroek News*, 28 December 2008 <http://www.stabroeknews.com/news/appoint-acting-public-servants-to-posts-gpsu/> accessed 27 Jul 2010.
28. See, e.g., Barbados Constitution s 84.
29. See Jamaica Constitution s 97(3).

the Consolidated Fund[30] and cannot be reduced to their disadvantage while in office.[31] This means, as it has been colourfully put elsewhere, that judges are not reduced to the position of mendicants dependent on executive largesse.

A. Post Retirement Extensions

Specific conditions are laid down for extending a judge's tenure following the attainment of retirement age – invariably dictated, as in The Bahamas Constitution, to be for such period 'as may be necessary to enable him to deliver judgment or to do anything in relation to proceedings' already underway.[32] Thus the omission to specify a fixed period as in other constitutions[33] would not necessarily sanction open-ended extensions, as these are mandated only for a stated objective. An extension in office for whatever period entitles the office-holder to perform all the functions of the office, so it is a substantive and significant facility. For this reason, the Privy Council has held in relation to Trinidad and Tobago that extensions beyond the specified three-month period should not be entertained.[34]

B. Premature Termination of Tenure

Premature termination is possible only in specific situations – invariably being the 'inability to discharge the functions of [the] office (whether arising from infirmity of body or mind or any other cause) or for misbehaviour,'[35] and only after a clearly detailed procedure is followed. For most of the countries of the Commonwealth Caribbean with the notable exceptions being Guyana and Belize, this procedure requires the ultimate sanction of the Privy Council, and it involves a three-tiered process involving (i) initiation by the Prime Minister or the Chief Justice, depending on who is being investigated; (ii) the appointment of a tribunal to investigate the question of removal and to advise the Governor General whether or not to refer it to the Privy Council; and (iii) consideration of the matter by the Privy Council, whose advice is to be followed by the Head of State.[36] Finally, these safeguards all enjoy varying degrees of

---

30. See ibid s 101(2).
31. See ibid s 101(1).
32. Bahamas Constitution 1973 s 96(2).
33. For example, as in the Barbados Constitution where a two-year limit is fixed [s 84(1A)], or in the Trinidad and Tobago Constitution (s 136).
34. *Sookoo v AG* [1986] AC 63, 72, (1985) 33 WIR 338, 376 (PC T&T).
35. Barbados s 84(3), Jamaica, s 100(4).
36. Barbados s 84(4)–(5), Jamaica s 100(5)–(6).

entrenchment in the constitutions, meaning that special parliamentary majorities are required for amendment.

The success of these provisions in ensuring an inviolable judiciary possibly rests on two critical conditions – one being their entrenchment in the constitutions, which means that a significant degree of political consensus is required in order to effect any changes, and the second being the retention of ultimate control by the Privy Council. Still, despite these safeguards judges have not been entirely immune from interference, and constant upheavals within the Trinidad and Tobago judiciary illustrate the potential for both executive and administrative abuse.

In *Rees v Crane*,[37] the respondent, the most senior puisne judge in the country, had been simply left off the roster of sittings for the upcoming term by the Chief Justice, following which the latter initiated the removal process by asking the Judicial and Legal Services Commission (JLSC) to consider whether they would recommend to the President to set up a tribunal to investigate the question of the respondent's removal. The JLSC did not give the respondent an opportunity to rebut the complaints before making the recommendation to the President, who duly established the tribunal and suspended the respondent. The respondent sought judicial review of the decisions of the Chief Justice and the JLSC, contending that they were *ultra vires* because he was not given an opportunity to make representations before they were made.

The Privy Council agreed with the Court of Appeal that there had been a breach of natural justice and prohibited the tribunal from proceeding with the inquiry. The Board held that the respondent ought to have been given the opportunity to reply to the charges before the representation was made to the President even though this was only the first stage of the removal process. Such an opportunity was required, they felt, because of the enormity of the proceedings, the seriousness of the charges against the respondent, including misbehaviour, the publicity surrounding both his suspension and the appointment of the tribunal of inquiry, and the damage to his reputation and position as a judge. The Privy Council also quashed the decision of the Chief Justice not to schedule the respondent on the roster for the following term, holding that this amounted to a de facto suspension. Their Lordships held that if judicial independence were to mean anything, then suspension and termination of judicial officers had to follow the strict letter of the law.

Rees v Crane is a classic example of the vulnerability of judges to administrative interference, despite all the protections itemized in the

---

37. *Rees v Crane* [1994] 2 AC 173 (PC T&T).

constitutions. As the head of the judiciary, Chief Justices are highly influential, in that they are in charge of the administration of the courts, they assign cases and they help to determine new appointees by virtue of sitting on the judicial (and legal) services commission. Such power helps to explain in turn why governments in the region have tried to influence the appointment to this office, for by controlling its incumbent governments can indirectly control the entire judiciary – not by insisting that judges must rule a certain way, but through the assignment of duties which may well determine the outcome of a case. Moreover, a chief justice aligned to the executive is a critical ally on the service commission, this being the body that chooses new appointees to the bench.

An example of executive machinations occurred more recently in Trinidad and Tobago in relation to the conduct of criminal proceedings brought against the Chief Justice, with the entire episode providing a perfect illustration of the lengths to which some governments are prepared to go in order to control the judiciary.

In *Sharma v Browne-Antoine*,[38] the Chief Magistrate alleged that the Chief Justice had tried to influence a case involving former Prime Minister Basdeo Panday. Facing imminent prosecution on a charge of attempting to pervert the course of public justice, the Chief Justice obtained leave to seek judicial review of an alleged decision to prosecute him by the Deputy Director of Public Prosecutions. Later, the trial judge made similar orders against the Assistant Commissioner of Police, restraining all of the respondents from taking steps to prosecute the Chief Justice. The trial judge refused an application by the respondents to set aside the leave, whereupon they appealed successfully to the Court of Appeal. Although the Privy Council dismissed an appeal by the Chief Justice on the ground that the trial judge had misdirected herself on the appropriate standard to be applied, in the account of the events detailed by their Lordships one can discern the influences that were at work behind the scenes.

A considerable period of time had elapsed between the first voicing of any complaint by the Chief Magistrate and the making of his statement, which in the context of criminal proceedings is a factor that impacts significantly on credibility. There was some suggestion that the Chief Magistrate had been implicated in a property transaction, from which he was extricated by the Attorney General, another factor which the Chief Justice held out as compromising the integrity of the Chief Magistrate and giving him a motive to lie. However, even though the state had

---

38. *Sharma v Brown-Antoine* [2006] UKPC 57 (T&T).

gathered considerable evidence relating to this transaction (some 20 statements or thereabouts), none was disclosed at any stage. Instead, information about the case was leaked by the government to the press, no doubt to prejudice the Chief Justice in advance of the proceedings. Uncontradicted evidence was led that prior to the laying of any charges both the Attorney General and the Prime Minister had urged the Chief Justice to resign on at least three separate occasions, a prejudgment of the issue that the Prime Minister either in his naiveté or plain contempt for the presumption of innocence (not to mention the separation of powers) actually repeated in Parliament.[39]

By the time the police were ready to lay charges, they obtained an arrest warrant which they attempted to execute at the home of the Chief Justice on a Friday at 5:00 p.m. Apparently some eight police cars turned up for the occasion, and though the Chief Justice was able to secure the intervention of his legal adviser and was not in the end taken away in handcuffs, this vulgar display of force – at the start of the weekend when arrested persons in the normal course would have to be detained until Monday morning – could only have been intended to intimidate the Chief Justice and secure his resignation, earlier solicited by the Prime Minister and his chief legal adviser in private meetings.

Irrespective of the merits of the allegations – the credibility of which is questionable given that the local committee dismissed the case to remove the Chief Justice and the matter never reached the Privy Council – what is particularly disturbing about this attempted removal were all the irregularities in the processes, both official and unofficial. While it may be difficult to come to any conclusions about motivations merely from the reported facts of a case, these events, particularly in the context of heterogeneous and politically polarized societies like Guyana and Trinidad and Tobago, highlight once again the inadequacies of the explicit constitutional provisions by themselves, however detailed they may be. In the absence of a mature political climate, resort to implicit constitutional norms (which reflect underlying values) could well provide a way for keeping governments in check and preventing the manipulation or other abuse of the actual text by an overreaching executive.

4. The Jurisdiction of Superior Courts

Finally, a critical element in ensuring the independence of the judiciary is the actual preservation of its jurisdiction. Obviously, if that

---

39. This was reported widely in the media, both locally and internationally. See 'Chief Justice Removal Being Discussed,' *BBC News (Caribbean)*, 12 May 2006 <http://www.bbc.co.uk/caribbean/news/story/2006/05/060512_ttjudgeweekend.shtml> accessed 27 Jul 2010.

jurisdiction could be reduced or taken away altogether, to be entrusted to a less secure body, then this would be a covert means of undermining the judiciary. The case that best articulates this principle in the Commonwealth Caribbean is *Hinds*, the Jamaica Gun Court case, where the constitutionality of a new court established by Parliament to try firearm offences was under review.[40] The Privy Council held that while the Jamaican legislature was perfectly entitled to create new courts or entrust existing courts with new names, what it could not do was vest in a new court composed of members of the lower judiciary, a jurisdiction that had previously formed part of the jurisdiction of the Supreme Court.

Delivering the judgment of the majority, Lord Diplock explicated in specific terms what the jurisdiction of the Supreme Court entailed, both from an examination of specific constitutional provisions as well as by extrapolation from the inherent nature of the institution itself. With regard to the former, the Jamaican constitutional provisions specified original and appellate jurisdiction in all litigation under the bill of rights as well as any disputes regarding the membership of the Houses of Parliament.[41] Aside from what was explicitly stated, Lord Diplock identified three types of jurisdiction which, in his view, were characteristic of a higher judiciary: unlimited original jurisdiction in all substantial civil cases; unlimited original jurisdiction in all serious criminal offences; and supervisory jurisdiction over the proceedings of inferior courts.[42] Taking away any of this power and conferring it on a differently constituted body, as attempted by the legislation under review, was a surreptitious means of subverting the constitution. Lord Diplock pointed out that if Parliament could simply strip the Supreme Court of all jurisdiction except that which was explicitly conferred on it in relation to the Bill of Rights and membership of Parliament, then what would be left would be such a restricted or limited jurisdiction that the label 'Supreme Court' would be misleading. According to him, what was most objectionable about this was that

> ...the individual citizen could be deprived of the safeguard, which
> the makers of the Constitution regarded as necessary, of having
> important questions affecting his civil or criminal responsibilities
> determined by a court, however named, composed of judges whose
> independence from all local pressure by Parliament or by the

---

40. *Hinds v R* [1977] AC 195 (PC Ja).
41. There are regional variations. In Guyana, for example, in addition to these matters the High Court also has exclusive jurisdiction to determine disputes over the conduct of elections: see Guyana Constitution 1980 art 163.
42. *Hinds* (n 40) 221.

executive was guaranteed by a security of tenure more absolute than that provided by the Constitution for judges of inferior courts.[43]

A. Removing the Jurisdiction of the Privy Council in Guyana

In Guyana, the assault on judicial independence has centred not only on the manner of appointment of judges, but has also involved this crucial element of jurisdiction. Post-independence, the first and arguably most effective step towards emasculating the judiciary was the removal of the Judicial Committee of the Privy Council as the country's final Court of Appeal. This was done in stages by the Burnham regime, first by abolishing the right of appeal in all criminal and civil matters not involving constitutional questions when the country attained Republican status in 1970,[44] as well as removing at the same time the right of appeal by special leave of the Judicial Committee.[45] This left appeals to the Privy Council only in constitutional cases, which was eventually removed three years later making the Guyana Court of Appeal the final court on all issues.[46] Once the neutral judges of the Privy Council were out of the picture, a local judiciary stacked with appointees of the ruling party provided no protection for the citizenry against an increasingly dictatorial and illiberal regime, and the reports are replete with cases that illustrate the consequences. Rights to freedom of expression and assembly and association were particularly endangered, no doubt on account of the threat they pose to a dictatorship. Thus, for example, the ability to criticize the government was stifled by a plethora of defamation suits brought by the President and senior ministers against newspaper editors and leading opposition politicians,[47] the existence of a free press was thwarted in other ways such as by the denial of newsprint and machinery,[48] and assembly and association rights were narrowly interpreted, notwithstanding grandiose declarations in the constitution regarding the political, economic and social system of the state.[49]

A compromised judge is most valuable in civil matters, but in serious criminal offences which are triable on indictment it is difficult to control

---

43. Ibid.
44. Guyana Republic Act 1970-9 s 8.
45. Judicial Committee (Termination of Appeals) Act 1970-14.
46. Constitution (Amendment) Act 1973-19 s 4.
47. *Jagan v Burnham* (1973) 20 WIR 96 (CA Guy). Many of the cases of this period are unreported, but have been comprehensively documented by contemporary journalists and academics. See, for example, Morrison (n 9), especially at 196–244, and R. James and H. Lutchman, *Law and the Political Environment in Guyana* (IDS, Turkeyen 1984) 143–65.
48. *Hope v New Guyana Co Ltd* [1979] 26 WIR 233 (CA Guy).
49. *AG v Alli* (1987) 41 WIR 176 (CA Guy).

the outcome when decisions of fact are made by a jury of 12 persons. In order to neutralize this safeguard, the government passed the Administration of Justice Act (AJA) in 1978, under which all indictable offences – except a very small number – were converted into hybrid offences. This meant that they could also be tried summarily, that is, before a single magistrate, which naturally made the outcome far more assured. Moreover, under the AJA, the election of how an indictable offence would be tried was taken away from the accused person and left in the discretion of the magistrate trying the case. The result of these changes was that the safeguard of jury trials was removed in all but a handful of extreme cases, clearing the way for politically motivated prosecutions against opponents of the government. Such trials were not left up to chance or fairness, which would be the case where they were determined by jury, but were entrusted to magistrates who could be relied on to imprison or at the very least terrorize political opponents.[50] According to Percy Hintzen and Ralph Premdas, commenting on these developments, '...the judicial system became integrated into the regime's coercive arsenal to be used against political dissidents arrested and charged with trumped-up offences by the loyal security forces.'[51]

Finally, in 1980, by which time oligarchic control had peaked, the independence constitution was repealed and replaced by another that created the office of Executive President while clothing its occupant with virtually imperial powers. Included among the package of new measures was one providing that 'Parliament may confer on any court any part of the jurisdiction of and any powers conferred on the High Court by this Constitution or any other law.'[52] This provision had not appeared in either of the two previous constitutions and seemed to be included specifically for the purpose of circumventing the ruling in *Hinds*, for it explicitly allowed Parliament to transfer the powers of the High Court to any other court, however constituted. Thus, the entrenched jurisdiction celebrated and upheld in *Hinds*, which precluded the government from transferring the jurisdiction of the Supreme Court to one with less protection by ordinary legislation, was removed in one fell swoop. This provision, unique in the Commonwealth Caribbean, has been described

---

50. P. Hintzen and R. Premdas, 'Guyana: Coercion and Control in Political Change' (1982) 24 J I-A Stud & World Affairs 337, 348–50. A notable example of the extent to which the menacing executive influenced litigation under the Bills is provided by the perverse outcome in *Ameerally v AG* (1978) 25 WIR 272 (CA Guy), where despite judicial acknowledgement that the particulars of the charge brought against the appellants disclosed no offence, the Court held itself powerless to intervene – even with a constitutional right providing 'protection of the law' (specifying therein various procedural protections for the criminally accused) – no doubt because the respondent was the state.
51. Hintzen and Premdas 349.
52. Guyana Constitution art 123(3).

by Dr Francis Alexis as a form of 'disentrenchment.'[53] It opened up a terrible vista for the survival of the higher judiciary as an institution, though ultimately, it never had to be invoked for so effective was the earlier AJA in achieving the same end of political control.

B. Abolition of the Privy Council Appellate Jurisdiction and Substitution with the Caribbean Court of Justice

More recently, the debates and litigation spawned in several territories over regional moves to establish an indigenous court of last resort bring into sharp focus the sensitive nature of judicial independence. In Jamaica, litigation was commenced by several public interest groups challenging the constitutionality of the legislation by which the Jamaican government sought to give domestic effect to the Caribbean Court of Justice (CCJ) Treaty. In *Independent Jamaican Council for Human Rights v Marshall-Burnett*,[54] the appellants accepted that the right of appeal to the Privy Council could have been abolished by legislation passed by a simple majority of each House of Parliament – an inevitable concession since section 110 of the Jamaican Constitution, in which this right of appeal was set out, was not specially entrenched. However, the appellants objected to the substitution of the CCJ for the Privy Council as the final court of appeal on the ground that the CCJ did not enjoy the same level of entrenched protections in the Constitution afforded to the Supreme Court and Court of Appeal of Jamaica. Therefore, according to their argument, any change to this structure could only be effected by constitutional amendment, and the failure to enact the relevant laws by the applicable majorities rendered the legislation ineffectual.

The Privy Council accepted these arguments and held that the Acts by which these changes had been purportedly made undermined the protection afforded Jamaicans by the entrenched provisions of Chapter VII of the Constitution. Since the procedures required for amendment of an entrenched provision were not followed, and since the two aspects of the legislation – abolition of the Privy Council and substitution of the CCJ – were inextricably bound up, there could be no severance and the legislation was declared wholly void.

The safeguards that currently exist in relation to the higher judiciary in Jamaica were identified as being their manner of appointment, security of tenure and conditions of service, all of which were designed to ensure their insulation from executive pressure or interference.

---

53. F. Alexis, *Changing Caribbean Constitutions* (Antilles Publications, Bridgetown 1983) 127–32.
54. [2005] UKPC 3 (Ja) (*IJCHR*).

Significantly, the *Agreement Establishing the Caribbean Court of Justice* provides similar safeguards for judicial independence, covering all the very same issues as appointment, service, remuneration, and so on as exist in relation to the higher judiciary of Jamaica. However, these were dismissed by their Lordships as inadequate, on the ground that the treaty could be amended by agreement of the parties followed by ratification, both executive acts which would thereafter take effect in Jamaican law by simple affirmative resolution. Notably, the Privy Council obtains no level of entrenchment in the Jamaican Constitution, nor are there any procedures by which the independence of that body can be guaranteed. But like Caesar's wife, their Lordships are apparently above reproach, unlike the judges of the CCJ and in spite of the fact that the latter are likely to be chosen from among only the best of Caribbean jurists.

The Privy Council's conclusion that the CCJ judges lack adequate independence was surely speculative. Furthermore, it is fanciful to suppose that the *CCJ Agreement*, which provides elaborate safeguards for judicial independence, can be easily changed so as to weaken or undermine the court's independence. To amend this *Agreement* in order to achieve such nefarious ends would require a conspiracy to subvert the rule of law of widespread and far-reaching proportions, an unthinkable prospect given that it would also require the consent of member states. That judicial independence is properly safeguarded under the *Agreement* therefore hardly seems to be in doubt.

At any rate, comparisons to their Lordships' Board and discussion of the potential dangers of amending the *Agreement* were unnecessary for this decision given the central problem identified with the legislation, which was its failure to entrench the right of appeal to the CCJ in the constitution. What their Lordships meant by this was that once the CCJ was established, there would be nothing to preclude any subsequent government from removing it as the final court of appeal and substituting its own court, so that in Lord Bingham's view, the 'three Acts give rise to a risk which did not exist in the same way before.'[55]

This possibility was not entirely speculative, given the precedent already set in the Caribbean by the United National Congress (UNC) while in power in Trinidad and Tobago assenting to the *CCJ Agreement* and then having second thoughts while in opposition.[56] But it does seem highly exaggerated. Any future attempt to replace the CCJ by a constitutionally less secure court could be invalidated by the reasoning in *Hinds*, at least where the holders of any new court are not appointed

---

55. Ibid 21.
56. *Sharma v AG* [2005] 1 LRC 148 (CA T&T).

on the same terms and in the same manner prescribed for persons exercising such jurisdiction. In other words, the jurisdiction conferred on any future court or tribunal could be scrutinized on the authority of *Hinds* to ensure, ultimately, its 'independence from political pressure by Parliament or by the executive.'[57] Exaggerated or not, however, as illustrated by the Guyanese experience tampering with the judiciary is the first step by which the executive is allowed to operate unrestrained and in violation of the rights of citizens. For all of its undiplomatic posturing and potential overreaching therefore, the decision of the Privy Council in this case underlines the premium placed on the independence of the judiciary. As pointed out by Lord Bingham, such independence is indispensable for the reason that '...the protection of judges from executive pressure or interference...is all but universally recognized as a necessary feature of the rule of law.'[58]

5. Implicit Constitutional Norms

The instances of subversion of the judiciary and general manipulation of the constitution described above are, ultimately, reflections of political immaturity – not unexpected given the nascent stage of development of our societies. These aberrations are by no means confined to the heterogeneous communities of Belize, Trinidad and Tobago, and Guyana. Indeed, in order to appreciate the critical role played by the judiciary in securing good governance across the region, one need only reflect on how enforcement of the Public Order Acts has impacted on expression and assembly rights (and by extension, democracy) in the OECS, particularly Antigua and Barbuda, and St Kitts and Nevis;[59] or the implications of expansive interpretations of the meaning of 'public interest' in emergency legislation in the OECS;[60] or the misuse of defamation laws by government officials to silence critics and stifle dissent.[61]

---

57. *Hinds* (n 40) 219, 222.
58. *IJCHR* (n 54) 12.
59. *AG v Antigua Times* (1975) 21 WIR 560 (PC A&B); *Francis v Chief of Police* (1973) 20 WIR 550 (PC St K-N); *AG v Hector* (1987) 40 WIR 135 (ECCA A&B); *St Luce v AG* (1975) 22 WIR 536 (CA WIAS A&B) – all of these being cases with overtly political implications.
60. *Maximea v AG* (1974) 21 WIR 548 (CA WIAS Dom).
61. *Simmonds v France* (7 May 1985) KN 1983 HC 1 (St K-N); *Barrow v Caribbean Publishing Co Ltd and Cozier* (1971) 17 WIR 182 (HC Bar); *Adams v Smith* (17 Feb 1982) BB 1982 HC 8 (Bdos) (also quoted in DeMerieux (n 9) 218). The author is also tempted to include *Panday v Gordon* [2005] UKPC 36, (2005) 67 WIR 290 (T&T) in this list, for even though the plaintiff was not a government functionary, the defendant was the Leader of the Opposition in Trinidad and Tobago, while the plaintiff was, ironically, the CEO of a large media house which controlled several newspapers as well as a television station. It seems that the defendant was to be silenced at all costs, and so held the Court of Appeal of Trinidad and Tobago by a majority, the lone dissenter being the later embattled Chief Justice Sharma.

While these are all cases with overtly political implications, there are other issues at stake. In the Commonwealth Caribbean, there has been a tendency to approach the Bills of Rights narrowly, and the effect has been to thwart the tremendous promise of the elaborate guarantees that were enshrined at independence.[62] It is perhaps no exaggeration to posit generally that where the state is involved, the courts have displayed excessive deference through notions of the presumption of constitutionality of legislation,[63] generous interpretations of the 'public interest'[64] and even by reading limitations into the Bills where none are stated.[65] While there have always been signs that that there is scope for innovative thinking free of common law restraints,[66] rights-based adjudication in the Commonwealth Caribbean has not been uniformly approached in an expansive or even purposive manner. It has had, at best, a very uneven trajectory. There are a number of reasons for this within the Bills themselves, in the form of opaque redress provisions, apparently unenforceable opening sections, generous savings of existing law and copious limitations on the actual rights. To be fair, judges have had a difficult task – grappling with this paradigmatically different way of approaching constitutional issues while at the same time having to balance age-old conflicts between community and individual in brand new states. But having acknowledged these realities of text and context, it would be futile to deny the blatant bias often on display, and one must wonder whether a more secure judiciary would operate with less deference to the state where it is a litigant in proceedings. In other words, the existence of an independent judiciary seems critical in order that the full vision of the constitutional guarantees may be realized, particularly in relation to the preservation of core values of human dignity, liberty and equality. But it is when these considerations are borne in mind that the limitations of the constitution become apparent, for not only has the text been insufficient to achieve its objectives independently of common law constraints, it has also not been able to secure an independent judiciary, which perhaps contributes to the problem.

Given this background, a recent decision of the Privy Council in an appeal from Mauritius holds significant promise. In the *State v*

---

62. See DeMerieux, 'The Common Law and the Litigation of Fundamental Rights and Freedoms before the Privy Council' (this volume).
63. *Mootoo v AG* (1979) 30 WIR 411 (PC T&T); *Suratt v AG* [2007] UKPC 55 [45] (T&T), (2007) 71 WIR 391, 409; *Chief of Police v Nias* (2008) 73 WIR 201 (CAECS St K-N).
64. *Sookermany v DPP* (1996) 48 WIR 346 (CA T&T); *DPP v Tokai* (1994) 48 WIR 376 (HC T&T).
65. *DPP v Nasralla* [1967] 2 AC 238, (1967) 10 WIR 299 (PC Ja); *AG v Caterpillar Americas Co* (2000) 62 WIR 135 (CA Guy); *Campbell-Rodriques v AG* [2007] UKPC 65 (Ja).
66. *Min Home Affairs v Fisher* [1980] AC 319, (1979) 44 WIR 107 (PC Ber); *Pratt and Morgan v AG* [1993] 4 All ER 769, [1993] 43 WIR 340 (PC Ja); *Gairy v AG No 2* [2001] UKPC 30 (Gren).

Khoyratty,[67] the respondent was charged with a non-bailable drug offence, whereupon he challenged an earlier constitutional amendment facilitating the refusal of bail as violating the principle of separation of powers and, by extension, s 1 of the Constitution which had declared Mauritius to be a democratic state. His argument, successful both in the Court of Appeal and the Privy Council, was that bail being intrinsically in the domain of the judiciary, the constitutional amendment in 1994 which denied its availability across the board for certain types of offences was a usurpation of judicial power by the legislature. The Privy Council agreed with the Court of Appeal of Mauritius that since the separation of powers is a vital feature of a democratic state, which Mauritius was declared to be in s 1, any law encroaching on this principle violated that section, which meant that to be effective it had to be passed in accordance with the higher majorities required for amendment. Since the 1994 amendment had been approved by a mere three-quarter majority in Parliament, it was accordingly void and of no effect.

Lord Steyn, delivering the principal judgment of the Board, identified 'democracy' as importing three distinct elements:

> The first is that the people must decide who should govern them. Secondly, there is the principle that fundamental rights should be protected by an impartial and independent judiciary. Thirdly, in order to achieve a reconciliation between the inevitable tensions between these ideas, a separation of powers between the legislature, the executive, and the judiciary is necessary.[68]

Lord Steyn noted that section 1 was not in the nature of a preamble, but was 'operative and binding';[69] further, its importance was underlined by two facts – its pride of place in the constitution and its exceptional degree of entrenchment.[70] In a separate concurring judgment, Lord Rodger of Earlsferry added that '...it would be wrong to say that the concept of the democratic state to be found [in s 1] means nothing more than the sum of the provisions in the rest of the Constitution, whatever they may be at any given moment. Rather, section 1 contains a separate, substantial, guarantee.'[71] As to what that separate guarantee entailed, Lord Rodger identified it in particular to be 'a separation of powers between the legislature and the executive, on the one hand, and the judiciary, on the other.'[72]

---

67. [2006] UKPC 13 (Maur).
68. Ibid 12.
69. Ibid 15.
70. Ibid 17.
71. Ibid 29.
72. Ibid.

In finding that a provision outside of the Bill of Rights captures substantive elements such as the protection of fundamental rights by an independent and impartial judiciary, separation of powers and even the rule of law itself, their Lordships have opened up new avenues for exploration independent of the schizophrenic Bills. For the Commonwealth Caribbean, where the term 'democracy' is also bandied about,[73] these developments surely hold tremendous implications for constitutional interpretation, judicial independence, and, by extension, governance in general. Their relevance is further accentuated by the fact that democracy is increasingly lumped together with other concepts like the rule of law, as done by Lord Bingham in 2005 where he stated that 'the function of independent judges charged to interpret and apply the law is universally recognized as a cardinal feature of the modern democratic state, a cornerstone of the rule of law itself.'[74] Surely one of the immediate benefits of *Khoyratty* (and there are others) is that their Lordships' *a priori* view of democracy leads us to ask a number of related questions, in particular whether our constitutions have been effective in securing key standards promoted therein such as the protection of fundamental rights and judicial independence. Can the written text, and especially references to democracy, support the meanings put on it, and further, do other implicit norms arise from the text or the constitution's basic structure? These are exciting issues, with all the potential of opening up a whole new frontier of constitutional interpretation in the Commonwealth Caribbean. Still, a cautionary note is in order. While the expansive reading of democracy is exciting for all of its possibilities, are we to assume that its meaning was exhausted in the judgment, or is it (or the constitution itself) capable of giving rise to other fundamental norms? If so, by what process or methodology are further norms to be ascertained? And does the fact that certain norms are dubbed 'fundamental' or 'intrinsic' mean that they are untouchable, beyond the scope of any Parliamentary majority?

This last inquiry is perhaps the most troublesome. Part of the difficulty in articulating a response lies in the prevarication displayed by the Privy Council on this subject. Just two years before its decision in *Khoyratty*,

---

73. See the Constitutions of Antigua and Barbuda s 1, The Bahamas art 1, Belize s 1, Guyana art 1, or the Preambles to the Constitution of Dominica and Trinidad and Tobago – all of which contain a reference to democracy or belief in a democratic society. Despite this, in at least one territory, the declaration of The Bahamas to be a 'sovereign and democratic State' was given a narrow interpretation, not encompassing a fundamental right to vote in absolute secrecy and possibly not even a right to vote at all: *Ingraham v McEwan* [2002] 65 WIR 1 (CA Bah).

74. *A v Secretary of State for the Home Department, X v Secretary of State for the Home Department* [2004] UKHL 56, [42] (Eng).

the Privy Council rejected an argument in an appeal from Trinidad and Tobago that the mandatory death penalty was unconstitutional on the basis of contravening the principle of separation of powers.[75] According to the majority in that case, 'the principle of the separation of powers is not an overriding supra-constitutional principle but a description of how the powers under a real constitution are divided.'[76] Given the aversion of their Lordships to proffer detailed reasons for their rulings, their Damascene conversion to the existence of a doctrine of separation of powers a mere two years later in *Khoyratty* stands in stark, irreconcilable contrast.

At any rate, accepting that the later decision in *Khoyratty* is consistent with previous authority and therefore more likely to be correct, still unresolved is the status of this and any other principle found to exist by implication. In India and Canada, where several identical principles (including the rule of law and separation of powers) have been read into their constitutions, the end result has been the elevation of those principles into a pre-eminent position. For the first time ever this year, a Commonwealth Caribbean court has relied on the Indian 'basic structure doctrine' (as well as the principle of separation of powers) to invalidate a constitutional amendment by which the government sought to exclude the protection of property from applying to sub-surface resources wherever they might be found within the country. In *Bowen v AG*, Conteh CJ held that the effect of a constitutional amendment should not be destructive of the basic structure of the constitution itself.[77] He rejected the government's position that all amendments are valid so long as they conform to the provisions of s 69 – the amending section – which merely set out, according to him, manner and form requirements for alteration. In addition to s 69, amendments must conform to the normative requirements encompassed in art 68, which subjects Parliament's law-making power to the constitution. Applying these principles, Conteh CJ found that fundamental rights and in particular the protection of certain rights form part of the basic structure of the Belize constitution. This meant that even though the amending legislation had passed with the required majority it was nonetheless tainted, for by purporting to 'disapply' one such fundamental right it violated the basic structure of the constitution.

Positivists will naturally recoil from this decision – here was an amendment duly passed, but invalidated by reference to a natural law-type argument in which the Belizean constitution was held to embody

---

75. *Matthew v State* [2004] UKPC 33 (T&T).
76. Ibid 28.
77. *Bowen v AG* (13 Feb 2009) BZ 2009 SC 2 (Bze).

an irreducible minimum content. Completely ignored by the trial judge was the legitimacy of frustrating the democratic will of the majority, or more profound questions as to the why the constitution should occupy this privileged position in the first place. Admittedly, Conteh CJ may have gone too far, but fidelity to purely mechanistic approaches to constitutional change (or, one could add, the rule of law and democracy) would subject constitutions to all the caprice of our 'fragile democracies.'[78] Thus, *Bowen* is not some maverick decision to be dismissed out of hand, but one in which the unmistakable parallels to *Khoyratty's* interpretation of democracy signals a new direction in human rights jurisprudence in the context of the problematic Commonwealth Caribbean constitutions. By bearing in mind the questions they raise, judges and lawyers stand a better chance of formulating a more meaningful indigenous jurisprudence as they work out the nature and scope of implicit constitutional rights, and how the latter may be legitimately utilized to secure – not only an independent judiciary – but ultimately a more substantive notion of democracy and the rule of law.

---

78. As Trinidad and Tobago was described by Jamadar J in *Northern Construction v AG* (31 July 2002) TT 2002 HC 104 (T&T). TRS Allan describes parliamentary majorities as a 'concentration of power,' which in his view poses a serious risk to fundamental rights and liberties. This possibility is what legitimates the existence of constitutional restraints against irresponsible legislative encroachment on such rights, and mandates a substantive view of the Rule of Law concept: 'Legislative Supremacy and the Rule of Law: Democracy and Constitutionalism' (1985) CLJ 111.

Constitutionalism in Belize: Lessons for the Commonwealth Caribbean?

Godfrey P. Smith

1. Introduction

The Belize Constitution, like most Commonwealth constitutions, is based on the eponymous Westminster model of parliamentary democracy. In terms of the structures of governance they created, the Commonwealth constitutions substantially mirrored Westminster's. In using the term 'Westminster model,' one is mindful of SA de Smith's caution that 'the Westminster model will never be a term of art, and the political scientist may also prefer to handle it circumspectly'[1] as well as Professor Carnegie's repartee 'that when we speak of Westminster model constitutions, we are not being lawyers or even political scientists. We are at best being poets.'[2] To avoid issues of constitutional taxonomy, the label 'Westminster model' is used here simply to describe those Commonwealth constitutions which reproduced the essential features of parliamentary democracy as it obtained in England at the time of their independence, described by Professor Albert Fiadjoe as the 'barest bones of the "Westminster model."'[3]

The bare bones of the Westminster model included: a ceremonial head of state who is the Queen's representative, a legislature with at least one chamber democratically elected by the people, an executive of cabinet ministers accountable to the legislature, safeguards for an independent judiciary, an office of Leader of the Opposition and a public service. But there were also some key differences. Commonwealth constitutions, unlike the old Westminster constitution, contained clauses declaring the supremacy of the written constitutions and had entrenched bills of rights which, together, sourced the principle of separation of powers and the tool of judicial review.

---

1. S.A. de Smith, 'Westminster's Export Models: the Legal Framework of Responsible Government' (1961–63) 1 J of Commonwealth Political Studies 2.
2. A.R. Carnegie, 'Floreat the Westminster Model? A Commonwealth Caribbean Perspective' (1996) 6 Carib LR 1, 12.
3. A. Fiadjoe, 'The Westminster Transplant in the Commonwealth Caribbean-Some Pertinent Issues' (1987) 11 WILJ 64, 67.

By the time of the promulgation of the Constitution of Belize in 1981, the Commonwealth already had 20 plus years of experience with Westminster-style constitutions. While in many Commonwealth African countries there had been by 1981, fundamental departures from the Westminster model, in the Caribbean countries and Pacific Islands of the Commonwealth, there was little that could be termed as fundamental change.[4] Caribbean judiciaries and the Judicial Committee of the Privy Council had already begun shaping the region's constitutional jurisprudence through such seminal cases like *Thornhill v AG*,[5] *Collymore v AG*,[6] *DPP v Nasralla*,[7] *Minister of Home Affairs v Fisher*,[8] *Hinds v R*,[9] *Maharaj v AG*.[10] Thus, when Belize attended the constitutional conferences in London in the months leading up to independence, it had the benefit of the Commonwealth's two decades of constitutional experience to guide it. In terms of the drafting of its constitution, Belize could avoid some of the deficiencies that had been exposed in the working of the Westminster transplant in the Caribbean, if not the Commonwealth. In terms of interpreting the Constitution, the Belizean judiciary, with the benefit of the Caribbean's 20 years of constitutional adjudication, could help to exorcise the spectre of hesitancy and conservatism that haunted the region's early constitutional judgments.[11] The lateness of its independence, therefore, presented Belize with an opportunity to make a strong and early contribution to the defining of a distinct Caribbean jurisprudence.[12]

The framers of the Belize Constitution introduced some significant alterations to the Westminster transplant model which, as will be shown, assisted the judiciary in expanding the frontiers of Caribbean constitutional interpretation. But the advancement of constitutionalism in Belize was not the exclusive province of the judiciary. Unlike many legislatures throughout the Commonwealth, the Belizean legislature was proactive, even aggressive, in discharging its role of developing the

---

4. See generally, W. Dale, 'The Making and Remaking of Commonwealth Constitutions' (1993) 42 ICLQ 67. Ghana, for example, which became independent in 1957, had introduced republican form of government by 1960 and had a one-party system by 1964.
5. (1981) 31 WIR 498 (PC T&T).
6. (1969) 15 WIR 229 (PC T&T).
7. (1967) 10 WIR 299 (PC Ja).
8. (1979) 44 WIR 107 (PC Ber).
9. (1975) 24 WIR 326 (PC Ja).
10. (1978) 30 WIR 310 (PC T&T).
11. See L. Jackson's 'Fi Wi Law,' Chapter 1 which provides an engaging, if withering, account of the region's tentative and formalistic approach to constitutional interpretation.
12. Jamaica and Trinidad and Tobago were the first to gain their independence in 1962 with Barbados and Guyana following in 1966. Belize in 1981, Antigua and Barbuda in 1981 and St Kitts-Nevis in 1983 were the final three of the independent Caribbean countries to gain independence.

Belize Constitution. Since the enactment of the Belize Constitution in 1981, the legislature has amended the Belize Constitution six times. By these amendments the Belizean legislature, regardless of the degree of its consciousness of this philosophical truth, grasped the fundamental importance of constitutional reform as an equally important, if not more efficient process, alongside adjudication, for ensuring that the Constitution remained true to its purpose.

Professor Simeon McIntosh makes the point that constitutional reform – the amending of a democratic constitution according to its own terms – aims to make changes to the constitution 'that experience reveals to be required by justice or the general good, in order to strengthen the political values to which the society has committed itself.'[13] The values to which the Belizean society committed itself can only be found in one place, that is, the preamble of the Belize Constitution which states that the people of Belize:

> ...desire that their society shall reflect and enjoy [certain] principles, beliefs and needs and that their Constitution should therefore enshrine and make provision for ensuring the achievement of the same in Belize.[14]

The principles, beliefs and needs referred to include faith in human rights, the dignity of the human person, the equal protection of children, respect for the principles of social justice, belief in a meritocracy, democracy, the rule of law and that the resources of the community should be so distributed as to serve the common good. The framers of the Belize Constitution were then tasked with making 'provisions for ensuring the achievement' of those principles, beliefs and needs in the body of the Constitution.[15]

But a society does not remain static. While the framers of the Belize Constitution devised a set of core structures and institutions for the achievement of the people's aspirations, there had to be appropriate mechanisms to ensure that those structures and institutions were able, despite the passage of time, to remain relevant. The Belize Constitution therefore gave the judiciary, through the process of adjudication, the power to ensure that the Constitution has continuing relevance, regardless of the times. Through the process of constitutional reform, the legislature was given the power to introduce changes to the Constitution

---

13. S. McIntosh, *Caribbean Constitutional Reform: Rethinking the West Indian Polity* (The Caribbean Law Publishing Co, Kingston 2002) 54–56.
14. Belize Constitution preamble s (f).
15. Ibid.

to achieve, as Simeon McIntosh puts it, 'the most appropriate ends or purposes for which the text was constructed.'[16]

As the Belizean judiciary interpreted the Constitution, and as the legislature responded with reforms, what emerged in Belize was a symbiotic, mutually re-enforcing dynamic between the judiciary and the legislature. This was an actualization of roles implicitly envisioned for them under the Belize Constitution to ensure its own resilience. It is worth mentioning that four of the six constitutional amendments were based either on recommendations of a broad-based political reform commission or manifesto promises of political parties. The point here is that the bulk of Belize's constitutional reforms emanated from a process of consultation with the people. This dynamic for constitutional development produced some results worthy of emulation elsewhere in the Commonwealth.

2. Judicial Review and Rights Constitutionalism

It is axiomatic that constitutionalism begins with the readiness of citizens to challenge governmental action and insist upon adherence to constitutional government. This chapter includes some cases that involve judicial review of administrative action because the principle that decision-makers must act within their lawful powers is nothing more than a technical derivative of the broader constitutional norm of the rule of law. Two years after independence in 1981, litigation to compel compliance with the Constitution was decidedly underway in Belize. *Card v AG*[17] established that the Head of State had no powers under the Constitution to discipline public officers, a function that resided exclusively with the Public Service Commission. The late Chief Justice of Belize, Sir George Brown, remarked that this decision 'demonstrated ...that no one was above the law, not even the Executive Head of State, the Governor General.'[18] *Smith v AG*[19] and *Carr v AG*[20] followed in quick succession, both re-enforcing the paramountcy of access to the courts for the purpose of securing compliance with the Constitution.

The judiciary has been fairly robust in enforcing fundamental rights and freedoms. *Belize Broadcasting Authority v Courtenay*,[21] for example, enforced the protection from discrimination and freedom of

---

16. McIntosh (n 13) 54.
17. 1 BzLR 270, BZ 1983 SC 15 (Bze).
18. G. Brown, 'Landmark Decisions in Belize since Independence' (1995) 5 Carib LR 540, 543.
19. 1 BzLR 275, BZ 1983 SC 16 (Bze).
20. 1 BzLR 281, BZ 1983 SC 12 (Bze).
21. (1986) 38 WIR 79, 3 BzLR 403 (CA Bze).

expression. Recently, in *Wade v Roches*,[22] the Court of Appeal upheld the decision of the Chief Justice that Wade, the General Manager of Roman Catholic Schools had discriminated against Roches in terminating her employment as a teacher after she became pregnant. Earlier, *Alonzo v DFC*[23] had firmly established that redress for breach of constitutional rights could not lie against a body that was not a public body endowed by law with coercive power. *Wade v Roches* was distinguishable since the management authority of the schools had been clothed by legislation with powers that gave it a public character.

A. Interpreting Saving Law Clauses

The clearest illustration that the framers of the Belize Constitution, in drafting the Belize Constitution, were alert to some of the challenges that had emerged from the region's experience with constitutional interpretation was their approach to the savings law clause in the Belize Constitution. The general and special savings law clauses have been described as 'probably the most contradictory feature of Caribbean constitutions [which] Courts now adopt a restrictive reading...because they are so devastating to the protection of fundamental rights and freedoms.'[24] The general savings law clause in the Belize Constitution appears in Part II, 'Protection of Fundamental Rights and Freedoms,' the bill of rights, at section 21. It states that 'Nothing contained in any law in force immediately before Independence Day nor anything done under the authority of any such law shall, for a period of five years after Independence Day, be held to be inconsistent with or done in contravention of any of the provisions of this part.' In examining section 21, Lord Bingham in *Reyes v R*[25] observed that '...unusually if not uniquely, the continuing savings clauses found in many other if not all Caribbean constitutions, whether in the wider form found in some constitutions or the narrower form found in others, have no close counterpart in the constitution of Belize.'[26]

Henry P in *San Jose Farmers' Cooperative Ltd v AG*[27] gave a fuller explanation for the singularity of section 21 when he observed that:

> In certain territories where the 'Westminster model' Constitution had been adopted, provision had been made for the continuing

---

22. (9 March 2005) BZ 2005 CA 6, (Bze).
23. 1 BzLR 82, BZ 1984 CA 20 (Bze).
24. T. Robinson, 'Inherent Constitutional Rights: Recalibrating the Common Law Constitution,' paper presented at the UWI Faculty of Law Faculty Workshop Series, Barbados (18 October 2007).
25. (2002) UKPC 11, [2002] 60 WIR 42 (Bze).
26. Ibid 6.
27. (1991) 43 WIR 63 (CA Bze).

validity of existing laws, notwithstanding their inconsistency with fundamental rights and freedoms provisions of the constitution of the territory. In others, such existing laws become instantly unconstitutional when the Constitution of the territory came into force because they were afforded no such protection. Both provisions created problems and section 21 of the Belize Constitution was designed to overcome both problems by providing a breathing space during which the Governor-General and Parliament could effect the necessary legislative changes.[28]

A majority of the Court of Appeal consisting of Henry P and Liverpool JA, having found certain sections of the Land Acquisition (Public Purposes) Act to be inconsistent with the Constitution, went on to effect minor textual amendments to the sections to bring them into conformity with the Belize Constitution. The dissent by Smith JA that this amounted to the creation of new law and could not be done by the court was met by the mild rebuke of Liverpool JA that in fact this was a task entrusted to the court which it was obliged to undertake 'with an approach akin to that which Lord Atkin in *Liversidge v Anderson* [1942] AC 206 would have required of his "bold spirits."'[29] Parliament shortly after that judgment effected the amendments to the legislation pointed out in the judgment to bring the Act into conformity with the Constitution.

In contrast, in *Melendez v R*,[30] the Court of Appeal was astute to the implied constraints on the power to modify and adapt unconstitutional laws to bring them into conformity with the Belize Constitution. The appellant, a minor at the time of his commission of murder, was, in accordance with the Indictable Procedure Code, sentenced to be detained at Her Majesty's pleasure. The court found that this was a provision that obliged the court to delegate to the executive the power to determine the length of detention of a convicted person and was 'a patent infringement' of the principle of separation of powers. The court was invited to utilize section 134 of the Belize Constitution to modify that provision of the Code to bring it into conformity with the Constitution. Justice Telford Georges, President of the Court of Appeal, declined the invitation. He was very much alive to the fact that the circumstances here were different from the *San Jose Farmers* case. Even though the insertion by the court of simple wording could have effected conformity, the Court of Appeal observed that the 'area of punishment is quite different. There is no clear principle of the common law or constitutional criterion to chart

---

28. Ibid 70.
29. Ibid 88.
30. 3 BzLR 289, BZ 1995 CA 4 (Bze).

the path for one seeking to amend with modifications. It remains very much a matter of social policy.'[31] He made a clear distinction between the prescription of a fixed penalty which was a matter for Parliament and the selection of a penalty for a particular case, the latter being a matter for the courts. The court found an escape route from its constitutional quandary in the Criminal Code which had recently been amended to empower a court to impose life imprisonment in special and extenuating circumstances where a murder of the type in issue in that case had been committed.[32]

B. The Parameters of the Right to Work

Another noteworthy difference between Belize's bill of rights and that of its Caribbean counterparts is the provision of the right to work as a substantive and enforceable right under section 15 of the Belize Constitution. That section provides that no person 'shall be denied the opportunity to gain his living by work which he freely chooses or accepts, whether by pursuing a profession or occupation or by engaging in a trade or business, or otherwise.' McIntosh argued that 'the problem with the constitutionalization of...the right to work means that the State...would be in violation of the citizens' fundamental right whenever its economic policies fail to...provide work for anyone willing and able to work.'[33] He argues that its dependency on social and economic contingencies makes it meaningless as a constitutional right. In *Belize Petroleum Haulers Association v Habet*,[34] the Belize Court of Appeal found that the requirement in the Belize Petroleum Haulers Association Act that before the Department of Transportation could grant a licence to haul petrol to an applicant it had to have regard to whether the applicant was a member of the association and was prohibited from issuing a hauler's licence to anyone unless recommended by the association, was a breach of the right to work. Carey JA dismissed the association's argument that the right to work was not enforceable but more in the nature of a constitutional privilege and liberty, as 'semantic Terpsichore.'[35]

In *Brown Sugar Marketplace v AG*,[36] the right to work again arose. The allegation was that a wall erected by the cruise ship docking facility

---

31. Ibid 299.
32. Compare *DPP v Mollison* (2003) UKPC 6, (2003) 64 WIR 140 (Ja) where a similar law was modified to read 'at the pleasure of the court' rather than at the pleasure of the executive.
33. McIntosh (n 13) 245.
34. (24 June 2005) BZ 2005 CA 14 (Bze).
35. Ibid 9.
36. (unrep) 11 March 1998, No 28 & 29 of 2007 (SC Bze).

which prevented its competitors from having direct access to cruise ship tourists on a boardwalk abutting all their properties was in breach of the competitors' right to work. The case attracted immense media publicity. The Chief Justice found that the maintenance of the walls infringed the claimants' right to work. The Court of Appeal took the view that since the cruise tourists could exit the docking facility and access the facilities of the claimants, albeit in a roundabout manner, their opportunity to earn a livelihood was not infringed.[37] The approach of the Belizean courts in interpreting the right to work seems to be that what is guaranteed is the opportunity to pursue a trade or profession without unlawful hindrance by legislation or administrative action.

C. The Rule of Law and Protection of the Environment

The 2004 Privy Council decision of *Belize Alliance of Conservation NGOs v Department of the Environment and Belize Electricity Ltd*[38] has become a cause célèbre. The Department of the Environment, the department charged with ensuring environmental compliance, had granted approval for the electric company to build a massive hydroelectric dam in the pristine rainforest of Belize. An association of environmental NGOs challenged the *vires* of the process all the way to the Privy Council. It is noteworthy that the *locus standi* of the NGOs to challenge the process was never an issue and the Supreme Court readily embraced as fundamental the citizen's right to challenge decisions affecting the public interest that might breach the rule of law. In a 3–2 decision, the Privy Council found that the process of obtaining environmental approval had complied with the country's environmental laws.

In a passionate dissenting judgment, Lord Walker of Gestingthorpe was of the view that the last minute disclosure before the Board that crucial geological reports as to the integrity in the dam design had been withheld from the decision-making body was enough to quash the approval. He said:

> Belize has enacted comprehensive legislation for environmental protection and direct foreign investment, if it has serious environmental implications, must comply with that legislation. The rule of law must not be sacrificed to foreign investment, however desirable (indeed, recent history shows that in many parts of the

---

37. *Fort Street Tourism Village Ltd v AG* (2008) 74 WIR 133 (CA Bze).
38. [2004] UKPC 6, (2004) 64 WIR 68 (Bze). The alliance of non-governmental organizations (NGOs) called 'BACONGO' brought this action on the principle that the dam was bad for Belize. Environmental NGOs are particularly strong and active in Belize.

world respect for the rule of law is an incentive, and disrespect for the rule of law can be a severe deterrent, to foreign investment) ...The people of Belize are entitled to be properly informed about any proposals for alterations in the dam design before the project is approved and before work continues with its construction.[39]

Lord Walker framed what was a technical environment case squarely as a case about respect for the rule of law. While the majority preferred to view the process as 'a political decision about the public interest,' Lord Walker felt that the geological error in the Environmental Impact Assessment considered and approved by the Department of the Environment vitiated the approval. His dissent manifests a punctilious regard for the over-arching pre-eminence of the rule of law. Although the point was not taken before any of the courts, the requirement in the preamble of the Belize Constitution that there be policies of the state 'which protect the environment' – a requirement absent from the preambles of most Caribbean constitutions – could arguably have provided the normative basis for Lord Walker's dissent. It could be argued that the inclusion in the preamble of the Belize Constitution of a requirement that 'policies of state...protect the environment' signalled that the framers of the Belize Constitution intended that environmental policies be especially scrutinized for compliance with the rule of law.[40]

D. The Reformed Preamble and the Protection of Indigenous People

In contrast, *Cal v AG*,[41] better known as the Maya land rights case, is notable for the open prominence accorded to the preamble of the Belize Constitution in the reasoning of the Chief Justice of Belize. The case raised before the Supreme Court the unprecedented issue of determining whether the protection from deprivation of property extended to cover customary land tenure of the Mayan people, the indigenous inhabitants of Belize. This issue, litigated often enough in other parts of the Commonwealth, was a novel one for the Caribbean. The case was a test case brought by villagers from the two Mayan villages of Santa Cruz and Conejo.[42] In essence, their argument was that by failing to demarcate and recognize the boundaries of their lands and by continuing to issue leases, grants and concessions over their lands, the government had failed to respect their customary land rights which were based on traditional land

---

39. Ibid 120.
40. Belize Constitution preamble s (e).
41. (2007) 71 WIR 110 (SC Bze).
42. They were backed by organized local indigenous organizations as well as powerful international indigenous rights organizations.

use and occupation of the Mayan people dating back before the time of English settlement of Belize. They contended that the government by its actions and inactions had breached several of their constitutional rights, namely, their right to life, to not be deprived of property and to not be discriminated against. They also contended that there was a breach of section 3, the opening section of Part II of the Constitution, the bill of rights, which set out the omnibus rights, including the right to 'life, liberty, security of the person and the protection of the law.'[43]

After finding that there existed in southern Belize Maya customary land tenure and that the villagers of Santa Cruz and Conejo had proprietary interests in land, the question for the Supreme Court then was whether such interest constituted 'property' protected under the Constitution. The starting point in the reasoning of Conteh CJ was the preamble to the Belize Constitution 'which by an amendment...now makes explicit reference to the collective group to which the claimants undoubtedly belong, namely, the indigenous peoples of Belize.'[44] The preamble provides:

> Whereas the people of Belize...(a) affirm that the Nation of Belize shall be founded upon principles which acknowledge...faith in human rights and fundamental freedoms...(e) require policies of state which protect...the identity, dignity and social and cultural values of Belizeans, including Belize's indigenous peoples....

The Chief Justice adopted the approach that 'a generous and purposive interpretation is to be given to constitutional provisions protecting human rights and that a court is required to consider the substance of the fundamental right at issue and ensure contemporary protection of that right in the light of evolving standards of decency that mark the progress of a mature society.'[45] The Chief Justice concluded that the Maya right to land based on customary land tenure formed

> a kind or species of property that is deserving of the protection the Belize Constitution accords to property in general. There is no doubt this form of property, from the evidence, nurtures and sustains the claimants and their very way of life and existence.[46]

It is difficult to take issue with the prominence accorded to the preamble by Conteh CJ. It was the legislature, after all, the elected representatives of the people, which, by a constitutional amendment in

---

43. Belize Constitution s 3(a).
44. *Cal* (n 41) 96.
45. Ibid 102.
46. Ibid.

2001, introduced a specific reference to 'Belize's indigenous peoples' in the preamble, requiring that state policies protect them. The case was not appealed by the government. The notion that the preamble plays an important role as the normative or philosophical basis for interpreting the Constitution should be applauded. The extent to which issues of ethnicity, gender and minorities should be given recognition is topical in constitutional reform discourse in the Commonwealth.[47] Included in the constitutional reforms to the preamble of 2001 were also references to 'ethnicity,' 'gender equality' and persons with disability. These, however, have not yet attracted litigation. The constitutional amendment to recognize the indigenous people by the Belizean legislature and the ready application of it by the judiciary is illustrative of the dynamic complementarity of these two institutions in creating a 'constitutional space' for indigenous people in Belize.[48] The legislature and the judiciary were discharging their implied role of ensuring that the Constitution fulfils the aspirations of citizens of the state as reflected in the preamble.

The Maya also argued that their human security was being threatened. They hunted, fished, farmed and gathered communally for their physical survival. This, they said, was being threatened by the government's refusal to respect their right to communal lands. Other than section 3 of the Belize Constitution which recognized 'security of the person' as one of the fundamental rights and freedoms to which each individual is entitled, the Belize Constitution contained no separate, detailed or enumerated right to 'security of the person.' In most other Caribbean constitutions, the equivalent to Belize's section 3 is non-justiciable and considered by the Caribbean Court of Justice in *AG v Joseph* to be 'in the nature of a preamble.'[49] This is because in those constitutions that opening section of their bill of rights is specifically excluded in the section that lists the rights that are enforceable. In Belize, the framers were wise to make that opening section specifically enforceable.[50] The Chief

---

47. The High Court of South Africa declared recently that South Africans of Chinese descent fall within the ambit of the definition of 'black people' in section 1 of the Employment Equity Act of 1988 and in the Broad-based Black Empowerment Act of 2003. *Chinese Association of South Africa v Minister of Labour* HC RSA (Transvaal Provincial Division) 18 June 2008. This might at first blush appear an improbable conclusion. But the improbability of it is only skin deep. This is a good example of a judiciary eschewing the kind of formal and legalistic approach to interpretation famously proclaimed by Lord Wilberforce in *Minister of Home Affairs v Fisher* (1979) 44 WIR 107 (PC Ber) and embracing a realistic interpretation that reflects the evolving socio-economic realities of the day.

48. This amendment was requested by representatives of the indigenous people who were at the time engaged in negotiations with the government of Belize over their rights to a homeland. The writer was intimately involved in the negotiations.

49. [2006] CCJ 3 (AJ), (2006) 69 WIR 104 (Bdos) [58].

50. See also Antigua and Barbuda Constitution 1981 s 3 and St Kitts-Nevis Constitution 1983 s 3.

Justice was, therefore, not detained by doubts as to the justiciability of section 3. He found that

> ...the land they traditionally use and occupy plays a central role in their physical, cultural and spiritual existence and vitality... without the legal protection of their rights to and interests in their customary land, the enjoyment of their right to life and their very lifestyle and well-being would be seriously compromised and be in jeopardy. This, I find, will not be in conformity with the Constitution's guarantees.[51]

The failure of most of the Caribbean to make the opening section of their bill of rights enforceable has hindered unnecessarily the development of human rights in the region. It has resulted in 30-year evolutionary creep by Caribbean judiciaries towards finding a meaningful role for that opening section. Tracy Robinson, for example, makes an argument for the opening section of Caribbean bill of rights to assume greater weight in constitutional interpretation as a normative guide.[52] It is entirely open to Caribbean legislatures through constitutional reform to amend their constitutions to give enforceability to it in the manner of Belize, St Kitts-Nevis, and Antigua and Barbuda.

3. Constitutional Reform and the Liberal Legislature

A. Expanding Access to Justice

Compared to many Commonwealth legislatures that display of a reflexive reluctance to expand citizens' right to access the courts to test their constitutional rights, the Belizean legislature may be regarded as having adopted a liberal approach. Included in the Belize Constitution (Third Amendment) Act 2001 was an amendment to Part II containing the bill of rights. Section 20 which provided the right of access to the courts for redress contained a proviso that if the Supreme Court dismissed an application on the grounds that it was 'frivolous and vexatious,' no appeal would lie. The amendment deleted that proviso. Such a proviso had been unique to Belize and no counterpart could be found, for example, in the constitutions of Jamaica, Barbados or Trinidad and Tobago. No doubt the framers of the Belize Constitution at that time were influenced by considerations of efficient use of precious court time. The proviso lay dormant until the advent of the phenomenon of constitutional challenges to the death penalty. A couple of illustrations will contextualize the rationale for the amendment.

---

51. *Cal* (n 41) 117.
52. T. Robinson, 'Our Inherent Constitution,' Chapter 11.

In *Lauriano v AG*[53] the appellant, a death row inmate who had exhausted all appeals, brought a constitutional motion challenging the constitutionality of his death sentence. The Supreme Court, pointing out that the appellant had had the opportunity to canvas the issues before the courts, dismissed the motion as frivolous and vexatious. Before the Court of Appeal, the state made a preliminary objection that the Court of Appeal had no jurisdiction in light of the proviso. Georges P rejected the submission that, despite the proviso, the court could examine whether the basis on which the Chief Justice had arrived at his conclusion that the grounds were frivolous and vexatious was sound. He concluded that to do that 'would be to allow an appeal against the determination itself.'[54] A few other cases followed this emerging pattern.

Finally, in *Mejia, Bull and Guevara v AG*,[55] the Court of Appeal revisited its position. Georges P said that a 'literal interpretation of the proviso...makes serious inroads in the scheme for the enforcement of the protective provisions of the Constitution.'[56] Because the proviso was unique to Belize, no cases could be cited indicating the relevant matters to be considered in exercising the power to dismiss an application as frivolous and vexatious in the area of fundamental rights and freedoms of a constitution. The court reasoned that, in exercising the jurisdiction to dismiss a constitutional application on the ground that it was frivolous and vexatious, a judge should act judicially. Finding that there was no basis for dismissing the application as frivolous and vexatious, the court allowed the appeal.

Through judicial activism, the court introduced a qualification to the apparent absoluteness of the proviso. But the Legislature was not content with this judicial amelioration of the severity of the proviso. It deleted it from the Constitution along with another proviso commonly found in Caribbean constitutions. That other proviso was to the effect that the Supreme Court could decline to exercise its jurisdiction where it is satisfied that adequate means of redress for constitutional contravention are available under another law. Together, these amendments conferred upon the citizenry unhindered access to the courts where they alleged breach of their fundamental rights and freedoms.

---

53. (1995) 47 WIR 74 (CA Bze).
54. Ibid 87.
55. 3 BzLR 248, 25 June 1996 (CA Bze).
56. Ibid 255.

B. Refining a Constitutional Convention

The Belize Constitution (Fourth Amendment) Act 2001 introduced a curious amendment into the Belize Constitution. The amendment provided that the Governor General could not exercise his constitutional powers to make appointments to offices established by the Constitution or a public office after the National Assembly has been dissolved. The seeds of this amendment were sown in February of 1999 when Belize came close to a constitutional crisis. The government of the day made a number of appointments to the judiciary, including the appointment of a Chief Justice, one day before the general elections scheduled for 27 August 1998. The Secretary to the Cabinet had written to the Leader of the Opposition on 19 August 1998 inviting his comments on the proposed Chief Justice. The Opposition Leader replied that he stood ready to meet to present his views. On 24 August, the Governor General signed and sealed the instrument appointing the Chief Justice. That same day, the Secretary to the Cabinet invited the Leader of the Opposition to a meeting with the Prime Minister in the capital on 25 August. The Leader of the Opposition replied suggesting that the meeting take place in Belize City on the 26 August 1998. On 25 August 1998, the Prime Minister replied, regretting that he was unable to accede to the request for a change in the appointment for a meeting. On 26 August 1998 the Chief Justice was sworn into office. The general elections were held. The government of the day lost the elections and the Leader of the Opposition became the Prime Minister of Belize.

Nearly six months after the appointment of the Chief Justice and the holding of the general elections, a Belizean citizen in *J Mohammed v AG*[57] challenged the constitutional validity of the appointment of the Chief Justice and sought prohibition, restraining the Chief Justice from continuing to act as Chief Justice.[58] Section 97(1) of the Belize Constitution states that 'The Chief Justice shall be appointed by the Governor General acting in accordance with the advice of the Prime Minister given after consultation with the Leader of the Opposition.' But the Belize Constitution also contained a provision not to be found in any other constitution in the Caribbean. This provision set out the effect of consultation and the requirements of consultation. It stated that:

> Where any person or authority is directed by this Constitution to exercise any function after consultation with any other person or authority, that person or authority shall not be obliged to exercise

---

57. (unrep) 2 February 1999, No 73 of 1999 (SC Bze).
58. The Chief Justice was not a party to the case and had no knowledge that it was before the courts.

that function in accordance with the advice of that person or authority.

Where any person or authority is directed by this Constitution or any other law to consult any other person or authority before taking any decision or action, that other person or authority must be given a genuine opportunity to present his or its view before the decision or action, as the case may be, is taken.[59]

Section 34(4) of the Belize Constitution also contained a clause ousting enquiry by the courts of those functions of the Governor General requiring him to act in accordance with the advice of, or after consultation with any person or authority. There is force in the judge's conclusion that the ouster clause could only protect from review the question of whether the Governor General himself had actually acted in accordance with advice or after consultation. That was not what was being questioned. What was being challenged was the failure by the Prime Minister to comply with the constitutional requirement to consult prior to advising the Governor General to appoint the Chief Justice. The judge found that when the Prime Minister wrote to the Leader of the Opposition inviting him to a meeting on Tuesday, 25 August 1998 to consult on the matter of the judicial appointments, the Governor General had already signed and sealed the instrument appointing the Chief Justice on that same day. The judge said:

> This is the most telling piece of evidence and shows that the proposed meeting scheduled for Tuesday, 25th August, 1998, was a mere sham ...the appointment had been perfected by the Governor-General even before the scheduled meeting which had been specifically arranged to hear the views of the then Leader of the Opposition on the proposed appointment, had taken place.[60]

The judge added *obiter*:

> I also take judicial notice of the fact that general elections of members of the House of Representatives was due to be held on the 27th day of August 1998 and the proposed appointment of Mr. Sosa as Chief Justice became effective a day before the election, i.e., 26th August 1998. Such a course of action is unheard of in a parliamentary democracy based on the Westminster model where the government of the day after the issue of the Writ of Election acts merely in a caretaker capacity and refrains from taking any major decisions. To my mind, to appoint a Chief Justice substantively just

59. Belize Constitution s 129.
60. *J Mohammed* (n 57).

a day before the general elections makes a mockery of parliamentary democracy.[61]

The two ends of the rule of law were tied in a Gordian knot. The case did not go before the Court of Appeal so whether that court would have untied the knot, or like Alexander the Great, slice it, must remain a matter of speculation. On the one hand, the Belize Constitution, like other Caribbean constitutions, provided that a judge could be removed from office *only* for inability to discharge the functions of his office or for misbehaviour. On the other hand, the Constitution had provided a defined procedure for the appointment of a judge and had gone further than its Caribbean counterparts in explaining what consultation was to involve. The clear intention was that the procedure be respected. The Wooding Commission, set up in the early 1970s to review Trinidad and Tobago's Constitution, had cautioned about the dangers of transplanting the Westminster model into 'societies without political cultures which support its operative conventions.'[62] The Belize framers had the foresight to avoid *legis non scripta* and reduce the convention of consultation into constitutional text. In the end, the deposed Chief Justice and the government reached an out-of-court settlement and the legislature two years later removed the possibility of a re-occurrence of this kind of matter in a constitutional amendment.

C. Strengthening Judicial Independence

What differentiates *Meerabux v AG*[63] from other cases around the Commonwealth involving the removal of a high court judge is that it was not politically motivated. Complaints against the judge were initiated by the Bar Association of Belize and by a practising senior counsel.[64] They invoked the constitutional procedures for removal on the ground of misbehaviour in office. The Constitution empowered the Governor General to remove a justice of the Supreme Court on the advice of the Belize Advisory Council, sitting as a tribunal, after it had inquired into a referred complaint. The judge alleged bias because the Chairman of the Belize Advisory Council, who was an attorney-at-law (and was required by the Belize Constitution to be an attorney-at-law), was a member of the Bar Association of Belize, the body that complained to the Belize

---

61. Ibid.
62. Constitution Commission of Trinidad and Tobago, *Report of the Constitution Commission* (Port of Spain 1974) (Wooding Commission) 27.
63. [2005] UKPC 12, (2005) 66 WIR 113 (Bze).
64. This was the same judge who presided over the deposing of the Chief Justice.

Advisory Council. The Privy Council accepted that the answer could be found in the doctrine of necessity. They were of the view that:

> ...it must be taken to have been within the contemplation of the framers of the Constitution that the Chairman who was directed by the first proviso to section 54(11) to preside over an inquiry into the question whether a judge of the Supreme Court should be removed for inability or misbehaviour would be a member of the Bar Association...it must also have been appreciated that complaints alleging inability or misbehaviour on the part of a justice of the Supreme Court would be a matter of concern to the Bar Association, and that it would be likely to be involved in the presentation of such complaints to any tribunal that was convened to inquire into the matter under section 98(5)(b)...in this context mere membership of the Association is not to be taken, in itself, as a ground of disqualification in the case of the Chairman.[65]

The appellant also alleged that his section 6(8) constitutional right was also infringed. Section 6(8) required that all proceedings of every court or other authority be held in public. The Belize Advisory Council had held its inquiry in camera. The Privy Council found that section 6(8) is designed to reinforce the fundamental guarantee in section 6(1) that all persons are equal before the law and are entitled without discrimination to the equal protection of the law. But, they held, it must be assumed:

> that the framers of the Constitution had that fundamental guarantee in mind when they were addressing themselves to the composition and powers of the BAC and the functions that it was to perform. It must also be assumed that they had it in mind when they were devising the procedure that should be followed for the removal from office of a justice of the Supreme Court. They had the opportunity, if they were so minded, to make it clear that the guarantee in section 6(8) applied to these proceedings. The provisions which deal with these matters in sections 54 and 98 of the Constitution contain no hint that they must be read subject to the provisions of section 6(8)...it is not engaged upon the determination of the existence or extent of any civil right or obligation within the meaning of section 6(8).[66]

The judges of the Supreme Court, the Court of Appeal and the Privy Council all reached the same conclusion in the *Meerabux* case. At no stage was any serious issue taken with the operation of the removal procedures. Yet, on such a momentous matter as the removal of a judge, the legislature felt that the procedure ought to be tightened up.

---

65. *Meerabux* (n 63) 28.
66. Ibid 33.

The existing procedure was that complaints for the removal of a judge were made directly to the Governor General who would consider whether the question of the judge's removal ought to be referred to the Belize Advisory Council. The Belize Constitution (Fourth Amendment) Act now requires complaints to be made to the Judicial and Legal Services Commission which then considers whether the question of a judge's removal ought to be referred to the Belize Advisory Council.[67] This removes from the Governor General the onus of deciding whether there is enough in a complaint that merits referral to the Belize Advisory Council and places the onus on the Judicial and Legal Services Commission, a four-person panel comprised of the Chairman of the Public Services Commission, the Chief Justice, the Solicitor-General and the President of the Bar Association.[68] It also removes the Head of State, as it were, from the political fray that sometimes accompanies something as weighty as the removal of a judge.

In 2005, the legislature, in its fifth constitutional amendment, introduced two other amendments intended to further strengthen the independence of the judiciary.[69] The first recognized the Magistracy as an integral part of the judiciary and provided security of tenure for qualified magistrates in the same manner as that provided for Justices of the Supreme Court.[70] Of the people who come before the courts, the great majority do so at the magistrates courts. Public perception of justice, to a large extent, is therefore fashioned there. It would therefore seem appropriate that the magistrates also be given security of tenure. The benefit of this is, however, yet to take effect. Of the 16 magistrates in Belize in 2008, only five were qualified as attorneys. There is currently no plan in place for the systematic training of magistrates which would professionalize the magistracy within a specified time period.

The Second Amendment introduced is somewhat opaque; it provides that 'the budgets presented by the offices of the Auditor-General...the Supreme Court and the Court of Appeal shall be given first priority calls on the Consolidated Revenue Fund.'[71] No doubt this was intended to prevent the more indirect methods of judicial interference such as budget attenuation or the diminution of judicial salaries or pensions by allowing the judiciary to design its own budget and present it which, along with other listed constitutional offices, would take a first bite out of the budget regardless of the other demands on the budget. In practice this has not

---

67. Belize Constitution s 98(4), Belize Constitution (Fourth Amendment) Act 2001-39.
68. Belize Constitution s 98(5)(a).
69. Belize Constitution (Fifth Amendment) Act 2005-23.
70. Belize Constitution ss 93(A)(3), (4).
71. Ibid s 118(6).

worked out as the budget for the judiciary is routinely whittled down by the Ministry of Finance and consistently represents less than one per cent of the national budget.

D. Reforming Parliament

Another instance of the Belize legislature being sensitive to deficiencies in the Belize Constitution concerned the issue of floor-crossing. Floor-crossing is also a topic of constitutional reform discourse that has been debated for a long time across the Commonwealth. The legislature, however, amended the Constitution in 2001 to provide that if a member of the House of Representatives crosses the floor his seat shall be declared vacant resulting in a by-election to fill the vacant seat.[72] More controversial is the provision in the Belize Constitution (Sixth Amendment) Act of August 2008 that allows for the recall of elected representatives before the expiry of their normal term of office, the mechanics of which are fleshed out in the Recall of Elected Representatives Act.[73]

The question of the role and relevance of the Senate has been a live issue in Commonwealth Caribbean constitutional discourse since the 1970s. The Wooding Commission of Trinidad and Tobago had recommended its abolition.[74] Constitutional amendments introduced in 2001 restructured the Belize Senate, giving it new powers unprecedented in the Caribbean.[75] The senate was originally comprised of eight members: five appointed on the advice of the prime minister, two on the advice of the opposition leader and one on the advice of the Belize Advisory Council. This was expanded to 12; six on the advice of the prime minister; three on the advice of the opposition leader; and one each by the Belize Council of Churches and Evangelical Association of Churches, the Belize Chamber of Commerce and the National Trade Union congress along with the Civil Society Steering Committee.[76] The senate's powers and functions were expanded to include approving any bill to alter the bill of rights, authorizing the ratification of any treaty by the government of Belize, approving the establishment in Belize of any new, foreign military bases and approving the appointment of ambassadors, judges, the Director of Public Prosecutions, the Contractor-General and the Ombudsman.[77]

---

72. Belize Constitution s 59A, Belize Constitution (Third Amendment) Act 2001-2 s 9.
73. Belize Constitution (Sixth Amendment) Act 2008-13 s 6, Belize Recall of Elected Representatives Act 2010.
74. Wooding Commission (n 62) 194–95.
75. Belize Constitution s 61A, Belize Constitution (Fourth Amendment) Act 2001-39 s 6.
76. Belize Constitution s 61(1).
77. Ibid s 61A.

Since the restructuring of the senate, the value of the senate as a revising chamber has improved.[78] The number of instances in which bills sent by the House of Representatives have been improved upon in substance and in drafting has dramatically increased. It has also been observed that the scrutiny of and proposed amendments to the draft bills comes from the independent senators representing the churches, the business community, the trade unions and civil society.

Emboldened by its new powers, the senate sought to extend the ambit of its oversight to an extent unprecedented in the Caribbean. Following a huge public controversy over the alleged mismanagement of Belize Social Security Board (BSSB) funds in high risk, failed investments, the senate passed a resolution appointing a special select committee of the senate to inquire into the management and operation of the BSSB. Almost two years later, it concluded its report which was debated by the senate and accepted. One of the recommendations was that the CEO of the BSSB should be terminated. Following her termination, the CEO challenged, *inter alia,* the jurisdiction of the senate to embark on the inquiry.[79] The Supreme Court decided that under the National Assembly (Powers and Privileges) Ordinance 1962, which was still in force in Belize, the senate could have embarked on such an inquiry. While the Belize Constitution did not confer any specific power to embark upon such an inquiry, neither did it prohibit it. The Constitution, the judge found, was *merely silent about those matters.* Since there was no conflict between the National Assembly (Powers and Privileges) Ordinance and the Belize Constitution, the court was happy to conclude that the inquiry had not been unlawful.[80]

The Belize Constitution (Sixth Amendment) Act of 2008 has further reformed the Senate ensuring that the senators nominated by the Opposition and the non-government organizations together constitute the majority.[81] It expands the senate's powers to initiate and conduct public inquiries into mismanagement or corruption by persons in central government or statutory bodies, removing the basis for the challenge of the senate's jurisdiction that was relied upon in the *Garcia* case.[82] The most far-reaching reform as it relates to the executive has been the three-term limit for holders of the office of prime minister that was introduced in the sixth constitutional amendments.

---

78. The writer was a parliamentarian from 1999–2008.
79. *Garcia v Hulse* (2 July 2008) BZ 2008 SC 15 (Bze).
80. There was no appeal from the decision of the Supreme Court to the Court of Appeal.
81. Belize Constitution s 61A, Belize Constitution (Sixth Amendment) Act 2008-13 s 8.
82. *Garcia* (n 79).

4. Constitutional Debasement or Development?

With both the legislature and the judiciary vigorously embracing their respective roles in developing the Belize Constitution, it was perhaps only a matter of time before they differed about *how* the Constitution should be developed to best reflect the aspirations of the people. Differ they did, and sharply in *Vellos v Prime Minister of Belize*.[83] Two of the biggest issues of the day, crime and oil, which was discovered in commercial quantities in 2005, provided the basis for the disagreement. In response to spiralling crime, the Belize Constitution (Sixth Amendment) Bill proposed to derogate from the guaranteed right of liberty of the person by detaining persons for up to seven days where such persons are suspected of committing or likely to commit defined serious crimes.[84] It also proposed to derogate from the right not to be deprived of property as it related to mineral rights.[85] Could a parliament which had the requisite majority amend the Constitution to derogate from already existing rights? This was the high seas of constitutional interpretation. The waters, though not unchartered in the Commonwealth, were very unfamiliar. The Supreme Court of India had declared that the Parliament's power to amend the Constitution by a special majority does not include the power to amend its basic structure or basic features.[86]

However, the Belize Supreme Court did not go that far. But the amendments faced an obstacle. The Referendum Act provided that a referendum shall be held on 'any amendment to Part II of the Constitution which derogates from the fundamental rights and freedoms guaranteed therein.'[87] To circumvent this, an amendment to the Referendum Act repealing that clause was tabled at the same time as the sixth amendment bill. The thinking no doubt was that the Referendum Bill would be enacted well before the constitutional amendment which required a 90-day delay before the second reading. Before the Referendum (Amendment) Bill could be enacted, a group of registered voters sought mandamus against the Prime Minister to compel him to initiate a referendum on the amendment to the bill of rights. The Chief Justice granted an interim injunction prohibiting the presentation of the bill for the signature of the Governor General pending the trial.

At the stage of final judgment, the Chief Justice found that the constitutional amendment bill if enacted, would derogate from the rights

---

83. 28 July 2008, BZ 2008 SC 22 (Bze).
84. Belize Constitution (Sixth Amendment) Act 2008-13 c 2.
85. Ibid c 3.
86. *Kesavananda v Bharati* 1973 (4) SCC 225 (SC Ind).
87. Belize Referendum Act 1999 s 2(2)(a).

to protection of personal liberty and from deprivation of property and that clause 2(2) of the Referendum Act 'was intended to protect against the amending powers by a cyclical majority' and without it 'no fundamental right or freedom...would be immune from alteration or derogation.'[88] He concluded that:

> ...in introducing the two bills on the same day, there was a clear attempt to remove from consideration or to deny an opportunity the electorate of Belize to have a say on the proposed changes to... the Belize Constitution...it does not make one whit of a difference that the statutory requirement of a referendum on such a proposed constitutional change may be repealed or abolished.[89]

He lifted the injunction, declined to order mandamus against the Prime Minister, but declared that a referendum should be held on the relevant clauses of the constitutional amendment bill.

The decision to injunct the amendment to the Referendum Act, an ordinary piece of legislation which was not itself unconstitutional appears untenable. But for the interim injunction, the amendment to the Referendum Act would have gone ahead, removing the basis for the judicial review action. The decision of the Chief Justice was affirmed on appeal.[90] The Privy Council confirmed the decision of the courts below that the Referendum Act made provision for referenda to serve an advisory or consultative purpose.[91] It imposed an obligation that could be enforced by proceedings for judicial review, but did not impose a fetter on the legislative process. The Privy Council held that the requirement for a consultative or advisory referendum did not alter the Constitution. The Board also ruled that the obligation to hold a referendum in relation to the proposed Sixth Amendment of the Constitution did not survive amendments made to the Bill on the second reading. Given this ruling, the Board deemed it unnecessary to decide the effect of the Referendum (Amendment) Act on the obligation to hold a referendum.

5. Conclusion

The story of constitutionalism in Belize has been one in which both the judiciary and the legislature have tried to ensure that the Belize Constitution does not remain inflexible, like the hieroglyphs on a Mayan

---

88. *Vellos* (n 83) 42.
89. Ibid 59.
90. *Prime Minister v Vellos* (17 October 2008) BZ 2008 CA 30 (Bze).
91. *Prime Minister v Vellos* [2010] UKPC 7 (Bze).

stelae, but 'evolve[s] organically over time to reflect the developing needs of society.'[92] If one accepts the view that the constitution should be the institutionalization of the people's will, then undoubtedly the dénouement of the story is that much of the constitutional reforms had the benefit of the active participation of the people.[93] Should it matter that a particular piece of reform demanded by the people, such as the right of recall, on careful reflection, might debase rather than enhance democracy?[94]

Perhaps what is more important is that Belize has not been coy in testing reforms to its Westminster-bequeathed constitution to find a form that fits well with the thinking of a restive citizenry as to how best it should be governed. The reforms have not been regressive but reflect a genuine attempt at improving the Constitution. If constitutional development is a road over which the citizenry must pass in fulfilling its aspirations, it is not without some potholes caused by the appalling delay in delivering judgments that undermines the rule of law, the failure to develop ADR mechanisms to ease the cost and time of court processes and the anomaly of a British head of state. Horace Walpole observed of the centuries-old British constitution that 'It is Time that composes a good constitution....'[95] In a fast-paced world in which the changing demands of the people consistently outstrip the state's ability to respond, might we not be forgiven for using the innovative tool of constitutional reform to shortcut the time-intensive process of constitutional adjudication?

---

92. *DPP v Mollison* (2003) 64 WIR 140 [16].
93. As expressed in political reform consultations, on talk-shows, in civil society consultations and in party political consultations.
94. See G. Smith, 'Recall to the Political Pandora's Box' (Belize 13 August 2008) accessed < http://www.flashpointbelize.com/flashpointarticles/tabid/103/EntryId/62/Recall-to-the-Political-Pandoras-Box.aspx> accessed 8 August 2010.
95. H. Walpole, *Letters of Horace Walpole* (vol 4, Clarendon Press, Oxford 1892) 649.

Our Inherent Constitution

Tracy Robinson

1. Introduction

The Caribbean Court of Justice's (CCJ) first major decision, *AG v Joseph*,[1] an appeal in a death penalty case from Barbados, invites us, albeit not plainly, to look beyond the texts of Caribbean constitutions and to have regard to unwritten principles, especially the rule of law, as a fundamental source of Caribbean constitutional law. The Court held that capital defendants have a legitimate expectation that their petitions before international human rights tribunals would be dealt with before carrying out the death sentence. The joint decision of de la Bastide P and Saunders J justified this entitlement with reference to the 'inherent jurisdiction' of the superior courts to grant constitutional relief to give full effect to the 'protection of the law.' Wit J had a similar tack. He described the constitutional text as 'merely *a reflection of* the fundamental right to the protection of the law.'[2] The CCJ's analysis suggests that the 'protection of the law,' an aspect of the rule of law, is elevated to an implied justiciable constitutional norm.

This chapter starts where many discussions of Caribbean constitutional law do, with the doctrine of constitutional supremacy. But here with a caution that this doctrine cannot resolve all important questions in constitutional law and that there will always be the need to rely on unwritten norms. I go on to look briefly at the role of the rule of law in Caribbean constitutional law as a precursor to examining *Joseph's* analysis of the right to the protection of the law. Since *Hinds v R*[3] lays the strongest foundation for *Joseph's* provocative talk of an 'inherent' constitution, some attention is paid to the lessons we can learn from it and its progeny. Next are some less noticed decisions that begin to take seriously the idea that Caribbean constitutions have a normative foundation, which is a critical starting point for discussion around unwritten constitutional norms. And finally, it will be explained more

---

1. [2006] CCJ 3 (AJ), (2006) 69 WIR 104 (Bdos).
2. Ibid 20 (emphasis added).
3. [1977] AC 195, (1975) 24 WIR 326 (PC Ja).

fully why treating the rule of law as an unwritten constitutional norm can be a good development for Caribbean constitutional law.

2. Supremacy's Inadequacies

Early Caribbean public law scholarship shed light on the distinctiveness of postcolonial Caribbean public law: the paradigm shift brought about by constitutional supremacy and justiciable bills of rights, the demise of parliamentary sovereignty as it had been known,[4] and the basis and scope of judicial review, both of legislation[5] and administrative action.[6] Professor Albert Fiadjoe has offered up a public law that has come of age, a revolution in Caribbean public law as a result of the written constitutions and new judicial review legislation.[7]

But as jurists underlined the primacy of the written constitutions they faced a dilemma: how seriously should one take supreme laws that marginalize protection of fundamental rights with savings law clauses[8] and explicitly exclude the possibility of judicial review through ouster clauses.[9] The texts of Caribbean constitutions have internal contradictions that cannot be resolved satisfactorily by referring to constitutional supremacy. Identifying 'opaque redress provisions, apparently unenforceable opening sections, generous savings of existing laws and copious limitations on the actual rights,' Arif Bulkan bluntly concludes that Caribbean bills of rights are schizophrenic.[10] We evidently need modes of interpretation that honour the commitment to fundamental rights and freedoms in the bills of rights without being entirely undone by the textual restrictions within them.

---

4. See F. Alexis, 'The Classical Doctrine of Parliamentary Sovereignty as a Current Issue in West Indian Law' (1997) Guy LJ 41.

5. See A.R. Carnegie, 'Judicial Review of Legislation in the West Indian Constitutions' (1971) PL 276, F. Alexis 'The Basis of Judicial Review of Legislation in the New Commonwealth and the United States of America: A Comprehensive Analysis' (1975) 7 Lawyers of the Americas 567.

6. F. Alexis, 'Aspects of Judicial Review of Administrative Action in the Commonwealth Caribbean in comparison with Great Britain' (DPhil thesis, University of Cambridge 1980).

7. A. Fiadjoe, 'An Overview of the Public Law Revolution in the Commonwealth Caribbean' (1992) 21 Anglo-American LR 310. An earlier version of this paper was presented at the special UWI Faculty of Law Faculty Workshop Series 2007–8 in honour of Prof Albert Fiadjoe.

8. See F. Alexis, 'When is an Existing Law Saved?' (1976) PL 256.

9. See E. Thomas, 'The Application of an Ouster Clause in the Constitution and the Public Service Commission in the Exercise of Its Disciplinary Powers' (on file UWI Faculty of Law Library, 1980), A. Fiadjoe, 'Judicial Approaches to Constitutional and Statutory Exclusion of Judicial Review in Commonwealth Caribbean Public Law' in G. Kodilinye and P. Menon (eds), *Commonwealth Caribbean Legal Studies* (Butterworths, London 1992) 161.

10. A. Bulkan, 'Judicial Independence as an Indispensable Feature of the Rule of Law and Democracy: Implications for the Commonwealth Caribbean,' in David S. Berry and Tracy Robinson (eds), *Transitions in Caribbean Law: Law-Making, Constitutionalism and the Convergence of National and International Law* (The Caribbean Law Publishing Co, Kingston 2013).

Quite apart from contradictions in the texts, the written constitutions cannot answer all the complex questions of governance and liberty that arise from our constantly changing global, regional and local spheres. In many instances, the texts simply do not say enough to resolve the questions at hand because they are drafted in some critical places with a high level of generality. When, for example, is a punishment inhuman or degrading?[11] Or what balance between private property and legitimate public interests will secure the just economic system that many constitutions speak about?[12] Our written constitutions are at best a rough blueprint for governance.[13]

While constitutional supremacy is undeniably our starting point as public lawyers, it has not been enough to brace a maturing Caribbean public law. The usual argument for giving pre-eminence to the text, that the written constitution reflects choices and institutional arrangements made by 'the people,' has considerably less weight in respect of Caribbean independence constitutions which were not generated by highly democratic processes. For Professor Simeon McIntosh, this introduces a profound question of moral and political legitimacy – that these constitutions are not really *our own*.[14] While McIntosh is evidently pressing for constitutional reform using democratic processes, constitutions also can be *owned* or made more autochthonous through processes of interpretation and developing particular 'habits of constitutionalism.'[15] The comparison of constitutional texts to ill-fitting uncomfortable leather shoes that adapt to meet the feet of the wearer over time is an apt one.[16]

Ultimately, constitutional meaning cannot be derived *solely* from reading the constitutional texts as drafted, not if we expect the constitutions to endure. The fundamental law can never entirely be captured in a written constitution. There will always be a need to 'resort to implicit or unwritten principles of legal decency.'[17] It must be the business of Caribbean constitutional law to sort out far more clearly what those implicit and unwritten principles are, when they apply and their role in our constitutional order.

---

11. For example, Barbados Constitution 1966 s 15(1).
12. For example, ibid preamble (d).
13. A. Harding and P. Leyland, 'Comparative Law in Constitutional Contexts' in E. Orucu and D. Nelken (eds), *Comparative Law: A Handbook* (Hart Publishing, Oxford 2007) 313, 318.
14. S. McIntosh, *Caribbean Constitutional Reform: Rethinking the West Indian Polity* (The Caribbean Law Publishing Co, Kingston 2002) 41.
15. L. Ackermann, 'The Obligations on Government and Society in Our Constitutional State to Respect and Support Independent Constitutional Structures' (2000) 3 Potchefstroom Electronic Law Journal/Potchefstroomse Elektroniese Regsblad 1, 4.
16. Harding and Leyland (n 13) 316.
17. L. Fuller, *The Anatomy of Law* (Frederick A. Praeger, New York 1968) 94.

Since *Hinds v R*,[18] it has been acknowledged that Caribbean constitutions 'leave much to implication'[19] and unwritten constitutional principles have served as 'gap-fillers.' Strong inferences are made from the constitutions and their structure; these fill gaps in the written constitutional schemes and are treated virtually as if they are part of the written constitutions.[20] Another shade of this approach sees unwritten principles as 'constitutional values,' ideals that influence the interpretation of explicit provisions of the constitutions.[21] If asked, we likely would say that this process gives depth and meaning to the *written texts* themselves. In both approaches, the boundary between written and unwritten is blurred but constitutional authority and justiciability is strongly tied to the texts themselves.[22]

There is serious disputation among constitutional scholars and judges about an even more expansive role for unwritten constitutional principles in the constitutional order that *Joseph* tentatively aligns itself to, in which 'the constitutional text is not just supplemented by unwritten principles; it rests upon and reflects them.'[23] These principles are foundational and will in certain circumstances be treated as supreme, binding all state actors, even in the .absence of and, in extraordinary cases, in spite of, an explicit constitutional provision. Radically, it might be argued that certain indefensible constitutional amendments could be challenged on the ground that they amount to a pernicious violation of unwritten constitutional norms.[24]

3. The Rule of Law in Caribbean Constitutional Law

Joseph is yet another Caribbean case that invokes the 'multi-layered'[25] and contested concept, the rule of law. There is no coherent theory about the place of the rule of law in Caribbean constitutional law. Still, we can discern an underlying principle, that the rule of law eschews the exercise of arbitrary power and implies principles of rationality and fairness as a bulwark against arbitrariness.[26]

---

18. *Hinds* (n 3).
19. *Suratt v AG No 1* [2007] UKPC 55, (2007) 71 WIR 391 (PC T&T) [18] (Lord Bingham, dissenting).
20. M. Walters, 'Written Constitutions and Unwritten Constitutionalism' in G. Huscroft (ed), *Expounding the Constitution: Essays in Constitutional Theory* (CUP, Cambridge 2008) 245, 264.
21. P. Hogg and C. Zwibel, 'The Rule of Law in the Supreme Court of Canada' (2005) UTLJ 715, 718.
22. Walters (n 20) 269.
23. Ibid 264–65.
24. M. Walters, 'The Common Law Constitution in Canada: Return of Lex Non Scripta as Fundamental Law' (2001) 51 UTLJ 91, 140. See also *Bowen v AG* (13 February 2009) BZ 2009 SC 2 (Bze) [124].
25. *Joseph* (n 1) 20 (Wit J).
26. Ibid.

Often it is invoked in Caribbean public law cases as a general value that must influence how laws are made and administered, including judicial decision-making. Judges routinely remind us that no one is above the law. From the 'prime minister down to a junior clerk,' everyone is responsible for their actions before the law.[27] The law must be applied without favour. Conversely, the principle of equality means no one should be singled out for adverse treatment just because they are high-ranking public officers.[28] Forcefully, but still in a general way, Lord Hoffmann's renowned dissent turned to legal certainty as an aspect of the rule of law to castigate the majority in *Neville Lewis*.[29] His peers overruled many of the Privy Council's earlier decisions and Lord Hoffmann warned that: 'If the Board feels able to depart from a previous decision simply because its members on a given occasion have a "doctrinal disposition to come out differently", the rule of law itself will be damaged and there will be no stability in the administration of justice in the Caribbean.'[30]

Beyond these general references to the rule of law, the constitutions and specific provisions within them are understood to embody the principle of the rule of law. The concept thus influences the interpretation of those provisions. Judges have gone further in relation to certain aspects of the rule of law – legal certainty, procedural fairness and access to the courts. They give them considerable weight and have begun to treat them as overarching constitutional principles, even though they do not consistently name the rule of law as the fundamental value in operation.

A. The Constitutions Express a Commitment to the Rule of Law

Very directly, the preambles of most Caribbean constitutions state that freedom is premised on the rule of law.[31] Other provisions, especially those in the bills of rights, are understood to embody the principle as well. The hallowed constitutional right to due process is widely accepted to invoke 'the concept of the rule of law and universally accepted standards of justice observed by civilised nations which observe the rule of law.'[32] As Wit J puts it, '[t]he law cannot rule if it cannot protect' and the principles of fairness, reasonableness and rationality implied in the due process right are all designed to protect against arbitrariness

---

27. Ibid.
28. *Sharma v Antoine* [2006] UKPC 57, (2006) 69 WIR 379 (PC T&T) [14].
29. *Lewis v AG (2000)* 57 WIR 275 (PC Ja).
30. Ibid 309.
31. *Gairy v AG* [2001] UKPC 30, (1999) 59 WIR 174 [11] (Gren); *Lasalle v AG* (1972) 20 WIR 361 (CA T&T); *Mohammed v State* (1998) 53 WIR 444, 447 (PC T&T).
32. *Thomas v Baptiste* [1999] 3 WLR 249, (1998) 54 WIR 387 (PC T&T) (*Baptiste*).

and abuse of power.[33] 'Due process,' language used in the Trinidad and Tobago Constitution,[34] connotes procedural fairness and covers the same ground as the right to the 'protection of the law' found in other Caribbean constitutions.[35] The detailed right to the protection of the law in Caribbean constitutions contains standard elements of the rule of law, like the right to a fair hearing by an independent and impartial tribunal and the non-retrospective application of criminal laws.[36] The redress clauses in Caribbean bills of rights are associated with the rule of law's demand for access to justice and effective relief. [37] Citizens must have access to an independent and impartial judiciary to resolve all justiciable disputes. Recently, the Privy Council added that a wholesale contempt for the rule of law might warrant an additional award akin to exemplary damages to ensure effective relief.[38]

The bills of rights as a whole are viewed as aimed at securing the rule of law.[39] This understanding is very evident in the interpretation of the proviso within section 13 of the Trinidad and Tobago Constitution which deals with Special Acts. These are Acts of Parliament passed by certain special majorities, in accordance with section 13, that are valid even though they are inconsistent with the bill of rights. The proviso within section 13(1) permits a challenge to a Special Act if it is shown that the law is not reasonably justifiable in a society that has a proper respect for the rights and freedoms of the individual. In *Lassalle v AG*,[40] Phillips JA treated this proviso as 'intended to operate against the introduction of a system of administration of justice which is contrary to the precepts of the rule of law.'[41] It is said to establish due process, an element of the rule of law, as an 'irreducible minimum standard' for constitutionality.[42]

Judges root core constitutional norms like separation of powers and judicial independence in the rule of law. Separation of powers is described as a principle of good governance based on the rule of law which involves checks and balances designed to prevent abuse of governmental power

---

33. *Joseph* (n 1) 20 (Wit J).
34. Trinidad and Tobago Constitution 1976 s 4(a), Jamaica Constitution 1962 s 16.
35. *Lewis* (n 29).
36. Barbados Constitution ss 18(1),(4),(8).
37. The rule of law is assumed to be a key component of the Revised Treaty of Chaguaramas Establishing the Caribbean Community Including the CARICOM Single Market and Economy (2001), implying the availability of appropriate remedies where rights under the Treaty are infringed by member states. See *TCL v Caribbean Community* [2009] CCJ 4 (OJ), (2009) 74 WIR 319 [46]; *TCL v Guyana* [2009] CCJ 5 (OJ), (2009) 74 WIR 302 [27].
38. *Merson v Cartwright* [2005] UKPC 38, (2005) 67 WIR 17 (Bah).
39. *Lassalle v AG* (1971) 18 WIR 379 (CA T&T) 383 (Phillips JA).
40. Ibid.
41. Ibid 394.
42. *Northern Construction v AG* (31 July 2002) TT 2002 HC 104 (T&T).

and its concentration in one arm.[43] Judicial independence, the strongest element of the separation of powers, is also said to be implicit in the rule of law.[44] Judges cannot rule in accordance with the law and provide access to impartial justice if they are subject to undue pressure or influence from other branches.

More controversially, the rule of law's demand for the 'creation and maintenance of an actual order of positive laws to govern society'[45] is the latest explanation for the Caribbean's restrictive savings law clauses. It has been suggested that they may be explained by the need to ensure an orderly transfer of power to new independent democracies through the continuity of law.[46] This pragmatic explanation has given some impetus to a restrictive interpretation of these damning clauses.[47]

B. Legal Certainty and Limits on Fundamental Rights

The rule of law demands that laws be certain so that citizens can regulate their conduct. This is exemplified in the constitutional proscription of retrospective criminal laws.[48] It has been little noticed that legal certainty, a version of the European human rights principle of legality, has become an implied precondition for determining whether a statute that limits fundamental rights is constitutional. In *de Freitas v Permanent Secretary*,[49] the question was whether a statute that unreasonably infringed the right to freedom of expression could be saved by the application of the presumption of constitutionality used as a canon of construction; put differently, could words be implied into the statute to remedy the constitutional defect? Lord Clyde said that such a solution would only be acceptable if it met the standard of legal certainty, that is, if the modified provisions were formulated with sufficient precision to allow the citizen to know what was prohibited and to regulate his or her conduct. The standard applies to statutes that limit liberty in general and not only where the presumption of constitutionality has been applied to try and save an unconstitutional law.[50] The impact of non-compliance

---

43. See *DPP v Mollison* [2003] UKPC 6, (2003) 64 WIR 140 (Ja); *Ahnee v DPP* [1999] 2 AC 294 (PC Maur).
44. *Independent Jamaica Council for Human Rights (1998) Ltd v Marshall-Burnett* [2005] UKPC 3, (2005) 65 WIR 268 (Ja) 276 (Lord Bingham).
45. *Re Manitoba Language Rights* [1985] 1 SCR 721 (SC Can) 724.
46. *Watson v R* [2004] UKPC 34, [2004] 64 WIR 241 (Ja) [46].
47. Ibid.
48. For example, Barbados Constitution s 18(4).
49. *De Freitas v Permanent Secretary Ag & Fisheries* [1999] 1 AC 69, (1998) 53 WIR 131 (PC A&B); see also *Observer Publications Ltd v Matthew* [2001] UKPC 11, (2001) 58 WIR 188 (A&B).
50. *Sabapathee v State* [1999] 1 WLR 1836 (PC Maur), *Ahnee v Director of Public Prosecutions* [1999] 2 WLR 1305 (PC Maur).

is clear. Legislation that is 'hopelessly vague must be struck down as unconstitutional.'[51]

The requirement of certainty is not explicitly mentioned in the constitutions but it could be located in the fundamental rights and the permissible limits on them.[52] The standard approach in Caribbean bills of rights is to declare the right, and then say 'nothing contained in or done under the authority of *any law* shall be held to be inconsistent with or in contravention of this section to the extent that *the law* in question makes provision....'[53] We might say that a statutory provision that restricts fundamental rights will not be viewed as a 'law' that is justified if a citizen cannot reasonably predict what the law seeks to regulate or constrain. An alternate explanation for the rule of certainty does not rely on the text itself, but claims that legal certainty is a constitutional standard that arises from the implied justiciable norm of the rule of law.

The standard of legal certainty, as an aspect of the rule of law, should apply to other laws whose validity the constitutions protect, notwithstanding their infringement of fundamental rights and freedoms. The general savings law clauses immunize 'laws' in existence before the appointed date from judicial review on the ground that they infringe a fundamental right.[54] We should conclude either that a statute that fails to meet the requirements of legal certainty is not a 'law' for the purpose of these clauses and cannot enjoy their protection, or that legal certainty as an aspect of the rule of law is a fundamental constitutional standard that transcends the bill of rights, and thus also transcends savings law clauses. The immunity in respect of judicial review provided by the general savings law clauses is limited to bill of rights complaints. It does not provide protection against challenges on grounds of legal certainty. The same reasoning should apply to 'Special Acts' as provided for in section 13 of the Trinidad and Tobago Constitution. Special Acts are valid despite their inconsistency with the bill of rights. The constitutional provisions dealing with Special Acts provide no protection against a challenge on a non-bill of rights ground, and arguably legal certainty is such a ground.

C. Due Process, Access to Justice and Constitutional Ousters

The rule of law demands access to justice. You must be able to 'get to the court room door' and once in the door, you are entitled to procedural fairness and an effective remedy. These aspects of the rule of law have

---

51. *Sabapathee* ibid, 1840.
52. Ibid.
53. For example, Antigua and Barbuda Constitution 1981 s 12(2) (emphasis added).
54. For example, Bahamas Constitution s 30(i).

functioned as trumps that settle the tension between different provisions of the constitutions. For instance, the constitutions give parliament the power to determine its parliamentary privileges in ordinary legislation and those privileges are subject to the right of access to effective relief for breaches of fundamental rights.[55] In *Toussaint*,[56] the Privy Council said that the rule of law and separation of powers meant that judges should not be impeded in determining the scope of fundamental rights.

Courts have restricted the application of constitutional ouster clauses limiting judicial review in respect of the operation of service commissions and the exercise of the prerogative of mercy on the basis that giving full effect to them would undermine the right to due process and redress under the bill of rights. The Privy Council's more formalistic reasoning in *Thomas v AG*[57] – that the maxim of interpretation *generalia specialibus non derogant* when applied meant that the specific right to due process and redress could not be undermined by the general no-judicial review clause – is over time being replaced by a more normative claim that the limit on access to justice and procedural fairness contravenes core expectations of the rule of law and respect for fundamental rights.

In *Joseph*, de la Bastide P and Saunders J said that as a general principle courts would not be discouraged by constitutional ouster clauses from inquiring into whether a body performed its functions in contravention of the bill of rights, particularly the right to procedural fairness.[58] The litigants in *Joseph* did not need to prove that they fell within the detailed provision of the bill of rights, section 18, which deals with protection of the law because the 'court quite independently of [the redress clause in the bill of rights], has an implied or inherent power to give redress for such a violation.'[59]

4. An Expansive Protection of the Law

It took some work for the CCJ to locate in the Barbados Constitution 1966 an expansive right to protection of the law on which the legitimate expectation of exhausting the international human rights process could hang. Section 11(c) of the Barbados Independence Constitution 1966, the opening section to the bill of rights, provides that every person in Barbados is entitled to all the fundamental rights and freedoms

---

55. *Toussaint v AG* [2007] UKPC 48, (2007) 70 WIR 167 (St V&G).
56. Ibid.
57. (1981) 32 WIR 375 (PC T&T).
58. *Joseph* (n 1) 40.
59. Ibid.

including 'the protection of the law.'[60] The joint judgment described section 11 as being 'in the nature of a preamble.'[61] Familiarly, the judges turned to section 24, the redress clause in the bill of rights, to explain this conclusion. In its list of provisions that gave rise to redress, that section skipped the opening section and included only the sections that followed detailing the fundamental rights and freedoms.[62] The judges also considered section 18, one of the detailed provisions, noted in the margins of the text as dealing with 'the protection of the law.' It mostly protects fair trial rights, especially for criminal defendants. Section 18 was specific and narrow and, on the face of it, could not accommodate the expansive understanding of protection of the law and procedural fairness, with the legitimate expectations derived therefrom, invoked by de la Bastide P and Saunders J.

A. Distinguishing Rights: Exhaustive and Inexhaustive Rights

The judges plainly identified the dilemma. The question was whether the court's constitutional power to enforce the right to protection of the law was limited to contraventions of section 18. They held that it was not so constrained, reasoning that section 18 was different from the other detailed provisions. While the Barbados Constitution dealt comprehensively with the other rights in the detailed provisions and there was no scope for enforcement outside that, they said that section 18 was not exhaustive because it focused only on the impact of the right on criminal and civil proceedings and it was not possible to encapsulate that right in a single provision. Signalling their intention to elaborate a much broader constitutional right, they opined: 'The protection which this right [protection of the law] was afforded by the Barbados Constitution would be a very poor thing indeed if it were limited to cases in which there had been a contravention of the provisions of s 18.'[63]

De la Bastide P and Saunders J's distinction between exhaustive and inexhaustive rights is an appealing one but it faces a problem. It does not prove enough. There are a few detailed provisions in the conventional Caribbean bill of rights that cast rights in very broad and general terms, such as the right not to be held in slavery or servitude or not to be

---

60. I deliberately use the terminology 'opening section' and not 'preamble' because the latter begs the very question which is in issue, as to significance of this section, including its separate enforceability.
61. *Joseph* (n 1) 58.
62. See the Constitutions of Antigua and Barbuda 1981 s 18, Belize 1981 s 20, and St Kitts-Nevis 1983 s 18 in which the opening section is explicitly included in the provisions giving rise to redress under the redress clause.
63. *Joseph* (n 1) 60.

subjected to inhuman or degrading punishment.[64] But for the most part, the detail in the provisions that follow the opening section to the bill of rights is detail *limiting* the scope of the right. Arguably, almost all the detailed rights are 'inexhaustive' since this means the detailed right is not comprehensive or is constrained.

Why couldn't we extend the distinction to say that the freedom from discrimination in Barbados under the detailed provisions is inexhaustive because it does not include protection from sex discrimination?[65] Or alternatively, that the right to privacy in the detailed section is inexhaustive because it only covers protection from arbitrary searches and seizures.[66] Or even that property rights focused only on compulsory acquisition do not exhaust the larger concerns about deprivation and enjoyment of property.[67] That some of the rights detailed are not comprehensive or do not represent the fullest articulation of the right is a given. The crux is a normative one: should we assume that the narrow articulation represents the full extent of constitutional recognition and justiciability? Without much more, the CCJ's distinction between exhaustive and inexhaustive is purely descriptive and does not answer such questions.

B. Inherent Constitutional Jurisdiction: How the Trick Is Done

The conundrum remained, that the right to the protection of the law was very broadly and generously articulated in the opening section to the bill of rights, a section described by the judges themselves as a preamble, while the detailed section dealing with this right, which indisputably could give rise to constitutional redress, failed to include the compelling aspects of the right in issue before the court.

In 2005, in the Anguillan case *AG v Lake*,[68] Saunders CJ (Ag) as he then was, struggled with this well-worn and vexed issue of the status of the opening section to the bill of rights and had concluded that '[o]ne searches the Constitution in vain however for any provision that tells a person in Anguilla whether, or how, that person can enforce the rights declared in section 1 [the opening section to the bill of rights].'[69] The Court of Appeal was urged by counsel to give effect to the protection of enjoyment of property rights in section 1 of the Anguilla Constitution,

---

64. Barbados Constitution ss 14–15.
65. Ibid s 23(2).
66. Ibid s 17(1).
67. Ibid s 16(1).
68. *AG v Lake* (4 April 2005) AI 2005 CA 2 (Ang).
69. Ibid 41.

the opening section to the bill of rights.[70] The detailed right was much narrower, covering only the right not to have one's property compulsorily acquired without compensation.[71] Saunders CJ (Ag) insisted that there was no flexibility in the Anguilla Constitution and said that the conclusion that the opening section did not give rise to enforceable rights was 'inescapable' because the redress clause clearly excluded the opening section.'[72] He continued,

> The rights declared in section 1 are incapable of being enforced save in so far as they are contained in some section lying between sections 2 and 15 (inclusive) and then, only to the extent that the relevant section permits. In effect, what can be enforced is not section 1 but rather the particular section that contains the right in question. Section 1 is a mere statement of the broad principles upon which the fundamental rights and freedoms adumbrated in sections 2 to 15 are crafted. Any purported breach of section 1 is not justiciable.[73]

Eighteen months later in *Joseph*, Saunders J, now in the CCJ found a way to enforce the right to the protection of the law broadly declared in the opening section of the Barbados Constitution, adding a new plank to the debates about the opening section. The answer did not lie in a specific provision in the Constitution. Instead, 'the trick [was] done'[74] by pointing to inherent constitutional relief. In a provocative and frustratingly cryptic response, de la Bastide P and Saunders J concluded that 'pursuant to s 11, a condemned man has a constitutional right to procedural fairness as part of his right to protection of the law. Correspondingly, the courts have an inherent jurisdiction, and duty, to grant an appropriate remedy for any breach of that right.'[75] The CCJ judges seemed to be suggesting that protection of the law was intrinsic to, or an essential constituent of, the Constitution. It did not matter if the Constitution explicitly provided a remedy, it already inhered in the Constitution. In effect, the judges looked beyond the text of the constitutions to unwritten constitutional values. The joint decision also accepted the earlier Privy Council rulings in *Thomas v Baptiste*[76] and *Lewis*[77] that protection of the law was the

---

70. Anguilla Constitution 1982 s 1.
71. Ibid s 7.
72. *Lake* (n 68) 41.
73. Ibid.
74. In *Lewis* (n 29) 307, Lord Hoffmann, dissenting, famously stated that the majority have found in the ancient concept of due process of law a philosopher's stone, undetected by generations of judges, which can convert the base metal of executive action into the gold of legislative power. It does not, however, explain how the trick is done.
75. *Joseph* (n 1) 64.
76. *Baptiste* (n 32).
77. *Lewis* (n 29).

same as *due process of the law* which connoted procedural fairness, and that due process invoked the concept of the *rule of law*. Protection of the law is therefore substantially or an important element of respect for the rule of law.

Following their statement about 'inherent jurisdiction,' the big question is the nature of the relationship between the right to the protection of the law and section 11. One way of reading the joint decision is that it implies that protection of the law is what Mark Walters calls a 'text-emergent unwritten constitutional norm,' that is, a norm that emerges from the constitution itself.[78] The expansive right to the protection of the law, and we can now add *the rule of law*, on this interpretation is not dependent on section 11 or 18 or even the bill of rights more generally. Sections 11 and 18 declare the right but they do not create it or, to use the judges' language, exhaust it. Crucially, there is now an explanation for why the sections do not exhaust the right: protection of the law, or the rule of law, is a foundational constitutional value, an implied and enforceable constitutional norm that pervades the entire constitution and which also has a textual basis. Wit J addressed this more straightforwardly. Protection of the law or the rule of law, he said, demanded the availability of effective remedies. This guarantee inhered in the constitutions, and the redress clause reflected this aspect of the rule of law but was not its sum total.

In the end, the CCJ judges resisted the conventional approach that assumes the text of our constitutions, and the concept of supremacy, can answer all important questions that arise. Regrettably, the joint decision made no attempt to associate their nascent method with or distinguish it from the earlier cases relying on the rule of law or the landmark *Hinds* decision which treated certain constitutional norms like separation of powers as implied from the texts and structure of Caribbean constitutions, and justiciable. *Hinds*, its weightiness and the hesitations about its scope and meaning would have provided a template and invaluable guidance for clarifying the basis of and charting the extent and boundaries of implied justiciable constitutional norms.

5. Implied Justiciable Constitutional Principles

More than anything, the distinctive approach in *Joseph* – the *inherent constitutional jurisdiction* – strongly echoes the foundational implication of the doctrine of the separation of powers in Caribbean constitutions by

---

78. Walters (n 24) 98.

Lord Diplock in *Hinds v R*[79] 30 years before in 1976. Although *Hinds* is usually identified as the first time Caribbean courts plainly articulated an implied justiciable constitutional norm, the power of judicial review of legislation outside bill of rights matters is an even earlier and as monumental implication in the older Caribbean constitutions.

A. The Unwritten-Written Jurisdiction: The Implication of Judicial Review

The power of judicial review of legislation and administrative action that violate the provisions of the constitutions is the Caribbean's first (postcolonial) unwritten constitutional fundamental. It is now so taken for granted that we forget that in the older constitutions it is still an implied jurisdiction in non-bill of rights matters. The older independent Caribbean countries – Jamaica, Trinidad and Tobago, Guyana, Barbados and The Bahamas – explicitly provided for judicial review in respect of breaches of fundamental rights in their constitutions. They said nothing about access to the superior courts to challenge compliance with non-bill of rights provisions in the constitutions.

The legacy of United States Supreme Court decision in *Marbury v Madison*[80] made the implication of the power of judicial review in twentieth century written constitutions a given. Still, we should not overlook the labour of early Caribbean jurists in elucidating judicial review as an *unwritten* constitutional fundamental and an 'inherent constitutional jurisdiction.'[81] This expansive judicial review in respect of non-bill of rights matters was *implied* primarily from the supreme law clause, the writtenness of the constitutions, the textual restrictions on the authority of Parliament and the doctrines of separation of powers and the rule of law. Although implied, many today treat this power of judicial review as one *virtually written into* the texts of all Caribbean constitutions, blurring the distinction between written and unwritten norms.

B. 'Westminster Model': A Gap-Filling Concept

In *Hinds v R*, Lord Diplock used the label 'Westminster model constitutions' borrowed from SA de Smith as a device for implying constitutional principles.[82] Westminster modelled constitutions had

---

79. *Hinds* (n 3).
80. 5 US (1 Cranch) 137 (1803) (SC US).
81. See Carnegie (n 5), *Collymore v AG* (1967) 12 WIR 5 (CA T&T) 9 (Wooding CJ).
82. S.A. de Smith, 'Westminster's Export Models: the Legal Framework of Responsible Government' (1961–63) 1 J Commonwealth Political Studies 2.

a certain structure, dealing in separate chapters with each organ of government and providing for the independence of superior court judges, he said. As important, these constitutions were said to be 'negotiated as well as drafted by persons nurtured in the tradition of that branch of the common law of England that is concerned with public law and familiar in particular with the basic concept of separation of legislative, executive and judicial power as it had been developed in the unwritten constitution of the United Kingdom.'[83] The new constitutions drafted 'were evolutionary not revolutionary [providing]...for continuity of government through successor institutions....'[84]

Thus 'Westminster modelled' signified that the constitutions could be 'filled-in' from sources exterior to the written text consistent with two related but distinct notions of continuity. First, a temporal continuity; that the constitutions provided for continuity with colonial institutions and through existing laws. If a Westminster modelled constitution established a Supreme Court but said nothing about the powers and jurisdiction of the court, for instance, one could look back, as Lord Diplock did in *Hinds*, at what the colonial Supreme Court did to determine that the new court had similar original jurisdiction in serious crimes and substantial civil matters and supervisory jurisdiction over inferior tribunals. The second notion of continuity was an imperial one; it meant the continuity of British constitutional practices. Gaps in the constitutions could be filled by referring to colonial law and imperial habits.

Professor Ralph Carnegie famously said, 'When we [in the Caribbean] speak of our Westminster model Constitutions, we are not being lawyers or even political scientists. We are at best being poets.'[85] Amongst other things, he was pointing out that the notion that Westminster incorporated a strong separation of powers, imitated by Caribbean constitutions, could not be grounded in law or political science. 'Westminster modelled' was in good part a romantic idea that expressed a desire and feeling of common law kinship between the UK and the Caribbean. *Chandresh Sharma*,[86] decided in 2007, illustrates the whimsical constitutional theorizing that easily can be aligned to the ideology of 'Westminster modelled.' In that case, the Privy Council concluded that there was an implied constitutional right belonging to parliamentarians to be paid.

---

83. *Hinds* (n 3) 331.
84. Ibid.
85. A.R. Carnegie, 'Floreat the Westminster Model? A Commonwealth Caribbean Perspective' (1996) 6 Carib LR 1, 12.
86. [2007] UKPC 41, (2007) 70 WIR 287 (T&T).

It was based on the colonial practice and convention at Westminster of paying parliamentarians *and* the 'inferred intention of the framers' of the Constitution to have the parliamentary system operate in a way that is fair and even-handed as between competing partisan interests. The Privy Council was filling a gap in the text produced by an 'extraordinary and obviously unintended contingency' that elected parliamentarians were denied their salaries because there was no Speaker to administer the oath due to the even split of seats between the two major parties.[87]

In this and a few other cases, the Privy Council appears to be trying to hold the balance between Trinidad and Tobago's then ruling party and its main rival in that country's divisive and racially charged political context in the period after the dramatic 2001 elections.[88] They have made the operation of the parliamentary system in an even-handed way a fundamental *justiciable* unwritten constitutional norm in Trinidad and Tobago. This demands far more careful and explicit justification. Unlike separation of powers and judicial independence, this inference had no meaningful textual grounding. Laying this goal at the feet of the 'framers' and what they would have intended is not credible, nor is resorting to past political practices because that tells us little about whether courts should be arbiters when disputes arise. The conception of Caribbean constitutions as 'Westminster modelled' elides the questionable legitimacy of these moves by promoting the idea that the framers can be properly associated with the project of constitutional continuity and maintaining traditions. In the Caribbean, public law must be an unending project of figuring out what democracy means. We do need precepts that guide the courts in navigating our fiercely partisan political environment which increasingly is not the performance of democracy but its abasement. However, the inferred intention of the framers as a justification for those rules will not do.

C. Defining the Implied Rule: The Separation of Powers

Hinds ruled that separation of powers was fundamental to the constitution, part of the supreme law and justiciable. It had a direct force of its own, and could function as if it were an explicit provision of the Jamaica Constitution. This weighty assumption about the place of separation of powers in the constitutional order begged the question, what

---

87. Ibid 9.
88. See, e.g., *Bobb v Manning* [2006] UKPC 22; *CBS v AG* [2006] UKPC 35, (2006) 68 WIR 459; *Suratt No 1* (n 18); *Suratt v AG No 2* [2008] UKPC 38, (2008) 73 WIR 437; *Sanatan Dharma Maha Sabha v AG* [2009] UKPC 19; *Manning v Sharma* [2009] UKPC 36.

does 'separation of powers' mean? Lord Diplock's sweeping suggestion that Caribbean constitutions provided for the *exclusive* control by each organ of government of its functions is an overstatement. As Professor Fiadjoe noted, there are no 'watertight' compartments in government.[89] While it was accepted that *Hinds* ignored the overlap of functions and personnel between the legislature and executive, there was broad agreement on the principles it articulated about judicial power: that separation of powers meant that judicial power could not be vested in non-judicial bodies and that the jurisdiction of superior courts is specially protected.[90] In *DPP v Mollison*,[91] Lord Bingham observed that: 'Whatever overlap there may be under Constitutions on the Westminster model between the exercise of executive and legislative powers, the separation between the exercise of judicial powers on the one hand and legislative and executive powers on the other is total, or effectively so.'[92]

The majority decision of the Privy Council in *Suratt*, a 2007 appeal from Trinidad and Tobago, does violence even to this 'sacred cow.'[93] An Equal Opportunities Tribunal, headed by a Chair who did not enjoy the constitutional protections for his or her independence afforded to a superior court judge, was given jurisdiction to decide on discrimination cases that overlapped with and potentially excluded the High Court's jurisdiction to hear anti-discrimination cases under the redress clause of the bill of rights in the Constitution. Baroness Hale, giving the majority decision, acknowledged that it interfered with High Court jurisdiction, just not *seriously* so. Consequently, there was no constitutional breach of the separation of powers doctrine as articulated in *Hinds*. The majority's approach, which has not been well-received in the Caribbean, would have been more persuasive if it made a candid assessment that *Hinds* went too far in suggesting the protection of the jurisdiction of the superior courts was absolute. It should have attempted to lay the foundation for a more realistic and grounded understanding of separation of powers, and in doing so, it would have been obliged to properly explain why its understanding should be preferred to that of the four local judges, one High Court and three Court of Appeal judges, about what the doctrine meant in Trinidad and Tobago.

Courts have found themselves being asked to invalidate executive and legislative action on the basis of a very strict and naïve idea of separation

---

89. A. Fiadjoe, *Commonwealth Caribbean Public Law* (3rd edn, Routledge-Cavendish, London 2008) 172.,
90. *Hinds* (n 3).
91. [2003] UKPC 6, (2003) 64 WIR 140 (Ja).
92. Ibid 13.
93. *Suratt No 1* (n 19).

of powers attributed to *Hinds*. Judges have been unsure about how to tackle this aspect of *Hinds'* excess, especially when the quixotic version of separation of powers appears to conflict with the express provisions of the constitutions. In the death penalty cases *Boyce* and *Matthew* in 2004, lawyers claimed that the mandatory death penalty combined with the executive power granted by the constitutions to exercise the prerogative of mercy violated the separation of powers doctrine by allowing the executive to make the final determination of sentence.[94] The Privy Council in these cases said that to the extent that separation of powers is a constitutional principle, it is not an overriding one but just 'a pithy description of how the constitution works.' They noted that the constitutions can themselves provide for an overlap of functions, as with the prerogative of mercy, and constitutional supremacy dictates that effect be given to that.

The Privy Council was correct to discourage the formulation of a strict, abstract *and justiciable* notion of separation of powers. The provisions of the actual constitution must guide how the doctrine is formulated. We must look how the doctrine is 'operationally defined' by the constitutions.[95] Still, the texts will not always be sufficient to resolve all questions about how governmental power is distributed. As Professor Lawrence Tribe explains, sometimes 'it will be necessary to extrapolate what amounts to a blueprint of organizational relationships from the fundamental structural postulates one sees as informing the Constitution as a whole....'[96] But once the proper parameters of the doctrine are determined in a given case, the doctrine cannot be described as merely 'a pithy description of how the Constitution works.'[97] Contravention of the principle leads to constitutional invalidity.

D. Extending the Implied Principles: Tribunal Independence

In *Suratt*, the concept of implied constitutional norms as expressed in *Hinds* was both contained and extended. In her majority decision in *Suratt*, Baroness Hale concluded that even if it was determined that the new equal opportunities tribunal did not interfere substantially with the jurisdiction of the High Court (i.e., breach the Chapter in the Constitution dealing with the Judicature), there was a 'question as to

---

94. *Boyce v R* [2004] UKPC 32, (2004) 64 WIR 37 (Bdos); *Matthew v State* [2004] UKPC 33, (2004) 64 WIR 412 (T&T).
95. L. Tribe, *American Constitutional Law* Vol I (3rd edn, Foundation Press, New York 2000) 127.
96. Ibid 130.
97. *Boyce* (n 94) 70.

whether the protection given to the tribunal is adequate.'[98] She then went on to evaluate the adequacy of the independence of the tribunal and concluded that the independence provided for was sufficient. Baroness Hale's approach here represents a potentially dramatic development in Caribbean constitutional law. Although she barely acknowledged this herself, she in effect found that there was a constitutional requirement that the protection enjoyed by a tribunal or court must be sufficient to afford it the necessary degree of independence of the legislature and executive. Hitherto, the contours of judicial independence had been parsed out in relation to courts and judicial officers specifically mentioned in the constitutions, namely superior court judges and, to some degree, magistrates. The Privy Council left us with little more than suggestive language in *Suratt*. It made no attempt to explain the basis of this norm.

On one view, this implied principle of tribunal independence could be anchored to constitutional provision dealing with the protection of the law which guarantees the right to a fair hearing in accordance with the principles of fundamental justice for the determination of one's rights and obligations under the Trinidad and Tobago Constitution.[99] Other constitutions speak more directly about the right to a determination of one's rights and obligations by an independent tribunal.[100] Conversely, it may be viewed as an unwritten norm linked to the protection of other implied principles like separation of powers. The crux is that the value of tribunal independence which gives rise to a holding that executive or legislative action is unconstitutional cannot be an abstract strict or fixed standard. The standard will differ for inferior and superior courts and it will evolve and should be assessed having regard to the provisions of the constitutions and our legal and constitutional history.[101]

Like the other implied constitutional norms discussed here – judicial review and separation of powers – judicial independence represents a grand general concept that is 'uncontroversial when stated in abstract form.'[102] These principles are all strongly interrelated and seen as aspects

---

98. *Suratt No 1* (n 19) 41.
99. Trinidad and Tobago Constitution 1976 s 5(1)(e).
100. Barbados Constitution 1966 s 18(8).
101. *S v Van Rooyen* [2002] ZACC 8, 2002 (5) SA 246 (CC RSA) [75]. An implied constitutional principle of judicial or tribunal independence would open up the possibility of challenging ordinary legislation dealing with magistrates and magistrates' court as well as the terms of magistrates' contracts that deal with issues relating to independence other than appointment, discipline and removal, which are now addressed by the constitutions. See *Fraser v JSLC* [2008] UKPC 25, (2008) 73 WIR 175 (PC St Luc).
102. M. Walters, 'Incorporating Common Law into the Constitution of Canada: *Egale v Canada* and the Status of Marriage' (2003) 41 Osgoode Hall LJ 75, 112.

of the basic structure of the constitutions.[103] At the same time, we are left with thorny questions about their precise definition as justiciable constitutional rules.

6. Normative Core of the Constitutions

Unwritten constitutional principles will have the greatest legitimacy when they are suggested by and reflected in the constitutional texts themselves as core values and standards that 'animate' and 'breathe life' into the texts.[104] There is now an embryonic practice of identifying such values in Caribbean constitutions that has been championed by very prominent judges. If the concept of implied justiciable constitutional norms owes its roots to *Hinds*, then the notion of core constitutional values and the need for resistance to over-legalistic and literal approaches to interpretation take their cue from Lord Wilberforce's famous judgment in *Minister of Home Affairs v Fisher*.[105] In *Joseph*, Wit J presented our constitutions as 'qualitative and normative document[s]' and not just formal technical instruments.[106] As such, their interpretation must avoid 'the austerity of tabulated legalism'[107] in order to give effect to the values and standards expressed in the text.[108]

Judges now take it for granted that separation of powers is a fundamental core constitutional value. The dignity of the human person, protection of fundamental rights and freedoms and respect for the rule of law have also found some acceptance as the normative core or conscience of the Caribbean constitutions.[109] Conteh CJ of Belize in *Bowen v AG*[110] is the most unrestrained in naming the core. Attracted to the Indian concept of a 'basic structure' to our constitutions, he includes separation of powers, the rule of law, judicial independence, democracy, protection of fundamental rights within the core values. Until recently, judges stopped short of claiming these core values were separately enforceable. Instead, they gave them considerable force in guiding the interpretation of the texts. But Wit J in *Joseph* and Conteh CJ in *Bowen* go further; for them the normative core or basic structure establishes what is *inherent* and virtually unassailable in Caribbean constitutions.

---

103. Ibid.
104. *Bowen* (n 24) 54 (Conteh CJ).
105. *Minister of Home Affairs v Fisher* [1980] AC 319 (PC Ber).
106. *Joseph* (n 1) 18 (Wit J).
107. S.A. de Smith, *The New Commonwealth and its Constitutions* (Stevens, London 1964) 194; *Fisher* (n 105) 328.
108. *Matthew* (n 94) 34 (Lords Bingham, Nicholls, Steyn and Walker dissenting).
109. Ibid.
110. *Bowen* (n 24).

A. Preambles

All Caribbean independence constitutions, except Jamaica, have preambles. They begin, 'we the people of ...,' establishing the authorship of the constitutions. They express the moral and political aspirations of the political community. This includes affirmation of the principle of the rule of law, human dignity and the pre-eminence of individual freedom and human rights. Many also express a strong desire for social and economic equality and some mention regard for civil, political, social, economic and cultural rights.[111] Caribbean judges have turned to the language of the preambles – 'Men and institutions only remain free when freedom is founded on the rule of law' – to confirm the rule of law as a constitutional value. Judges must uphold it[112] and have regard to it in interpreting constitutional provisions, like the redress clause in the bill of rights that expresses the rule of law's commitment to access to justice.[113]

The place of the preamble in constitutional interpretation is receiving growing attention by modern courts. Although not separately enforceable, increasingly courts are stressing that that they are not 'pure embellishment'[114] or 'meaningless verbiage or empty rhetoric.'[115] In *Bowen v AG*, Conteh CJ said that there was 'an indissoluble link, an umbilical cord, if you will, between the Preamble of the Constitutions and its dispositive provisions'; the preamble, he argued, 'animates' the constitutions.[116] In *Matthew v State,*[117] the dissenting opinion, which is destined to gain more prominence and force, noted that while the preamble could not override the clear words of the constitutions, courts could have regard to the preambles in interpreting the texts. It added that interpretations that conflicted with the preambles would be suspect.[118]

De la Bastide CJ, as he then was, argued that the Trinidad and Tobago republican constitution was 'resilient and amorphous,' capable of change in response to the needs of the people.[119] He acknowledged that it would be difficult to figure out the appropriate direction in which to chart progress through constitutional interpretation, but said that

---

111. Grenada Constitution 1973, preamble.
112. *Lasalle* (n 39).
113. *Gairy* (n 31).
114. *Boodram v AG* (1995) 47 WIR 459 (AC T&T) 467 (Sharma JA).
115. *Matthew* (n 108) 46.
116. *Bowen* (n 24) 54.
117. *Matthew* (n 108).
118. Ibid 46.
119. *Boodram* (n 114).

if 'we bear in mind the right principles and we focus on the preamble our task can be made a little lighter.'[120] Conteh CJ recently went a bit further, saying that the new preamble to the Belize Constitution was more than an aid to interpretation because 'it fills the text with meaning and gives the Constitution itself a shape and form reflecting the very essence, values and logic of the Belizean people.'[121] The preambles of the republican constitution of Trinidad and Tobago and the reformed Belize constitution are post-independence preambles crafted and approved in Caribbean lawmaking spheres. In a turn around, the Chief Justices in both territories relied on them to counter the traditional critique of Caribbean constitutions – that they are not really our own – treating the preambles as the best evidence of the values, desires and hopes of 'we the people.'

B. Opening Sections to Bills of Rights

The bills of rights, and particularly their opening section, are the other normative nerve centre of Caribbean constitutions. As already mentioned, there has been a fierce debate about whether these opening sections give rise to enforceable rights. The descriptions of most of the opening sections as mere preambles and purely declaratory is at best misleading because the section has been at the heart of rights adjudication under the constitutions for over four decades. The opening section has been one of the most judicially cited provisions in the bill of rights precisely because of its clear enunciation of core values and standards around human rights, human dignity and liberty.[122] Courts refer to it as a relevant provision in examining the scope of fundamental rights and freedoms under the bill of rights.[123] In exploring a detailed right, it has been said that 'it is important to reiterate the basis on which [the bill of rights] was drafted' and that the opening section is material to that inquiry.[124]

In *Fisher*,[125] the *locus classicus* on interpretation of Caribbean constitutions' bills of rights, Lord Wilberforce said that the generality of

---

120. *Peters v AG* (2001) 62 WIR 244 (CA T&T).

121. *Bowen* (n 24) 57.

122. Recent examples include *Bowe v R* [2006] UKPC 10, (2006) 68 WIR 10 (Bah); *Grant v R* [2006] UKPC 2, (2006) 68 WIR 354 (Ja); *Ingraham v McEwan* (2002) 65 WIR 1 (CA Bah); *Worme v COP* [2004] UKPC 8, (2004) 63 WIR 79 (Gren); *R v Hughes* [2002] UKPC 12, (2001) 60 WIR 156 (St Luc); *Benjamin v Minister of Information and Broadcasting* [2001] UKPC 8, (2001) 58 WIR 171(Ang); *Observer Publications* (n 48); *Cable and Wireless (Dominica) Ltd v Marpin* (2000) 57 WIR 141 (PC Dom).

123. *Fisher* (n 105), *Hector v AG* (1990) 37 WIR 216 (PC A&B).

124. *Heron v DPP* (2000) 61 WIR 319, 337 (CA Ja).

125. *Fisher* (n 105).

this section, 'Whereas *every person* in Bermuda is entitled to fundamental rights and freedoms...' underlies the whole of the chapter and helped him to conclude that a broad interpretation of 'child' should be adopted. More recently, Lord Craig accepted in *Watson v R*,[126] that the rights and freedoms declared in the opening section of the Jamaica Constitution must be generously interpreted to give full effect to the protection of fundamental rights and freedoms.[127]

Calling a constitutional provision a preamble used to be a tidy way of dismissing it, but prominent Caribbean judges have shown very persuasively that there is an 'umbilical cord' between such provisions and the rest of the constitutions. Even if what we think of as preambles are not the source or originator of rights or norms, they might underscore them and often are the strongest expression of fundamental norms that inhere in the constitutions. They are indispensable, not peripheral to the interpretation of Caribbean constitutions.

7. The Rule of Law as a Fundamental Justiciable Constitutional Norm

The direction *Joseph* obliquely points us in – acknowledging that the rule of law or certain aspects of it are independent implied justiciable constitutional norms – can be cautiously defended with reference to both principle and precedent. We are more at ease in saying our constitutions have a normative core that guides interpretation. We have accepted that separation of powers, a core element of the rule of law, is a fundamental unwritten justiciable constitutional principle. We seem to now view judicial independence, another aspect of the rule of law, as a norm that is enforceable beyond the explicit provisions of the constitutions. In addition, we have given some shape to aspects of the rule of law – legal certainty, procedural fairness and access to the courts – as pre-eminent constitutional values that find expression in particular constitutional provisions but whose applicability is not confined to those sections. Procedural fairness and access to the courts as aspects of the rule of law have trumped explicit constitutional provisions limiting judicial review.

All of these strands of Caribbean constitutional law have a measure of inscrutability. The new interest in the rule of law provides an opportunity to shed light on them and settle some old disputes in an honest way – including what the seminal Privy Council decision *Hinds v R* stands for today. *Hinds* is a pioneering case with a panoramic read of Westminster-

---

126. *Watson* (n 46).
127. Ibid 42.

styled constitutions and has become a foundational authority in Caribbean and Commonwealth constitutional law. That very quality – its expansive assertions about these decolonization constitutions – also has made it susceptible to a growing list of judicial and academic provisos. However, so much in Commonwealth constitutional law has come to depend on the 'very important and salutary principle' of separation of powers derived from *Hinds* as an expression of the rule of law and an essential component of democracy, that the Judicial Committee is very reluctant to overtly disrupt it.[128] Awkwardly, it has undercut some of the key assumptions we have made about what the case means, without providing any clarity about the basis of implied norms, how they function, their relationship with the constitutional provisions and their precise meaning. The CCJ must do more than talk about inherent constitutional principles, it needs to make sense of a generation of disjointed jurisprudence around *Hinds* and establish a principled basis for thinking about implied constitutional norms. Appreciating that the boundary between written and unwritten is less distinct than we might think is a critical starting point.

Beyond this, I am attracted to the idea of thinking of the rule of law as an implied justiciable constitutional norm, part of the substructure of Caribbean constitutions, because it offers a way of making the constitutions more *our own*, 'resilient and amorphous.' This has a counterintuitive ring to it since the usual critique of the unwritten constitution lies in democracy, that it cedes power to the judiciary to reshape our constitutions, doing violence to the supremacy of the texts as drafted and the constitutions' democratic requirements for amendments.[129] Put another way, it allows judges to usurp the lawmaking powers of the legislature and engage in judicial activism, promoting their own views, rather than national values.

This is an important criticism but it is far removed from the present predicament of Caribbean constitutional law and politics. The argument from democracy, that it should be left to our legislatures to generate any changes as to how we think about our constitutions, must pay attention to the fiercely partisan political scene in the Caribbean. The conventional mechanism of higher lawmaking through constitutional amendments is incapacitated by oppositions that have sufficient parliamentary force to veto important constitutional reforms entirely on partisan political grounds. Alternatively, the amendment process is exploited for 'normal

---

128. *Mollison* (n 43) 13.
129. J. Leclair, 'Canada's Unfathomable Unwritten Constitutional Principles' (2002) 27 Queens LJ 389, 441.

politics' by governments who have the overwhelming majorities in parliament required for constitutional reform. With this stalemate, Caribbean people likely will turn increasingly to the courts to articulate and uphold the society's fundamental constitutional values and to temper the vagaries of the political scene.[130]

Rather than avoid unwritten norms like the rule of law, judicial legitimacy demands that our judges face directly the scope and place of unwritten constitutional norms. Judges must do justice and not engage simply in 'tabulated legalism.' Not surprisingly, a small group of leading Caribbean judges – de la Bastide P, Wit J and Conteh CJ – appreciate that constitutional legitimacy and development depend in part on articulating the core values of our fundamental law. Unwritten constitutional norms offer the potential for a principled response to the tensions and contradictions within our constitutions by looking at their ethos. To return to my earlier argument, our constitutions are incomplete and in some key areas unclear and contradictory. We cannot over-privilege the texts of independence Caribbean constitutions as an expression of the will of the Caribbean peoples. We should search for some articulated political theory that gives coherence to the constitution as a whole and, having regard to those principles, attempts to resolve constitutional provisions that on the surface appear to conflict with each other, particularly those in the bills of rights.[131]

True, concepts like the rule of law are contested and hard to define. There is interminable disagreement about its meaning. The rule of law in particular is sometimes taken to mean any and everything about good governance and a just society. Our constitutional law will face some uncertainty if it gives serious weight to unwritten norms.[132] But the interpretation of written provisions in our constitutions that are 'drafted in a broad and ample style which lay down principles of width and generality'[133] – the meanings of which we know evolve over time – present equal uncertainties. From this perspective, the chasm between the interpretation of written constitutional provisions and unwritten norms is not as great as it seems. Much of our constitutional law is already comprised of judicial precedents.

The post *Hinds* lesson is that if we recognize an implied justiciable constitutional norm like separation of powers, we must also accept that the meaning of the norm is not self-evident or fixed; rather it will

---

130. D. Dyzenhaus, 'The Unwritten Constitution and the Rule of Law' (2004) 23 SCLR (2d) 383, 412.
131. McIntosh (n 14) 253–55.
132. Leclair (n 129) 400–27.
133. *Fisher* (n 105) 112.

unfold through the process of interpretation over time. There will be disagreements about what it means, and understandings of it will evolve. But it is suggested we start by using the texts of the constitutions as a guide, having regard to our distinctive political history and our contemporary context. We should be slow to promote implied constitutional norms that have no textual grounding and the provisions of the constitutions should remain important to constitutional interpretation even when we accept that they rest on or are evidence of implied norms. Judges will have the exacting task of deciding whether the provisions reflect an implied principle but do not exhaust it.

There is a risk that the 'common law' might derail the progressive development of implied constitutional norms. Caribbean common law constitutionalism relied heavily on existing laws and the common law as the source of constitutional fundamentals. Post independence common law constitutionalism gained a bad reputation for elevating ordinary existing or colonial laws to higher order norms, giving them normative force as the repository of constitutional and human rights principles. There have been repeated calls for models of interpretation less burdened by coloniality. Implied norms cannot ethically be made to rest on fantasies of empire or the 'inferred framers intentions.'

Fraser JA's judgment in *Lassalle v AG*[134] opens the door to a less tortured role for the common law. He acknowledged that the common law was relevant in ascertaining the meaning of due process under the Constitution but he did not think that reference to the common law necessarily stagnated the development of the principle of due process.[135] He viewed the common law as a 'pragmatic system of rules and principles fashioned by the courts to meet the needs of society as those needs changed from time to time.'[136] As a result, he saw due process as a multi-dimensional concept that could be adapted and interpreted as justice demanded to meet the changing needs and situation in a country.[137] His description of procedural due process rights in the constitution as not being 'a comprehensive or exhaustive code'[138] resonates with the joint judgment in *Joseph*. This thinking is also consistent with the understanding that the constitutions as living instruments whose protections change over time and in light of new circumstances.[139]

In establishing how that pragmatic system of rules and principles evolves to meet the needs of the society we should look to the courts, *but not*

---

134. *Lassalle* (n 39).
135. Ibid 404.
136. Ibid.
137. Ibid 406.
138. Ibid 407.
139. *Boyce* (n 94) 28.

exclusively so. The legislature, executive and popular constitutionalism can generate shifts in fundamental values. For example, although Barbados has no plain provisions in its Constitution dealing with the right to health, education and social welfare, the provision of those social goods is an undeniably fundamental value in Barbados and central to that nation's identity. Or consider the failure of Barbados and The Bahamas to explicitly name sex as a prohibited ground of discrimination in their anti-discrimination clauses. It would be hard in the face of legislative advances and policy initiatives to protect the human rights of women and girls, and our international commitments to do the same, to say that protection against sex discrimination has not emerged as a fundamental principle of good governance and a just society and arguably an element of the protection of the law. We could reshape and recalibrate what we mean by respect for the common law to recognize these shifts in how we think and live while not holding Caribbean constitutional law hostage to common law supremacy or imperial romanticism.

The question of whether we should imply substantive rights from the rule of law is a contentious one.[140] Peter Hogg and Cara Zwibel reject a doctrine of rule of law that is all encompassing. They candidly say that 'the notion that the rule of law requires our laws to respect equality, human dignity and other good moral values is really just natural law in disguise.'[141] *Lassalle* left the question of substantive due process rights to an appropriate case in the future.[142] But it also conceded that the bill of rights as a whole – a source of substantive rights – was designed to give effect to the rule of law. *Joseph* clearly shows that gaps exist in the detailed enumeration of fundamental rights and freedoms in Caribbean constitutions that are hard to defend in our changing world. Rather than conclude that only the right in its narrower form was intended to be protected, the CCJ came to the opposite conclusion: that the narrow articulation in the detailed provisions could not prejudice the inherent constitutional jurisdiction to secure the protection of the law. Nothing forecloses this concept and other implied constitutional norms from becoming an avenue for elaborating an evolving constitutional protection of substantive rights in a principled way over time.

---

140. See J. Raz, 'The Rule of Law and its Virtue' (1977) 93 LQR 195.
141. Hogg and Zwibel (n 21) 718.
142. *Lasalle* (n 39) 405.

8. Conclusion

Mark Walters asserts that the 'challenge for judges is identifying for the legal system a theory of fundamental law that somehow fits within the matrix of doctrinal, institutional, and traditional assumptions that together define the character of the legal system.'[143] Our courts have declared that judicial review on constitutional grounds, a semblance of separation of powers and judicial independence rest at the core of our constitutions, and that these concepts can be located within our constitutional texts but do not depend on textual expression. Even though judges have not always established these tenets of Caribbean constitutional law with the desired conceptual precision, implied constitutional norms are now, without question, an indispensable part of our constitutions.

Not surprisingly, the rule of law is emerging as part of our inherent constitution. It is the foundation of separation of powers, judicial independence and judicial review. Given its overarching concern with constraining the arbitrary exercise of state power, it can provide some guidance on the proper limits of the other implied norms. The rule of law, for example, demands an appropriate distribution of state power to ensure accountability and limit abuse of state power. A very strict separation of powers is not necessary to meet those goals, and indeed might undermine them if it generates independence without accountability. Likewise, *Suratt's* extension and containment of the principle of judicial independence could be explained using the overarching principle of the rule of law. It could be argued that the doctrine promotes the expansion of access to justice through the establishment of new judicial bodies while, at the same time, insisting that new tribunals enjoy the appropriate protection for their independence. The rule of law as an implied constitutional norm and part of our fundamental law fits in with traditional understandings of constitutional law in the Commonwealth Caribbean. It could clarify the meaning of already accepted implied constitutional norms and it can also help to make our constitutions our own and attentive to our needs.

---

143. Walters (n 24) 92.

Contributors

Kamille Adair is an attorney-at-law in Jamaica and graduated with an LLB degree from the Faculty of Law, University of the West Indies, Mona Campus, in 2009.

Rose-Marie Antoine is the Professor of Labour Law and Off-Shore Law in the Faculty of Law, University of the West Indies, Cave Hill Campus.

David S. Berry is Dean of the Faculty of Law, University of the West Indies, Cave Hill Campus.

Arif Bulkan is a lecturer in the Faculty of Law, University of the West Indies, St Augustine Campus.

Margaret Demerieux was the Professor of Human Rights Law in the Faculty of Law, University of the West Indies, Cave Hill Campus. She died in 2003 and the previously-unpublished chapter in this book is published with the permission of her estate.

Suzanne Goldson is a lecturer in the Faculty of Law, University of the West Indies, Mona Campus.

Leighton M. Jackson is a senior lecturer in the Faculty of Law, University of the West Indies, Mona Campus.

Tracy Robinson is a senior lecturer in the Faculty of Law, University of the West Indies, Mona Campus.

Godfrey P. Smith is an attorney-at-law in Belize and former Attorney-General of Belize.

Eddy D. Ventose is the Professor of Intellectual Property and Public Law in the Faculty of Law, University of the West Indies, Cave Hill Campus.

Lesley A. Walcott is a senior lecturer in the Faculty of Law, University of the West Indies, Cave Hill Campus.

Index